Advance Praise for

BRIGHT GREEN LIES

"*Bright Green Lies* dismantles the illusion of 'green' technology in breathtaking, comprehensive detail, revealing a fantasy that must perish if there is to be any hope of preserving what remains of life on Earth. From solar panels to wind turbines, from LED light bulbs to electric cars, no green fantasy escapes Jensen, Keith, and Wilbert's revealing peek behind the green curtain. *Bright Green Lies* is a must-read for all who cherish life on Earth." —JEFF GIBBS, WRITER, DIRECTOR, AND PRODUCER OF THE FILM *Planet of the Humans*

"*Bright Green Lies* lays out in heartbreaking and sometimes disgusting detail the simple fact that to maintain the growth of techno-industrial civilization by replacing fossil fuels with solar panels, wind turbines, hydropower, electric cars, and whatever other green machines we might construct still requires the continuing rape of Mother Earth and the poisoning of her water, air, soil, wildlife, and human populations. The authors tell us unequivocally: Green growth is a doomed enterprise, and there is no future for humankind living in harmony with nature in which we fail to recognize that unlimited economic and population growth on a finite planet is ecological suicide. Environmental groups that blithely refuse to question the industrial growth paradigm should be fearful of this book, as it exposes with a sword point their hypocrisies and falsehoods. I suggest they seek the immediate burning of all copies." —CHRISTOPHER KETCHAM, AUTHOR OF *This Land: How Cowboys, Capitalism, and Corruption Are Ruining the American West*

"*Bright Green Lies* is a tour de force. The authors expose many of the fallacies of mainstream environmentalism and economics. Their main thesis is that much of what passes for environmental concern today is geared primarily toward sustaining an unsustainable 'lifestyle.' Most so-called 'sustainable' practices are just a slower way to degrade the earth's ecosystems. For years, I have been harping on the fact that society needs to do a full accounting of the real costs of our lifestyles. This book exposes much of what is missing in our flawed accounting system, and the genuine costs of this failure. I thought I knew a lot about the environmental impacts of the consumer society, but Jensen and his co-authors have shown me that I, like many people, only had a superficial appreciation of these costs. *Bright Green Lies* takes off where William Catton's book *Overshoot: The Ecological Basis for Revolutionary Change* left off and provides a stimulating roadmap of how to think about our environmental crisis. It makes a powerful case for what society needs to do to reevaluate its present and unsustainable pathway. Hopefully, *Bright Green Lies* will result in more thoughtful, insightful, and ultimately productive environmental activism."
—GEORGE WUERTHNER, ECOLOGIST, WILDLANDS ACTIVIST, PHOTOGRAPHER, AND AUTHOR OF 38 BOOKS, INCLUDING *Wildfire: A Century of Failed Forest Policy*

"*Bright Green Lies* is a book I've been keenly awaiting, a book made of numbers, clear thinking, wit, and love. *Bright Green Lies* urges the protection of the natural world in all its sacred and manifest diversity. Arm yourself with the precision and honesty that this book fiercely inspires and demands; recognize that life itself is the sole bearer of effective solutions, that organic, ecological, elemental, and biomic life can indeed save the planet from catastrophe."
—SUPRABHA SESHAN, RAINFOREST CONSERVATIONIST AT INDIA'S GURUKULA BOTANICAL SANCTUARY

"*Bright Green Lies* is a much needed wakeup call if we are to avoid sleepwalking to extinction—joining 200 of our fellow creatures and relatives that are being driven to extinction per day by an extractivist, colonizing money machine that is lubricated by limitless greed, and guided by the mechanical mind of industrialism. This destructive machine is labelled 'civilization,' and its violent and brutal imposition on indigenous cultures and communities is legitimized as the 'civilizing mission' for which exterminations of the rich cultural and biological diversity of the earth is necessary for the linear, blind rush to progress. Religions change, extermination continues. But there are other ways: the ways of indigenous cultures to whom we must turn to learn how to walk lightly on the earth."
—DR. VANDANA SHIVA, FOUNDER OF NAVDANYA AND THE RESEARCH FOUNDATION FOR SCIENCE, TECHNOLOGY, AND ECOLOGY; AUTHOR OF *Earth Democracy* AND *Making Peace with the Earth*

"*Bright Green Lies* is the book we've all been waiting for. Jensen and his co-authors explode the myth that we can somehow grow our way out of the mess that we've created by using 'renewable' energies to prop up the lie that endless growth is possible without continuing to destroy the planet and the life-support systems that it provides. May *Bright Green Lies* be the first step toward shifting us to a different future—one which doesn't continue to borrow from the future to give us an unlivable planet." —THOMAS LINZEY, SENIOR COUNSEL FOR THE CENTER FOR DEMOCRATIC AND ENVIRONMENTAL RIGHTS AND COFOUNDER OF COMMUNITY ENVIRONMENTAL LEGAL DEFENSE FUND

BRIGHT GREEN LIES

How the Environmental Movement Lost Its Way

and What We Can Do About It

DERRICK JENSEN
LIERRE KEITH
MAX WILBERT

Politics of the Living Series

•

Monkfish Book Publishing Company
Rhinebeck, New York

Bright Green Lies: How the Environmental Movement Lost Its Way and What We Can Do About It © 2021 by Derrick Jensen, Lierre Keith, and Max Wilbert

Politics of the Living Series (m-1)

Paperback ISBN 978-1-948626-39-2
eBook ISBN 978-1-948626-40-8

Library of Congress Cataloging-in-Publication Data

Names: Jensen, Derrick, 1960- author. | Keith, Lierre, author. | Wilbert, Max, author.
Title: Bright green lies : how the environmental movement lost its way and what we can do about it / Derrick Jensen, Lierre Keith, Max Wilbert.
Description: Rhinebeck, New York : Monkfish Book Publishing Company, [2021] | Series: Politics of the living series | Includes bibliographical references.
Identifiers: LCCN 2020044348 (print) | LCCN 2020044349 (ebook) | ISBN 9781948626392 (Paperback) | ISBN 9781948626408 (eBook)
Subjects: LCSH: Environmentalism. | Environmentalism--History. | Environmentalists.
Classification: LCC GE195 .J457 2021 (print) | LCC GE195 (ebook) | DDC 304.2/8--dc23
LC record available at https://lccn.loc.gov/2020044348
LC ebook record available at https://lccn.loc.gov/2020044349

Book and Cover Design by Colin Rolfe
"Leaf" by Isis França

Monkfish Book Publishing Company
22 East Market Street, Suite 304
Rhinebeck, NY 12572
(845) 876-4861
monkfishpublishing.com

A thing is right when it tends to preserve the integrity,

stability, and beauty of the biotic community.

It is wrong when it tends otherwise.

—ALDO LEOPOLD, *THE LAND ETHIC*

CONTENTS

A NOTE FROM THE AUTHORS ON LANGUAGE

It's customary when writing about nonhumans to use the relative pronoun *that* rather than *who*: "We cut down the tree *that* used to grow by the pond," not "We cut down the tree *who* used to grow by the pond."

The authors of this book use *who* when speaking of nonhumans because we believe that how we speak of the world profoundly affects how we perceive and experience the world, which in turn profoundly affects how we act in the world. If we perceive the life around us as a collection of resources to exploit, then exploit them we will—and ultimately, we will destroy the world in our attempts to control it. As we see happening now.

If, on the other hand, we perceive the world as consisting of other beings with whom we share our home, then share our home with them we will—with all of the richness, beauty, and wisdom that this entails.

Changing language is no substitute for organized resistance to the ongoing destruction of this once-fecund and now-wounded planet, and it's no substitute for the protection and restoration of wild places and wild beings, but it's an important step toward changing our values, priorities, and actions.

PREFACE

This book began to take form in 2010, when co-author Derrick Jensen was asked to debate a so-called "bright green" environmentalist. According to bright green environmentalism, neither capitalism nor industrial civilization (the state of civilization following the Industrial Revolution, characterized by commonplace use of machinery and technology) is inherently unsustainable.

From the bright green perspective, the unsustainable aspects of our way of life today—including large cities—are not functional problems, but rather are solvable by readily available technologies and processes: photovoltaic cells, wind power generators, recycling, and the like.

During the debate, when the bright green proponent claimed that cities can indeed be sustainable, Derrick responded with several questions: "Where do you get the food, the energy, the water? Where does the human waste go? Cities have always depended upon finding a countryside and denuding that countryside of resources."

Sustainability can be defined as a way of life that doesn't require the importation of resources. So, if a city requires the importation of resources, it means that city has denuded its landscape of that particular resource. Quite naturally, as a city grows, it denudes a larger area; in fact, cities have been denuding countrysides for the last 6,000 years. More than 2,000 years ago, the Chinese philosopher Mencius wrote: "There was once a time when the forests of the Niu Mountain were beautiful. But can the mountain any longer be regarded as beautiful, since being situated near a big city, the woodsmen have hewed the trees down?"

"I'm not saying that people shouldn't reduce their ecological footprint, or that cities are more unsustainable than suburbs," Derrick argued. "I'm saying we need to be honest with ourselves and recognize that you can't have an electrical system without a mining infrastructure because you need copper or other metals for wiring."

Just as a modern city would be impossible without an electrical grid, so is electricity unthinkable without metals being mined to create it. "You can't take individual technologies out of context," Derrick said, because every system, every object relies upon humans extracting resources from the earth. To make his point, he took off his glasses and held them up as an example. "They're made of plastic, which requires oil and transportation infrastructures, and metal, which requires mining, oil, and transportation infrastructures," he explained. "They've also got lenses made of glass, and modern glassmaking requires energy and transportation infrastructures. The mines from which to get the materials to make my reading glasses are going to have to be located somewhere, and the energy with which to manufacture them also has to come from somewhere.

"We need to stop being guided by the general story that we can have it all," Derrick concluded, "that we can have an industrial culture and also have wild nature, that we can have an oil economy and still have polar bears."

The bright green responded with his movement's most common

argument and statement of faith: that every system we are currently using that is unsustainable was designed by humans and is therefore capable of being redesigned. "It is entirely possible," the bright green argued, "to create a zero-impact, closed-loop, carbon-neutral method of generating prosperity that most people would accept as reasonable."

But what, asked Derrick, is an example of a system that could be redesigned to be sustainable?

"You mentioned mining," replied the bright green. "It is, in fact, possible to recapture minerals and metals, to design things for disassembly so that minerals are easily pulled from objects as they cease to be of use, and to turn those elements into parts for new things. We know that it is at least theoretically possible to have an absolutely zero-waste economy, and we know that it is practically possible right now to have a very-close-to-zero-waste economy."

Sounds great, right? The only problem—and this is the case with all the bright green arguments—is that this idea doesn't correspond to physical reality. As we prove in this book, the process of recycling materials itself requires an infrastructure that is harmful to both the environment and humanity. Not only does the recycling process very often cause more waste and pollution, but it frequently relies upon nearby populations living in unsafe conditions and workers being subjected to both toxins and slave labor.

But bright green environmentalism has gained so much attention over the past 20 years that it has effectively colonized mainstream environmentalism. That's because bright green proponents tell a lot of people what they want to hear, which is that you can have it all: industrial civilization and a planet too. Or, put another way, you don't have to change your lifestyle at all; you can have a planet and consume it too.

But we can't have it all. And if we want our planet to survive, we do have to change our lifestyle—radically. Bright green environmentalism and other forms of denial about our situation do great harm by wasting time we don't have on "solutions" to sustainability that cannot work.

This book is an introduction to some of the lies common among the bright greens. We reveal many of these lies, analyze why and how they are false, and make clear the tricks the bright greens are pulling—possibly on themselves as well as the rest of us—to perpetuate these lies. Our hope is that once we've revealed these lies, our readers can use what they've learned to debunk other bright green claims.

We're not saying innovation is never helpful. Nor are we saying we shouldn't recycle, or that some forms of production aren't more or less unsustainable than others, or that cities can't be made less unsustainable.

We're simply saying that we shouldn't lie to ourselves, or to each other. Especially with the world at stake, we should tell the truth. We're saying that these bright green solutions are lies that allow us to maintain an unsustainable way of living while pretending that we are not killing the planet.

PROLOGUE

Lierre Keith

We are in peril. Like all animals, we need a home: a blanket of air, a cradle of soil, and a vast assemblage of creatures who make both. We can't create oxygen, but others can—from tiny plankton to towering redwoods. We can't build soil, but the slow circling of bacteria, bison, and sweetgrass do.

But all of these beings are bleeding out, species by species, like Noah and the Ark in reverse, while the carbon swells and the fires burn on. Five decades of environmental activism haven't stopped this. We haven't even slowed it. In those same five decades, humans have killed 60 percent of the earth's animals. And that's but one wretched number among so many others.

That's the horror that brings readers to a book like this, with whatever mixture of hope and despair. But we don't have good news for you. To state it bluntly, something has gone terribly wrong with the environmental movement.

Once, we were the people who defended wild creatures and wild places. We loved our kin, we loved our home, and we fought for our beloved. Collectively, we formed a movement to protect our planet. Along the way, many of us searched for the reasons. Why were humans doing this? What could possibly compel the wanton sadism laying waste to the world? Was it our nature or were only some humans culpable? That analysis is crucial, of course. Without a proper diagnosis, correct treatment is impossible. This book lays out the best answers that we, the authors, have found.

We wrote this book because something has happened to our movement. The beings and biomes who were once at the center of our concern have been disappeared. In their place now stands the very system that is destroying them. The goal has been transformed: We're supposed to save our way of life, not fight for the living planet; instead, we are to rally behind the "machines making machines making machines" that are devouring what's left of our home.

Committed activists have brought the emergency of climate change into broad consciousness, and that's a huge win as the glaciers melt and the tundra burns. But they are solving for the wrong variable. *Our way of life doesn't need to be saved. The planet needs to be saved from our way of life.*

There's a name for members of this rising movement: *bright green environmentalists.* They believe that technology and design can render industrial civilization sustainable. The mechanism to drive the creation of these new technologies is consumerism. Thus, bright greens "treat consumerism as a salient green practice."[1] Indeed, they "embrace consumerism" as the path to prosperity for all.[2] Of course, whatever prosperity we might achieve by consuming is strictly time limited, what with the planet being finite. But the only way to build the bright green narrative is to erase every awareness of the creatures and communities being consumed. They simply don't matter. What matters is technology. Accept technology as our savior, the bright greens promise, and our current way of life is possible for everyone and forever. With the excised species gone

---

[1] Julie Newman, *Green Ethics and Philosophy: An A-to-Z Guide* (Thousand Oaks, CA: SAGE Publications, 2011), 40.
[2] Ibid., 39.

from consciousness, the only problem left for the bright greens to solve is how to power the shiny, new machines.

It doesn't matter how the magic trick was done. Even the critically endangered have been struck from regard. Now you see them, now you don't: from the Florida yew (whose home is a single 15-mile stretch, now under threat from biomass production) to the Scottish wildcat (who number a grim 35, all at risk from a proposed wind installation). As if humans can somehow survive on a planet that's been flayed of its species and bled out to a dead rock. Once we fought for the living. Now we are told to fight for their deaths, as the wind turbines come for the mountains and solar panels conquer the deserts.

"May the truth be your armor," urged Marcus Aurelius. The truths in this book are hard, but you will need them to defend your beloved. The first truth is that our current way of life requires industrial levels of energy. That's what it takes to fuel the wholesale conversion of living communities into dead commodities. That conversion is the problem "if," to borrow from Australian antinuclear advocate Dr. Helen Caldicott, "you love this planet." The task before us is not how to continue to fuel that conversion. It's how to stop it.

The second truth is that fossil fuel—especially oil—is functionally irreplaceable. The proposed alternatives—like solar, wind, hydro, and biomass—will never scale up to power an industrial economy.

Third, those technologies are in their own right assaults against the living world. From beginning to end, they require industrial-scale devastation: open-pit mining, deforestation, soil toxification that's permanent on anything but a geologic timescale, the extirpation and extinction of vulnerable species, and, oh yes, fossil fuels. These technologies will not save the earth. They will only hasten its demise.

And finally, there are real solutions. Simply put, we have to stop destroying the planet and let natural life come back. There are people everywhere doing exactly that, and nature is responding, sometimes miraculously. The wounded are healed, the missing reappear, and the exiled return. It's not too late.

I'm sitting in my meadow, looking for hope. Swathes of purple needlegrass, silent and steady, are swelling with seeds—66 million years of evolution preparing for one more. All I had to do was let the grasses grow back, and a cascade of life followed. The tall grass made a home for rabbits. The rabbits brought the foxes. And now the cry of a fledgling hawk pierces the sky, wild and urgent. I know this cry, and yet I don't. Me, but not me. The love and the aching distance. What I am sure of is that life wants to live. The hawk's parents will feed her, teach her, and let her go. She will take her turn—then her children, theirs.

Every stranger who comes here says the same thing: "I've never seen so many dragonflies." They say it in wonder, almost in awe, and always in delight. And there, too, is my hope. Despite everything, people still love this planet and all our kin. They can't stop themselves. That love is a part of us, as surely as our blood and bones.

Somewhere close by there are mountain lions. I've heard a female calling for a mate, her need fierce and absolute. Here, in the last, final scraps of wilderness, life keeps trying. How can I do less?

There's no time for despair. The mountain lions and the dragonflies, the fledgling hawks and the needlegrass seeds all need us now. We have to take back our movement and defend our beloved. How can we do less? And with all of life on our side, how can we lose?

THE SPECTRUM OF ENVIRONMENTALISM

DEEP GREENS

The living planet and nonhumans both have the right to exist. Human flourishing depends on healthy ecology. To save the planet, humans must live within the limits of the natural world; therefore, drastic transformations need to occur at social, cultural, economic, political, and personal levels.

LIFESTYLISTS

Humans depend on nature, and technology probably won't solve environmental issues, but political engagement is either impossible or unnecessary. The best we can do is practice self-reliance, small-scale living, and other personal solutions. Withdrawal will change the world.

BRIGHT GREENS

Environmental problems exist and are serious, but green technology and design, along with ethical consumerism, will allow a modern, high-energy lifestyle to continue indefinitely. The bright greens' attitude amounts to: "It's less about nature, and more about us."

WISE USE / ENVIRONMENTAL MANAGERS

Ecological issues exist, but most problems are minor and can be solved through proper management. Natural resources should be protected primarily to enable their continued extraction and human well-being.

CORNUCOPIANS

The earth is made up of resources that are essentially infinite. Ecological problems are secondary. Technology and the economic system—whether free-market capitalism or socialism—will solve all ecological problems.

TECHNOCRATS / TRANSHUMANISTS

Humans should transcend biology by investing heavily in technology. We can also avoid the possibility of human extinction by leaving planet Earth behind, and we should ultimately move toward cybernetic enhancement and uploading human consciousness into machines in order to defeat death.

Chapter 1

THE PROBLEM

Once our authoritarian technics consolidates its powers,
with the aid of its new forms of mass control, its panoply of
tranquilizers and sedatives and aphrodisiacs, could democracy
in any form survive? That question is absurd: Life itself will
not survive, except what is funneled through the mechanical
collective.[1]

— **LEWIS MUMFORD**

There is so little time and even less hope, here in the midst of ruin, at the end of the world. Every biome is in shreds. The green flesh of forests has been stripped to grim sand. The word *water* has been drained of meaning; the Athabascan River is essentially a planned toxic spill now, oozing from the open wound of the Alberta tar sands. When birds fly over it, they drop dead from the poison. No one believes us when we say that, but it's true. The Appalachian Mountains are being blown to bits, their dense life of deciduous forests, including their human communities, reduced to a disposal problem called "overburden," a word that should be considered

[1] Lewis Mumford, "Authoritarian and Democratic Technics," *Technology and Culture* 5, no. 1 (Winter, 1964), 7.

hate speech: Living creatures—mountain laurels, wood thrush fledglings, somebody's grandchildren—are not objects to be tossed into gullies. If there is no poetry after Auschwitz, there is no grammar after mountaintop removal.

As above, so below. Coral reefs are crumbling under the acid assault of carbon. And the world's grasslands have been sliced to ribbons, literally, with steel blades fed by fossil fuel. The hunger of those blades would be endless but for the fact that the planet is a bounded sphere: There are no continents left to eat. Every year the average American farm uses the energy equivalent of three to four tons of TNT per acre. And oil burns so easily, once every possibility for self-sustaining cultures has been destroyed. Even their memory is gone, metaphrastic now, something between prehistory and a fairy tale.

All that's left is carbon, accruing into a nightmare from which dawn will not save us. *Climate change* slipped into *climate chaos,* which has become a whispered *climate holocaust.* At least the humans whisper. And the animals? During the 2011 Texas drought, deer abandoned their fawns for lack of milk. That is not a grief that whispers. For living beings like Labrador ducks, Javan rhinos, and Xerces blue butterflies, there is the long silence of extinction.

We have a lot of numbers. They keep us sane, providing a kind of gallows' comfort against the intransigent sadism of power: We know the world is being murdered, despite the mass denial. The numbers are real. The numbers don't lie. The species shrink, their extinctions swell, and all their names are other words for *kin*: bison, wolves, black-footed ferrets.

Before me (Lierre) is the text of a talk I've given. The original version contains this sentence: "Another 120 species went extinct today." The *120* is crossed clean through, with *150* written above it. But the *150* is also struck out, with *180* written above. The *180* in its turn has given way to *200*. I stare at this progression with a sick sort of awe. How does my small, neat handwriting hold this horror? The numbers keep stacking up, I'm out of space in the margin, and life is running out of time.

Twelve thousand years ago, the war against the earth began. In nine places,[2] people started to destroy the world by taking up agriculture. Understand what agriculture is: In blunt terms, you take a piece of land, clear every living thing off it—ultimately, down to the bacteria—and then plant it for human use. Make no mistake: agriculture is biotic cleansing.

That's not agriculture on a bad day, or agriculture done poorly. That's what agriculture actually is: the extirpation of living communities for a monocrop of humans. There were perhaps five million humans living on earth on the day this started—from this day to the ending of the world, indeed—and there are now well over seven billion.

The end is written into the beginning. As geologist David R. Montgomery points out, agricultural societies "last 800 to 2,000 years ... until the soil gives out."[3] Fossil fuel has been a vast accelerant to both the extirpation and the monocrop—the human population has quadrupled under the swell of surplus created by the

---

[2] There exists some debate as to how many places developed agriculture and civilizations. The best current guess seems to be nine: the Fertile Crescent; the Indian subcontinent; the Yangtze and Yellow River basins; the New Guinea Highlands; Central Mexico; Northern South America; sub-Saharan Africa; and eastern North America.
[3] David R. Montgomery, *Dirt: The Erosion of Civilizations* (Berkeley, CA: University of California Press, 2007), 236.

Green Revolution—but it can only be temporary. Finite quantities have a nasty habit of running out.

The name for this diminishment is *drawdown*, and agriculture is in essence a slow bleed-out of soil, species, biomes, and ultimately the process of life itself. Vertebrate evolution has come to a halt for lack of habitat. With habitat taken by force and kept by force, Iowa alone uses the energy equivalent of 4,000 Nagasaki bombs every year. Agriculture is the original scorched-earth policy, which is why permaculturist Toby Hemenway and environmental writer Richard Manning have written the same sentence: "Sustainable agriculture is an oxymoron." To quote Manning at length: "No biologist, or anyone else for that matter, could design a system of regulations that would make agriculture sustainable. Sustainable agriculture is an oxymoron. It mostly relies on an unnatural system of annual grasses grown in a monoculture, a system that nature does not sustain or even recognize as a natural system. We sustain it with plows, petrochemicals, fences, and subsidies, because there is no other way to sustain it."[4]

Agriculture is what creates the human pattern called *civilization*. Civilization is not the same as culture—all humans create culture. A culture is, broadly, the set of customs, traditions, and values particular to a group of people. *Civilization* is the word for one specific way of life: people living in cities. Most definitions of *city* reference permanence, population density, and division of labor as a city's salient features. Rarely stated is the reality of people living in numbers large enough to require the importation of resources: city dwellers need more than the land can give. Food, water, and energy have to come from somewhere else. From that point forward, it doesn't matter what lovely, peaceful values people

---

[4] Richard Manning, *Rewilding the West: Restoration in a Prairie Landscape* (Berkeley: University of California Press, 2009), 185.

hold in their hearts. The society is dependent on imperialism and genocide because no one willingly gives up their land, their water, their trees. But since the city has used up its own, it has to go out and get those from somewhere else. That's the last 10,000 years in a few sentences. Over and over and over, the pattern is the same. There's a bloated power center surrounded by conquered colonies, from which the center extracts what it wants, until eventually it collapses.

The conjoined horrors of militarism and slavery begin with agriculture. Agricultural societies end up militarized—and they always do—for three reasons. First, agriculture creates a surplus, and if it can be stored, it can be stolen. So the surplus needs to be protected. The people who do that are called *soldiers*.

Second, the drawdown inherent in this activity means that agriculturalists will always need more land, more soil, and more resources. They need an entire class of people whose job is war, whose job is taking land and resources by force—agriculture makes that possible as well as inevitable.

Third, agriculture is backbreaking labor. For anyone to have leisure, they need slaves. By the year 1800, when the fossil fuel age began, three-quarters of the people on this planet were living in conditions of slavery, indenture, or serfdom.[5] Force is the only way to get and keep that many people enslaved. We've largely forgotten this because we've been using machines—which in turn use fossil fuel—to do that work for us.

The symbiosis of technology and culture is what historian, sociologist, and philosopher of technology Lewis Mumford (1895-1990) called a *technic*. A social milieu creates specific technologies which in turn shape the culture. Mumford writes, "[A] new

---

[5] Adam Hochschild, *Bury the Chains: Prophets and Rebels in the Fight to Free an Empire's Slaves* (Boston: Mariner Books, 2006), 2.

configuration of technical invention, scientific observation, and centralized political control ... gave rise to the peculiar mode of life we may now identify, without eulogy, as civilization.... The new authoritarian technology was not limited by village custom or human sentiment: its herculean feats of mechanical organization rested on ruthless physical coercion, forced labor and slavery, which brought into existence machines that were capable of exerting thousands of horsepower centuries before horses were harnessed or wheels invented. This centralized technics ... created complex human machines composed of specialized, standardized, replaceable, interdependent parts—the work army, the military army, the bureaucracy. These work armies and military armies raised the ceiling of human achievement: the first in mass construction, the second in mass destruction, both on a scale hitherto inconceivable."[6]

Technology is anything but neutral or passive in its effects: Ploughshares require armies of slaves to operate them and soldiers to protect them. The technic that is civilization has required weapons of conquest from the beginning. "Farming spread by genocide," Richard Manning writes.[7] The destruction of Cro-Magnon Europe—the culture that bequeathed us Lascaux—took farmer-soldiers from the Near East perhaps 300 years to accomplish. The only thing exchanged between the two cultures was violence. "All these artifacts are weapons," writes archaeologist T. Douglas Price, with his colleagues, "and there is no reason to believe that they were exchanged in a nonviolent manner."[8]

---

[6] Mumford, op. cit., 3.

[7] Richard Manning, *Against the Grain: How Agriculture Has Hijacked Civilization* (New York: North Point Press, 2004), 45.

[8] T. Douglas Price, Anne Birgitte Gebauer, and Lawrence H. Keeley, "The Spread of Farming into Europe North of the Alps," in Douglas T. Price and Anne Brigitte Gebauer, *Last Hunters, First Farmers* (Santa Fe: School of American Research Press, 1995).

Weapons are tools that civilizations will make because civilization itself is a war. Its most basic material activity is a war against the living world, and as life is destroyed, the war must spread. The spread is not just geographic, though that is both inevitable and catastrophic, turning biotic communities into gutted colonies and sovereign people into slaves. Civilization penetrates the culture as well, because the weapons are not just a technology—no tool ever is. Technologies contain the transmutational force of a technic, creating a seamless suite of social institutions and corresponding ideologies. Those ideologies will either be authoritarian or democratic, hierarchical or egalitarian. Technics are never neutral. Or, as ecopsychology pioneer Chellis Glendinning writes with spare eloquence, "All technologies are political."[9]

Biologist David Ehrenfeld has written that not only is nature more complex than we think, it's also more complex than we *can* think. Here's one example: A teaspoon of soil can contain a billion living creatures. We can picture a number with nine zeroes, but our minds could never hold that many actual items at once. The number of things we can store simultaneously in our brains—which have been two million years in the making—turns out to be a humble four.

The nine unfolding zeroes in that one billion signal incredible complexity. But that complexity swells into still more. Each of those billion creatures interacts with the others. The number of relationships between a billion organisms is five times 10^{17}. We'd get lost in seeing that many zeroes written out—never mind that many beings laid out before us—so we condense the number to

[9] Chellis Glendinning, "Notes toward a Neo-Luddite Manifesto," *Utne Reader*, March–April 1990, 50.

the exponent *17*. Or, to put it simply, 500 quadrillion. We can do nothing else, even with our brains' 100,000 miles of blood vessels and 100 billion neurons: A quadrillion is so much bigger than four.

Each of those unseen creatures has its own majesty. Bacteria are tiny—maybe one-tenth the size of a typical nucleated cell—but as a biomass, they exceed all of the plants and animals on earth combined. The meek have already inherited the earth. A single bacterium can become 16 million more in one day. Some bacteria live alone; others join together to form chains, filaments, and spirals of eldritch grace. They also aggregate into dense mats, called biofilms, building an armored fortress, which makes them dramatically harder to kill. For instance, methicillin-resistant *Staphylococcus aureus* (MRSA) builds biofilms. So do the bacteria in our mouths—including the hard, dental plaque that only specialized tools and a fair amount of force can scrape from our teeth. Not so meek at all.

A few bacteria can turn themselves into endospores, reducing themselves to bare DNA and an integument of fantastical abilities—surviving extreme heat, cold, pressure, chemical agents, radiation, desiccation, and time. There are viable endospores that are 40 million years old.

And that's just the bacteria in that teaspoon of soil. There are other creatures there too. There are fungi, with filament bodies a mile long, and there are several thousand protozoa, hunting and gathering bacteria and organic matter. In consuming bacteria, protozoa produce nitrogen, making the world green: 80 percent of the nitrogen in plants comes from bacteria-eating protozoa. None of us are in this alone.

That single teaspoon of soil is also home to approximately 1,000 tiny arthropods. These include crustaceans so small their armored exoskeletons are thin to the point of transparency. And the soil also contains scores of nematodes—roundworms—feeding on fungi, algae, tiny animals, dead creatures, and living tissues.

These beings make life possible. "It is to the bacteria of the soil," writes soil scientist James Nardi, "that most of the credit for the constant renewal of our earth is due."[10]

And how have we repaid these extraordinary, infinitesimal creatures who ensure life on earth? By skinning the planet alive. Topsoil on the North American prairie was 12 feet deep when the farmer-soldiers arrived in the early 1800s. In less than a century, it could only be measured in inches. And the "Great Plowing" was done before the invention of the internal combustion engine, with only the power of oxen and horses. Fossil fuel is an accelerant, but the impulse to subdue the planet—and dominate it to its very death—was already there.

The mechanistic mind is built on an epistemology of domination. It wants a heirarchy. It needs to separate the animate from the inanimate and then rank them in order of moral standing. In his book, *History of Animals*, Aristotle arranged life with minerals at the bottom, serving as an insensate substrate. Plants are next, then various animals, with humans at the top. This system, which he named *la scala naturae*, meaning "the great chain of being," has held sway for 2,000 years.

This mind and its *scala* are wrong. Moment to moment, the world is kept alive only by the bacteria doing the basic work of life, which no one else can do, and by maintaining relationships more complex than any we could ever understand. *We are all here only because of other beings.* Biologist Robert Rosen argues that the mechanistic paradigm of Western science cannot explain living communities, which are always built from relationship "between

---

[10] James Nardi, *Life in the Soil: A Guide for Naturalists and Gardeners* (Chicago: University of Chicago Press, 2007), 51.

the part and the whole." The word he uses to define living communities: *nonfractionability*.

The mechanistic mind is also wrong across geologic time. Scientists and lay people alike have tried to draw a line between life and inanimate matter. Chemists, for instance, divide their field into the organic and inorganic. Organic matter is that which is produced by the "vital chemistry" of living creatures. Inorganic refers to "forms of matter which exist independently of the operation of living beings."[11] Rocks, metals, minerals, and water, for instance, are considered inorganic. But given a few billion years, rock will become living creatures who will eventually get pressed back into rock. And with a few plate shifts, the sediment of the ocean floor, built from the bodies of sea creatures, will become dry land. That land—comprised of those compressed dead bodies—is once more taken up by living creatures. Hence Russian scientist V. I. Vernadsky called life on earth "a disperse of rock." Writes evolutionary biologist and futurist Elizabet Sahtouris, "This view of living matter as continuous with, and as a chemical transformation of, nonliving planetary matter is very different from the view of life developing on the surface of a nonliving planet and adapting to it."[12] In Sahtouris's words, it's the difference between "a living planet" and a "planet with life on it."[13]

This is not just clever semantics. According to one viewpoint, the planet is for humans and maybe a few other creatures. According to another, everything on earth is part of a process called life. As Sahtouris writes, "Planetary life is not something that happens

[11] Henry Alleyne Nicholson, *A Manual of Zoology for the Use of Students. with a General Introduction on the Principles of Zoology* (Ann Arbor, MI: Scholarly Publishing Office, University of Michigan Library, November 30, 2006), 2.
[12] Elizabet Sahtouris, *EarthDance: Living Systems in Evolution* (Lincoln, NE: iUniverse Press, 2000), 69.
[13] Ibid., 4.

here and there on a planet—it happens to the planet as a whole."[14] Life is not a kind of matter, but a process.

Particles attract to form atoms; atoms form matter; matter condenses into stars and rocks and rain, which transform into elegant spirals of proteins that replicate themselves through oceans and then over land and into 300-foot-long redwoods; the startling, saturated green of tree frogs; and the night silence of owls' wings. Each new level of complexity depends on the one before; each new arrangement of atoms can't exist without the others. As the late Pueblo writer Paula Gunn Allen explained, "The thing about tribal systems, about the old, old stories is that they recognize multiplicity at every single level. It's always about interaction. There isn't any other way to talk about it.... All life's plural and there are lots and lots of circles.... Within those circular, circular, circulars, everything has an interactive capacity with everything else.[15]

For 2.5 million years, some version of humans has lived on this planet, and we weren't monsters and destroyers. Over that time our brains got bigger, our tools got better, letting our brains get bigger still. We didn't make war: we made art. Specifically, we rendered the megafauna and the megafemales,[16] because that was who gave us life. The moment our brains got big enough to know that, we said thank you. That was the beginning of religion. The sacredness of awe and thanksgiving was built into us, body and brain. We were humble participants in a living cosmos. And it was good.

We are none of us frozen objects. We take, we give, we need, and

---

[14] Ibid., 39.

[15] Paula Gunn Allen, "She Is Us: Thought Woman and the Sustainability of Worship," in *Original Instructions: Indigenous Teachings for a Sustainable Future,* ed. Melissa K. Nelson (Rochester, VT: Bear & Company, 2008), 139.

[16] Megafemales is a reference to the myriad early pottery figurines of females.

we are only possible because of the others here with us. Plankton make oxygen, bacteria seed rain, plants turn sun into sugar and carbon into soil. Bison don't exist without grasses, and grasses don't exist without bison. Given enough time, each being will become the other. As the late biophysicist Harold J. Morowitz said, "Life is a property of an ecological system rather than a single organism and species."[17]

Information about the tiniest members of the universe—from microbes to atoms to quarks—has grown broad and deep. Yet the truth about the world—that it is alive, all of it—is still rejected by the culture at large. This is not an argument so much as an observation: the declaration that matter is lifeless has led to a planet laid to waste. The story we tell is the story we live. And every being on earth must surely be begging for a different story now.

No technology is neutral. That sentence carries our only hope. There are the fish who famously cannot see water; we, too, are submerged in the only culture we have ever known. The defense of this culture lies somewhere between catechism and cliché: technology is neutral, the problem is who controls it or how we use it. Left and right, atheist and religious, capitalist and socialist, even most environmentalists will state the same platitude—that technology is neutral—with certainty. Yet it is observably untrue. And since observation is the basis of the scientific method, let us observe how and why it is untrue.

All tools require materials and energy—they are built from something. A nuclear power plant, for instance, is made almost entirely from concrete and steel, which account for "over 95 percent" of the

---

[17] Harold J. Morowitz, *Beginnings of Cellular Life: Metabolism Recapitulates Biogenesis* (New Haven, CT: Yale University Press, 1992), 31.

power plant's "material energy inputs,"[18] according to a University of California, Berkeley report. Concrete is made from aggregates—sand, gravel, crushed stone—and cement. Cement, in turn, is made from limestone, clay or shale, and gypsum. Steel is made from iron ore, alloying elements, and coking coal.

All of these substances are mined. It hardly matters which material we examine—the horrors are the same. The life stripped to bare rock, the rock hacked, bludgeoned, or bombed into cavernous pits, the pits engulfing sweeps of land that will not recover until the next ice age recedes. Surrounding the devastation is always more: the leach ponds, the toxic tailings, the acid rain, the ulcerated fish, the fine particulates shredding lung tissue with every breath. In the eight centuries of its rule, the Roman Empire covered Greenland in 800 tons of copper and 400 tons of lead from its mines.

Try to imagine the scale: windborne dust from 4,000 miles away, captured in the crystals of snowflakes, one by one by one, accreting to 800 tons.[19] Victims of Rome's industrial pollution may have numbered in the millions across Europe and the Middle East. The health impacts, then as now, are ghastly: convulsions, vomiting, diarrhea, anemia, stunted fetal growth, mental retardation, and cancer.

The seasonal river valley Wadi Faynan, in modern-day Jordan, is the site of an ancient Roman copper mine. Two thousand years has not been enough time to heal the damage from the mine. To this day, "the growth of the plants is stunted and their reproductive

---

[18] Per F. Peterson, Haihua Zhao, and Robert Petroski, "Metal and concrete inputs for several nuclear power plants," *Report UCBTH-05-001* (University of California—Berkeley), February 4, 2005.
[19] Steve Connor, "Ice pack reveals Romans' air pollution," *Independent*, September 23, 1994.

systems severely damaged."[20] The sheep there still have disturbing concentrations of copper in their feces, urine, and milk. Goats
from the area are in high demand because they have no parasites,
"but this is almost certainly because their guts are poisonous." A
deathly monument of slag still rises 30 meters high.

These things happen in a half-mythical "somewhere else,"
unless you live there, in which case it's your water and air, your
lungs and skin, your cancer, and your child's asthma. Which is why
mines are always fiercely opposed by the people condemned to
endure them.[21]

But mining is dangerous, regulated or unregulated, under capitalism or any other system. This is what mining is: extracting minerals from inside the earth at concentrations that life, both current
and future, cannot possibly withstand.

Extractive processes are energy intensive. Mining is, in essence,
the destruction of rocks. They have to be drilled, blasted, hauled,
crushed, and transported. To state the obvious, rocks are hard and
heavy. The scale of industrial civilization has reached grotesque
proportions, and the mined substances it requires can only be
provided by fossil fuel. But mining has always required machines,
as Mumford described so precisely. He writes, "Ruthless physical coercion, forced labor and slavery ... created complex human
machines ... [which] raised the ceiling of human achievement: the
first in mass construction, the second in mass destruction, both on
a scale hitherto inconceivable." And, 2,000 years later, the generative organs of living creatures at Wadi Faynan are still bearing the
damage.

Rome's mines served both as penal colonies and death penalty.

---

[20] David Keys, "How Rome Polluted the World," *Geographical* (Campion Interactive
Publishing) 75, no. 12 (December 2003), 45.
[21] And why these locals are often ignored or derided as NIMBYs.

A sentence of *damnatio in metalla* turned a citizen into a penal slave in a mine "until they died, which usually didn't take long."[22]

And so, the work army requires the military army: Slaves must be conquered and then controlled. The silver mines of ancient Greece funded its vast imperial navy—with devastation, destruction, and slavery spawning more of the same. That is the totalizing scale of authoritarian technics, which both creates and then requires hierarchical social relations, turning humans into machines that convert more life into more machines.

Here is the full technic of the nuclear power plant: Its physical components require mines and their attendant assaults on life, but it also needs a specific social arrangement that is patriarchal, hierarchical, militaristic, specialized, and mechanistic. And all of that requires an internal theological rationale that life is a series of disconnected objects—things we might call "plants" or "animals" or "rivers"—not complex beings with whom we are engaged in relationships. Mechanical objects are not self-willed creatures; they don't call respect from us; in fact, they barely deserve notice. They exist to be used.

René Descartes bragged, "I have described this earth, and indeed this whole visible world, as a machine."[23] Our science is a series of discoveries designed to let us use them better—and use them we have. There is no brake in the system; why would there be? Indeed, violation is built into mechanistic science. Sir Francis Bacon, who is credited with the creation of the scientific method, was also a legal inquisitor at witch trials. His practical objective was bluntly "dominion over creation," which could be achieved by

---

[22] Carol Ashby, "Crime and Punishment," CarolAshby.com.

[23] René Descartes, *René Descartes: Principles of Philosophy: Translated, with Explanatory Notes,* trans. Valentine R. Miller and Reese P. Miller (Dordrecht: Kluwer Academic Publishers, 1982), 276.

"the inquisition" of mechanical experimentation.[24] The late social psychologist Erich Fromm describes sadism as "the passion to have absolute and unrestricted control over a living being."[25] Is there a more apt description of industrial civilization? Its technology has emptied rivers, crushed mountains, damaged the climate, and broken the boundaries of the atom itself. And the end point of sadism is necrophilia, says Fromm, "the passion to transform that which is alive into something un-alive; to destroy for the sake of destruction; the exclusive interest in all that is purely mechanical."[26]

We are long out of time to break through our cultural denial about this fact: *No technology is neutral.* "An industrial society," writes social critic Kirkpatrick Sale, "has its own inevitable logic, simply because its needs and values are determined by its technology.... [T]he artifacts are not something added on, like a coat of paint or a caboose; they are basic, central, the revelation of its heart and mind."[27] Industrial technics produce speed, efficiency, ease, uniformity, fungibility, and centralization. The word for that is "machine." Having declared the cosmos lifeless, industrial humans are now transforming the biosphere into the technosphere, a dead world of our own artifacts that life as a whole may not survive.

"To maximize energy, speed, or automation," writes Mumford, "without reference to the complex conditions that sustain organic life, have become ends in themselves."[28] Mumford named this drive and its social processes the "megamachine." Sale calls it "the

---

[24] Francis Bacon, *Novum Organum*, Book 2, Aphorism 52 (Works, vol. 4), ed. Joseph Devey, M.A. (New York: P.F. Collier, 1902), 247–248.

[25] Erich Fromm, *The Anatomy of Human Destructiveness* (New York: Holt, Rinehart & Winston, 1973), 332.

[26] Ibid., 332.

[27] Kirkpatrick Sale, *Rebels Against the Future: The Luddites and Their War on the Industrial Revolution: Lessons for the Computer Age* (Reading, MA: Addison-Wesley Publishing Company, 1995), 213.

[28] Mumford, op. cit., 5.

industrial regime." Its existence as a system is barely acknowledged, despite its near total domination of both human affairs and
the planet. As Sale points out, "The industrial regime hardly cares
which cadres run the state as long as they understand the kind of
duties expected of them. It is remarkably protean in that way, for
it can accommodate itself to almost any national system—Marxist
Russia, capitalist Japan, China under a vicious dictator, Singapore
under a benevolent one, messy and riven India, tidy and cohesive
Norway, Jewish Israel, Moslem Egypt—and in return asks only
that its priorities dominate, its markets rule, its values penetrate,
and its interests be defended."[29]

Once, we defended the land. Every last one of us descends from
a line of people who fought, as civilization is universally resisted.
Agriculture takes the forests, the grasslands, the wetlands, everything that it can. The trees go to build the cities and the giant navies
needed to take more. The first written story of this culture and
the second-oldest religious text is *The Epic of Gilgamesh*, which
mythologizes the destruction of the cedar forests of the Middle
East and the murder of its spiritual guardian. "We have reduced
the forest to a wasteland," says the eponymous hero: "How shall
we answer our gods?"

Four thousand years later, here we are. Ninety-eight percent
of the world's old-growth forests are gone. And almost none of us
remember what we all once knew: We—the human race—belong
to one tiny species that's utterly dependent on a million others, and the relationships between all these species—what Gunn
Allen called "circular, circular, circulars"—are more complex than
we could ever know. Wolves restore rivers. Salmon feed forests.
Prairie dogs bring the rain. They are, all of them, our kin.

This is our last chance. Facts must be faced, and our loyalties,

---

[29] Sale, op. cit., 267–8.

finally, declared. Here are the facts as they stand, according to Sale: "The record of the last five thousand years of history clearly suggests that every single preceding civilization has perished ... as a result of its sustained assault on its environment, usually ending in soil loss, flooding, and starvation.... Industrial civilization is different only in that it is now much larger and more powerful than any known before, by geometric differences in all dimensions, and its collapse will be far more extensive and thoroughgoing, far more calamitous."[30] And there is also this fact: The only people who want a nuclear power plant, or a solar panel, or a wind turbine, are people who demand industrial levels of energy. Those levels are needed for a single purpose: the wholesale conversion of the living to the dead, the longest war ever. And our choice is now very stark: Stand with the living or go down with the dead.

This way of living cannot last. And when it is over it would be far better that there be more of the world left rather than less. This is why our actions now are so important. What we do now determines what life is like—or, indeed, whether it exists at all—for those humans and nonhumans who come after us.

We have written this book because life has been broken and is now fast draining away through the cracks. The cultures that have done that breaking need to be abandoned and their ruling sociopaths dethroned. Make no mistake, this will require a serious and dedicated resistance movement. It will also require an unsentimental understanding of which human activities constitute that breaking,

---

[30] Ibid., 278.

and some understanding of how the fractured parts could be rejoined. But in the end, that won't be up to us to decide. The parts—the beavers and the lush abundance of wetlands, the bison and the tenacious grip of grass—will know how to make the whole. We just need to stop destroying and let them do it. And then we need to remember how to bring our own offering to the endless prayer of life creating life, which is life itself.

Chapter 2

SOLVING FOR THE WRONG VARIABLE

What this adds up to should be clear enough, yet many people who should know better choose not to see it. This is business-as-usual: the expansive, colonizing, progressive human narrative, shorn only of the carbon. It is the latest phase of our careless, self-absorbed, ambition-addled destruction of the wild, the unpolluted, and the nonhuman. It is the mass destruction of the world's remaining wild places in order to feed the human economy. And without any sense of irony, people are calling this "environmentalism."[1]

—PAUL KINGSNORTH

Once upon a time, environmentalism was about saving wild beings and wild places from destruction. "The beauty of the living world I was trying to save has always been uppermost in my mind," Rachel Carson wrote to a friend as she finished the manuscript that would become *Silent Spring*. "That, and anger at the senseless, brutish

---

[1] Paul Kingsnorth, "Confessions of a recovering environmentalist," *Orion Magazine*, December 23, 2011.

things that were being done."[2] She wrote with unapologetic reverence of "the oak and maple and birch" in autumn, the foxes in the morning mist, the cool streams and the shady ponds, and, of course, the birds: "In the mornings, which had once throbbed with the dawn chorus of robins, catbirds, doves, jays, and wrens, and scores of other bird voices, there was now no sound; only silence lay over the fields and woods and marshes."[3] Her editor noted that *Silent Spring* required a "sense of almost religious dedication" as well as "extraordinary courage."[4] Carson knew the chemical industry would come after her, and come it did, in attacks as "bitter and unscrupulous as anything of the sort since the publication of Charles Darwin's *Origin of Species* a century before."[5] Seriously ill with the cancer that would kill her, Carson fought back in defense of the living world, testifying with calm fortitude before President John F. Kennedy's Science Advisory Committee and the U.S. Senate. She did these things because she had to. "There would be no peace for me," she wrote to a friend, "if I kept silent."[6]

Carson's work inspired the grassroots environmental movement; the creation of the Environmental Protection Agency (EPA); and the passage of the Clean Air Act, the Clean Water Act, and the Endangered Species Act. *Silent Spring* was more than a critique of pesticides—it was a clarion call against "the basic irresponsibility of an industrialized, technological society toward the natural world."[7]

Today's environmental movement stands upon the shoulders of giants, but something has gone terribly wrong. Carson didn't save

---

[2] Rachel Carson, *Silent Spring* (Greenwich, CT: Fawcett Publishing, 1962), 9.

[3] Ibid., 10.

[4] Ibid., 8.

[5] Ibid., 8.

[6] Ibid., 8.

[7] Ibid., 8.

the birds from DDT so that her legatees could blithely offer them up to wind turbines. We are writing this book because we want our environmental movement back.

Mainstream environmentalists now overwhelmingly prioritize saving industrial civilization over saving life on the planet. The how and the why of this institutional capture is the subject for another book, but the capture is near total. For example, Lester Brown, founder of the Worldwatch Institute and Earth Policy Institute—someone who has been labeled as "one of the world's most influential thinkers" and "the guru of the environmental movement"[8]—routinely makes comments like, "We talk about saving the planet.... But the planet's going to be around for a while. The question is, can we save civilization? That's what's at stake now, and I don't think we've yet realized it." Brown wrote this in an article entitled "The Race to Save Civilization."[9]

The world is being killed *because of* civilization, yet what Brown says is at stake, and what he's racing to save, is precisely the social structure causing the harm: civilization. Not saving salmon. Not monarch butterflies. Not oceans. Not the planet. *Saving civilization.*

Brown is not alone. Peter Kareiva, chief scientist for The Nature Conservancy, more or less constantly pushes the line that "Instead of pursuing the protection of biodiversity for biodiversity's sake, a new conservation should seek to enhance those natural systems that benefit the widest number of people.... Conservation will measure its achievement in large part by its relevance to people."[10]

Bill McKibben, who works tirelessly and selflessly to raise awareness about global warming, and who has been called

[8] "Biography of Lester Brown," Earth Policy Institute.
[9] Lester Brown, "The Race to Save Civilization," *Tikkun*, September/October 2010, 25(5): 58.
[10] Peter Kareiva, Michelle Marvier, and Robert Lalasz, "Conservation in the Anthropocene: Beyond Solitude and Fragility," *Breakthrough Journal*, Winter 2012.

"probably America's most important environmentalist," constantly stresses his work is about saving civilization, with articles like "Civilization's Last Chance,"[11] or with quotes like, "We're losing the fight, badly and quickly—losing it because, most of all, we remain in denial about the peril that human civilization is in."[12]

We'll bet you that polar bears, walruses, and glaciers would have preferred that sentence ended a different way.

In 2014 the Environmental Laureates' Declaration on Climate Change was signed by "160 leading environmentalists from 44 countries" who were "calling on the world's foundations and philanthropies to take a stand against global warming." Why did they take this stand? Because global warming "threatens to cause the very fabric of civilization to crash." The declaration concludes: "We, 160 winners of the world's environmental prizes, call on foundations and philanthropists everywhere to deploy their endowments urgently in the effort to save civilization."[13] Coral reefs, emperor penguins, and Joshua trees probably wish *that* sentence would have ended differently. The entire declaration, signed by "160 winners of the world's environmental prizes," never once mentions harm to the natural world. In fact, it never mentions the natural world at all.

Are leatherback turtles, American pikas, and flying foxes "abstract ecological issues," or are they our kin, each imbued with their own "wild and precious life"?[14]

---

[11] Bill McKibben, "Civilization's Last Chance," *Los Angeles Times*, May 11, 2008.

[12] Bill McKibben, "Global Warming's Terrifying New Math," *Rolling Stone*, August 2, 2012.

[13] "Environmental Laureates' Declaration on Climate Change," European Environment Foundation, September 15, 2014. It shouldn't surprise us that the person behind this declaration is a solar energy entrepreneur. It probably also shouldn't surprise us that he's begging for money.

[14] "Wild and precious life" is from Mary Oliver's poem "The Summer Day." *House of Light* (Boston, MA: Beacon Press, 1992).

Wes Stephenson, yet another climate activist, has this to say: "I'm not an environmentalist. Most of the people in the climate movement that I know are not environmentalists. They are young people who didn't necessarily come up through the environmental movement, so they don't think of themselves as environmentalists. They think of themselves as climate activists and as human rights activists. The terms 'environment' and 'environmentalism' carry baggage historically and culturally. It has been more about protecting the natural world, protecting other species, and conservation of wild places than it has been about the welfare of human beings. I come at it from the opposite direction. It's first and foremost about human beings."[15]

Note that Stephenson calls "protecting the natural world, protecting other species, and conservation of wild places" *baggage.*

Naomi Klein states explicitly in the film *This Changes Everything*: "I've been to more climate rallies than I can count, but the polar bears? They still don't do it for me. I wish them well, but if there's one thing I've learned, it's that stopping climate change isn't really about them, it's about us."

And finally, Kumi Naidoo, former head of Greenpeace International, says: "The struggle has never been about saving the planet. The planet does not need saving."[16]

When Naidoo said that, in December 2015, it was 50 degrees Fahrenheit warmer than normal at the North Pole, above freezing in the winter.

[15] Gabrielle Gurley, "From journalist to climate crusader: Wen Stephenson moves to the front lines of climate movement," *Commonwealth: Politics, Ideas & Civic Life in Massachusetts*, November 10, 2015.

[16] Emma Howard and John Vidal, "Kumi Naidoo: The Struggle Has Never Been About Saving the Planet," *The Guardian*, December 30, 2015.

I (Derrick) wrote this for a friend's wedding.

> *Each night the frogs sing outside my window. "Come to me," they sing. "Come." This morning the rains came, each drop meeting this particular leaf on this particular tree, then pooling together to join the ground. Love. The bright green of this year's growth of redwood trees against the dark of shadows, other trees, tree trunks, foliage, all these plants, reaching out, reaching up. I am in love. With you. With you. With the world. With this place. With each other. Redwoods cannot stand alone. Roots burrow through the soil, reaching out to each other, to intertwine, to hold up these tallest of trees, so they may stand together, each root, each tree, saying to each other, "Come to me. Come." What I want to know is this: What do those roots feel at first touch, first embrace? Do they find this same homecoming I find each time in you, in your eyes, the pale skin of your cheek, your neck, your belly, the backs of your hands? And the water. It is evening now, and the rain has stopped. Yet the water still falls, drop by drop from the outstretched arms of trees. I want to know, as each drop lets go its hold, does it say, and does the ground say to it, as I say to you now, "Come to me. Come."*

In the 15 years since that wedding, the frogs in my pond have suffered reproductive failure, which is science-speak for their offspring dying, baby after baby, year after year. Their songs began to lessen. At first their songs were so loud you could not hold a (human) conversation outside at night, and then you could. The first spring this happened I thought it might just be a bad year. The second spring I sensed a pattern. The third spring I knew something was wrong. I'd also noticed the eggs in their sacs were no longer small black dots, as before, but were covered in what looked like white fur. A little internet research and a few phone calls to herpetologists revealed the problem to me. The egg sacs were being killed by a mold called *saprolegnia*. It wasn't the mold's fault. Saprolegnia is ubiquitous, and eats weak egg sacs, acting as part of a clean-up crew in ponds. The problem is that this culture has depleted the ozone layer, which has allowed more UV-B to come through: UV-B weakens egg sacs in some species.

What do you do when someone you love is being killed? And what do you do when the whole world you love is being killed? I'm known for saying we should use any means necessary to stop the murder of the planet. People often think this is code language for using violence. It's not. It means just what it says: any means necessary.

UV-B doesn't go through glass, so about once a week between December and June, I get into the pond to collect egg sacs to put in big jars of water on my kitchen table. When the egg sacs hatch, I put the babies back in the pond. If I bring in about five egg sacs per week for 20 weeks, and if each sac has 15 eggs in it, and if there's a 10 percent mortality on the eggs instead of a 90 percent mortality, that's 2,400 more tadpoles per year. If one percent of these survive their first year, that's 24 more tadpoles per year who survive. I fully recognize that this doesn't do anything for frogs in other ponds. It doesn't help the newts who are also disappearing from this same pond, or the mergansers, dragonflies, or caddisflies. It doesn't do anything for the 200 species this culture causes to go extinct each and every day. But it does help these.

I don't mean to make too big a deal of this.

One of my earliest memories is from when I was five years old, crying in the locker room of a YMCA where I was taking swimming lessons, because the water was so cold. I really don't like cold water. So, I have to admit I don't get all the way into the water when I go into my pond to help the frogs. I only get in as far as my thighs. But this isn't, surprisingly enough, entirely because of my cold-water phobia. It's because of a creature I've seen in the pond a few times, a giant water bug, which is nicknamed Toe-Biter. My bug book says they're about an inch and a half long, but every time I get in the pond, I'm sure they are five or six inches. And I can't stop thinking about the deflated frog-skin sacks I've seen (the giant water bug injects a substance that liquefies the frog's insides, so they can be sucked out as through a straw). I've read that the bugs sometimes catch small birds. So, you'll note I only go into the pond as deep as my thighs—and no deeper. Second, I have to admit that sometimes I'm not very smart. It took me several years of this weekly cold-water therapy to think of what I now perceive as one of the most important phrases in the English language—"waterproof chest waders"—and to get some.

What do you do when someone you love is being killed? It's pretty straightforward. You defend your beloved. Using any means necessary.

We get it. We, too, like hot showers and freezing cold ice cream, and we like them 24/7. We like music at the touch of a button or, now, a verbal command. We like the conveniences this way of life brings us. And it's more than conveniences. We know that. We three co-authors would be dead without modern medicine. But we all recognize that there is a terrible trade-off for all this: life on the planet. And no individual's conveniences—or, indeed, life—is worth that price.

The price, though, is now invisible. This is the willful blindness of modern environmentalism. Like Naomi Klein and the polar bears, the real world just "doesn't do it" for too many of us. To many people, including even some of those who consider themselves environmentalists, the real world doesn't need our help. It's about us. It's *always* "about us."

Decades ago, I (Derrick) was one of a group of grassroots environmental activists planning a campaign. As the meeting started, we went around the table saying why we were doing this work. The answers were consistent, and exemplified by one person who said, simply, "For the critters," and by another person who got up from the table, walked to her desk, and brought back a picture. At first, the picture looked like a high-up part of the trunk of an old-growth Douglas fir tree, but when I looked more closely, I saw a small spotted owl sticking her camouflaged head out of a hole in the center of the tree's trunk. The activist said, "I'm doing it for her."

The goal has been shifted, slowly and silently, and no one seems to have noticed. Environmentalists tell the world and their organizations that "it's about us." But some of us refuse to forget the last spotted owls in the last scrap of forest, the wild beings and wild places. Like Rachel Carson before us, there will be no peace for us if we keep silent while the critters, one by one, are disappeared. Our once and future movement was for them, not us. We refuse to solve for the wrong variable. We are not saving civilization; we are trying to save the world.

Chapter 3

THE SOLAR LIE
PART I

Alternative energy technologies rely on fossil fuels through
every stage of their life. They rely on fossil fuels for raw material
extraction, for fabrication, for installation and maintenance,
and for decommissioning and disposal.[1]

—OZZIE ZEHNER

If you're near a computer, go to your search engine and type in the words *solar power will save the world*. You'll get millions of hits, with headlines we could have predicted, like: "Top Five Reasons Solar Energy Will Save the World,"[2] "Ten Reasons Renewable Energy Can Save the Planet,"[3] "This [Economic] Boom Might Save

---

[1] Mark Hand, "'*Green Illusions*' author dissects 'overly optimistic expectations' for wind, solar,'" *S&P Global Market Intelligence*, April 1, 2013.
[2] Juan Cole, "Top 5 Reasons Solar Energy Will Save the World," *Informed Comment*, April 23, 2014.
[3] Stefanie Spear, "10 Reasons Renewable Energy Can Save the Planet," *EcoWatch*, October 30, 2014.

the World,"[4] and of course, "Seven Ways Solar Panels Will Save the Planet and Make You Rich."[5]

Solar is being pushed relentlessly as an environmental choice, from universities to Amazon and Fortune 500 companies to major nonprofits and NGOs. Almost every major centrist and progressive institution in the United States, from 350.org to Greenpeace to Democracy Now to prominent members of the Democratic Party, seems committed to a solar-powered future they call "earth friendly."

Meanwhile, a mass movement, able to mobilize hundreds of thousands of people around the world, has been built to stop global warming. If you ask many of the people who march for the environment why they're mobilizing, they'll tell you they're trying to save the planet; but if you ask for their demands, they often respond that they want additional subsidies for solar manufacturers.

Given all this, one could easily be forgiven for concluding that much environmentalism has become a de facto lobbying arm of the solar industry. That's a hell of a PR/marketing coup. And the blame shouldn't go to individual protestors. They're not the problem. The problem is that *this is what capitalism does.*

Subsidizing the energy industry is standard practice. The International Monetary Fund estimates that fossil fuel subsidies cost $5 trillion annually, with coal leading the way at about $2.5 trillion, followed by petroleum at nearly $2 trillion. If you look at the IMF's figures, you'll discover that most of the $5 trillion is

[4] Kaisa Kosonen, "This 'boom' might save the world—10 quick facts about renewable energy," *Greenpeace*, October 30, 2014.
[5] Randy Nelson, "7 Ways Solar Panels Will Save the Planet and Make You Rich," *Movoto Real Estate Blog*, August 8, 2015.

nonmonetary; in other words, they are assigning a dollar amount on externalities such as pollution. Now, if our only choices are to put numbers on externalities or not put numbers on externalities, we'd rather do the former, although we'd prefer to eliminate these externalities altogether. But the real point is that the study, which explicitly calls for increased subsidies for "renewables," fails to mention any of the externalities associated with solar, wind, hydropower, and so on. In fact, the words "solar," "wind," and "hydro" don't even appear in the article.[6] The conclusions of this article have been broadcast widely and repeatedly by proponents of solar subsidies, with never a mention of what was conveniently left off.

Attempts by environmentalists to try to monetize the harmful effects of the industrial economy are one sign of our collective insanity. Here's an example.

Once when I (Derrick) was doing a talk via Skype at an Ivy League school, a few of the faculty and students kept insisting that putting dollar values on nature is a good thing to do—in fact, some environmentalists claim that this is the only way to save wild nature. I finally said to one of the students, "I agree with you. In fact, the same is true for putting dollar values on human beings."

He concurred, noting that insurance companies do this all the time. So do capitalists in general.

So, I asked him, "Since you're at an Ivy League school, shall we say your estimated future earnings run about four million dollars, with a present value then of about a million?"

He said, "Sure, since we're just making up numbers."

"So, imagine this: I talked with your parents," I said, "and we

---

[6] David Coady, Ian Parry, Louis Sears, and Baoping Sheng, "IMF Working Paper: How Large Are Global Energy Subsidies," *International Monetary Fund*, May 2015.

made a deal. The bad news for you is that I'm going to kill you. The good news for you and your parents is that, according to these earnings estimates, I way overpaid. I gave your parents five million dollars for you. They did the math on the back of a napkin, thought it was a fantastic deal, and jumped at the chance. So, are you ready to die?"

He didn't get it.

Assigning dollar values to living oceans or rivers or other natural communities presumes dollar values can mimic real values—that is, the intrinsic values of the oceans, rivers, or natural communities, and the relationships between all of these. For me to assign a dollar value to, say, a river, presumes I know what that river's value is (or else I can at least guess at it), and, more importantly, that this value can be in any reasonable way represented by a dollar amount—which, of course, is nonsensical and arrogant. How can I know the full value of salmon to a forest or the full value of phytoplankton, who provide oxygen for two out of three of animal breaths? How can I know the full value of wind on a hilltop or tidal energy to oceans or sunshine to a desert? How can I know the full value of prairie dogs to prairies, or even shadows of their full values? Why can't we just accept that prairies and prairie dogs know best their value to each other?

For capitalists to assign dollar values to the lives of others presumes capitalism has the capacity to assign accurate value to these others. But if someone paid you a trillion dollars for all the phytoplankton in the world, what would you (or any other animal) breathe?

In fact, if we assign dollar values to "ecosystem services" provided by the natural world, no sector of the industrial economy would be profitable. None. Not even the coal, oil, and gas sectors. Not one of them.[7]

The industrial economy is based on systematic theft from land bases, and the conversion of these living communities into dead products. That's what an industrial economy *is*. The economy does not create value for the real world: It destroys the real world.

Let's say your community has been invaded by a terrifying occupier. It doesn't matter who the invader is. It could be anyone from the Romans to the Imperial British to the Nazis to capitalists to space aliens to conspiracy theorist David Icke's Lizardmen. These conquerors install a violent and exploitative extractive economy (sorry for the redundancy, but, once again, all extractive economies are violent and exploitative). They perceive you and everyone else in your community as inferior to them, and of less value. Indeed, none of you has any inherent value whatsoever; you are valued only to the degree that you're useful to the occupiers.

The crassest occupiers place value on you only insofar as they can convert you directly into cash. If they value your labor, they'll enslave you or pay whomever owns you for this labor. If you have no value to them as a laborer, they'll put monetary values on other ways they can use you. Can they sell your flesh for food? Can your skin be made into jackets? Can your fat be made into soap? Can your teeth be carved into trinkets, or your bones be made into fertilizer? Can your body be used for housing? Can you be burned or otherwise exploited for fuel? Each of these uses adds value, and those values are determined by the overlords. Your value is not

---

[7] David Roberts, "None of the world's top industries would be profitable if they paid for the natural capital they use," *Grist*, April 17, 2013.

determined by you or by those you love, those who love you, or other members of your community.

But why would you put a financial value on yourself anyway? And why, unless you're a sociopath, would you name a financial value for any other member of your community? For how many pieces of silver would you sell your mother?

The slightly more sophisticated of the occupiers recognize that it's possible for you to serve them in ways that can't be immediately monetized, so they'll put dollar values on your "ecosystem services" instead. For example, if your poop can fertilize the soil they're using to grow their crops, then they'll tolerate you being on their agricultural fields so long as you only poop but do not eat their cash crops or otherwise interfere with them.

Because the occupiers are inflicting an extractive economy on your community, it begins to crumble. In fact, your community crumbles so much that it begins to interfere with the occupier's ability to exploit and, ultimately, the occupier's economy.

At that point a few of the occupiers begin to grow concerned, not for your health or the health of your community, of course, because your health and the health of your community never seem to do it for the occupiers, but for the potential failure of their occupation. Some of the occupiers insist the only way to save your community (in order to preserve their economy) is to become ever more obsessed with putting a dollar value on every way they can think of that your existence serves their occupation. Others come up with Plans A through D to Mobilize to Save the Occupation, perhaps making statements like, "We talk about saving the community of subhumans we've conquered and enslaved. Those of us working on taking care of the subhuman community have been talking about the need to save subhumans for some time. But the subhumans are going to be around for a while. The question is, can we save the occupation? That's what's at stake now, and I don't think we've yet realized it."

Next, let's say there's an organization called the Subhuman Conservancy, and its chief scientist states, "Instead of pursuing the protection of subhumans for subhumans' sake, a new conservation should seek to enhance those processes of the subhumans that benefit the widest number of occupiers.... Conservation will measure its achievement in large part by its relevance to occupiers." A typical occupier states, "I'm not a subhuman liberationist. Most of the people in the movement to save the occupation aren't subhuman liberationists. The term 'subhuman liberation' carries baggage historically and culturally. It has been more about protecting the subhumans than it has been about the welfare of the occupiers. I come at it from the opposite direction. It's first and foremost about the occupiers and maintaining the occupation." Another says, "But the subhumans? They still don't do it for me. I wish them well, but if there's one thing I've learned, it's that it's about us." And yet another says, "The struggle has never been about saving the subhumans. The subhumans do not need saving."

It takes tremendous energy to maintain the lifestyle of the occupiers, and 160 especially enlightened occupiers state that the occupiers need to switch from one energy source to another, or else the very fabric of their occupation might crash.

The most reliable numbers show that in 2013, the United States subsidized the solar industry by more than $5 billion (almost $3 billion in direct expenditures, more than $2 billion in tax credits, and almost $300 million in research and development). Wind received almost six billion. Coal received a little over a billion in subsidies, nuclear received almost $1.7 billion, and "natural gas and petroleum liquids" received about $2.4 billion.[8] No matter who makes up these numbers, they contain a lot of fudge factors.

So far, Americans aren't getting a lot of brightness for the buck, as solar accounts for far less than 1 percent of U.S. electricity generation.[9]

Using another set of numbers, if you calculate the subsidies per "energy unit" produced, then coal, oil, and gas receive the smallest financial subsidy, at 0.8 cents per kilowatt hour, followed by nuclear at 1.7 cents per kilowatt hour, and so-called renewables and so-called biofuels at 5.0 and 5.1 cents per kilowatt hour, respectively.[10]

For many environmentalists, Germany is the shining city upon a hill. Certainly, it's a success story for investors in the solar industry, as Germany has provided the solar industry with subsidies of well over $10 billion a year,[11] with some sources estimating these

---

[8] "Direct Federal Financial Interventions and Subsidies in Energy in Fiscal Year 2013," United States Energy Information Administration, March 12, 2015, revised March 23, 2015. This is an example of how tricky these subsidies are to tease out, since, among other problems, these figures don't include any of the externalities foisted on humans and nonhumans by these industries. Subsidies for natural gas and petroleum liquids don't include deaths from oil or gas extraction; those for nuclear don't include military expenditures on nuclear programs; coal subsidies don't include the destruction of entire mountain communities; and solar subsidies don't include the horrors of rare earths mining.

[9] Calculated from Table ES-3 in "Direct Federal Financial Interventions and Subsidies in Energy in Fiscal Year 2013," op. cit.

[10] "Relative Subsidies to Energy Sources: GSI Estimates," Global Subsidies Initiative, April 19, 2010. Some of these energy sources, like fossil fuels, aren't normally measured in kilowatt-hours. Please see original source for their underlying assumptions.

[11] Alexander Neubacher, "Solar Subsidy Sinkhole," *Der Spiegel*, January 18, 2012.

subsidies at $26 billion a year.[12] But what are the results of these subsidies? Have they helped the living world?

The answer depends on whom you ask. Bill McKibben says the results of these subsidies "are un-fucking-believable. Munich's north of Montreal, and there were days this month [December] when they got half their energy from solar panels. It has nothing to do with technology or location—it's all political will, and they have it."[13]

Unfortunately, McKibben is right: these results literally are not believable, since such a claim is physically impossible. Because solar panels *only* generate electricity, and because about 80 percent of Munich's energy consumption is *not* in the form of electricity, half of Munich's energy *can't* come from solar panels. Further, when McKibben said this in 2012, it was during the month of December, when solar power is at its weakest and supplies perhaps 5 percent of Munich's electricity. He may have been referring not to "days" or even "one day" during "this month," but rather to a single short period the previous May when, for about *two hours* (on a Saturday, i.e., not a business day), Munich got 50 percent of its *electricity* from solar.[14]

If you talk to longtime solar booster Thomas Friedman of the *New York Times*, he may tell you that "Germany today deserves a Nobel Peace Prize." Why? He cites Ralf Fücks, president of the German Green Party's political foundation. Writes Friedman, "In my view, the greatest success of the German energy transition was giving a boost to the Chinese solar panel industry." This subsidy

---

[12] Leonid Bershidsky, "Germany's Green Energy Is an Expensive Success," *Bloomberg View*, September 22, 2014.

[13] Stephen Markley, "The Rumpus Interview with Bill McKibben," *The Rumpus*, December 10, 2012.

[14] Robert Wilson, "Bill McKibben Mistaken on German Solar Energy," *The Energy Collective*, May 14, 2013.

reduced the price of solar photovoltaics; hence, Friedman's suggestion that Germany receive the Nobel Peace Prize. Germany gave the Chinese solar panel industry this boost, Friedman acknowledges, through a surcharge—not on industrial consumers, but on German households, which paid on average $220 a year. So, in effect, Germany deserves a Nobel Peace Prize for the forced contributions of private German citizens to Chinese corporations. Friedman concludes by urging Germany to stop its post-World-War-II pacifism and become not just a "superpower" but "Europe's first green, solar-powered superpower."[15]

If ending a pacifism that was born of the shame and horror of waging aggressive wars that cost tens of millions of lives and destroyed an entire continent for a couple of generations doesn't put Germany in line for a Nobel Peace Prize, we don't know what would.

The notion that a "superpower" can be "green" reveals the bankruptcy of the bright green ethos. Bright green supporters presume you can have the material benefits of a colonial social and economic system, including an industrial infrastructure, without the horrors and exploitation of a colonial social and economic system. We hope by the end of this book it's clear there can be no such thing as a "green superpower," a "green industrial system," or a "nonextractive industrial system." Those are all oxymorons.

If you ask mainstream environmentalists what they think of Germany's solar policies, you'll hear the words "miracle" and "success" again and again. A Google search yields headlines like, "Germany leads way on renewables...."[16] and "Germany's renewable

[15] Thomas Friedman, "Germany: The Green Superpower," *New York Times*, May 6, 2015.
[16] "Germany leads way on renewables, Sets 45% target by 2030," *Worldwatch Institute*.

energy sector is among the most innovative and successful world-wide."[17] Or: "Germany's impressive streak of renewable energy milestones continued, with renewable energy generation surging...."[18] Or: "Germany's transition to renewable power has been a stunning success."[19]

Sounds great! But, on the other hand, if you read the German magazine *Der Spiegel*, the answer you get might be the subhead of the 2012 article "Solar Subsidy Sinkhole": "The costs of subsidizing solar electricity have exceeded the 100-billion-euro mark in Germany, but poor results are jeopardizing the country's transition to renewable energy. The government is struggling to come up with a new concept to promote the inefficient technology in the future."[20]

Let's ignore for a moment the fact that all of these answers are about solar power's effects on the economy, not the real, physical world. Have these subsidies been an economic success?

The answer, according to solar lobbyists, is a resounding *yes*. Isn't it great that Germany now has solar panels on lots of rooftops and solar-powered funfairs and soccer stadiums? Who could complain about that? (Well, maybe some soccer fans, like those of Germany's Werder Bremen football club, since its solar-powered stadium is so expensive that Werder Bremen can't afford to pay decent players without subsidies from the government: "[Klaus] Filbry [the Werber Bremen Club's CEO] admits that the club had

---

[17] "Renewable Energy in Germany," Wikipedia.

[18] Kiley Kroh, "Germany Sets New Record, Generating 74 Percent of Power Needs from Renewable Energy," *Climate Progress*, May 13, 2014.

[19] Chris Nelder, "Myth-Busting Germany's Energy Transition," *ZDNet*, October 12, 2013.

[20] Alexander Neubacher, "Solar Subsidy Sinkhole: Re-Evaluating Germany's Blind Faith in the Sun: Part 2: Solar Energy's 'Extreme and Even Excessive Boom,'" *Der Spiegel*, January 18, 2012.

less money to spend on players for a time but stoutly denies any link to the club's current position at the bottom of the Bundesliga.")[21]

A crappy football team, however, is trivial compared to saving the planet. Germany has subsidized lots of utility-scale solar and rooftop solar generators. That is precisely the transformation this society needs to become sustainable and save the earth! Right?

Wrong! Because these solar panels, so loved by the bright greens, produce only tiny amounts of electricity: about 3 percent of the total electrical supply.[22]

Fossil fuel provided 84 percent of Germany's energy in 2000. Writes science journalist Paul Voosen, "Then the country embarked on a historic campaign, building 90 gigawatts of renewable power capacity, enough to match its existing electricity generation. But because Germany sees the sun only 10 percent of the time, the country is as hooked as ever on fossil fuels: In 2017, they still supplied 80 percent of its energy.... The nation doubled its hypothetical capacity to create electricity but has gotten minimal environmental benefit."[23]

And that's not even the real point. The real point is that all of this investment in solar has done a great big nothing to reduce global warming emissions. And it was never meant to: German investment in wind and solar is an explicit attempt to move away from nuclear, not coal, oil, and gas. From 2011 to 2013, electrical generation by coal and lignite (which receive about 2.8 billion per year in subsidies) increased by 2 percent, up to 45 percent.[24] Despite its own coal and lignite fields, Germany imports coal from China and

---

[21] Arthur Nelson, "German solar ambitions at risk from cuts to subsidies," *The Guardian*, November 5, 2014.

[22] Neubacher, op. cit.

[23] Paul Voosen, "Meet Vaclav Smil, the man who has quietly shaped how the world thinks about energy," *Science*, March 21, 2018.

[24] Arthur Nelson, op. cit.

Australia. Further, Germany is the fifth-largest consumer of oil in the world. Even with huge subsidies to "renewables," wind and solar combine for a whopping 3.3 percent of all German energy consumption.[25]

"But wait!" you may say. "How can you say wind and solar account for only 3.3 percent of German energy consumption, when bright greens say 'renewables' account for 25 percent, I mean 30 percent, I mean 74 percent, I mean 78 percent, I mean, soon-to-be 100 percent of German energy or power?"

We are fully aware that energy and power are not the same. We are not conflating them. Part of the point of the following discussion is that too many bright greens inaccurately conflate energy and power in ways that serve their political ends. Here are some examples of the claims being made about Germany's renewable energy production:

In 2014, Naomi Klein, author of *This Changes Everything: Capitalism vs. the Climate* and board member of 350.org, stated during an interview with Democracy Now: "Twenty-five percent of Germany's energy now comes from renewable energy, particularly wind and solar, much of it small-scale and decentralized."[26]

Avi Lewis, director of the documentary film version of *This Changes Everything*, says: "Germany is ... one of the top economies

[25] Robert Wilson, "Germany gets only 3.3 percent of its energy consumption from wind and solar. Ignore the headlines," *Carbon Counter: Observations on energy and climate change from Robert Wilson*, July 31, 2015.
[26] "Capitalism vs. the Climate: Naomi Klein on Need for New Economic Model to Address Ecological Crisis," *Democracy Now*, September 18, 2014.

in the world. And in the last 15 years they've shifted their electricity system to 30 percent renewable."[27]

Bill McKibben once cited a *Bloomberg Business* article with the headline, "Germany Reaches New Levels of Greendom," then tweeted: "German renewables continue to soar: 31 freaking percent of its power already. Coal use falling."[28]

"Lefty Coaster," a writer for *The Daily Kos*, says: "Germany has reached the point where it had gotten over 74 percent of its electrical power from renewable sources the other day. That's a huge milestone, and it demonstrates that renewable sources can power a large industrial nation. Germany shows us that renewables aren't a potential source of power for some time in the future; they are a viable alternative *today*."[29]

Kiley Kroh, senior editor at ThinkProgress, reports: "On Sunday, Germany's impressive streak of renewable energy milestones continued, with renewable energy generation surging to a record portion—nearly 75 percent—of the country's overall electricity demand by midday."[30]

Fellow ThinkProgress writer Ari Phillips noted in 2015: "On Saturday, July 25, Germany set a new national record for renewable

[27] Jon Queally, "As 'This Changes Everything' Debuts in US, Leave Your Climate Despair at the Door," *Common Dreams*, October 1, 2015. It often seems like it's more important for many mainstream environmentalists and progressive journalists to avoid feeling despair than it is for them to stop the horrors.

[28] Bill McKibben (@billmckibben), "*Business Week*: German renewables continue to soar: 31 freaking percent of its power already. Coal use falling," Twitter post, August 19, 2014. And for the record, coal use wasn't falling. Lignite use fell slightly. Coal and lignite aren't the same thing. Lignite is a type of soft coal. Please note also that McKibben is seeming to imply a correlation—or even causation—between "soaring" renewables and "falling" coal. But that's not been shown. As said in the text: Renewables are explicitly meant to replace nuclear, not coal.

[29] Lefty Coaster, "Germany got 74% of its electrical power from Renewable Sources the other day," *The Daily Kos*, May 18, 2014. Italics in original.

[30] Kiley Kroh, "Germany Sets New Record, Generating 74 Percent of Power Needs from Renewable Energy," *Climate Progress*, May 13, 2014.

energy by meeting 78 percent of the day's electricity demand with renewable sources."[31]

Melanie Mattauch, 350.org's Europe communications coordinator, says German solar power "floods the power grid."[32]

So how do we make sense of it all? Which is it: 3 percent or 25 percent or 78 percent? How can the claims be so varied? Don't some of them have to be false? What's really going on?

We should start by getting clear on what is meant by "renewable energy." The term usually refers to wind and solar. But "renewables" also includes hydroelectricity and biofuels (as well as geothermal energy, tidal energy from oceans, ocean thermal energy conversion, and a few other forms, but these forms are all trivial or nonexistent in Germany).

Let's get hydropower out of the way first, since it only accounts for about 3.5 percent of Germany's electricity (and less than 1 percent of Germany's energy demand). While hydropower is certainly renewable, at least for the 50-to-100-year operational existence of a dam,[33] dams are profoundly destructive of the natural world. They kill the creatures in the riparian zones—interfaces between land and rivers or streams—that they inundate. And they kill the riparian zones themselves. They deprive rivers above dams of nutrients from anadromous fish. They deprive floodplains below of nutrients flowing downstream. They destroy habitat for fish and other creatures who live in flowing rivers and cannot survive in warm, slow-moving reservoirs. And they aren't, as bright greens,

---

[31] Ari Phillips, "Germany Just Got 78 Percent of Its Electricity from Renewable Sources," *Climate Progress*, July 29, 2015.

[32] Melanie Mattauch, "Power struggle: after Germany's renewables surge, can it keep its coal in the ground?" *The Ecologist*, May 22, 2015.

[33] And presuming global warming and water theft by agriculture and industry don't dry up the entire region. See, for example, Tanzania, which is converting back to fossil fuels because reservoirs are drying.

governments, and capitalists in general falsely claim, "carbon-neutral." Dams have been called "methane bombs" and "methane factories" because they emit so much methane, an extremely potent greenhouse gas. They are, in fact, methane's single-largest anthropogenic (human-created) source, accounting for 23 percent of all methane emitted because of humans.[34] Dams can release up to three and a half times as much greenhouse gases per unit of energy as is released by burning oil, primarily because, as an article in *New Scientist* points out, "Large amounts of carbon tied up in trees and other plants are released when the reservoir is initially flooded and the plants rot. Then after this first pulse of decay, plant matter settling on the reservoir's bottom decomposes without oxygen, resulting in a buildup of dissolved methane. This is released into the atmosphere when water passes through the dam's turbines."[35]

From the perspective of the health of the planet, the best thing we can say about dams is that, eventually, they fail.

So, when bright greens give you a number for how much electricity is consistently generated by renewables in Germany, if you care about the health of the real, physical world, take 3.5 percent off the top, since that electricity comes from dams. (In some countries, like Costa Rica or Norway, you have to take off much more, because 50 to 100 percent of their "renewable" electricity comes from hydro.)

While you're at it, cut the bright greens' "renewable electricity" number by about another third, because 30 percent of all renewable electricity in Germany comes from what bright greens call "biofuels" or "biomass"—biofuels like ethanol are derived from

---

[34] Gary Wockner, "The Hydropower Methane Bomb No One Wants to Talk About," *EcoWatch*, October 6, 2015.
[35] Duncan Graham-Rowe, "Hydroelectric power's dirty secret revealed," *New Scientist*, February 24, 2005.

living materials, like corn; and biomass, in this sense, is just a fancy word that means burning living materials like wood—and what you and I might call "planting monocrops to use as fuel," or "cutting down forests to burn." The salient points are that a) "biofuels" are counted as "renewables"; b) they're counted as "carbon-neutral"; and c) countries are legally and financially encouraged to deforest in the name of being "green" and "environmentally responsible." This is the Orwellian world into which bright green environmentalism—with its prioritization of fueling the economy over saving the real world—drives us: This culture is cutting down forests to stop global warming and cutting down forests to save the planet.

Because of encouragements (read: subsidies and propaganda) to go green—albeit a perverse shade of green—the use of biomass and biofuels has exploded over the past 30 years. In 1990, biofuels accounted for about a quarter of 1 percent of Germany's electricity generation, and most of that came from burning wastes from other forms of processing (essentially sawdust, agricultural wastes, and so on). By 2015 biofuels in Germany had increased 35 times. As of 2020, biomass accounts for about 60 percent of EU renewable energy production.[36] There obviously isn't enough waste material to burn, so up has gone the percentage of land devoted to "biofuels." As energy analyst Robert Wilson states, "The production of bio-energy is also now a significant form of land-use in Germany. According to official statistics a total of 2 million hectares is devoted to crop-based biofuels. This is 17 percent of arable land and approximately 6 percent of total land in Germany."[37]

Forests in the United States, Canada, South Africa, Germany,

---

[36] Saul Elbein, "Europe's renewable energy policy is built on burning American trees," *Vox*, March 4, 2019.

[37] Robert Wilson, "Biomass: the hidden face of the Energiewende," *Energy Post*, May 14, 2014. These 2 million hectares produce only 2 percent of Germany's energy, which Robert Wilson points out is "a remarkably inefficient use of land."

Sweden, Czech Republic, Norway, Russia, Belarus, Ukraine, and many other countries are being felled to feed Europe's demand for biofuels. There are dozens of huge pulp mills just in the southeastern United States exporting *100 percent* of this biomass to Europe. The wetland forests located in the Southern states are right now being "drained, logged, burned, shipped across the Atlantic, and converted to monoculture pine plantations."[38] Somewhere between 50 and 80 percent of Southern wetland forests is already gone. Let that settle in before you take on the next horror: The Southern wetland forests area is being logged four times faster than the South American rainforests—the term "logged" serving as a nice ellipsis of the devastation. The Southern Coastal Plain is a designated biodiversity hotspot, which means there are creatures who live there and nowhere else. Losing these individual creatures' lives is bad enough, but at risk are entire species because they have nowhere else to go.

For instance, the Florida yew, a small evergreen tree, is critically endangered because its home is a 15-mile length of the Apalachicola River. That's all they've got, and once it's gone, so are they. Also endangered is the Southeastern American Kestrel, the smallest falcon in North America. Their lives depend on red-cockaded woodpeckers, who are built for hollowing out nest cavities. Raptors are not, so the kestrels need the woodpeckers' abandoned nests. This is just one example of the mutual dependence that aggregates—everywhere, always—into life as a whole. It goes without saying that the logging of the Apalachicola River also endangers the red-cockaded woodpecker and longleaf pines.

Last in this elegiac sample is the gopher tortoise. The tortoise digs burrows that are 40 feet long and 10 feet deep. That is

---

[38] Rachel Fritts, "Why are America's wetlands being destroyed in the name of renewable energy?" *Pacific Standard*, June 14, 2018.

extraordinary enough, but there's more: Nearly 400 other species depend on those burrows. Four hundred other mammals, birds, reptiles, amphibians, and insects cannot survive without the protective cover created by the tortoises who are now critically endangered.

These relationships of give-and-take, need-and-help, feed-and-be-fed are what create the whole. To scale up a phrase: An insult to one is a permanent injury to all, with insults as catastrophic as an entire biotic community pelleted, shipped to Europe, and burned.

This is the magnitude in time and numbers. This forest has been an ancient refugium since the Pleistocene. The biological diversity is "virtually unparalleled in North America."

There are 190 tree species in the Southern Coastal Plain, with 27 endemic plants and animals. Beneath the trees, there are "3,417 species of native herbaceous and shrub species, and among the highest levels of endemism found in North America"; and the forest is lush with "reptiles, amphibians, butterflies, and mammals"[39] who exist nowhere else and are barely hanging on. They are our kin—our fragile, wondrous, desperate kin—and right now environmentalists would have them reduced to pellets while calling their slaughter "green."

One pro-industry researcher blandly describes Germany's increasing reliance on biofuels: "As North West European wood resources are not sufficient for this sudden demand, the region relies on imports from abroad."[40] Germany also deforests its own lands:

---

[39] "Southeastern conifer forest," World Wildlife Fund.

[40] Clemens von Wülsch, "Financial analysis of the transport of wood chips as an option among other solid fiber-based combustibles from the USA to Germany" (Master's Thesis, abstract, University of North Carolina—Wilmington / Bremen University of Applied Sciences, 2011).

almost half of Germany's timber production is simply cutting down trees, pulping them, drying them into pellets, and burning them.

It's even worse than this. As *Climate Central* reporter John Upton makes clear, "Burning wood pellets to produce a megawatt hour of electricity produces 15 to 20 percent more climate-changing carbon dioxide pollution than burning coal, analysis of [biomass corporation] Drax data shows. And that's just the CO_2 pouring out of the smokestack. Add in pollution from the fuel needed to grind, heat and dry the wood, plus transportation of the pellets, and the climate impacts are even worse. According to [biomass corporation] Enviva, that adds another 20 percent worth of climate pollution for that one-megawatt hour."[41]

So, how can the bright greens call this carbon neutral?

One argument is that because trees originally sequestered carbon in their bodies as they grew, and will eventually release this carbon when they die, we may as well cut them down now and burn them. As the industry lobbying group American Forests and Paper Association (AFPA) puts it: "As forests grow, carbon dioxide (CO_2) is removed from the atmosphere via photosynthesis. This CO_2 is converted into organic carbon and stored in woody biomass. Trees release the stored carbon when they die, decay, or are combusted. As the biomass releases carbon as CO_2, the carbon cycle is completed. The carbon in biomass will return to the atmosphere regardless of whether it is burned for energy, allowed to biodegrade, or lost in a forest fire."[42]

Their argument boils down to this: If you're going to die someday anyway, why don't I just kill you now?

And it's profoundly misleading. As forests grow, they sequester more and more carbon. Individual trees (and whole forests)

---

[41] John Upton, "Pulp Fiction," Climate Central, October 21, 2015.

[42] "Biomass Carbon Neutrality," American Forest and Paper Association, July 2014.

sequester more carbon per year with age. Forests also create soil, which can store carbon for tens of thousands of years. Logging destroys that soil, which is one reason logging in states like Oregon is by far the largest source of carbon emissions.[43] As one researcher wrote, "The [carbon emission] accounting rules were written by loggers for loggers."[44]

The AFPA's argument also ignores the importance of dead trees to the health of forests. Dead trees—the ones being "allowed" to biodegrade—are habitat to even more species than are live trees (think, for example, of birds nesting in holes in standing dead trees).

It shouldn't surprise us that the AFPA ignores the role of dead trees to forest health, not only because the AFPA lobbies for an industry, and therefore lies, but also because the entire industry for which it lobbies is based on systematically devaluing the role of *live* trees to the health of forests; otherwise, it couldn't cut them down.

Another way to put the argument for the "carbon neutrality" of biomass is that, since the carbon was already stored when the trees grew, all that's being done is the rereleasing of previously stored carbon—which is kind of like spending money we already put in savings. That, too, is crap, for a few reasons. The first is that we didn't store that carbon. Trees did. This is analogous to you putting money into your savings account, and someone else taking it out and spending it, then calling it even. You might call that theft, but bright greens might call that "dollar neutral": *A dollar was put in, and a dollar was taken out, so what's your problem?* It's also

---

[43] Carl Segerstrom, "Timber is Oregon's biggest carbon polluter," *High Country News*, May 16, 2018.

[44] Michael Le Page, "Logging study reveals huge hidden emissions of the forest industry," *New Scientist*, September 10, 2019.

crap because you can make the same argument about coal and oil: *The carbon got sequestered by algae in the time of dinosaurs, and we're just taking it back out.*[45]

And it's crap for yet another reason: Trees do not exist to clean up our messes. Nor are they dollars on the stump. Nor do they exist just for us to burn. They have their own lives and play their own roles in their own natural communities. There are five million species who directly depend on forests[46]—fully 80 percent of terrestrial biodiversity.[47] Ursula K. Le Guin said the same with more poetry and fewer numbers: "The word for world is forest."[48] Now, humans have killed more than 50 percent of forest animals in the last 40 years.[49] Do these forest animals count? What of the trees themselves—beings who feel, learn, communicate, and care for each other? Dr. Suzanne Simard writes that she was "staggered" to discover that paper birches were feeding firs "like carers in human social networks,"[50] and that, over time, the trees took turns being the carer, depending on the season: "Mother trees recognize and talk with their kin, shaping future generations.... Injured trees pass their legacies on to their neighbors, affecting gene regulation, defense chemistry, and resilience in the forest community." There has been careful scientific research discovering plant sentience. They are beings not so different from us, as it turns out.

---

[45] It's like an inheritance, and there's no money more fun to spend than money you didn't earn! As we see, the same is true for energy.

[46] Benjamin Jones, Carolyn Ciciarelli, Eric Dinerstein and Michael Anderson, "Forests Housing Rare and Endangered Species Lost 1.2 Million Hectares of Trees Since 2001," World Resources Institute, May 6, 2015.

[47] "Forest Habitat," World Wildlife Fund.

[48] Ursula K. Le Guin, *The Word for World is Forest* (New York: Berkley Books, 1976).

[49] Jane Dalton, "More than half of world's forest wildlife lost in 40 years, study finds," *Independent*, August 13, 2019.

[50] Suzanne Simard, "Note from a forest scientist," in Peter Wohlleben, *The Hidden Life of Trees: What They Feel, How They Communicate: Discoveries from a Secret World* (Vancouver, Canada: Greystone Books, 2015).

A discussion of whether deforestation is carbon neutral without a simultaneous discussion of whether deforestation is morally neutral is only possible if you believe humans are the only beings who subjectively exist on the planet. Understanding that trees—and the five million species they cradle, nourish, and protect—also subjectively exist changes everything.

A related argument for carbon neutrality is that although you may be cutting down trees and releasing carbon, since trees grow back, the carbon will be resequestered in the future, thereby rendering the process carbon neutral. As John Upton writes, "When power plants in major European countries burn wood, the only carbon dioxide pollution they report is from the burning of fossil fuels needed to manufacture and transport the woody fuel. European law assumes climate pollution released directly by burning fuel made from trees doesn't matter, because it will be reabsorbed by trees that grow to replace them. The assumption is convenient, but wrong. Climate science has been rejecting it for more than 20 years. It ignores the decades it can take for a replacement forest to grow to be as big as one that was chopped down for energy—or the possibility that it won't regrow at all. The assumption also ignores the loss of a tree's ability to absorb carbon dioxide after it gets cut down, pelletized and vaporized. The accounting trick allows the energy industry to pump tens of millions of tons of carbon dioxide into the air every year and pretend it doesn't exist."[51]

The argument is that biomass is carbon neutral because the trees will grow back, and the carbon will be recaptured over the next 100 years. But this is accounting fraudulent enough to make Enron

---

[51] Upton, op. cit.

envious. Can you imagine what would happen to even a corpora-tion (although nothing ever happens to corporations) that tried to claim its books were balanced because it was spending money now, and *hoping* to accumulate that same amount of money over the next 100 years?

It's worse than this. Because the (de)foresters didn't sequester the carbon, but rather the forest did, the more accurate analogy would be an Enron-style company stealing from people, then say-ing this is not theft because in time their victims will earn more money to put back into the bank (which will then again be stolen—we mean, harvested—by the company).

"Growth of renewable energy [in the EU] since 2000...only really came from three energy sources: wind, solar and biomass," writes Wilson. "The absolute growth of biomass was 1.5 times greater than in wind and solar, and so far, the majority of new renewable energy since 2000 has come from biomass, not wind and solar."

He continues, "Biomass is also the biggest source of renew-able energy, on a final energy consumption basis, in all but two EU countries.... Denmark may get 30 percent of its electricity from wind farms, but it still gets more than twice as much of its final energy consumption from biomass than from wind farms."

As for the German success story, he says, "The supposedly rapid expansion of solar power gets a lot of attention. The even more rapid expansion of biomass however has received absolutely no attention.... Absolute growth of biomass in Germany has ... been three times higher than for wind and solar combined."

Forgotten in all of this, of course, are the forests themselves. Seventy percent of Germany's "renewable" energy comes from biomass, from the wholesale slaughter of forests. *Will you "speak for the trees, for the trees have no tongues"?*[52] There's not a forest in the world that has survived more than three rotations of being cut.[53] You can't cut down a forest, take out all of that biomass (read: the bodies of those who live in and make up the forest), and expect the forest to continue to live. Yet bright greens, capitalists, and nations continue to count biomass as carbon neutral, and count it and its numbers as part of the German "success story," while spring grows ever more silent.

Earlier we stated that 30 percent of Germany's "renewable" electricity comes from biomass. This may seem like a contradiction, but the first statement concerns energy while the second is about electricity. Most biomass is used for purposes other than generating electricity. Two examples would be burning wood for heat and converting corn or turnips into methane or other gases to be burned for heat or transportation.

---

[52] Dr. Seuss, *The Lorax* (New York: Random House), 1971.

[53] Chris Maser, "Logging to Infinity," *Anderson Valley Advertiser*, April 12, 1989. Maser said, "I know of no nation and no people that have maintained, on a sustainable basis, plantation managed trees beyond three rotations. The famous Black Forest in Europe is a plantation; it and other forests are dying at the end of the third rotation. The eastern pine plantations are dying. It's the end of their third rotation. We do not have any third rotations here. I was quoted on this in a newspaper article, a little out of context, but not badly. One of the gentlemen from the industry said, 'Well, geez, we're in our third rotation and trees are growing better than ever.' But he counted nature's old-growth as one of those rotations. We're only now cutting the second rotation, and the forest is not producing as it did. We do not value the land if we harvest the land's products to a maximum and make payments in minimums. We spend the least amount possible on every acre and harvest the maximum amount possible. We are not in any sense willing to reinvest in any natural, renewable resource."

We're going to suggest what is for this culture a radical redefinition of what it means for an action to be "green" or "environmental," which is that the action must tangibly benefit the natural world on the natural world's own terms. Not that the action helps fuel the industrial economy. Not that the action makes your life easier. Not that the action seems like a success, such that it helps you not feel despair. The action must tangibly help tigers, or hammerhead sharks, or Coho salmon, or Pacific lampreys, or sea stars, or the oceans, or the Colorado River, or the Great Plains.

Environmentalism for the real world: what a concept.

There's a difference between "energy" and "power." Energy is defined as the capacity to do work, with work defined as a force moving an object. I know that sounds complicated, but examples make it clear: It takes energy to do the work of moving your car (or you) from your house to the grocery store. It takes more energy to move a heavier car, and it takes more energy to move a car farther. Likewise, it takes energy to heat water.[54] The hotter you want the water, the more energy it takes: it takes more energy to heat water sufficiently to boil eggs than it does to heat it to bath temperature. And, obviously, the more water you have, the more energy it takes to heat it: it takes more energy to heat a bathtub full of water than it does to heat a small pan to the same temperature. The energy that has gone into the water then remains in the water (as heat), before eventually dissipating into the room. This is why one of my (Derrick's) physics professors advised never draining warm

---

[54] In the case of heating water or anything else, the objects being moved are molecules. That's what heat *is*: the hotter something is, the faster the molecules are moving.

bathtubs: it lets all that heat (energy) go down the drain. Instead, he said, we should let it warm our homes. For years I followed his advice, until one day, while lying in the tub with my feet against the wall, the wall collapsed, leaving me wondering why the physics professor hadn't mentioned that letting all that warm, moist air stay in the room would rot the drywall. It took energy to carry the broken tiles and ruined drywall from the bathroom to my truck, energy to drive the truck to the dump, and so on. At the time, I lived in a double-wide manufactured home with two bathrooms, so for the next year and a half, until a friend fixed the master bath, I also used energy to walk to use the other bathroom.

Energy can come from burning things (like wood or oil); from an object in motion (like a car or a bullet—a car has more mass but a bullet probably has more velocity, and if either one hits you it will probably do work on your body); from metabolizing food (moving your body is work, too, and that energy has to come from somewhere); and from other sources.

Some common measures of energy are joules, calories, British thermal units, kilowatt-hours, and so on.

Power, on the other hand, is the rate at which this work is done. More power means the work is done faster. As one analysis of energy versus power puts it: "While energy measures the *total quantity* of work done, it doesn't say how fast you can get the work done. You could move a loaded semi-trailer across the country with a lawnmower engine if you didn't care how long it took. Other things being equal, the tiny engine would do the same amount of work as the truck's big one. And it would produce the same amount of energy and burn the same amount of fuel. But the bigger engine has more power, so it can get the job done faster."[55] This is why so many auto enthusiasts get all jazzed about an engine's horsepower, which is a measure of how fast your car's engine can convert the energy in the gasoline into mechanical energy to make your ride peel out from the stoplight, leaving all the "scrubs" and "lamers" behind.

The primary unit for measuring power is the watt (1/746th of a horsepower). The most common way most of us think of watts is in lightbulbs or other electronics. The same principle holds here: a 120-watt bulb consumes electricity (electrical energy), turning it into light and heat twice as fast as a 60-watt bulb. If you leave a 60-watt bulb (60 watts being the *power* of the bulb) on for an hour, you've used 60 watt-hours of energy. If you run it for 16 hours and 40 minutes, you'll have used one kilowatt-hour of energy. If you leave it on longer than that, your mother will probably tell you to turn it off.

Now, you've probably noticed from your power bill that you're charged for the number of kilowatt-hours you use (recall that kilowatt-hours are energy, not power). This should upset the pedant in all of us, since this means, of course, that your power bill should rightly be called your "energy bill."

Which brings us to the distinction between energy and power as concerns this discussion. Because the amount of energy you get from burning a barrel of a certain type of oil or a ton of a certain type of coal or a cord of a certain type of firewood (or, for that matter, by eating a Twinkie) is predictable, and because this energy can be stored at will (coal and oil, evidently, for tens of millions of

---

[55] Rob Lewis, "The Great 'Power versus Energy' Confusion," *Clean Technica*, February 2, 2015. And please note that he's oversimplifying to make a point, in that he's presuming, among other things, that the cross-country trek would be completely flat. A lawnmower engine obviously couldn't pull a semi load up a hill.

years, and my understanding is that the same is true for Twinkies), we normally speak of these in terms of "energy" and not "power."[56] If you burn a barrel of a certain type of oil, you'll release about 1.7 million watt-hours (MWh). It doesn't matter how quickly or slowly you burn it. Or how quickly or slowly you eat a Twinkie. It's going to release the same amount of energy. It doesn't matter to the oil or to ExxonMobil whether the barrel is burned to keep a 60-watt bulb lit for 28,333 hours, or a 120-watt bulb for half that long (and in either case, your mother will *surely* tell you to turn off the light). On both individual and economic scales, fossil fuels, wood, Twinkies, and so on are considered in terms of energy.

Electricity, however, while sometimes talked about in terms of energy, is more often discussed in terms of power. This is primarily because the electrical grid is based on alternating current (AC), which can't be stored. You can use AC to charge direct current (DC) batteries, or to store mechanical energy (by, for example, pumping water uphill, to be stored in a reservoir and released through a dam's turbines when you need more electricity), but you can't store it directly. Consequently, electric utilities have been forced to build generation systems and grids in terms of having enough capacity to reliably meet peak demand for power (which is defined as how much energy is being delivered *right now*): hospitals, factories, and stores (and refrigerators) cannot reasonably be expected to stop functioning when the sun goes down and the wind calms. Total quantity of energy delivered is necessarily considered secondary to the capacity to meet whatever demand is placed on the grid at any (and every) moment. And demand, of course, changes by the hour of the day ("on-peak" is usually considered from 7:00 a.m. to 10:00 p.m.); by the day of week (weekends and holidays

---

[56] In the case of Twinkies, it's about 135 kilocalories per Twinkie, which is a little over 150 watt-hours, or enough to light a 60-watt bulb for 2.5 hours.

have less demand); by the weather; by the time of year (in many places, summer and winter have higher demand because of air conditioning and electric heating, respectively); and so on. Peak demand is often 200 percent or more of minimum demand. So, when discussing electricity, it often makes more sense to speak of power than energy.

This means the pedant inside each of us can relax a little: even though we pay for electricity in terms of energy used, it does make some sense to talk about power companies and power grids, hence, power bills.

Now that we know that when someone talks about oil or coal they usually speak in terms of *energy* and when they talk about electricity they usually speak in terms of *power*, we're almost ready to talk about where the bright green enthusiasts get their numbers.

Remember—and we're sorry to repeat this, but this is a source of some of the errors—"energy" is not the same as "power," and "energy" is not the same as "electricity." Power is the *rate* at which energy is transformed into work. And electricity is just one *form* of energy. In Germany, electricity accounts for only about 20 percent of the energy consumed:[57] transportation and heating, for example, rely mainly on sources other than electricity for their energy.

Primary energy consumption in Germany for 2013 was 13,908 petajoules. That's about 3,863 terawatt-hours, or enough to run a 60-watt bulb for more than 7.3 billion years, almost twice as long as the earth has existed. Put another way, the same amount of energy would be produced by "processing" about 30 billion humans.

---

[57] Craig Morris, "What German Energy Supply Looks Like," *Energy Transition: The German Energiewende*, December 29, 2014. As of 2019, electricity was a slightly smaller percentage of total energy use.

Of course, Germany's industrial economy, like all other industrial economies, isn't fueled by consuming the bodies of humans (except politically, socially, spiritually, and metaphorically).

We're using 2013 numbers since that was the year Naomi Klein used in *This Changes Everything*. We also provide more recent numbers to show that in the intervening years, things have not gotten better for the planet.

The following chart shows how Germany's primary energy consumption broke down in 2013:[58]

Primary Energy Consumption in Germany in 2013

Source: AGEB, AGEE

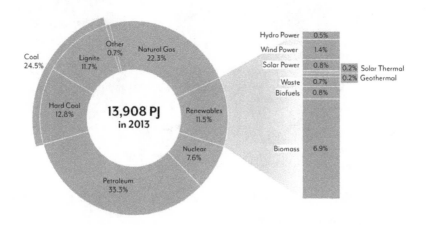

As you can see, petroleum accounted for a third of all energy consumed in Germany, followed by the combined forms of coal at 24.5 percent, then natural gas at a bit over 22 percent. "Renewables" came in at 11.5 percent, of which the majority, as we've seen, was biomass. Solar and wind together accounted, according to these figures, for about 2.4 percent of Germany's primary energy production.

Only 2.4 percent? That's the great German success story?

---

[58] Craig Morris, op. cit.

And the 2019 numbers are similar. "Renewables" have risen to 14.7 percent of primary energy consumption, with wind accounting for 3.6 percent and solar for 1.6 percent, for a total of 5.2 percent. Biomass still provides almost exactly the same share of energy, at 7.6 percent. Oil and natural gas have—wait for it—increased.[59]

Here is a chart of those numbers.

German Energy Mix in 2019: Energy Sources' Share in Primary Energy Consumption.
Source: AG Energiebilanzen 2020

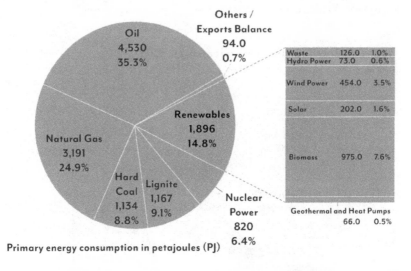

Primary energy consumption in petajoules (PJ)

Well, that's disappointing. So, where do the bright greens get their impressive numbers?

Let's start with Naomi Klein's quote from an interview with *Democracy Now*: "Twenty-five percent of Germany's energy now

---

[59] Kerstine Appunn, Yannick Haas, and Julian Wettengel, "Germany's energy consumption and power mix in charts," *Clean Energy Wire*, January 28, 2020.

comes from renewable energy, particularly wind and solar, much of it small-scale and decentralized."[60]

This one's easy. She's just plain wrong. But *how* is she wrong? How did 11.5 percent, with solar and wind together making up 2.4 percent, become "25 percent ... particularly wind and solar"?

This one's easy, too. Klein said that "25 percent of Germany's energy now comes from renewable energy," but what is true is that "25 percent of Germany's *electricity* now comes from renewable energy." There's a big difference between providing 25 percent of some amount, and 25 percent of 20 percent of that amount. The latter is, of course, only 5 percent of the original amount.

Here's a breakdown of German electrical generation (which is, remember, only 20 percent of total energy), also from 2013.[61]

Gross Electricity Production in Germany in 2013, by Percent

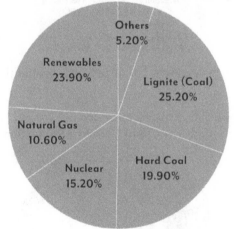

[60] "Capitalism vs. the Climate: Naomi Klein on Need for New Economic Model to Address Ecological Crisis," *Democracy Now*, September 18, 2014. One of the interviewers, Juan Gonzalez, stated in a question the falsehood that Germany is "close to 25 percent renewable energy." Not only did Klein not correct him, but she doubled down by stating (incorrectly), "the number that you cited is correct," and then gave her inaccurate statement.
[61] Data from "Gross Electricity Production in Germany from 2012 to 2014," *DeStatis: Statistiches Bundestamt*, Economic Sectors/Energy/Production.

As you can see, "renewables" made up 23.5 percent, which is probably close enough to 25 percent (and did cross the 25 percent line the following year).

And here's the same chart from 2019.

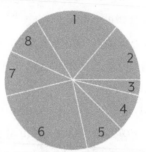

German Electricity by Source in 2019

1. Brown Coal: 102.18 TWh (19.9%)
2. Nuclear: 71.09 TWh (13.8%)
3. Hydro: 19.23 TWh (3.7%)
4. Biomass: 44.42 TWh (8.7%)
5. Solar: 46.54 TWh (9.1%)
6. Wind: 127.22 TWh (24.8%)
7. Natural Gas: 54.05 TWh (10.5%)
8. Hard Coal: 48.69 TWh (9.5%)

Here is the breakdown for electricity production by "renewables" for 2013.[62]

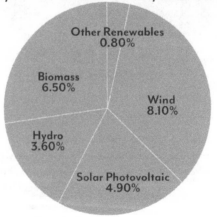

Renewable Electricity Generation in Germany in 2013, by Percent of Total Electricity Production

Other Renewables 0.80%
Biomass 6.50%
Wind 8.10%
Hydro 3.60%
Solar Photovoltaic 4.90%

---

[62] Ibid.

So, wind and solar combined for 13 percent of Germany's electrical generation. Recall that electricity is only 20 percent of Germany's energy usage. Thirteen percent of 20 percent takes us right back to where we started, with solar and wind accounting for between 2 percent and 3 percent of Germany's energy.

And here's the same chart for 2019.

Renewable Electricity Generation in Germany in 2019, by Percent of Total Electricity Production

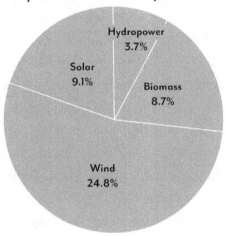

Now, nobody really cares if auto mechanics, neurosurgeons, or cricket players say *energy* when they actually mean *power* or *electricity*. But for those who write about energy policy, this is neither trivial nor the sort of one-off mistake we all make occasionally. And it happens routinely with bright greens. For example, in *This Changes Everything*, Klein claims that Frankfurt and Munich "pledged to move to 100 percent renewable energy by 2050 and 2025, respectively."[63]

Well, no. Frankfurt and Munich did *not* pledge to move to 100 percent "renewable" *energy* by 2050 and 2025. They pledged to

---

[63] Naomi Klein, *This Changes Everything: Capitalism vs. the Climate* (New York: Simon & Schuster, 2015), 97.

move to 100 percent "renewable" *electricity* by 2050 and 2025. Cars and motorcycles and semi-tractors in Munich and Frankfurt aren't going to suddenly switch to solar. Boilers that heat big buildings aren't going to suddenly switch from coal to solar. And remember, 30 percent of the "renewable electricity" comes from "biofuels."

Here's more of the same sort of inaccuracy: In *This Changes Everything,* Klein effectively claims that rooftop solar provides 25 percent of Germany's electricity; she cites Bill Gates as "writing off energy solutions like rooftop solar as 'cute' and 'noneconomic' (despite the fact that these cute technologies are already providing 25 percent of Germany's electricity)." That certainly sounds better than saying that the "cute" technologies provide 4.9 percent of Germany's electricity and about 1.0 percent of Germany's energy.[64]

Of course, Klein isn't the only bright green to make these inaccurate claims. The same is true for the Sierra Club and the leaders of the cities, counties, and one state in the United States all claiming to switch to "100 percent renewable energy." Not a single person associated with the Sierra Club or any of those governmental offices has bothered to do the slightest fact-checking. Either that or, having checked facts, they've decided to ignore them. We don't know which is worse.

Recall Bill McKibben's claim that "there were days this month when they [Munich] got half their energy from solar panels." Even ignoring that he said this in December, and that he was referencing a two-hour period on a single day (not "days") in the previous May, Munich did *not* get half its *energy* from solar panels. First, it got half its *electricity* from "renewables," which means, if Munich follows the German pattern of electricity accounting for 20 percent

---

[64] Ibid., 237. Or, if we include wind as one of the "cute" technologies then it's 13 percent of Germany's electricity and 3.3 percent of its energy.

of total energy, then "renewables" provided about 10 percent of Munich's energy (for about two hours, on a Saturday). That doesn't sound quite so exciting. And second, solar provides only about 20 percent of the total "renewable" electricity, so if Munich is typical of Germany, this drops the actual percentage of Munich's energy provided by solar photovoltaics down to about 2 percent.

Even accounting for the possibility that Munich might have far more solar panels than anywhere else in Germany (which makes McKibben's assertion problematical on another level, in that he would still be citing an atypical example and generalizing from there), his numbers don't add up.

So, we've covered the 25 percent number. What about the really big ones, like 75 percent and 78 percent?

Here are a few excerpts from articles touting Germany's "success" with renewable energy. First, from the *Daily Kos*: "Germany has reached the point where it had gotten over 74 percent of its electrical power from renewable sources the other day. That's a huge milestone, and it demonstrates that renewable sources can power a large industrial nation. Germany shows us that renewables aren't a potential source of power for some time in the future; they are a viable alternative *today*."[65]

From *Climate Progress*: "Germany's impressive streak of renewable energy milestones continued, with renewable energy generation surging to a record portion—nearly 75 percent—of the country's overall electricity demand by midday."[66]

And again from *Climate Progress:* "Germany set a new national

---

[65] Lefty Coaster, "Germany got 74% of its electrical power from Renewable Sources the other day," *Daily Kos*, May 18, 2014. Italics in original.
[66] Kiley Kroh, "Germany Sets New Record, Generating 74 Percent of Power Needs from Renewable Energy," *Climate Progress*, May 13, 2014.

record for renewable energy by meeting 78 percent of the day's electricity demand with renewables sources."[67]

These figures are profoundly misleading for several reasons. First, once again, bright greens consistently fail to mention that electricity is only 20 percent of Germany's energy usage, so 78 percent of electricity demand is, all things being equal, still less than 16 percent of energy demand. Reduce each number in the above quotes by four-fifths and see if the numbers sound as impressive. Second, remember that demand is lower on weekends, and those record-setting percentages took place on a Saturday and a Sunday, when power demands were about 15 to 25 percent below weekday demands. It should be obvious, but we need to make this plain: It's easier to capture a larger percentage of a small number than the same percentage of a larger number. The point is that if you're wanting to power a working economy—which we don't particularly want to do, but they sure seem to want to—you've got to drop each of their numbers by another 20 percent or so. That would lower that 16 percent number (already down from 78 percent by the conversion from percentage of electricity to percentage of energy) to about 13 percent of a workday energy requirement.

The third and far more important reason these numbers are misleading is that the data points the bright greens are (mis)using are completely atypical. It's worth quoting University of Strathclyde marine biologist Robert Wilson at length, from an article entitled, "Germany gets only 3.3 percent of its energy from wind and solar. Ignore the headlines." He explains: "The obvious problem with these headlines is that many people come to the mistaken conclusion that these record highs are somehow representative of what goes on the rest of the time. They are not. Let's quantify this. The

[67] Ari Phillips, "Germany Just Got 78 Percent of Its Electricity from Renewable Sources," *Climate Progress*, July 29, 2015.

record high renewables output (which included biomass and hydro, a fact rarely pointed out) occurred on the 25th July. The total wind and solar output was about 39 GW [gigawatts: there are a billion watts in a gigawatt] according to Fraunhofer ISE data. How often does this happen? This is relatively easy to find out. All we need to do is add up all hourly wind and solar output and see how it is distributed throughout the year. I have done this in the graph below.... Each bracket covers the average output over an individual hour, in GW. In total we have about 40 brackets, starting at 0 GW. Yes, German wind and solar falls to zero gigawatts, rounded to the nearest gigawatt. Resist that temptation to write 'German wind and solar now meeting 0.1 percent of Germany energy needs' headlines."[68]

Why shouldn't we write those headlines instead? It would be more accurate to say Germany met 0.1 percent of its power needs than it is to say it met 78 percent, since there were far more hours in the year where solar and wind met 0.1 percent of Germany's power needs than hours where it provided what these bright green headlines claim.

"Flooding the power grid" indeed.

Wilson's graph follows on the next page.

---

[68] Ibid.

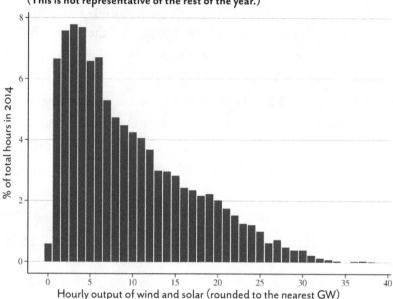

Germany's record-high wind and solar output was 39 GW on July 25, 2014. (This is not representative of the rest of the year.)

Do you see that data point at 39 GW? The one way off to the right? Yeah, we don't see it either. But it's presumably there. *That* is the data point trumpeted by the bright greens, the one that "demonstrates that renewable sources can power a large industrial nation," the one that "shows us that renewables ... are a viable alternative *today*." Yes, a data point that occurs far less than 1 percent of the time.

Wilson continues, "Mean hourly output of German wind and solar was 9.6 GW in 2014, while the median output was 8 GW [out of a total German electrical demand of 60 to 80 GW]. The maximum output was almost 39 GW; four times greater than the average, no matter how you define the average. Furthermore, total wind and solar output was above 30 GW only 2.1 percent of the time. It was above 25 GW only 9.6 percent of the time. The heavily skewed distribution shown above has clearly led to heavily skewed perceptions about German renewables. So, each time you see headlines about record high renewables output remember this: average output of combined German wind and solar is roughly one quarter of these record highs, and German wind and solar is still just over 3 percent of final energy consumption in Germany."[69]

We know this is a lot of math. We're hoping that the numbers and graph together made clear the level of misrepresentation by the bright greens. In case they haven't, let's try a few nonmathematical examples of misrepresentation of outlier data points.

Have you ever ridden a bike down a hill? Did you have to pedal? No? Really? Let's write a headline: "Person rides bike without having to pedal!" Then bright green enthusiasts can write books and articles about how renewable energy companies just need investments to develop stationary bikes that don't need to be pedaled that will power the economy.

Let's try again. It's me, Derrick, here. When I was 17, I evaded a police chase. It wasn't so exciting as it sounds. I was in the left lane at a stop light when I realized I was going the wrong direction. A sign prohibited left turns at this busy intersection, but I observed it did not say no U-turn, so I popped on my signal and waited for a break in traffic—I was, after all, 17, and therefore this logic made sense to me. An RV directly behind me started honking, but eventually I was able to pull a Uey. Just behind the RV was a cop, who pointed at me, then pointed at the side of the road. I responded as many 17-year-olds might: I floored it. I turned left at the next corner, right at the next, left at the corner after that, then pulled into the parking lot of a large apartment complex, ditched my car between two large vehicles, ran into the building's lobby, leaned against a wall, and did a poor impression of belonging there. I saw the cop drive by on the street a few times, but he evidently didn't see my car (or me), and when I hadn't seen him for 10 or

---

[69] Ibid.

15 minutes I got in my car and this time drove the right direction. We should publish a headline: "Jensen details teenage life on the run from police." Depending on the audience, we could use that to either harm or improve my reputation.

Let's try one final time. The other day I went to the doctor's office. I had to wait in the reception area. I sat down. As I was waiting, what was happening to the world? It was being killed by industrial civilization. Headline: "As industrial civilization kills the planet, Derrick Jensen sits on his ass."[70]

Just like most everybody else, I guess.

The misrepresentation by bright greens, whether intentional or not, is far worse than I've made it seem. Recall that electric utilities must have enough capacity to *reliably* meet whatever demand for power is placed on the grid at any and every moment. But solar photovoltaics only provide electricity during sunny days, and windmills only provide electricity when the wind's blowing. Do you see the problem yet? Recall also that AC electricity can't be stored. In other words, barring conversion to DC or mechanical energy, a grid based on solar and wind is completely unreliable for running an industrial economy. You could strap cute li'l solar photovoltaic cells to every mailbox and to the backs of all the hedgehogs in the Black Forest (I guess we should call it the Black Biomass Production Zone); and replace every flag pole outside every municipal building and every spire on every cathedral with gigantic windmills; and then what happens to your factory (or your washing machine or refrigerator; or your ventilator at the hospital) on a calm night,

---

[70] I (Derrick) want to be as clear as possible. I'm not complaining when writers make simple mistakes. We all do that all the time. Hell, in the sentence above in the text, I had a typo and mispelled my own name and didn't catch it until my fifth or sixth draft. Nobody's perfect. What I am talking about here is a consistent pattern of "mistakes" that, significantly, support their position. At some point they're no longer mistakes, and they are either denial or deceit.

when solar and wind provide 0.1 percent of Germany's industrial power demand? As one analyst states, "The output of wind and solar generators varies wildly with weather and the time of day; during most hours they produce a small fraction of their name-plate [that is, theoretical maximum] power—or nothing at all."[71] In other words, if you want to run an industrial economy, you'd *still* need coal, oil, biomass, and hydro to provide stability. Or, as a report of the German Physical Society (the world's second-largest organization of physicists) concludes, "Essentially, solar energy cannot replace any additional power plants."[72] Complete predict-ability and reliability are crucial to the power needs of an industrial society. It is remarkably dishonest to pretend that "renewables" meeting 74 or 78 percent of electricity needs for a couple of hours on a sunny, windy, weekend afternoon even remotely implies that "renewable sources can power a large industrial nation."

Der Spiegel reports, "Solar lobbyists like to dazzle the public with impressive figures on the capability of solar energy. For example, they say that all installed systems together could generate a nomi-nal output of more than 20 gigawatts, or twice as much energy as is currently being produced by the remaining German nuclear power plants. But this is pure theory."[73] The reporter points out, as the math and graph did above, that this theory doesn't match reality on the ground.

Der Spiegel continues, "Because of the poor electricity yield, solar energy production also saves little in the way of harmful carbon dioxide emissions, especially compared to other possible

[71] Will Boisvert, "Green Energy Bust in Germany," *Dissent*, Summer 2013.

[72] Alexander Neubacher, "Solar Subsidy Sinkhole," *Der Spiegel*, January 18, 2012.

[73] Ibid.

subsidization programs. To avoid a ton of CO_2 emissions, one can spend €5 on insulating the roof of an old building, invest €20 in a new gas-fired power plant or sink about €500 into a new solar energy system.[74] The benefit to the climate is the same in all three cases. 'From the standpoint of the climate, every solar system is a bad investment,' says Joachim Weimann, an environmental economist in the eastern German city of Magdeburg. Hans-Werner Sinn of the Munich-based Ifo Institute for Economic Research calls solar energy a 'waste of money at the expense of climate protection.'"[75]

In addition to being a waste of money, some solar may be a waste of energy. One paper published in 2015 calculates that solar systems in northern Europe have a negative energy return on energy invested (ERoEI). The study found that energy used for production, transport, installation, maintenance, and financing of solar PV power facilities in Switzerland and Germany was greater than the total energy produced by these panels during their operational duration.

The study concludes that "the ERoEI [for solar systems in regions of moderate insolation] is significantly below 1 ... [indicating that] an electrical supply system based on today's PV technologies

---

[74] Of course, one could also help restore prairies, forests, wetlands, and so on, but that wouldn't serve the industrial agenda (or the desires of the financial elites), so it is not often enough mentioned. One could also begin deconstructing the industrial economy—this is the fate of life on this planet we're talking about, after all—but that certainly doesn't serve the industrial agenda (or the desires of the financial elites) so that sure as hell doesn't get mentioned.

[75] Neubacher, op. cit.

cannot be termed an energy source, but rather a non-sustainable energy sink."[76]

That leads to the real questions: Does industrial solar power help the natural world? More specifically, does it help stop global warming? Let's leave aside the misused statistics, and let's leave aside (for now) the fact that industrial civilization is inherently unsustainable and killing the planet. The explicitly claimed goal of bright greens is to find a way to maintain the industrial economy while reducing emissions. Wouldn't it be okay to subsidize the hell out of the solar industry, so long as it reduces emissions?

So, let's talk about German emissions and the German energy miracle. In 1997, Germany signed the Kyoto Protocol and pledged to reduce greenhouse gas emissions from 1990 levels by 21 percent between 2008 and 2012, and 40 percent by 2020. What follows is a chart of Germany's annual emissions, in millions of tons of carbon equivalent (carbon equivalent means that you've converted other greenhouse gases, like methane, into their equivalent of carbon dioxide).

---

[76] Ferruccio Ferroni and Robert J. Hopkirk, "Energy Return on Energy Invested (ERoEI) for photovoltaic solar systems in regions of moderate insolation," *Energy Policy* 94, 336–344 (April 26, 2016).

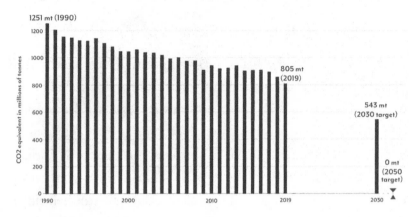

Greenhouse Gas Emission Trends in Germany 1991-2019
Data: UBA 2020

As you can see, in 1990 Germany emitted 1251 million tons (Mt) of carbon equivalent. By 2010, Germany's emissions were 942 Mt, a reduction of about 25 percent. Germany clearly made the first target. Before we celebrate this too much as a victory for industrial solar, we should note that more than half of this decline took place by 2000 (and in fact almost half of it took place before Germany even made the commitment), prior to solar "flooding the power grid" with a whopping 4.9 percent of Germany's power supply and 0.8 percent of Germany's energy supply. This means this reduction couldn't possibly have had anything to do with the installation of solar. Instead, much of the reduction came because of increased energy efficiency. And most of this increased efficiency came early on. From 1991 to 2001 efficiency improved by about 1.5 percent per year. But there are physical limits to how efficient processes can be made. From 2001 to 2006 efficiency increased only by .5 percent in total.

As you can also see, German emissions dropped sharply (and encouragingly) from 2008 to 2009, but reductions stalled from 2009 to 2014, going up for most of the intervening years, before dropping again in 2014 to 2009 levels. The 2009 reduction was, of course, caused by the banking crisis of 2008 and the consequent economic contraction, and frankly reveals the most obvious way to save the planet, presuming we care more about the planet than we do the economy. Not even bright greens try to claim the 2009 reduction was caused by an increase in "renewable" energy.

The 2014 reduction, however, is a different matter, with bright greens claiming it as proof that the great transformation has begun. For example, TriplePundit, an organization promoting "ethical, sustainable, profitable business" (a.k.a. the "triple bottom line or—three Ps—of sustainability—People, Planet, Profit," and no, we couldn't make this up), claimed that "2014 may have marked an inflection point in the transition to clean, renewable energy in Germany."[77]

Meanwhile, under the headline "Germany May Offer Model for Reining in Fossil Fuels," the *New York Times* said much the same thing in its own style: that Germany was now "reducing its overall energy consumption while still recording modest economic growth of 1.5 percent, breaking a traditional pattern in which nations see their energy use fall only during recessions." It cited World Bank President Jim Yong Kim as saying, "Germany is the first country in the world to show they can uncouple growth from [the] burning of fossil fuels."[78] All of these claims have been repeated until they've become accepted as truth among the bright green faithful.

Never mentioned is that most of the reductions were due to an extremely mild winter, in fact the warmest weather Germany's

---

[77] Andrew Burger, "Germany's Carbon Emissions Fall as Renewable Energy Takes the Lead," *TriplePundit: People, Planet, Profit*, January 13, 2015.

[78] Melissa Eddy, "Germany May Offer Model for Reining in Fossil Fuel Use," *New York Times*, December 3, 2015.

had since it began keeping records in 1881,[79] with, according to the National Oceanic and Atmospheric Administration, "a temperature 1.4°C (2.5°F) above the 1981–2010 average and 0.4°C (0.7°F) above the previous record warmth of 2000."[80]

And bright greens *know* this: the AGEB,[81] the group of utility experts and economists who gather the official statistics, *entitled their introduction* to that year's summary, "Strong downturn in energy consumption thanks to mild weather." This mild weather led to a 13.6 percent decline in consumption of heating oil and, interestingly, a small increase in diesel and gasoline consumption by vehicles. ("It's such a nice day, love, let's go for a drive, rather than staying home drinking hot cocoa.") Adjusting for the weather, Germany used about 1 percent less energy and emitted about 2.5 percent less greenhouse gas, a rate of reduction that would lead to Germany failing to reach its goal for 2020.[82]

Also ignored is the fact that, for reasons having nothing to do with slowing global warming, Germany's chemical sector—the country's biggest power consumer and second-biggest energy consumer[83]—shrank by nearly 7 percent in 2014.[84]

These claims of the bright greens/capitalists are crap, for the same reason so many of their other claims are crap: they're based on cherry-picking. One weather- and chemical-sector-decline-influenced data point does not constitute "breaking a traditional pattern in which nations see their energy use fall only during

[79] Craig Morris, "Lower Energy Consumption in Germany Explained," *The Energiewende Blog*, March 12, 2015.
[80] "Global Analysis—Annual Review 2014," *National Oceanic and Atmospheric Administration: National Centers for Environmental Information*.
[81] AGEB stands for Arbeitsgemeinschaft Energiebilanzen (Working Group Energy Balances).
[82] Morris op. cit., March 12, 2015.
[83] After metal production.
[84] Morris op. cit., March 12, 2015.

recessions," nor does it show that an industrial economy "can uncouple growth from burning of fossil fuels." Does no one associated with the *New York Times* or the World Bank understand anything about statistics? Should we go through examples of outliers again? Or should we just mention that in the first six months of 2015, energy use went back up by 3 percent, because it was a cold spring? Are the bright greens now going to announce that "2015 may have marked an inflection point back to business as usual in Germany"? Will the *New York Times* run an article noting that "Germany continues the longstanding pattern of using even more energy when it's cold"? Will the World Bank proclaim, "Germany shows, once again, that the industrial economy causes greenhouse gas emissions"?

Lost in all of this bright green self-congratulation is that Germany still emitted more than 900 million tons of carbon-equivalent greenhouse gases in 2014, more than any other country in Europe.

You can't claim a break in a pattern (in this case, a break in the pattern of increased economic growth implying increased energy use); or an uncoupling of two specific variables (in this case, the uncoupling of economic growth and fossil-fuel use), when you only have one data point going against the longstanding pattern, and when you haven't corrected or at least accounted for all the other variables and the causal or at least correlative relationships between them. To make such claims is inaccurate, unjustified, and disingenuous. And given that we're talking about life on this planet, they're irresponsible and extremely dangerous. Discussions of this magnitude necessitate thorough and rigorous analyses, not boosterism and grasping at whatever straws one can to maintain the illusion that this way of life, which is killing the planet, can continue without in fact killing the planet.

By the way, German greenhouse gas emissions rose again in 2015, 2016, and 2017. What does that say about the "German miracle"?

Two can play the cherry-picking game. From 2007 to 2012, Germany's greenhouse gas emissions went from 976 to 931 Mt. That's a decrease of about 4.6 percent. But during those same years emissions in the United States went from 7400 to 6546 Mt, a decrease of more than 11.5 percent. And yet bright greens trumpet Germany and not the United States as a miracle of "renewables"?

That's probably because the United States reduced emissions not primarily through subsidies for "renewables"—of course Germany didn't either—but through the not-nearly-so-sexy means of substituting natural gas for coal.

Most of this reduction occurred because of economic collapse: 2009 emissions were 6724 Mt: in other words, 676 out of the 854 Mt of reduction (almost 80 percent) were caused by economic contraction, suggesting, once again, the real way to reduce emissions.

In no way are we suggesting switching to natural gas from coal will "save the planet." We're merely pointing out that at the same time the German miracle was reducing emissions less than 5 percent, the U.S. was reducing emissions more than 11 percent.

And what does that prove about sustainability? Not a goddamn thing.

Cherry-picking, Volume 2. In 2014, Germany reduced emissions a little under 5 percent. In that same year another entity reduced emissions 23 percent. If bright green enthusiasts call Germany a "miracle" of "renewables," what will they call this other entity? Well, maybe they can call it by its name: the oil company ConocoPhillips. As an energy reporter commented, "ConocoPhillips Co.'s efforts to curb methane leaks in New Mexico's San Juan Basin resulted in major reductions to its greenhouse gas contributions in 2014— even as production continued to climb."

If we were the *New York Times,* we co-authors would, on the basis of this one sample point, comment that ConocoPhillips is "breaking a traditional pattern in which oil corporations see their greenhouse gases fall only when they reduce extraction." And if we were, collectively, the president of the World Bank, we would argue that ConocoPhillips "is the first corporation in the world to show it can uncouple growth from increasing emissions."

As it is, we'll just point out that this wasn't a miraculous transformation: they merely replaced some faulty equipment.

And what does that say about sustainability? Not a goddamn thing.

Cherry Picking, Volume 3. Emissions aren't even counted correctly. Greenhouse gas emissions in the U.S. dropped 11.5 percent between 2007 and 2012. Economic contraction was responsible for almost 80 percent of that dip but substituting natural gas for coal also helped. Or did it?

We talk about greenhouse gases, using the plural, because CO_2 does not sin alone. Methane is in some ways worse—84 times worse, at least for the first 20 years after it hits the atmosphere. This is why methane has been called global warming "on steroids."[85] Methane's

---

[85] Gayathri Vaidyanathan, "How bad of a greenhouse gas is methane?" *Scientific American*, December 22, 2015.

decay is rapid compared to CO_2, which can last for millennia. But when it does break down, it turns into—wait for it—CO_2.

Greenhouse gas accounting takes carbon as the standard. It uses a 100-year framework as a matter of convention, notated as "GWP100." "GWP" stand for "global warming potential" and "100" means 100 years. The GWP100 for methane is 34. Which is bad enough, but the GWP20 is 84.

By averaging the destructiveness of methane over a hundred years, the actual damage *while the planet is in crisis* is invisible in the accounting—accounting which extends into policy decisions. Countries like the U.S. that have swapped coal for gas are able to claim a smaller, cheaper climate impact. The wreckage here and now is uncounted, rendered invisible.

And there's more. One major source of anthropogenic methane (and let's be clear: anthropogenic methane is the kind that is breaking the planet) is leaks from natural gas infrastructure. The Environmental Defense Fund, along with 15 other groups, measured these leaks starting from wells all the way through to pipes entering private homes, in "the most comprehensive body of research of its kind."[86] They concluded that U.S. emissions of methane are 60 percent higher than EPA has estimated.

So, a substance that's 84 times worse than CO_2 is being released at a rate 60 percent higher than anyone was counting, while the world burns.

Germany's Commission on Growth, Structural Change and Employment, known as the Coal Commission, set 2038 as the target date for the end of coal, which currently accounts for 40

---

[86] Doyle Rice, "US emissions of methane—a potent greenhouse gas—are 60% higher than EPA thinks," *USA Today*, June 21, 2018.

percent of Germany's power. Greenpeace's Martin Kaiser said, "Germany finally has a road map for how to make the country coal-free."[87] Commission member Hans Joachim Schellnhuber celebrated: "This is an important step on the road to the post-fossil age."[88] Buried in 336 pages and all the media coverage is the unstated acceptance that industrial levels of consumption cannot be questioned, never mind curtailed.

So where will the energy come from? Imported fossil gas.

Greenpeace's Kaiser also said, "At least Germany is moving again after years in a climate policy coma."[89] Which is worse: a coma or schizophrenia? Because Greenpeace itself has stated categorically that "methane is actually a far more potent greenhouse gas than carbon dioxide.... [A] 100-year time scale ... vastly underestimates the damage methane will cause to the climate in the next two critical decades. Scientists say that methane could push the climate over a 'tipping point' in the next 18-25 years, causing runaway global warming, and making a 100-year timeline obsolete."[90]

Swap gas for coal, methane for carbon dioxide, and it's not even rearranging the deck chairs. It's telling the drowning and the terrified that you're bailing out water—and maybe even believing it— while filling the hull with more.

Measuring a single country's emissions gives some information, but it fails to give a full picture.

One problem is that the global economy in general is a giant

---

[87] Michael L. Buchsbaum, "Germany's Coal Commission proposes a nebulous 20-year coal-exit pathway," *Energy Transition*, January 30, 2019.

[88] Adam Vaughan, "Germany agrees to end reliance on coal stations by 2038," *The Guardian*, January 26, 2019.

[89] Buchsbaum, op. cit.

[90] "Natural gas: methane's contribution to global warming," Greenpeace.

money- and atrocity-laundering machine. In go the lives of impoverished children, and out comes chocolate, wrapped in foil and ready for Mother's Day. In go the limbs of workers hacked off by machetes, and out come diamond rings, to be delivered with the understanding that "every kiss begins with Kay." In go lowland mountain gorillas, and out come cell phones. In go the Columbia River and millions of salmon, lamprey, sturgeon, and all those beings who depend on them, and out comes "green," "sustainable," and "renewable" energy. In go the Colorado River and its delta, and all those who live there, and out come Las Vegas, golf courses, citrus orchards, alfalfa fields. In go the marshes and prairies of Iowa—once one of the most biodiverse places in North America, called by early explorers "a country so full of game"—and out come cornfields and "clean" and "green" and "sustainable" biofuels. In go forests and out comes "biomass." In go mountains, and out comes coal. In go lakes, rivers, meadows, entire islands, and out come the materials to build solar panels and windmills. In goes the whole planet, and out come the luxuries that characterize this way of life, the luxuries for which the bright greens are fighting so hard.

The global economy is not only a money- and atrocity-laundering machine, it's also an emissions-laundering machine. Although superficially it should be easy to figure out which countries emit which emissions, it can get complicated pretty quickly because the global economy is, well, global. Here's the easy part: emissions are counted in the country where the gases are emitted. Except of course for those gases emitted by some forms of "renewable" energy, like hydro or biomass, in which cases the emissions aren't counted at all. So, if you live in Milwaukee, Wisconsin, and buy a Chinese-made "Down with U.S. Emissions" T-shirt, China will take the hit for the emissions caused by the production of the shirt.

Now, here's how it gets complicated. Remember how we got

tepidly excited a few paragraphs above about how U.S. emissions are dropping and said that's partly due to substituting natural gas for coal? Well, bright greens have not surprisingly used this substitution to declare "the end of coal." As far back as 2008, former President Obama claimed that if someone wanted to build a new coal plant, it would "bankrupt them." Both Obama-backers and -bashers loved to talk about "Obama's war on coal." And after pledging that Los Angeles would no longer buy electricity from coal-fired generating stations (by 2025), the mayor of Los Angeles proclaimed—and bright greens and liberals echoed—that "the era of coal is over." Great for the environment!

But this is more accounting shenanigans. It's not true that "the era of coal is over." In 2008, about 7.5 billion short tons of coal were extracted worldwide. In 2009 that number went up to 7.6 billion (and the only reason it didn't go up more is because of global economic recession). In 2010 it was about 8 billion. In 2011 and 2012 it was about 8.4 and 8.6 billion, respectively. Coal extraction continued to rise through 2014, then dropped about 12 percent over the next two years. It has since rebounded, in 2019 reaching about 8.7 billion tons.[91]

Typically, a lot of bright greens have asked, with no evidence to support their question, "Will the decline of coal solve the climate crisis?"[92] A friend of mine from Austria couldn't contain himself from answering, "The decline of coal will solve the climate catastrophe about as much as the glorious German victory at Stalingrad allowed the expansion of the Reich's *Lebensraum* way beyond the Urals if not all the way to the Pacific, and made the *Endsieg* inevitable."

---

[91] "Coal Information: Overview," International Energy Agency, July 2020.
[92] Sharon Kelly, "Will the Decline of Coal Solve the Climate Crisis," *The Real News*, December 24, 2015.

Now, while it's true that new coal facilities aren't being built in the U.S., it's also true that until 2016 coal extraction in this country basically held steady. In 1980 it was about 830 million short tons. It reached 1 billion short tons in 1990, and then hovered between about 900 million and 1.15 billion tons until 2016, when it dropped to 730 million tons.[93]

It's just that the U.S. is now *exporting* the coal (and emissions). As recently as 2003 the U.S. exported "only" about 20 Mt of coal per year. When Obama and his "war on coal" took over in 2008, exports were about 50 Mt/year. They dropped in 2009 because of the recession (are we seeing a pattern?), then by 2012 climbed to a record 126 Mt before dropping back to just under 100 Mt/year. More recently, exports have fluctuated between 60 Mt (three times the 2003 level) to 93 Mt in 2019.

Emissions from this coal are counted by buyer countries, where the coal is burned. Meanwhile U.S. carbon emissions go down. Yay! The era of coal is over in the United States!

It's not over in Australia, either. In 2018, the deputy prime minister stated bluntly that his country will "absolutely" use and export its coal.[94] When coal fuels 60 percent of Australia's electricity and is its largest export, how could it be otherwise? Meanwhile the German environment minister called global demand for coal "unrelenting."[95] Germany itself, despite passage of a federal plan to phase out coal, is not facing "the real debate," according to one German MP. "How do we replace it?"[96] His answer:

---

[93] U.S. Energy Information Administration, op. cit.

[94] Lorraine Chow, "Australia to 'absolutely' exploit and use coal despite IPCC warning," *EcoWatch*, October 9, 2018.

[95] Sören Amelang and Benjamin Wehrmann, "Targeted action needed to curb unrelenting global demand for coal power," *Clean Energy Wire*, December 12, 2019.

[96] Julian Wettengel, "Without innovation leaps, Germany will fail on climate action— conservative German MP," *Clean Energy Wire*, December 16, 2019.

"renewables-based hydrogen in Northern Africa," which might as well be fairy dust.

There has been no decline in coal. Wishing will not make it so. The Statistical Review of World Energy is a report put out by energy colossus BP. The 2018 edition is a stark catalogue of assaults against the planet. Primary energy consumption increased "sharply," coal is growing "quickly," and coal's percentage of global power generation hasn't changed.[97] In 1998 it was 38 percent. In 2017, it was the same 38 percent. The true horror in those two small digits is that since global power generation has increased, the flat 38 percent is a grossly larger amount. The report states bluntly: "no net decarbonization progress has been made."

Why are we being told that coal is dead? That's not so much a rhetorical question as a bewildered one. We could understand if the architects of the apocalypse wanted to keep burning coal (they do) and didn't want us to know. But that's not who is carrying this tale. It's organizations committed to the cause. And we don't understand. Is it an attempt to stave off our collective despair? If so, there is only more bad news: In the battle between mood management and reality, reality is always going to win. We understand reality is unbearable. But will we soothe ourselves to sleep with stories of gentle, giant blades turning wind into gold as life itself slips into extinction? Because the world doesn't need a lullaby of lies, no matter how much we might. It needs us to fight.

---

[97] David Roberts, "The most depressing energy chart of the year," *Vox*, June 16, 2018.

The global economy is a sticky web.

My (Derrick's) niece and her family recently visited. My niece's husband is from China. He's in his mid-thirties. During the visit he complained to me about Walmart: "All these Americans buy all these cheap consumer goods made in China, and that has been good for the Chinese economy, but not good for the air. In my lifetime I have seen the sky in China go from blue to gray to black. All so Americans and others can have cheap goods. I understand this is the price we have to pay so a country can develop its economy, but I don't like it."

He also said he has old friends who've been forced by the economy to become de facto slaves in these factories, to work standing for 12 hours at a time without breaks. He told me of friends who work in high-rise factories with nets around the buildings to prevent workers from jumping to their deaths, and friends whose coworkers have joined together anyway to kill themselves, anything to end the ceaseless torment of their slave labor.

China is by far the world's biggest user of coal, both extracting and using almost 50 percent of all coal consumed. The U.S. and other countries get cheap consumer goods; and the Chinese get black skies, emissions, slave labor, a completely devastated natural world, and a financial surplus. It works for governments in all these countries. For the real world, not so well.

And what does this have to do with the German miracle? Well, do you remember the words of Ralf Fücks, president of the German Green Party's political foundation? "In my view the greatest success of the German energy transition was giving a boost to the Chinese solar panel industry."

At this point, China is, as *Fortune* put it, "utterly and totally dominating solar panels."[98]

In Germany, local environmentalists—the grassroots kind, not the solar lobby kind—have time and again protested the installation of solar infrastructures, including massive powerlines and 230-foot transmission towers. Representatives of a Dutch corporation building some of this infrastructure were met in 2014 by hundreds of protestors carrying signs like, "Stop the power-line madness." Local mycologist, botanist, and protest organizer Ingo Queck told the *Wall Street Journal*, "The corridor they're planning would destroy everything we've done to improve the environment in this region."[99]

We could tell similar stories of how solar-lobbying-cum-environmentalism has been used to subsidize the solar industries in Spain, Italy, the United Kingdom, the United States, and China, at the expense of nature. All over the world. And we could tell stories of local grassroots environmentalists across the world fighting industrial solar (and wind, and hydro) facilities. Here's a typical sample headline: "Here Comes the Sun: Local Environmentalists Oppose University Solar Project." Why? Because Georgetown University is going to clearcut 218 acres in "one of the most ecological valuable areas in Maryland"—to install a solar facility.[100]

---

[98] Katie Fehrenbacher, "China is utterly and totally dominating solar panels," *Fortune*, June 18, 2015.

[99] Matthew Karnitschnig, "Germany's Expensive Gamble on Renewable Energy," *Wall Street Journal*, August 26, 2014.

[100] Noah Telerski, "Here Comes the Sun? Local Environmentalists Oppose University Solar Project," *The Georgetown Voice*, December 7, 2018.

China is by far the leading producer of solar panels, with more than 50 percent of the world market. It has accomplished this through—what else?—massive subsidies. In China, solar cell manufacturers and other high-tech corporations are allowed to buy land at about one-third the official price, and are often given land for free, land that might otherwise sell for about $750,000 an acre. This land can be used to manufacture solar cells, or it can be used for golf driving ranges for employees. The government also provides low-cost loans. And it spends up to $1 billion per day "intervening," as the *New York Times* puts it, "in the currency markets so that Chinese exports become more affordable in foreign markets."[101] (Of course, this intervention in the currency market helps not just the export of solar photovoltaics, but also all exports from China, including most of the plastic crap at Walmart.) The solar industry in China benefits from subsidized labor, which runs from engineers being paid a few thousand dollars per year all the way to slave labor.

These solar installations in Germany and elsewhere are only possible through consistent and expensive subsidies. And frankly, many countries, like Germany, can no longer afford them (never mind poor countries that could never afford them in the first place: we recently saw a ridiculous piece by solar lobbyists arguing that Greece can solve its debt crisis by somehow purchasing solar photovoltaic cells for every rooftop, then selling the electricity to rich countries).

In his book *Green Illusions: The Dirty Secret of Clean Energy and the Future of Environmentalism*, engineer Ozzie Zehner makes clear the level of subsidy necessary to build and maintain a solar infrastructure big enough to fulfill Lester Brown's (and others') fantasies of a solar economy: "By comparing global energy

---

[101] Keith Bradsher, "On Clean Energy, China Skirts Rules," *New York Times*, September 8, 2010.

consumption with the most rosy photovoltaic cost estimates, courtesy of the solar proponents themselves, we can roughly sketch a
total expense. The solar cells would cost about $59 trillion; the
mining, processing, and manufacturing facilities to build them
would cost about $44 trillion; and the batteries to store power for
evening use would cost $20 trillion; bringing the total to about
$123 trillion plus about $694 billion per year for maintenance.
Keep in mind that the entire gross domestic product (GDP) of the
United States, which includes all food, rent, industrial investments,
government expenditures, military purchasing, exports, and so on,
is only about $14 trillion. This means that if every American were
to go without food, shelter, protection, and everything else while
working hard every day, naked, we might just be able to build a
photovoltaic array to power the [economy] in about a decade. But,
unfortunately, these estimates are optimistic."

He continues, "If *actual* installed costs for solar projects in
California are any guide, a global solar program would cost roughly
$1.4 quadrillion, about one hundred times the United States GDP.
Mining, smelting, processing, shipping, and fabricating the panels
and their associated hardware would yield about 149,100 mega-
tons of CO_2. And everyone would have to move to the desert, otherwise transmission losses would make the plan unworkable."[102]

Zehner's calculations lead him to ask important questions:
"Could manufacturing and installing photovoltaic arrays with
today's technology on *any scale* be equally absurd? Does it just not
seem as bad when we are throwing away a few billion dollars at a
time?"

These are questions never asked by the environmental cheer-
leaders of the solar industry.

---

[102] Ozzie Zehner, *Green Illusions: The Dirty Secrets of Clean Energy and the Future of Environmentalism* (Lincoln, NE: University of Nebraska Press, 2012), 8–9.

Financial subsidies aren't quite so necessary for oil, coal, and gas as they are for solar, because oil, coal, and gas are such dense forms of energy that, at first, they were somewhat capable of being economically self-sustaining. When oil could be scooped out of seeps and sold directly, oil extraction could make money without subsidies. Later, as oil became incrementally more difficult to extract, subsidies became required. These subsidies could be in the form of research, free or cheap access to public lands, building a road system to facilitate oil consumption, the military acting as muscle to protect (or steal) oil fields across the world, and so on, but in terms of energy return on energy invested, oil at least had the potential to be somewhat financially self-sustaining.

This can't be said for solar. Without subsidies, the industry would collapse even more quickly than would most industries. And even with subsidies, it can't, as we've seen, power, much less fuel, the economy.

We also understand that the free market is a lie, that capitalism requires subsidies or it will collapse, and that it's better to subsidize good things than bad. Given our choice, subsidies would be immediately diverted from the military toward everything from battered women's shelters to free education to free health care to wildlife and stream restoration to massive projects of dam removal, reforestation, and revivification of prairies and wetlands. As long as industrial capitalism lasts, we'd like to see subsidies that help the world.

So, given all that, why shouldn't the government subsidize the solar industry, even if it makes no economic sense? Isn't the solar industry a social good?

Well, even if we had the money, and even if solar power were a social good, it's not a planetary good. And that's the point. Industrial solar energy doesn't help the world. It's just another way to power industrial capitalism. At root, it's an industrial product designed and built in the global capitalist marketplace to make a profit. Like other products, it leaves behind the wreckage of destroyed land, poisoned water, and devastated communities.

Chapter 4

THE SOLAR LIE

PART 2

Any source of energy . . . enables civilization to further destroy

its environment through the extraction of matter.[1]

—TIM GARRETT

A photovoltaic (PV) panel is composed of a few main parts. The cells themselves are made of silicon refined to 99.99 percent purity and mixed with other elements to create conductivity. Solar panels don't work if the internals get wet, so a sheet of tempered glass covered with plastic film and sealed with ethylene-vinyl acetate resin is used for weather protection.

The PV electrical system uses copper wiring sheathed in plastic, with aluminum and silver pastes in the connections. A standard three-by-five-foot solar panel weighs about 40 pounds, not counting the mounting hardware.

The other essential component of a solar power system is an inverter to convert the DC electricity from the panel into AC,

---

[1] Tim Garrett, "Are renewables the answer?" Intermountain Network and Scientific Computation Center, University of Utah.

suitable for use with everyday appliances, lighting, and electronics. For the average solar installation on a single-family home, the inverter is a box about the size of a large computer and weighing 40 to 60 pounds, filled with magnets, inductors, capacitors, and oscillator circuits. It typically needs to be replaced every three to 10 years (which can be a big deal, since they cost a few thousand dollars).

Some of the raw materials in inverters include lead, indium, nylon, polypropylene and polyvinylchloride, silicon, zinc sulfide, gold, silver, chlorine, aluminum, copper, and tin.[2]

None of these materials grow on trees.

Solar systems linked to the electric grid also require (by proxy) everything the grid itself requires, including transformers, substations, transmission lines, a network of roads to provide maintenance access, vehicles, fuel for the vehicles, factories to build the vehicles, and so on.

Home installations of solar panels not connected to the grid require batteries to store power. Both energy storage and the grid itself are issues we'll tackle later on. The origin of the materials used in solar PV systems is an important story to tell as well, and we'll get to that after we talk about the other common type of solar harvesting facility.

Concentrated Solar Power (CSP) systems normally take one of two forms. In parabolic trough systems, a series of curved mirrors concentrate sunlight on a small tube containing a "working fluid"—often synthetic oil—heated to temperatures above 750°F. The other

---

[2] We owe a profound debt of gratitude to Wolf Dieter Aichberger, a.k.a. WDA, for his patience and technical expertise. He corrected many errors, saving us from embarrassing ourselves.

major type of CSP system is a solar power tower, in which a field of mirrors uses motorized mounts to track the sun from dawn to dusk and reflect light onto the apex of a tall central tower, heating a fluid inside of the tower to 1000 to 2000°F.[3]

An example of the latter type is Ivanpah, a 377 MW solar energy harvesting facility built in southeastern California and financed by BrightSource Energy, Bechtel, NRG Energy, the federal government (of course), and Google.

Before the project was installed, this 3,500-acre swathe of federal land was described by Mojave advocate Shaun Gonzales as "pristine desert." It's no longer pristine. Instead, it effectively no longer exists. The Ivanpah facility is so large it can be seen from space, and each of the three fields of mirrors surrounding each tower is more than a mile across.

Construction of the Ivanpah facility killed rare plants and destroyed habitat for threatened desert tortoises. The federal government claimed about 30 desert tortoises lived in the area, but eventually more than 170 tortoises were forcibly removed from their homes and relocated. It is believed that dozens more were killed during construction when underground burrows collapsed under the heavy equipment. Many of the relocated tortoises tried to go home, but found their way blocked by a chain-link fence. Outside this fence they paced back and forth, back and forth, until they died of heatstroke.

The Ivanpah project was originally set to destroy 4,000 acres (more than six square miles), but after environmentalists challenged the plan because of harm to wildlife, the site was reduced by about 13 percent. Joshua Basofin, an activist with Defenders of Wildlife, responded, "This reconfiguration is pretty minimal. It

---

[3] Christopher L. Martin and D. Yogi Goswami, *Solar Energy Pocket Reference* (Abingdon, U.K.: Routledge, 2005).

hasn't really addressed the core issues on the impact on desert tortoise and rare plants."[4]

Ivanpah also kills insects and birds. Insects seem to be attracted to light from the mirrors. Birds follow the insects, and predatory birds follow the insectivores. The concentrated sunlight burns and melts every creature who flies over. MacGillivray's warblers, blue-gray gnatcatchers, peregrine falcons, Wilson's warblers, mourning doves, yellow-rumped warblers, verdins, house finches, and others have been immolated, their wings burned off.[5]

Here's some of what went into the Ivanpah CSP plant: 173,500 heliostats (each composed of two mirrors), three 459-foot tall towers, three 2,100-ton Riley Power boilers capable of handling steam at over 1000°F and nearly 2,500 PSI, three Siemens turbine generators, three 110-ton mass dampers, 20,000 gallons per day of water, air-cooled condensers from SPX Cooling technologies, 42 million heliostat components, 7,500 tons of steel, 1,200 miles of cable, more than 36,000 cubic yards of concrete, a new power substation, and miles of 220 kV transmission lines.[6]

Industrial solar—this "green," "save the earth" industry—is entirely dependent on mining. Mining is, no matter how you look at it, an

---

4 Todd Woody, "BrightSource Alters Solar Plant Plan to Address Concerns Over Desert Tortoise," *New York Times*, February 11, 2010. The rare plants found in ecological surveys of the site included Mojave milkweed, desert pincushion, Utah vine milkweed, nine-awned pappus grass, Parish's club-cholla, Utah mortonia, Rusby's desert mallow, and desert portulaca.

5 Shaun Gonzalez, "Waking up to the Solar Power Tower Threat," *Mojave Desert Blog*, November 24, 2013.

6 Thomas W. Overton, "PLANT OF THE YEAR: Ivanpah Solar Electric Generating System Earns POWER's Highest Honor," *Power Magazine*, August 1, 2014.

ecological disaster. Ice cores from Mount Blanc, the Alps' highest peak, show levels of lead and antimony over 10 times background levels from Roman mining and smelting.[7] During Roman rule, people across Europe spent their lives breathing in toxic metals. Mines from the Roman Empire still produce toxic acid-mine drainage (a river-destroying cocktail of heavy metals and hydrochloric acid). Pollution from Roman copper mines at Wadi Faynan, in Jordan—remember the goats?—stunts plants and causes "severely damaged" reproductive systems. And it's not just plants. To this day, copper in these soils causes human health problems, including cancers and reproductive defects.[8]

That's what mines *do*, from the first mine until today. The environmentalist David A. Lien noted correctly, "There are no examples of hard rock mining operations without serious pollution."[9]

And mining is a necessary part of the industry that the bright greens say will save the world.

The pure silicon used in solar cells doesn't occur naturally; instead, raw silicon ores must be mined and then refined. This is an intensive industrial process, requiring specialized equipment, dangerous materials, and a wide range of toxic substances.[10]

It starts with the mining of silicon dioxide, or quartz, often in the form of sand. Since sand is also used in concrete, landscaping,

---

[7] "Lead from Roman mines pollutes ancient Alpine ice," *Nature*, May 13, 2019.

[8] David Keys, "How Rome Polluted the World," *Geographical* (Campion Interactive Publishing), vol. 75, no. 12, 45; December 2003.

[9] David A. Lien, "Don't buy PolyMet's assurances on environmental outcomes of sulfide mining," *Minnesota Post*, January 16, 2015.

[10] Eric Williams, "Global Production Chains and Sustainability: The Case of High-purity Silicon and its Applications in IT and Renewable Energy," United Nations University—Institute of Advanced Studies, 2000. In 1998, 99 percent of all solar panels were silicon-based. The number is only slightly smaller now.

and road construction, mining sand from open pits, beaches, dunes, rivers, and the ocean floor is common around the world.

Sand is strip-mined using earth-moving equipment that is, without exception, powered by diesel engines. The sand is purified by crushing, milling, washing, and screening. In the United States, annual extraction is about a billion tons; globally, extraction is about 40 billion tons. Fish kills, destruction of sensitive habitats, and the disappearance of entire beaches are the results of sand mining.[11] One species of Indian crocodile, the Gharial, has nearly been driven extinct. Since 2005, two dozen Indonesian islands have been entirely destroyed in the service of silicon. Understand: these islands no longer exist.

About 800 million tons of silicon is mined each year to create high-purity, metallurgical silicon. This quantity is growing. According to the Minor Metals Trade Association, "The biggest shift in recent years [in the metallurgical silicon market] has been the growth in the use of silicon for use in solar panels, mainly via the production of polycrystalline (or multi-crystalline) silicon (polysilicon).... Continued strong growth in silicon use in PV is expected to lead to market growth ... in excess of 10 percent [per year]."[12]

Refining silicon dioxide into metallurgical-grade silicon requires heating the crushed raw ore to about 4000°F in an electric arc furnace. Carbon, often in the form of coal or coke, is added and bonds with the oxygen to create carbon monoxide. This reaction, which of course leaves behind slag, produces 99.6 percent pure silicon. But still more purity is needed for solar cells.

The second refining step involves heating the material inside a steel furnace insulated with thick layers of graphite until the silicon is molten, around 2500°F. Hydrochloric acid and copper are

---

[11] Vince Beiser, "The Deadly Global War for Sand," *Wired*, March 26, 2015.
[12] "Silicon Market Overview," Minor Metals Trade Association, 2015.

added to the mixture, and they react with the silicon to produce trichlorosilane gas. Boron or phosphorus is introduced to the furnace to help make the silicon conductive. Finally, a "seed crystal" is inserted into the mixture and slowly withdrawn while spinning at a precise speed. This process, entirely controlled by computers, results in a single huge 99.99 percent pure silicon crystal in which all the atoms are aligned.[13] During that process, about 80 percent of the original metallurgical silicon is lost as waste.

A 2008 exposé of the Luoyang Zhonggui High-Technology facility in China found that silicon production was poisoning nearby fields and sickening local residents. The facility was supplying the then-largest solar PV company in the world.[14] A 2014 update noted that even then, "less than one-third of Chinese polysilicon producers meet China's own environmental and energy standards."[15] More recently, a professor of material sciences at Hebei Industrial University stated, "The land where you dump or bury it [silica tetrachloride] will be infertile. No grass or trees will grow in its place.... Human beings can never touch it."[16]

As an article entitled "China's Communist-Capitalist Ecological Apocalypse" put it, "Polysilicon production produces about four tons of ... liquid waste for every ton of polysilicon produced. In Germany, where Siemens produces solar panels, pollution recovery technology is installed to process the silicon tetrachloride waste and render it harmless. But such environmental protection technology is expensive. In 2008, the cost to produce polysilicon

[13] "Step 1: Crystal growing," SolarWorld USA, 2015.
[14] Ariana Eunjung Cha, "Solar Energy Firms Leave Waste Behind in China," *Washington Post*, March 9, 2008.
[15] Brian Lombardozzi, "The True Cost of Chinese Solar Panels: Part 2," Alliance for American Manufacturing, September 23, 2014.
[16] Richard Smith, "China's Communist-Capitalist Ecological Apocalypse," *Truth-Out*, June 21, 2015.

safely was about $84,500 a ton in Germany and would not have cost much less in China. [More recently,] Chinese companies have been producing it for $21,000 to $56,000 a ton, saving millions of dollars a month, by just dumping the toxic waste in rural areas on helpless village communities."[17]

This might be a good time for us to remind ourselves that solar power will save the world.

And do you remember how the bright greens say that sustainability is nigh because the price of solar panels is declining? Now we understand the drop in prices.

In 2011, another Chinese firm, Jinko Solar, was caught dumping hydrofluoric acid into the Yellow River, killing fish and pigs. Residents of a village near Haining in the Zhejiang Province rioted about the pollution—which has caused increased cancers and other diseases—and stormed the Jinko Solar facility, where they flipped over cars. Many were arrested.[18]

The next step consists of robotic wire saws shaping silicon crystals into square cells. Dust from the sawing, called kerf, can cause silicosis, and is a major worker hazard.[19] The individual wafers are then etched using plasma or acid solvents, a process which creates more surface area and increases efficiency. Next, the solar cells are moved into vacuum-sealed chambers and coated with silicon nitride, which further increases efficiency. Finally, conductive metals are printed onto both sides.

Here are just a few of the potentially hazardous chemicals used

[17] Ibid.

[18] Royston Chan, "China quells village solar pollution protests," *Reuters*, September 18, 2011.

[19] Dustin Mulvaney, "Hazardous Materials Used in Silicon PV Cell Production: A Primer," *Solar Industry Magazine*, September 2013.

during the production of solar cells: hydrogen fluoride, hydrochloric acid, sulfuric acid, nitric acid, sodium or potassium hydroxide, silane gas, lead, phosphine or arsine gas, phosphorous oxychloride and trichloride, boron bromide and trichloride, stannic chloride, tantalum pentoxide, titanium and titanium dioxide, diborane, and ethyl vinyl acetate.[20]

Solar panel production also directly contributes to global warming. Zehner notes in *Green Illusions*: "Solar panel production is now among the leading sources of hexafluoroethane, nitrogen trifluoride, and sulfur hexafluoride, three extremely potent greenhouse gases which are used for cleaning plasma production equipment. As a greenhouse gas, hexaflouroethane is 12,000 times more potent than CO_2, is 100 percent manufactured by humans, and survives 10,000 years once released into the atmosphere. Nitrogen trifluoride is 17,000 times more virulent than CO_2, and sulfur hexafluoride is 25,000 times more powerful than CO_2. Concentrations of nitrogen trifluoride in the atmosphere are rising 11 percent per year."[21] Nitrogen trifluoride and sulfur hexafluoride last 700 and 3,000 years, respectively, in the atmosphere.

In addition to copper and other metals, solar panels require 17 rare-earths minerals (used also in cell phones, batteries, wind turbines, and a host of other high-tech devices). These 17 rare-earths minerals are so-named because they're almost never found in high concentrations but are mostly scattered throughout the earth's crust. Nearly all of these rare earths are mined in China. Almost half of all rare earths in China are mined near the city of Baotou,

---

[20] "Health and Safety Concerns of Photovoltaic Solar Panels," Good Company via Oregon Department of Transportation.
[21] Zehner, op. cit.

a name which literally means "place with deer." Most of the rare earths come from one open-pit mine more than a half mile deep and covering more than 18 square miles.

Separating rare earths from the rest of the ore requires the use of sulfates, ammonia, and hydrochloric acid, and produces 2,000 tons of toxic waste for every ton of rare earths.

The mines, smelters, and factories of Baotou produce 10 million tons of wastewater per year. This "water" is pumped into tailings ponds, including one that covers almost four square miles and about which *The Guardian* has reported, "From the air it looks like a huge lake, fed by many tributaries, but on the ground it turns out to be a murky expanse of water, in which no fish or algae can survive. The shore is coated with a black crust, so thick you can walk on it." *The Guardian* also wrote, "The foul waters of the tailings pond contain all sorts of toxic chemicals, but also radioactive elements such as thorium which, if ingested, cause cancers of the pancreas and lungs, and leukemia. 'Before the factories were built, there were just fields here as far as the eye can see. In the place of this radioactive sludge, there were watermelons, aubergines and tomatoes,' says Li Guirong with a sigh.'" The soil and water near Baotou are so polluted that the local residents can no longer grow vegetables there. Many have fled. Many have been forcibly relocated. Many have died, and those who remain are suffering a host of diseases caused by this mining.[22]

Ignorance is easier to maintain with distance. Geography is one

---

[22] This paragraph is mostly put together from Cécile Bontron, "Rare-earth mining in China comes at a heavy cost for local villages: Pollution is poisoning the farms and villages of the region that processes the precious minerals," *The Guardian*, August 7, 2012; and Jonathan Kaiman, "Rare earth mining in China: the bleak social and environmental costs," *The Guardian*, March 20, 2014.

kind of distance, and the worst extraction is usually done far, far away, in the colonies, the hinterland. Hierarchy is another, and hence the dispossessed are targeted for industrial harm while the rest of us, safe in the center of empire, see nothing.

There is a third distance, built from denial. Because we surely know, no matter how little we let ourselves, that solar panels aren't born in the spring and wind turbines aren't the fruit of the turbine tree. They're manufactured. They're built from something. The getting of that something requires effort, energy. And the getting of that something, from inside a mountain or under the earth, cannot have been gentle or good. And that pile of something must be getting smaller.

But it's all so shiny, so new, so sweet with promises. Cars as clean as air, electricity from pure light, a future of plenty. Surely this is possible? We want to believe. We need to believe, so we keep our distance.

Right now, people along the Idaho/Washington border are fighting a proposed silicon smelter. The demand is bottomless. This is what's required. Six raw tons of silicon are mined for every ton of silicon metal produced.[23] Buried in the word "mined" is the devastation of blasting enormous holes in the ground, all over the world. One observer from Uttar Pradesh in India states the mines "have changed the region's topography ... scarred the landscape, disrupted ecosystems, and destroyed microbial communities."[24] Even the bacteria don't escape. The topsoil is lost forever, the water table sinks, the rivers are strangled by silt, and "fugitive" silica dust scars the lungs of every creature that breathes. Most people

[23] Eric de Place and Ahren Stroming, "Small town silicon smelter plan tees up big questions," *Sightline Institute*, June 25, 2018.

[24] Mishra Ashutosh, "Impact of silica mining on environment," *Journal of Geography and Regional Planning*, May 27, 2015.

reading this couldn't find Uttar Pradesh on a map, so: distance. What about Minnesota? Is that close enough to count? One report from Minnesota found that 138 threatened and endangered species are within one mile of silica sand "resources." That includes turtles, fish, and plants, as well as 3,000 acres of native prairie. Since 98 percent of the prairie is gone, the prairie itself is "extremely rare."[25]

Once taken, those millions of tons of sand have to be transported to a smelter. That means trains on tracks and trucks on roads slashed through habitat—the place somebody calls home—and the oil to fuel them. It takes 3000°F or higher to turn silicon into silicon metal for solar panels and electronics.[26] In Washington, that 3000°F is supposed to come from Pend Oreille Public Utility District's Box Canyon Dam. Only that dam produces 90 megawatts, and the smelter wants 105. In fact, the smelter would need four times the electricity "used by all of the utility's residential and small commercial customers combined."[27] Silicon metal also requires woodchips, those small, dead fragments once known as "forests." It also requires "bluegreen," a rare coal from Kentucky, 48,000 metric tons of it every year: mountains reduced to rubble.

The smelter in Idaho would produce not just the silicon metal for our shiny, green future, but also 320,000 tons of greenhouse gases, making it the fifteenth-largest producer in the state. It would also produce acid rain from its annual 760 tons of sulfur dioxide and 700 tons of nitrogen oxides.[28]

Make no mistake, this is poison. People who lived near a silicon smelter in Rykjanes, Iceland, got chemical burns in their throats.[29]

[25] Minnesota Environmental Quality Board, Report on Silica Sand, March 20, 2013, 54.
[26] de Place and Stroming, op. cit.
[27] Ibid.
[28] Ibid.
[29] Paul Fontaine, "Gasping for air: United Silicon's enduring problems," The Reykjavik Grapevine, September 8, 2017.

Arsenic was at 20 times the legal limit. The plant was closed, then reopened, and not much changed. The people say they're being held hostage by the smelter as they can't safely breathe outside. Of course, other animals have nowhere to go but outside.

The people of Washington and Idaho don't want the smelter. The Kalispell Tribe, on whose traditional homeland the smelter would be built, has firmly rejected it as posing "unacceptable risks" to their health and culture.[30] The Affiliated Tribes of Northwest Indians are also standing against it.[31] Neighboring tribes, a citizen group, and local environmentalists have all said no.

But the rest of us want this bright, happy future, and we refuse to close the distance. We don't want to know about the acid rain falling, the fish strangling, and the rubble that once was mountains going up in smoke.

And what happens when solar panels wear out?

Solar waste is an increasing problem. In 2011, the community watchdog group Silicon Valley Toxics Coalition wrote, "As the solar industry expands, little attention is being paid to the potential environmental and health costs of that rapid expansion. The most widely used solar PV panels have the potential to create a huge new source of electronic waste at the end of their useful lives, which is estimated to be 20 to 25 years. New solar PV technologies are increasing efficiency and lowering costs, but many of these use extremely toxic materials or materials with unknown

---

[30] Kalispel Tribe of Indians, Resolution #2018-16.
[31] Affiliated Tribes of Northwest Indians, Resolution #18-12.

health and environmental risks (including new nano materials and processes)."[32]

What about small-scale, community solar-power projects? Aren't they much better than the alternative? Well, as it turns out, they aren't. The majority of solar panels are produced far from the regions where they're used. More than 60 percent of the solar panels sold in the United States are manufactured in China, Korea, Japan, or Singapore.[33] Oceanic shipping is one of the most polluting industries on earth. Container ships burn bunker fuel, which is so polluting it's illegal to burn on land just about everywhere in the world. But on the ocean, it's completely legal. Global shipping is responsible for about 4 percent of all carbon dioxide emissions, and as much as 30 percent of global smog. One container ship can emit as much pollution as 50 million passenger vehicles.[34]

And even being a proponent of local solar energy doesn't address the supply chain. The materials used in solar PV and CSP aren't evenly distributed around the world. The biggest iron ore mine in the world is in Brazil, formerly in the Amazon Rainforest ("formerly" because the region surrounding the mine has been clear-cut). The biggest copper mine in the world is in Utah. The largest rare-earth mineral mine is, as we discussed, in Baotou, China.

Solar PV and CSP require a global scale economy. That means ships on the ocean, trains on the land, planes in the sky. It means highways and ports and shipping containers. It means stock

[32] "Towards a Just and Sustainable Solar Energy Industry," Silicon Valley Toxics Coalition, January 14, 2009, no. 4.

[33] "Where are solar panels manufactured, and should you care," *Energy Sage Solar Marketplace*.

[34] "Ocean Pollution: Global Shipping and the Cruise Industry," *Earthjustice*.

exchanges and economic systems to facilitate the movement of goods.

This is the economy that is killing the planet. These are not solvable issues. These are fundamental to the manufacture of solar PV and CSP. Tell us again, how is this is sustainable?

Here is something else Naomi Klein said, something that is both perceptive and brilliant. In the interview on *Democracy Now* we've already cited, in which she claimed 25 percent of Germany's energy is supplied by "renewables," she talked about something global warming deniers get right. She stated, "And when I interviewed the head of the [right-wing] Heartland Institute, Joe Bast, for this project, he was quite open that it wasn't that he found a problem with the science first. He said, when he looked at the science and listened to what scientists were saying about how much we need to cut our emissions, he realized that climate change could be, if it were true, it would justify huge amounts of government regulation, which he politically opposes. And so, he said, 'So then we looked at the science, and we found these problems,' right? So the issue is, they understand that if the science is true, their whole ideological project falls apart, because, as I said, you can't respond to a crisis this big, that involves transforming the foundation of our economy—our economy was built on fossil fuels, it is still fueled by fossil fuels. The idea in this—we hear this from a lot of liberal environmental groups, that we can change completely painlessly, just change your light bulbs, or just a gentle market mechanism, tax and relax, no problem. This is what they [the global-warming deniers] understand well, that in fact it [stopping global warming] requires transformative change [as in stopping the fossil fuel economy]. That change is abhorrent to them. They see it as the end of the world. It's not the end of the world, but it is the end of their world. It's the end of their ideological project. So, that is unthinkable, from [prominent climate change denier] Marc Morano's perspective and Joe Bast's perspective. So, rather than think about that, they deny the science."

She's right, of course. So much of this culture's discourse is not based on physical reality—and certainly not based on protecting life on this planet—but rather is based on attempting to maintain this way of life. Anything that threatens this way of life is unthinkable, and so physical reality must be denied. Understanding that helps make many of the lies of the global-warming deniers comprehensible.

And Klein is *so close* to understanding the many inaccurate statements made by bright greens as well. Let's change a few of her words:

"So the issue is, ~~global warming deniers~~ *bright greens* understand that if the science is true, their whole ideological project falls apart, because, as I said, you can't respond to a crisis this big, that involves transforming the foundation of our economy—our economy that's built on ~~fossil fuels~~ *functionally and systematically converting the world into products; in other words, destroying the planet, no matter how the destruction is fueled.* The idea in this—we hear this from a lot of ~~liberal environmental groups~~ *bright greens*, that we can change completely painlessly, just change your ~~light bulbs~~ *source of energy*, or just a gentle market mechanism, tax and relax, no problem. This is what bright greens understand well, that in fact it [stopping global warming] requires transformative change as in stopping industrial civilization. That change is abhorrent to them. They see it as the end of the world. It's not the end of the world, but it is the end of their world. It's the end of their ideological project. So, that is unthinkable, from *a bright green* perspective. So, rather than think about that, they deny the science, *and they deny what's really at stake.*"

Chapter 5

THE WIND LIE

I will do anything that is basically covered by the law to reduce
Berkshire's tax rate. For example, on wind energy, we get a tax
credit if we build a lot of wind farms. That's the only reason to
build them. They don't make sense without the tax credit.[1]

—WARREN BUFFET

The mountains and moors, the wild uplands, are to be staked
out like vampires in the sun, their chests pierced with rows of
500-foot wind turbines and associated access roads, masts,
pylons and wires.[2]

—PAUL KINGSNORTH

You're walking up Spring Valley in eastern-central Nevada, but not
seeming to make much progress. This is a big place, and you're
a small person. Sagebrush and bitterbrush stretch for miles on
either side, to where mountains don't so much loom as are solidly
present. Thick forests of single-leaf piñon pine and western juniper

---

[1] Michael Bastasch, "Here's Why This Warren Buffett-Owned Utility Wants to Use 100
Percent Wind Power," *Daily Caller*, May 31, 2018.
[2] Paul Kingsnorth, *Confessions of a Recovering Environmentalist and Other Essays*
(Minneapolis, MN: Graywolf Press, 2017), 70.

blanket the mountains' torsos before thinning toward their rocky shoulders and snow-clung heads. The sun is high, and the sunlight warms you, but when you pass into the shade of a cloud your skin chills immediately. It's springtime in the high desert.

The Western Shoshone and Goshute, who call themselves Newe, have lived here for thousands of years. This valley—one of the lushest in the region—was and is important to them. They ate pine nuts and rabbits and the seeds of grasses. Then, 150 years ago, the first settlers came with their shovels and picks, their dynamite and cattle. They found silver and gold in the mountains, and before long explosions destroyed the complex and delicate desert soundscape. The resultant ore needed to be smelted, and so the forests came down. All across Nevada, mountains for 50 miles in every direction from mining camps were stripped of every tree. Observers in the 1870s described "the terrible destruction of forest which follows ... every new discovery of the precious metals."[3]

As mines have devastated uplands, so cows have devastated valleys. The ground here used to be thickly speckled with native bunchgrass, wildflowers, and forbs. Even though the brush you walk through is beautiful, the ground between the shrubs is dusty; cattle have killed the natural soil crusts, so essential to life in this dry place.

You cross a wash; cows have mangled it. The ground around it is especially trampled and eroded. A hundred years ago it might have carried water for months every year, but no longer. Now it's only wet when spring thunderstorms bring a flood of silty water down the alluvial fan from the mountain.

That the forests of piñon pine and juniper have returned speaks

[3] Charles S. Sargent, "The forests of central Nevada, with some remarks on those of the adjacent regions." *American. Journal of Science and Arts*, third series, Art. 53 (1879), 417–426.

to the resilience of these forests—and to the hard work of forest-tending piñon jays and packrats.

Now the forests face new threats: clearcutting, herbicide sprays, "mastication," and chaining—all, in standard Orwellian fashion, described as "restoration."[4] And their most recent threats: sustainability and renewable energy.

You walk over a small hillock and see the northern expanse of the valley. You leave off cursing miners and ranchers and begin cursing environmentalists. The valley floor is littered with wind turbines: 66 of them, each 425 feet tall, each with a set of three fiberglass blades sweeping a 330-foot radius.[5] Access roads lead to the base of each turbine, spreading across the valley, further fragmenting the battered landscape and delivering seeds of weedy invasive plants like cheatgrass to freshly disturbed soil.

Directly adjacent to and east of the turbines, a grove of juniper trees grows on the valley floor. This is a sacred place to the Newe, who call it the Swamp Cedars or Shoshone Cedars. It has been a gathering place for generations. It also has a terrible history; two major massacres were committed here by whites, one in 1863 and another in 1897. The first left over 350 Newe dead, making it one of the worst massacres of American Indians.

This valley has seen too many atrocities, and wind turbines are merely the latest. And as with most atrocities, the "good-hearted" public supports this project. Despite all evidence, people simply refuse to see the harm caused by wind turbines.

---

[4] Learn more at pinyonjuniperforests.org. "Chaining" is where deforesters drag a huge anchor chain, weighing up to 20,000 pounds, between two bulldozers, yanking up all trees between them. It's a horrific practice.

[5] "Wind Turbine SWT-2.3-101, Technical Specifications," Siemens Energy.

If solar power has captured the imagination of the mainstream environmental movement, wind power has captured its wallet. Serious proponents of "renewable" energy rely heavily on wind power in their energy transition plans.

The Economist says, "Wind power is widely seen as the source of renewable energy with the best chance of competing with fossil-fuel power stations in the near term."[6]

Every mainstream environmentalist praises wind energy. Kumi Naidoo says it is a critical part of "an energy revolution on the scale [of] the industrial revolution ... [to] maximize all the renewable energy potential."[7] (And we all know how well the industrial revolution went for the planet, right?) According to environmentalist Lester Brown, "Our civilization needs to embrace renewable energy on a scale and at a pace we've never seen before"; he calls for the building of "roughly 300,000 wind turbines per year over the next decade."[8]

Mark Z. Jacobson, a professor of civil and environmental engineering at Stanford University, has become one of the highest-profile "renewable" energy boosters, primarily because he created detailed plans that purport to show how to transition global energy usage to 100 percent "renewable" energy by 2030. And, yes, he means energy, not just electricity, which means he's including transportation, heating, and so on. In his vision, wind power will provide a full half of global industrial energy needs, far more than any other source.

---

[6] *The Economist Technology Quarterly.* June 12, 2010, 12.

[7] Diane Toomey, "Greenpeace's Kumi Naidoo on Russia and the Climate Struggle," *Yale Environment 360*, January 14, 2014.

[8] Lester Brown, "The Great Transition: Building a Wind-Centered Economy," *Population Press*, April 16, 2013.

To make this possible, Jacobson calls for building 3.8 million 5 MW wind turbines by 2030.[9]

Yes, you read those numbers correctly. If Spring Valley was devastated by 66 of these machines, how many valleys would he destroy with his plan? Well, that would be 58,575.

In an article entitled "Windmills Are Things of Beauty," environmentalist David Suzuki acknowledges that there are grassroots activists who oppose wind energy facilities. He calls their efforts "hypocritical and counterproductive." He believes "windmills are beautiful" and states that if one day he looks out from the porch of his vacation cabin—valued at over $1 million, and one of at least four homes he owns—with a view of wilderness and sees "a row of windmills spinning in the distance, I won't curse them. I will praise them. It will mean we're finally getting somewhere."[10]

It's pretty easy for Suzuki to praise and not curse wind turbines, since it's only the view from his vacation home that's being destroyed. For the nonhumans, it's a little harder as it's their actual homes—as in where they live—being destroyed to serve the industrial economy.

Most people—even most wind-energy proponents—don't know what wind turbines are made of, because the materials used in these machines aren't usually part of the conversation about renewable energy. But an accounting of these materials is critical.

[9] Mark Z. Jacobson and Mark A. Delucchi, "Providing all global energy with wind, water, and solar power, Part I: Technologies, energy resources, quantities and areas of infrastructure, and materials," *Journal of Energy Policy* 39 (2011), 1154–1169.

[10] David Suzuki, "Windmills are things of beauty," *David Suzuki Foundation*, April 3, 2014. Thankfully, a significant number of the comments left below the article were sane.

Wind turbines consist of four main parts: tower, blades, nacelle (the bulbous bit on top of the tower), and foundation.

The tower holds the spinning blades aloft. Winds tend to be faster and more consistent the farther they are above the ground, which is one reason turbines are getting larger. Another reason is that as the length of a turbine's blades increases, the area swept, and thus the power that can be generated, increases as the square of the length. The largest wind turbine design in operation as of 2019, the Vestas V164 10 MW turbine, stands 722 feet tall—about 70 percent as tall as the Empire State Building—with each 263-foot-long blade weighing 38 tons. Even larger wind turbines are currently undergoing testing. A 12 MW offshore prototype from General Electric is more than 850 feet tall, and its 350-foot long blades "represent one of the largest single machine components ever built.[11]

The nacelle is the control center of the wind turbine, containing a gearbox that translates energy to a workable rotational speed and a generator that transforms this mechanical energy into electricity.

Because they're top-heavy and installed in windy areas, turbines need an especially sturdy foundation. On land, foundations are made of steel-reinforced concrete. In shallow areas offshore, wind turbines are built on foundations sunk into the sea floor. In deeper waters, turbines are built on floating platforms anchored to the sea floor with cables.

By mass, the main materials used in wind turbines are steel and concrete. Most of the steel is in the tower and the nacelle, and

---

[11] Tomas Kellner, "Extreme Measures: At 107 Meters, The World's Largest Wind Turbine Blade Is Longer Than A Football Field. Here's What It Looks Like," *General Electric*, April 18, 2019.

in the foundation in the form of structural reinforcements, often rebar. Concrete is generally used only in the foundation, but some wind turbines use concrete towers reinforced with steel instead of traditional steel towers.

Blades are manufactured from wood and composite materials like fiberglass and carbon fiber, which are energy-intensive plastics made from petrochemicals. As one analysis notes, "Resins [used in wind turbine blades] begin with ethylene derived from light hydrocarbons, most commonly the products of naphtha cracking, liquefied petroleum gas, or the ethane in natural gas.... To get 2.5 TW of installed wind power by 2030, we would need an aggregate rotor mass of about 23 million metric tons, incorporating the equivalent of about 90 million metric tons of crude oil."[12]

Nacelles contain large amounts of copper and rare earth metals like neodymium (used for powerful magnets to increase reliability and performance).

And of course, industrial wind-energy-harvesting facilities don't exist in a vacuum; they require substations, transmission lines, control facilities, vehicles to haul maintenance teams, and so on.

We call them harvesting facilities because they don't, as common usage suggests, generate energy. They harvest it from the wind, just like solar-harvesting facilities harvest it from the sun, dams harvest it from rivers, and so on. This is crucial, because if you generate something, it wasn't there before. If you harvest something, that thing being harvested already exists, and once harvested, is no longer available to others. This is as true of wind and sunlight as it is of trees, fish, water, and at this point the entire earth. As we shall see, removing energy from the wind changes climate.

The average 5 MW wind turbine is between 300 and 400 feet tall, with rotor blades more than 200 feet long, bringing the total

---

[12] Vaclav Smil, "To Get Wind Power You Need Oil," *IEEE Spectrum*, February 29, 2016.

height to 600 feet or more. That's about 50 stories. In a 5 MW turbine, the tower alone weighs around 400 tons, the nacelle 300 tons,
and the rotor blades 54 tons. The foundation is even more massive:
on land, several thousand tons. Offshore foundations can range
from 500 tons to more than 8,000 tons, depending on the depth of
the water and the type of sediment or bedrock.[13] All these numbers
are rising in the quest for greater energy production.

Let's do the math. Mark Jacobson calls for 3.8 million 5 MW
turbines by 2030. That's 19 million MW. First, let's subtract the
2017 installed capacity of 540,000 MW, taking us down to a little
under 18.5 MW: That reduces the number of new 5 MW wind turbines needed in his plan to about 3.7 million new turbines.

To build that many new wind turbines would require more than
1.4 billion tons of steel for towers, another billion tons of steel
and 1.9 million tons of copper for the nacelles, 133 million tons of
composite fiber materials for rotor blades, and around 2.6 billion
tons of concrete and steel for foundations (assuming a conservative average of 2,000 tons of material per turbine). In comparison,
construction of Hoover Dam used 211,500 tons of concrete and
22,500 tons of steel. The scale of this project, then, is the equivalent of building perhaps 60,000 Hoover Dams in 12 years, more
than 13 Hoover Dams per day.

Just what the world needs, right?

The everyday operation of wind turbines requires fossil fuels for
lubrication. ExxonMobil is one of the major providers; they have a
line of fossil-fuel based lubricants solely for use in wind turbines.[14]
The average 5 MW turbine contains several hundred gallons of oil
and hydraulic fluid; the transformer at the base of each turbine

---

[13] "Repower 5M," Database of turbines and manufacturers, the Windpower Wind
Energy Market Intelligence.
[14] "Energy portfolio diversification," ExxonMobil Fuels & Lubricants.

may contain another 500 gallons. Let's take a rough average, 700 gallons, and multiply it by the 3.8 million turbines Mark Jacobson and other bright greens want to build, and you get 2.6 billion gallons. These lubricants don't last forever: like oil in a car, they get gunked up and have to be replaced—on average every nine to 16 months. They also sometimes spill or leak. A worldwide fleet of 3.8 million wind turbines—or any number, for that matter—requires a steady supply of lubricants to keep them humming. This fleet would leak and spill an oily flood of these chemicals.[15]

The most critical ingredient in wind turbines is steel. According to the World Steel Association, the trade group that represents most of the world's large steel companies, "every part of a wind turbine depends on iron and steel."[16] And it's not just essential for the turbines themselves, either. Steel is required for other phases in the generation of wind power, from the mining machines that extract the ore that will become the steel in wind turbines to the massive ships carrying turbine components around the world to the cranes that lift and install these turbines.

And it's not just critical to wind power, either. Steel is one of the most important global commodities, essential to many parts of industrial civilization. Buildings, ships, cars and trucks, appliances, infrastructure, machinery, and weapons all require abundant, cheap steel.

Steel is made of iron alloyed with a smaller portion of at least one other element, most often carbon but sometimes manganese,

---

[15] Darren Lesinski, "Synthetics to Protect the Wind Turbine and the Environment," *Wind Systems Magazine*, January 2013. Note: EPA considers synthetic oil to be just as dangerous as conventional.

[16] "Steel Solutions in the Green Economy: Wind Turbines," World Steel Association, 2012.

chromium, nickel, or tungsten. About 2 billion tons of steel was produced in 2018, with more than half coming from China. Other major producers include Japan, Germany, Russia, the United States, and Brazil.[17]

Mark Jacobson's plan, revered by so many mainstream environmentalists, would require about 120 percent of the steel produced in 2018 across the entire world.

Increased mining: that can't be the plan that's going to save the earth, can it? That's just more of the same plan that's already killing the earth.

Just for the United States, Jacobson's plan would require "335,000 onshore wind turbines; 154,000 offshore wind turbines; 75 million residential photovoltaic systems; 275,000 commercial photovoltaic systems; 46,000 utility-scale photovoltaic facilities; 3,600 concentrated solar-power facilities with onsite heat storage; and an extensive array of underground thermal storage facilities."

His plan would require a 15-fold increase in hydroelectric capacity (i.e., dams), and would daily require these dams to release about 100 times the flow of the Mississippi River.

And this plan is supported by environmentalists?

Here are a few more insane assumptions of Jacobson's plan. He assumes an energy storage capacity more than twice the current generating capacity of all U.S. power plants combined. He assumes underground thermal-energy storage capacity more than 125,000 times that of the current largest facility of this sort. He assumes the United States will have enough hydrogen-storage facilities to cover an entire month of U.S. electricity usage. He assumes that power

---

[17] "World Steel in Figures 2019," *World Steel Association*, June 3, 2019.

equivalent to twice the entire U.S. supply will be used to isolate and prepare this hydrogen. He assumes that 6 percent of the land mass of the United States will be devoted to wind (presumably with much of the rest underwater from dams). He assumes that factories can run when solar and wind can't provide their power.[18]

Iron ore is the main raw precursor to steel and is mined around the world. Five of the 10 largest iron ore mines are in Brazil. Because iron ore mining is big business, worth hundreds of billions of dollars annually just in Brazil, the government does all it can to streamline mining permits, sidestep environmental regulations, and mute community opposition.

The world's largest iron-ore mine is the Carajás mine, located in the Amazon rainforest in Brazil. More accurately, the mine is located in what used to be the Amazon rainforest. Now, it's located in the center of a wasteland, a clearcut, an industrial chasm. Every year, more than 2,400 square miles of forest around Carajás are cut down, mostly to make charcoal used for smelting iron ore.[19] Yes, you read that number correctly. And yes, that's annually. The latest $17 billion mine expansion project has already destroyed mile after mile of rainforest, and threatens a unique part of the Amazon, a

---

[18] Cobbled together from Peter Fairley, "Can the U.S. Grid Work With 100% Renewables? There's a Scientific Fight Brewing," *Spectrum*, June 19, 2017; Nathaneal Johnson, "A battle royale has broken out between clean power purists and pragmatists," *Grist*, June 20, 2017; and Ronald Bailey, "Powering U.S. Using 100 Percent Renewable Energy Is a Total Fantasy," *Reason*, June 21, 2017. Please note that while Bailey's work in general is reprehensible, that doesn't mean his math is bad.

[19] Roger LeGuen, "Amazon Mining: Extracting Valuable Minerals and a Pandora's Box of Problems," World Wildlife Fund. Note that WWF's source is from 1997, and deforestation rates have gone up since then. We used that conservative estimate, but estimates run up to 4,000 square miles per year. Please note also that when environmentalists were opposing the mine back in the 1980s, they feared the mine would consume a little over 275 square miles per year. Isn't that the way it always goes?

savanna around two lakes, home to more than 40 endemic plant species found nowhere else on earth.

Toxic "tailings" sludge from these mining operations is impounded behind huge earthen dams, two of which have failed in recent years. A 2015 collapse near Mariana, Brazil destroyed two villages, killed 19 people, polluted water supplies for 400,000, and released more than 43 million cubic meters of toxic waste into 400 miles of rivers of streams and the Atlantic Ocean. According to a United Nations report, "Entire fish populations—at least 11 tons—were killed immediately when the slurry buried them or clogged their gills." The same report describes that "the force of the mud-flow destroyed 1,469 hectares (3,630 acres) of riparian forest."[20]

The report uses the term "eliminating all aquatic life" to describe what has happened to more than 400 miles of river. The Mariana tailings dam failure has been called the worst environmental disaster in Brazil's history.

The second major failure at a Vale iron-ore mine hit Brumadinho, Brazil, in January 2019. This time, the mudflow killed 270 people and released 12 million cubic meters of toxic sludge—destroying all life in another river, the Paraopeba. In the aftermath, Vale safety inspectors "failed to guarantee the safety" of 18 other Vale dams and dikes in Brazil.[21] As one researcher put it in the aftermath, "In Brazil and [the state of] Minas, it is the ore above everything and everyone."[22]

Iron ore mines in the Amazon basin have displaced tens of thousands of indigenous people, decimated newly contacted tribes through the spread of infectious diseases, and flooded remote areas

---

[20] "Mine Tailings Storage: Safety is No Accident," U.N. Environment, 2015.

[21] Samantha Pearson and Luciana Magalhaes, "Inspectors Fail to Guarantee Safety of 18 Vale Dams, Dikes in Brazil – 2nd Update," *MarketScreener*, April 1, 2019.

[22] Gabriel De Sá, "Brazil's deadly dam disaster may have been preventable," *National Geographic*, January 29, 2020.

with thousands of workers. A 2011 report from the International Federation for Human Rights attributes "incessant air pollution" to the iron ore mines. Forced labor and child slavery have been documented by the Brazilian government. Mines become the locus of networks of roads that cut into the jungle, leading to poaching and illegal logging in protected areas.

People in the region contend with cancers, birth defects, and lung diseases caused by pollution from processing facilities, factories, and constant traffic of industrial trucks and trains. In some towns, a fully loaded train passes every 20 minutes, day and night. "[The town of Piquiá de Baixo is] a place where practically the whole population is likely to get health problems and lung diseases," says local teacher Joselma Alves de Oliveira.[23]

Resistance has been widespread, with tribal people, students, and forest lovers blockading railways and holding public protests, but with little success.[24] Local business elites and politicians, many of whom have been powerful since the days of Brazil's military dictatorship, protect the mining operations with the help of police and paramilitary forces.

"In thirty years, iron exploitation [has left] deforested areas, slave labor, migration, and has torn apart the identification of the communities with their territories," says community organizer Padre Dario Bossi, who has been fighting iron ore mines for decades. "It has also left land conflicts, pollution, urban disorganization, and violence due to the intense exodus of people in search of work, the most affected being indigenous or African."[25]

[23] Fabiola Ortiz, "Brazil—The Polluted Face of Carajás. I," *Latin America Bureau*, September 17, 2014.

[24] Dom Phillips, "Another huge and open iron mine is carved out of Brazil's rain forest," *The Washington Post*, April 13, 2015.

[25] Raúl Zibechi, "Mining and Colonialism in Brazil's Giant Carajás Project," *CIP Americas Program*, May 31, 2014.

❁

Like all industrial projects, iron ore mines in the Amazon are not only a locus of roads but also sexual exploitation. Trafficking, sexual assault, prostitution, and other atrocities against women and children follow every mine. As Sheila Jeffreys writes in her book *The Industrial Vagina: The Political Economy of the Global Sex Trade*, "[Mining industries] open up new areas for new forms of colonial exploitation [and] they set up prostitution industries to service the workers. These industries have a profound effect on local cultures and relations between men and women."[26]

❁

Wherever it takes place, and with whatever regulations in place, iron ore mining and steel production are environmental and social disasters.

Cliffs Natural Resources, for example, is a mining company based in the United States. Two of their operations, the Tilden and Empire mines (both in Marquette County, Michigan) extract 20 percent of the iron ore in the U.S. (Cliffs also operates coal mines, and if you think this is an unnatural fit, you should know that coal is required for steel production.)

And what have their iron ore mines left behind? Toxic tailings ponds, selenium and mercury contamination, warnings against eating local fish, massive air pollution, acid rain that is particularly harmful to wild rice (a staple food for local indigenous people), and more than 100 square miles of devastated land.

The fuel use of these mines is stunning: The colossal diesel dump trucks used in the industry have 1,200-gallon tanks, which

---

[26] Sheila Jeffreys, *The Industrial Vagina: The Political Economy of the Global Sex Trade* (Abingdon, U.K.: Routledge, 2008), 7.

are filled twice a day. A few dozen of these trucks may be operating at any time.[27]

Regulations haven't made much of a difference. The mine at Keewatin, near the Tilden and Empire mines, opened in 2009 and was cited each of its first three years for air- and water-quality violations. A railway serving another nearby iron ore mine in Minnesota was cited multiple times for violating rules around hazardous waste and air quality. The Wisconsin Resources Protection Council calls iron ore mines "chronic polluters," and states that "all modern U.S. taconite [a type of iron ore] mines have violations and fines totaling more than $2.1 million; with [fines for] cleanups the total is over $10.5 million."[28]

These fines are trivial for companies with revenues in the billions. Regulations haven't been effective in cleaning up iron ore mines in the United States. But that shouldn't be surprising. After 20 years at the EPA, William Sanjour described the environmental regulatory system as "stupid, corrupt, ineffective, [and] inefficient."[29] Thomas Linzey, co-founder of the Community Legal Environmental Defense fund, explains well why the entire system of environmental regulations is foolish: it permits harm to continue. "Abolitionists never sought to regulate the slave trade," he says, "they sought to abolish it." He explains that the very concept of regulating industrial harms comes from industry and not concerned people, who would in most cases rather ban harmful activities altogether.

---

[27] "Empire & Tilden Mines," Keeweenaw Bay Indian Community, Natural Resources Department; and "The Tilden Mine," Michigan State University, Geology Department.

[28] "The Environmental Track Record of Taconite Mining: The Facts Exposing the False Premise that Iron Ore Mining is Safe," Wisconsin Resource Protection Council, January 2013.

[29] William Sanjour, "From the Files of a Whistleblower, or how EPA was captured by the industry it regulated," December 25, 2013.

☉

Most steel is made by alloying iron ore with coke as a source of carbon. Coke, also known as coking coal or metallurgical coal, is created from low-sulfur bituminous coal through a process called destructive distillation in which the feedstock coal is heated in the absence of air, breaking down large, volatile molecules that could interfere with steel production. Sometimes other gases or solvents are added to the reaction chamber to help with the process. Byproducts include coal gas (used as an industrial fuel), ammoniacal liquor (used in fertilizers), and coal tar (used to manufacture dyes, insecticides, artificial yarns, and other products).

The amount of coal used in steel production is not small—it's about 12 percent of global anthracite, the highest grade of coal.[30]

The production of steel and metallurgical coke is the third-largest source of greenhouse gas emissions, after fossil fuels and electrical generation, with a large gap to fourth.

Could steel be made without coal? There have been experiments to see if it's possible. The University of New South Wales in Australia developed a method that uses car tires instead of coal (of course, car tires are mainly made of synthetic rubber, which is derived from fossil fuels). Another process, called the Hisarna method, uses coal directly rather than requiring coke, which reduces the coal demand by 20 percent. The only hope of making steel without coal lies, at this time, with a process called molten oxide electrolysis. Originally developed as a theoretical process to produce oxygen on the moon, molten oxide electrolysis takes place

---

[30] Jeanette Fitzsimons, "Can we make steel without coal?" Coal Action Network Aotearoa, April 24, 2013.

in a vat of molten iron oxide kept at more than 2900°F, and is sealed using a special alloy of chromium and iron.[31]

None of this is sustainable. Nor does this process address any of the other issues with steel production, such as direct land destruction from mining, heavy equipment use, impacts on forests and indigenous communities, sexual exploitation, and so on.

Need another reason to be against mining? Just look at this headline: "U.S. Mines Pollute Up to 27 Billion Gallons of Water Annually."[32]

Wind turbines also require copper. Lots of it. Copper makes up about 35 percent of the mass in a wind turbine's generator, and is also used in wiring, power cables, transformer coils, and lightning-protection systems. The Copper Development Association, the main trade group, calls copper "an indispensable ingredient for wind energy."[33] Each 5 MW wind turbine has more than 1,000 pounds of copper inside, which means Mark Jacobson's plan would require, at minimum, 3.8 billion pounds of copper, or almost 2 million tons. That's not counting the copper in transmission lines, wiring, substations, electric transit, electronics, vehicles, and so on. One conservative estimate shows that about one-third of one year's global copper production would be required for the energy transition called for by Jacobson and the rest of the bright greens.[34]

[31] David Chandler, "Electrolyis method described from making 'green' iron," Phys.org

[32] Laura Beans, "U.S. Mines Pollute Up to 27 Billion Gallons of Water Annually," *EcoWatch*, May 2, 2013.

[33] "Copper: An Indispensable Ingredient for Wind Energy," *Copper Development Association, Inc.*, September 2010.

[34] Danny Chivers, "The Stuff Problem," *New Internationalist*, August 15, 2015.

Copper, like most minerals, is strip mined in vast open-pit mines. One of the largest in the world is the Kennecott Bingham Canyon Mine in the Oquirrh Mountain Range just outside Salt Lake City. You can see the mine from space. It's a pit that's 2.5 miles wide, dug more than half a mile into the root of the mountains. It looks like what it is: a mountaintop-removal mine.

Here's how it works. Explosives break up the rock, which is loaded onto two-story dump trucks and dropped on a five-mile conveyor belt leading to a facility where the rock is ground to dust by rotating crusher drums made of hardened steel. This dust is added to a slurry of water and chemicals like methyl isobutyl carbinol, potassium or sodium ethyl xanthate (which has sickened many workers and is "especially toxic to aquatic life"), or various dithiophosphates and dithiocarbamates. This process, called "flotation," separates the valuable minerals.

Next, the wet sediment slurry is sent through a 17-mile pipeline to a smelter facility in the town of Magna, Utah, where it's dried and injected into a superheated furnace. This heat oxidizes iron and sulfur, which can be removed. The sulfur becomes sulfur dioxide gas, which is captured and used to produce sulfuric acid, a valuable industrial material that facilitates resource extraction and pollution around the world. The copper sulfide material left behind is about 70 percent pure copper, which has to be processed again to reach the desired 99.99 percent purity.[35]

The harms of the Kennecott Mine include acid rain from smelter emissions, asbestos-related illness in workers, emissions of arsenic and mercury, and the spillage of more than 200 million gallons of highly contaminated process water (which has seeped into the nearby Jordan River and contaminated groundwater along a

[35] Bill Grosser, "Copper Mining and Refining (Redox)," November 3, 2012; and "Copper Info: Mining and Refining of Copper," *HowStuffWorks*, July 21, 2009.

72-mile plume). Kennecott has filled a tailings pond with more than a billion tons of toxic material, and worked with corrupt state regulators to hide the risk of dam failure which would have killed people in Magna, directly below it.[36] The mining company plans to expand this tailings pond, destroying an additional 700 acres of wetlands (the tailings pond is directly adjacent to the Great Salt Lake, one of the Western Hemisphere's most significant migratory bird habitats). The mine is also releasing acid mine drainage; causing severe dust pollution leading to health issues for nearby residents; and unleashing toxins like copper sulphate and selenium, which at one point killed more than 30 percent of the fish in the Jordan River.

Between 2000 and 2011, there were 18 documented spills and leaks related to the mine, which in total released more than 8 million gallons of contaminated water/tailings and more than 260,000 tons of concentrate and metals. In 2008, the Fish and Wildlife Service sued Kennecott for release of selenium, copper, arsenic, zinc, lead, and cadmium. In many states, the largest single source of pollution is a petrochemical facility or oil refinery. Not so in Utah. The Bingham Canyon mine produces 10 times as much pollution as the Chevron Oil refinery a few miles away. These are just a few of the documented harms caused by the mine.[37]

---

[36] Judy Fahys, "Special Report: How Kennecott concealed warnings of a possible disaster from the people of Magna," *Salt Lake Tribune*, March 24, 2008.

[37] Compiled from: "Problems with Bingham Canyon Mine," *Earthworks*, 2011; "Kennecott Copper Mine," Mesothelioma Cancer Alliance, Asbestos Exposure Program; Bonnie Gestring, "U.S. Copper Porphyry Mines Report: The Track Record of Water Quality Impacts Resulting From Pipeline Spills, Tailings Failures, and Water Collection and Treatment Failures," *Earthworks, Patagonia Area Resource Alliance*, November 2012; "Scoping Summary Report: Kennecott Utah Copper LLC Tailings Expansion Project," United States Department of the Army Corp of Engineers, August 2011; and Leonard J. Arrington and Gary B. Hansen, *The Richest Hole on Earth: A History of the Bingham Copper Mine* (Logan, UT: Utah State University Press, 1963).

The Kennecott Mine produces around 300,000 tons of copper per year. It would need to be operated continuously for more than six years to supply the copper needed for Mark Jacobson's wind turbines. That's in addition to the other copper needed for the "green economy."

🌍

Let's step away from this industrial nightmare and turn toward the land. The Oquirrh Mountains rise to almost 10,000 feet above the south end of Great Salt Lake. This is where the Great Basin meets the Colorado Plateau. The intersection of these two great ecosystems leads to an astounding variety of habitats, from exposed alpine tundra to sagebrush and rabbitbrush steppe. Springs nourish aspen and maple forests on cool north-facing slopes. Juniper and piñon pine live on western and southern slopes. Hardy, salt-tolerant wetland plants survive both wet and dry years and thrive near the lakeshore. Mountain lions, mule deer, butterflies, bald eagles, elk, waterfowls, red-backed voles, shrews, black bears, mice, American coots, blackbirds, great blue herons, yellow warblers, hummingbirds, hawks, western grebes, hermit thrushes, minks, ospreys, ruffled grouses, lark buntings, hairy woodpeckers, kingfishers, Bonneville cutthroat troutfish, redside shiners, speckled daces, Utah chubs, three species of sucker fish (including the endangered June sucker), and many more call this place home. In the spring and fall, migratory birds visit the area in (for now) still strong numbers.

Wolves and grizzly bears used to live in the Oquirrh mountains before they were deliberately exterminated. In the winter of 1848, Mormon colonists undertook a "varmint hunt" and killed as many as 15,000 predators in one month, including bears, wolverines, wildcats, wolves, foxes, minks, eagles, ravens, owls, and other birds.[38] The last Utah grizzly was killed in 1923, and wolves were exterminated by the early 1930s.

The mountains removed at the Kennecott Mine site had watched over countless generations of these creatures. Now the mountains themselves are being blasted into dust, then toxified. The creatures who've survived are now refugees on their own land. None of them, for example, can visit the tailings pond, where noisemakers and nets are required to prevent birds from landing on the contaminated surface.

On hillsides and in poisoned ponds around the smelter, only the hardiest creatures survive. With every bite, they ingest carcinogens and mutagens they will pass down to their offspring.

This is copper production, and it's a nightmare. And it's required for wind power.

According to the Kennecott smelter website, "Environmental stewardship is at the heart of Rio Tinto Kennecott's commitment to sustainable development.... Whenever possible, we prevent, or otherwise minimize, mitigate or remediate any potentially harmful effects of our operations on the environment."[39] But their operations are the harm. There's no kinder, gentler way to blow up mountains and apply an ocean of toxins to the rubble. This is what green energy is made from: the dust of shattered mountains, lakes of acid, and the agony of our winged and scaled kin.

---

[38] Twila Van Leer, "Young John D. Lee Helped Lead a Hunting Contest," *Desert News*, October 22, 1996.
[39] "About Us" and "Environment" Pages, Rio Tinto Kennecott.

Rare-earth minerals are critical components of wind turbines. Even more than other metals, rare earths are produced only through severe and grotesque environmental harm. Dan Harris writes, on his blog about legal issues in China, that "the rare earth neodymium is required for the batteries used in the engines of most current electric vehicles and in the generators of most wind power turbines.... As a result, the rare earth mining regions in Inner Mongolia are classified as some of the most polluted regions in the world.... The resulting poverty and health problems for the workers are well known."[40]

Projections show that wind turbines will likely play a major role in the growth in use of rare-earth minerals worldwide—and could even exhaust supplies completely. One study noted that "demand growth for these metals appears to be ... significant.... This is especially relevant because rare earths are considered critical [for wind turbines]."[41]

For a 2011 *National Geographic* article called "Can China Go Green?" Bill McKibben visited Baotou. Not once in his article, which contains more than 3,000 words, did he mention that the devastating pollution in the area—toxified soil and groundwater, illness in every family, water where no fish or algae can survive, a

---

[40] Dan Harris, "Rare Earths and Polysilicon. Does China Control Our Green Future?" *China Law Blog*, November 5, 2010.

[41] Zimmermann et al., "Material Flows Resulting from Large Scale Deployment of Wind Energy in Germany," *Resources*, 2013, 2, 303–334. Wind turbines can be made without rare earth metals, but they are far more expensive per unit of energy generated. And since the primary goal of creating wind turbines is to generate profit (and electricity), not to protect the planet, most contain these metals.

complete absence of wildlife—was created in part to make wind turbines, solar panels, and hybrid and electric cars.[42]

You know how we said demand for rare earths metals could exhaust them? Well, there's "good" news. In an article entitled, "Renewables' deep-sea mining conundrum," we find that "British scientists exploring an underwater mountain in the Atlantic Ocean have discovered a treasure trove of rare minerals." One of the minerals, Tellurium, "is used in a type of advanced solar panel, so the discovery raises a difficult question about whether the push for renewable energy may encourage mining of the seabed. The rocks also contain what are called rare earth elements that are used in wind turbines and electronics."

The article states that "if the entire deposit could be extracted and used to make solar panels, it could meet 65 percent of the U.K.'s electricity demand."

The scientist who made the discovery said, "If we need green energy supplies, then we need the raw materials to make the devices that produce the energy so, yes, the raw materials have to come from somewhere. We either dig them up from the ground and make a very large hole or dig them from the seabed and make a comparatively smaller hole. It's a dilemma for society—nothing we do comes without a cost."

The cost of ocean mining would be "killing marine life wherever digging machines are deployed and potentially devastating a far wider area. One major concern is the effect of plumes of dust, stirred up by excavation of the ocean floor, spreading for long

---

[42] Bill McKibben, "Can China Go Green?" *National Geographic*, June 2011.

    Also: Cécile Bontron, "Rare-earth mining in China comes at a heavy cost for local villages," *The Guardian*, August 7, 2012.

distances and smothering all life wherever it settles."[43] One biologist said that recovery from mining would take thousands or millions of years.[44]

That's worth it, though, right? Especially since the costs will be paid not by us, but by creatures at the bottom of the ocean, unknown and unnoticed, who will suffocate in silence while we carry on.

◊

By the way, that's not a dilemma. It's only a dilemma when you have to choose between costs you have to pay. When you choose to inflict these costs on others, the word you're looking for is exploitation.

◊

If the materials necessary for wind energy don't stir your soul, perhaps the impacts of installation will. It might seem like each 5 MW wind turbine has a relatively small direct footprint in that perhaps two acres are required. But to make turbines efficient, the surrounding land is also cleared of trees that can "interfere" with the wind. To prevent regrowth, herbicide treatments are sprayed for as long as the facility is operating.[45]

Industrial wind energy harvesting facilities also need wide, straight access roads. For example, the 84 MW Mount Lucas wind energy harvesting facility in Ireland required 12 miles of new access roads for its 28 turbines.

[43] David Shukman, "Renewables deep-sea mining conundrum," *BBC News: Science and Environment*, April 11, 2017.

[44] Maddie Stone, "The Future of Technology Is Hiding on the Ocean Floor," *Gizmodo*, April 5, 2016.

[45] Linda Ewing, "Stop poisoning our community! Herbicide spraying is wind industry's toxic secret," *East County Magazine*, May 2013.

The lands near large wind-energy-harvesting facilities are usually closed to humans. This is particularly true for areas near the blades themselves. Sometimes the blades fly off and careen hundreds of yards. And as a visit to any industrial wind-energy-harvesting facility will show you, the land around turbines can be considered wildlife habitat only in the most meaningless and degraded sense. When it's not cultivated for monocrops or grazed for livestock, it's a maze of compacted access roads, crumbling soils, and slash piles. And it's loud. Decibel levels of 33 to 43 have been recorded a mile away from turbines. That's loud enough to interfere with not just animal communication but with their "health and survival."[46] Spring will be silent except for the deafening drone of machines, and environmentalists are leading the charge.

Under Mark Jacobson's plan, about 2.5 percent of the land mass of California would be dedicated to industrial wind-energy-harvesting facilities. That is more than 4,000 square miles, an area of new industrialization four times the size of Yosemite National Park.

That's just in California. Other wildlands would be similarly devastated.

If we ignore the harm from mines and ignore the harm from the land clearance for wind-energy-harvesting facilities, won't the energy still be green? Won't the wind turbines just go on spinning merrily, harvesting clean energy and no problems whatsoever?

Well, no. One problem is that wind turbines kill birds and bats. A lot of birds and bats. They're killed in at least two ways. The first

[46] Mia Myklebust and Miriam Raftery, "Do wind turbines harm animals?" *East County Magazine*, May 10, 2012.

is direct collisions. Although when looked at from afar wind turbines seem to spin slowly, the tips of the rotor blades can move up to 200 mph. Birds and bats aren't used to anything moving this fast, and so creatures are struck out of the air. Many are killed instantly, but others are maimed, their beaks, wings, and/or legs shattered or shorn off.

But there's more. Because wind turbine blades displace so much air as they spin, they create a pressure drop in the air behind them so drastic it pulps the eardrums and cardiovascular systems of bats passing nearby. In other words, their eardrums, lungs, and hearts explode. Technically, this is called barotrauma, but more accurately, it should be called an atrocity. If you have a beating heart in your chest, you should feel the bats' pain.

In a 2015 report, The American Bird Conservancy estimated that more than 80,000 wind turbines have been (or are already planned to be) put up in "critical habitat corridors" for protected bird species. These often are, from an economic perspective, the best place to put up turbines. And in any conflict between the world and the economy, we know which one always takes precedence.

In another report, the Conservancy estimates that up to 573,000 birds were killed by turbines in 2012, and projects 1.4 million bird deaths per year if the U.S. expands wind-energy-generation facilities to produce 20 percent of the electricity demand.[47]

Now, let's go back to Jacobson's plan and examine a range of estimates of the effects on birds. Let's start with a 2012 study published in the Journal of Integrative Environmental Sciences, stating that wind turbines kill about 0.27 birds per GWh of energy harvested (and we're not cherry picking; this study has often

---

[47] James Conca, "Wind Industry Ignores Bird Conservationists," *Forbes*, June 4, 2015.

been cited by defenders of wind power).[48] As we've already noted, Jacobson calls for 19 million MW (19,000 GW, or 19 Terawatts) of wind turbines to be built. The average wind-harvesting facility has a capacity factor of about 31 percent (they never harvest as much power as they're rated for, since the wind doesn't blow all the time), which means these wind turbines would on average be generating 19,000 GW times .31 equals 5,900 GW. If they harvest this for one hour, they've harvested 5,900 GW-hours (remember, that's the conversion from power—GW—to energy—GW-hours). Since wind turbines kill .27 birds per GW-hour, these turbines would kill 5,900 times .27 equals almost 1,600 birds per hour, a little over 25 birds per minute, or nearly one every two seconds. Sixteen hundred birds per hour times 24 hours per day equals more than 38,000 per day or 267,000 per week. It equals about 14 million bird deaths per year.[49]

The numbers could be much higher. Because scavengers like coyotes often carry off dead animals soon after they're killed, studies often underestimate the number of bird and bat kills at wind turbines. Estimates of bird kills also don't include fatalities from birds colliding with power lines and towers associated with wind turbines, which could add millions.[50] Nor do they account for habitat destruction caused by wind-energy-harvesting facilities, roads, and transmission lines, and how this affects food gathering and childrearing for birds (as well as other species).

It also does not include bird deaths due to mining materials necessary for wind-energy-generation facilities.

---

[48] Benjamin K. Sovacool, "The Avian and Wildlife Costs of Fossil Fuels and Nuclear Power," *Journal of Integrative Environmental Sciences* 9, no. 4, (December 2012) 255–278.
[49] Thanks to Geoff Pearce, Carver Deron Lowe, and Wolf Dieter Aichberger (a.k.a. WDA) for help with these calculations.
[50] "Bird-Smart Wind Energy: Protecting Birds from Poorly Sited Wind Turbines," *American Bird Conservancy*.

But all these birds are just as dead.

According to Save the Eagles International, studies document-ing direct bird and bat kills (e.g., those smacked to death by wind turbines, not those whose habitat is destroyed by mines) underes-timate deaths by as much as 90 percent, since most carcasses are catapulted outside the area searched in studies—typically a small radius around each turbine.[51]

Here's another estimate of how many birds Jacobson's plan would kill. Recall that the American Bird Conservancy projects 1.4 million annual bird kills if 20 percent of U.S. electricity is gener-ated by wind. In 2014, the U.S. generated about four trillion kilo-watt-hours from all sources.[52] Twenty percent of that number is 800 billion kilowatt-hours, or 800 Terawatt-hours, or 800,000 GWh. Dividing the number of bird deaths (1,400,000) by the num-ber of GWh (800,000) reveals the number of bird deaths per GWh ≈ 1.75 bird kills per GWh (much higher than the estimate from the Journal of Integrative Environmental Sciences). Now, recall that Jacobson's plan calls for 19,000 GW of global-wind capacity (with a capacity factor of 31 percent) which means about 58.2 million GWh of wind energy harvested each year. That much wind energy harvested—58.2 million GWh—would lead to 1.75 bird kills/GWh x 58.2 million GWh equals more than 100 million birds per year, or more than three per second.

If the numbers don't horrify you, maybe the specifics will. In 2013, birdwatchers in the U.K. rushed to the Hebrides Islands to view a

---

[51] Mark Duchamp, "US windfarms kill 10-20 times more than previously thought," *Save the Eagles International*, April 2014.

[52] "What is U.S. electricity generation by energy source?" *U.S. Energy Information Administration*, March 31, 2015.

rare bird called the white-throated needletail sighted in the area. Needletails are swift, darting insectivores who snatch raindrops from the sky to quench their thirst. This species had not been seen in Britain for 22 years. Then, in front of their eyes, the bird was struck and killed by the blades of a wind turbine.[53] Another video from 2015 shows a dozen partridges at the base of a wind turbine, some dead and some maimed with broken bones. It's hard to watch; the birds are obviously in pain.[54] There aren't the only videos showing what wind turbines do to birds. If you want to spend an afternoon crying, search YouTube for "wind turbine bird."

In Scotland, a proposed industrial wind energy harvesting facility off the coast at Fife Ness and Angus poses a major threat to gannet populations. Nearby islands have the largest known colonies of gannets, with an estimated 70,000 breeding pairs visiting each year, each raising a single chick per year, those chicks not reaching sexual maturity for five years. A 2015 study found that 1,800 of the birds could be struck and killed by the proposed turbines each year, 12 times more than previously estimated.[55]

Another species harmed by wind turbines is the endangered greater sage grouse, a large and unusually beautiful bird who lives in the sagebrush country between the Rocky Mountains and the Cascades. It's estimated that sage grouse populations have gone down by 98 percent since 1988, mostly because of overgrazing, coal and uranium mining, and oil and gas drilling. And before 1988, the species had already been hit hard.[56] Now wind-energy-harvesting

[53] Will Robinson, "Rare bird last seen in Britain 22 years ago reappears – only to be killed by wind turbine in front of a horrified crowd of birdwatchers," *The Daily Mail*, June 27, 2013.

[54] Mastermax595, "Rebhuhn-Schwarm fliegt in Bubenheimer Windrad welches im Vogelschutzgebiet steht Dutzend Tote Tiere," YouTube, July 20, 2015.

[55] David Miller, "Offshore wind farms 'threaten gannets,'" *BBC*, September 28, 2015.

[56] "Emergency Order for the Protection of the Greater Sage-Grouse," *Canada Gazette* (Gatineau, Quebec: Minister of the Environment) 147 (25), December 4, 2013.

facilities, going up all over the valleys and rolling hills of this inter-mountain region (sometimes called "the sagebrush sea"), are a growing threat. "Nest success and brood survival was a lot lower in the habitats closer to turbines," says Chad Laboe, a biologist working with the birds in Wyoming. These birds need open space. According to the Center for Biological Diversity, any development within six miles of a lek (breeding area) hurts their children's chances for survival.[57]

Large species with slower breeding rates are disproportionately killed by turbines, since they tend to fly higher and in windier areas. A 2004 study from the Altamont Pass Wind Farm in California (nicknamed the "Cuisinart for birds") estimated that this facility alone killed 116 golden eagles, 300 red-tailed hawks, 333 American kestrels, 380 burrowing owls, 2,526 rock doves, 217 northern flickers, 2,557 western meadowlarks, 10 great horned owls, 49 barn owls, 48 ravens, 24 ferruginous hawks, and 215 mountain blue-birds (this is not a complete list of kills documented in this study: the full list would take a page).[58]

In December 2013, the federal government exempted the wind industry from federal protections of bald and golden eagles. For the next 30 years, wind turbines can legally kill federally protected bald and golden eagles with no penalty.[59]

---

[57] Diane Cardwell and Clifford Krauss, "Frack Quietly Please: Sage Grouse Is Nesting," *New York Times*, July 19, 2014.

[58] "Developing Methods to Reduce Bird Mortality in the Altamont Pass Wind Resource Area," The California Energy Commission, Public Interest Energy Research Program, August 2004.

[59] "White House gives wind farms 30-year pass on eagle deaths," Associated Press, *CBS News*, December 6, 2013.

Remember, this is a technology promoted by the modern environmental movement.

Remember, also, that these bird kills are occurring on top of ongoing population collapses. A March 2018 study found that bird numbers across France had declined by a third in the past 15 years. The population of birds across Europe has gone down more than 50 percent in the past 30 to 40 years.[60] Those numbers aren't unique to Europe. North America lost more than a billion birds in the last 40 years.[61] Major population declines are being observed across the world.[62]

Bat deaths from wind turbines in the United States alone were conservatively estimated at 600,000 in 2012.[63] Wind energy harvested 140,822 GWh in the U.S. that year. As always, let's do the math: 600,000 bat deaths divided by 140,822 GWh equals a little over four bats killed per GWh. Since Jacobson's plan calls for 58.2 million GWh per year, this would mean almost 250 million bat kills a year, about 4.75 million a week, almost 680,000 per day, more than 28,000 per hour, more than 400 per minute, more than 7 per second.

---

[60] Josh Gabbatiss, "'Shocking' decline in birds across Europe due to pesticide use, say scientists," *The Independent*, March 21, 2018.

[61] Eric Andrew-Gee, "Bird populations in steep decline in North America, study finds," *The Globe and Mail*, September 14, 2016.

[62] "Global trends in bird species survival," *Canada Environment and Natural Resources*, April 10, 2017.

[63] Mark A. Hayes, "Bats Killed in Large Numbers at United States Wind Energy Facilities," *BioScience* 63, no. 12 (2013): 975–979.

Wind turbines kill more bats than any other human industry or activity.[64] This has generated some backlash, and in response, the American Wind Energy Association published guidelines in 2015 that feather turbine blades during periods of low wind speed. They claimed this would reduce the killing of bats by 30 percent or more. The plan has been criticized as completely insufficient by biologists, who say that even with this plan (which is completely voluntary for each facility to implement), wind energy will cause a crash in global bat populations.[65]

Industry has responded, predictably, with another technology. Unable to prevent bat deaths, their latest response is to simply get rid of the bats using an ultrasound deterrent system that produces sound between 20 and 50 kilohertz, blocking bats ability to echo-locate, orient, and forage. The bats "respond by choosing to leave the area."[66]

Can you imagine if we played piercing sirens in your home day and night, and described your having to flee as "choosing to leave the area"?

This is, of course, a typical bright green response. Rather than do what is best for the bats (in other words, dismantle existing wind turbines and stop building any more), the wind industry is moving towards simply excluding the bats, as if they were the problem. Out of sight, out of mind. Never mind the fact that those bats may be starving, or have less success with mating, or have lower long-term survival without the habitat from which they have now been excluded.

---

[64] Thomas J. O'Shea et al., "Multiple mortality events in bats: a global review," *Mammal Review* 46, no. 3 (2016).

[65] Amy Mathews Amos, "Bat Killings by Wind Energy Turbines Continue," *Scientific American*, June 7, 2016.

[66] Mary Bates, "A New Deterrent System Could Help Save Bats from Wind Turbines," *Pacific Standard*, February 11, 2019.

This is no different from "wildlife" agencies shooting sea lions that congregate below dams on the Willamette and Columbia Rivers in a so-called effort to protect endangered salmon, or shooting wolves in a so-called effort to protect endangered Selkirk Caribou. Remove the dam, and the salmon will thrive. Stop the logging and close the roads, and the caribou will multiply. Shut down the wind turbines, and bats will survive.

Or maybe not. According to biologist Paul Cryan of the U.S. Geological Survey, "Bats are long-lived and very slow reproducers. Their populations rely on very high adult survival rates. That means their populations recover from big losses very slowly."[67]

The wind installation with which we started this chapter, the Spring Valley wind-energy-harvesting facility, is located four miles from the largest bat roost in the Great Basin, the Rose Guano Cave, which is home to a million Brazilian free-tailed bats during their fall migration.

A study by Bat Conservation International "that looked at hoary bat (Lasiurus cinereus) fatalities at wind energy facilities revealed the population of this species may plunge by a staggering 90 percent over the next 50 years—even if no new turbines are built." The study "used conservative figures of bat fatalities: 128,000 hoary bat fatalities annually in the U.S. and Canada, and assumed no new wind turbines are to come online in the future. They found, with

---

[67] Amos, op. cit.

the highest possible population estimate of 10 million hoary bats, the species could still experience a 50 percent decline over the next 50 years. With more conservative and likely population estimates, around 2.5 million individuals reproducing at a more realistic rate, that impact could deepen to a 90 percent decline within the next five decades."[68]

Wind-energy boosters usually respond to any discussion of bird and bat kills by pointing out that fossil fuels, cars, cats, and flying into buildings kill far more birds than do wind turbines. Art Sasse of the American Wind Energy Association, for example, writes: "Those who truly care about the fate of birds and wildlife know that climate change is by far their greatest threat."[69] David Suzuki plays this same game, saying that the risk to birds is "low" and "negligible" compared to the risk to birds from skyscrapers (which of course is an argument to get rid of skyscrapers, but Suzuki doesn't seem to see that part of it). It's even worse than this, though. Suzuki puts the word "negligible" in quotes, and he cites a blog post by the United Kingdom's Royal Society for the Protection of Birds (RSPB). If the RSPB says that windmills cause "negligible" harm to birds, he suggests, it must be true. But Suzuki fails to mention that the very blog post to which he's linking is a response to accusations

---

[68] Michelle Donahue, "Seeking answers in the wind," *Bat Conservation International*, February 24, 2017. The article suggests a number of technical fixes that may lower bat mortality. These include turning off the wind turbines at times when bats are most active, using ultrasonic deterrents, and so on. But the industrial economy is so sacrosanct that not even Bat Conservation International, which is supposed to have its primary loyalty to bats, dares to suggest not putting in wind turbines. The only people we know consistently opposing these industrial facilities are local grassroots environmentalists.

[69] Art Sasse, "Wind industry has a legacy of caring for wildlife," *American Wind Energy Association*, April 2, 2015.

that the RSBP is "in the pocket of the wind industry." Why would those accusations come up? Well, it might be because the RSBP actively "partners" with the big wind energy company Ecotricity. RSBP helps Ecotricity site new industrial wind-energy-harvesting facilities (including over the objection of local environmentalists), and Ecotricity gives RSBP £60 for every new customer Ecotricity signs up. It works for everyone, except of course the birds and those who love them. No wonder the RSBP says bird kills by wind turbines are "negligible."[70]

It's more than a little ironic that environmentalists now routinely use a classic technique of industrialists and developers to dismiss or deride descriptions of harm caused by the industrial sectors they represent. How many times have we heard this argument? "It could be worse," says the developer. "This mall will preserve some open space that would otherwise be destroyed." "Don't worry about this industrial pesticide application," says the factory farm operator. "The river gets much more pollution from other sources." "If you don't let us clearcut," says the timber company spokesperson, "we'll subdivide for ranchettes." Dam owners blame timber companies for extirpated salmon runs, and timber company flaks blame dams. It works out great for those whose primary concern is corporate profits: nobody takes responsibility, nothing gets done. How's it working out for salmon or, in this case, birds? Not so well.

This argument is what's called a double bind: You're presented with two options, both of which are bad—in this case, bird and bat kills from global warming, and those from wind turbines—and told that choosing the lesser of the two evils is the "best choice."

Some double binds are real. During World War II, people who were rounded up and sent to concentration camps often faced such

---

[70] Martin Harper, "Facing up to inconvenient truths," *RSBP*, April 4, 2013.

a choice: get shot or get into the cattle cars. Other double binds are false. This is one of the latter. There is an unspoken premise of the argument in favor of wind turbines: that harvesting energy is more important than birds and bats. That some sacrifices (billions of sacrifices, in this case) are justifiable to provide industrial humans with energy. This is, of course, the usual human supremacist assumption.

The only way out of a double bind is to smash it. That's what we must do.

Domestic cats, cars and trucks, fossil fuels, introduced invasive species, and destruction of habitat are killing birds and bats. There's no argument about this, which is why some of us have worked for decades to dismantle car culture and the fossil fuel economy, to fight invasive species and destruction of habitat. This is why some of us devote our lives to restoring habitat. But the wind industry is another blow to bird and bat species already hammered by pesticides, poisoning, overhunting, habitat destruction, and global warming. The arguments against even discussing bird and bat kills from wind turbines reveal once again that most people have more allegiance to machines than they do to our winged kin.

Another predictable response to bird and bat kills is to talk about bladeless wind turbines, which don't spin and therefore don't kill as many nonhumans. Unlike conventional wind turbines, bladeless turbines work on a vertical axis, harnessing vorticity (the spinning motion in the wind) to create oscillation or vibration in turbine "blades."

But there's a reason that traditional spinning-blade turbines make up nearly 100 percent of turbine installations. The energy harvested by a wind turbine is proportional to the area swept. For traditional wind turbines, it's relatively easier to make them taller and (crucially) increase the length of the blades to increase energy harvested. But bladeless turbines quickly run into fundamental engineering problems when they try to scale up. Larger designs tend to disrupt the airflow patterns that make them work, so beyond a certain size, you get a negative feedback loop. "When the cylinder gets very big and wind gets very high," says Sheila Widnall, an aeronautics and astronautics professor at MIT, "you won't be able to get as much energy out of it as you want to because the oscillation is fundamentally turbulent."

Further, Widnall also claims that large bladeless designs will be as loud as freight trains.[71]

Is it possible to be homesick for a place you've never been? As a child, I (Lierre) longed for the forest with an ache that's never stopped. The concrete, the houses, the cars were an open wound on the world, and I wanted them gone. It was a huge, inchoate hunger for things I had never known: ancient trees, dark shade, and animal secrets—all of it wild. On and on, for miles, for years. Forever.

It's universally noted that children are drawn to wild places. Even when they're offered playgrounds, and even when they help design the playground—castles, mazes, swings—they will find the spots where adults don't go, the abandoned ditches, the tiny edges no one owns and where wildness survives. In my school playground,

---

[71] Phil McKenna, "Bladeless Wind Turbines Offer More Form Than Function: Startup Vortex Bladeless makes a turbine that looks intriguing, but it may not solve wind power's challenges," *MIT Technology Review*, May 27, 2015.

there was one brave, single-file line of pine trees and shrubs at the very bottom of the field where my best friend and I returned. You couldn't even call it a scrap of wilderness; it was just a thin unraveling thread that we needed to lead us home. It couldn't, but we never stopped asking.

And I guess I'm still asking. The forest, sturdy with old-growth and swelling with species, will not return in my lifetime. My grief is my own, and it is also not the point. Full restoration will take longer than a human lifespan, but the world could be repaired. It could. But first the destruction has to stop.

Here's the question: Are we the people who love the forest? Or are we the people who demand the right to destroy the last traces of the wild? Right now, a huge swathe of Clashindarroch Forest in Scotland is under threat.

Environmentalists laid the groundwork for this catastrophe by demanding wind and solar for decades, and now Swedish energy giant Vattenfall is offering to meet those demands. A quarter of the forest will be felled for wind turbines and their attendant infrastructure, right through the last refugium of the Scottish wildcat.[72] The remaining wildcats number 35. There are no missing zeroes in that number: 35 are all who remain. That's more a whisper than a number, the stripped skeleton of a species. They are the only wild felines left on the island of Great Britain and they will be lost to willful extinction in the service of wind.

This destruction is not unusual. Since 2000, Scotland has cut down almost 14 million trees over more than 17,000 acres—more than 26 square miles—to serve wind-energy harvesting.[73]

---

[72] Greg Russell, "Almost a third of wildcat population at threat over windfarm plans, says group," The National, June 21, 2018.
[73] "Renewable developments on Scotland's national forests and lands: EIR release," January 21, 2020.

So, are we the people who love the forest? Or are we happy to trade in everyone who makes up a forest—trees, birds, wildcats, and all—for giant machines that will flash like 30 pieces of silver in the sun?

Our justified panic to address global warming has made us susceptible to seductive technological promises. In the face of concerted, sophisticated marketing techniques and the nearly complete cooptation of the big green groups, many people have come to believe the lies.

But some communities are resisting.

In Nantucket, Massachusetts, for example, an offshore wind project has been indefinitely stalled because of local opposition based on potential harm to the surrounding ocean and seafloor, increased boat traffic, and the possibility of oil spills. "It is beyond comprehension that a massive offshore industrial project of such magnitude; 130 wind turbines, 417 feet tall, in 15-foot waves, with spinning blades as wide as football fields, covering 24 square miles, in often foggy, noisy conditions, would be safe for any biologically sensitive location," says opponent Christine Morabito. "Nor can I imagine a parallel universe where we would accept this level of environmental risk, were it posed by an oil company."[74]

The thing is, some of these wind projects are run by oil companies.

In Ayrshire, Scotland, residents' water supplies were contaminated by toxic releases from what was—at the time—Europe's biggest industrial wind-energy-harvesting facility. A local doctor, in response to the contamination, said "It's highly unlikely that Airtnoch Farm is the only supply in Scotland that has been

---

[74] Christine Morabito, "Cape Wind Project: A Tale of Crony Environmentalism (Part 2) Did Mass Audubon Sell its Soul to the Wind Industry?" *The Valley Patriot*, June 2015.

contaminated. There may be hundreds of rural water supplies unknowingly affected by wind farm development."[75]

In Kenya, a facility at Lake Turkana (the largest alkaline lake in the world) displaced an indigenous village through the privatization of 150,000 acres of their land. The facility is set to be the largest industrial wind-energy-harvesting facility in Africa (310 MW).[76]

In southern Mexico, more than 15 major wind-energy-harvesting facilities (the largest would install more than 130 turbines for a total of 400 MW of capacity) are under construction or already built in the states of Oaxaca, Chiapas, Tabasco and Veracruz, despite almost unanimous opposition from the people. "This is an assault on the way of life and the sacred places of the indigenous communities who live in the region," writes Santiago Navarro, a Mexican journalist. Most of these projects are being built on land held communally by local peoples who have defended it for generations; now they are being cheated or intimidated out of it. Industrial lubricants are polluting aquifers, and noise from the turbines and changes to wind patterns have scared away fish and birds and harmed traditional food practices. "We are worried because they are attacking our way of life, our health, and the sea," says Carlos Sanchez, a community activist in Oaxaca. These wind-energy-harvesting facilities are just another expression of colonialism; most of the energy harvested by the projects is planned for use for major corporations like Walmart, Coca-Cola, and Heineken.[77] One human rights observer wrote that due to lack of public consultation, local people "see the wind industry as 'new

---

[75] Marcello Mega, "Power company knew residents' water supply was heavily polluted," *The Times* [U.K.], September 21, 2013.

[76] "COP19: Carlo Van Wageningen talks about wind power in Africa," Responding to Climate Change, *Climate Change TV*, November 2013.

[77] Santiago Navarro, "On Mexican Isthmus, Indigenous Communities Oppose Massive Energy Projects," CIP Americas Program, April 2, 2014.

conquistadors.'" Opposition has been widespread, with indigenous groups using protests, blockades, grievances, and courts to fight wind projects.[78]

Another example is the Wayuu, the indigenous people of the Guajira Peninsula, on the border of Colombia and Brazil. Due to fierce defense of their land—at one point, they had 20,000 members under arms—they were never fully subjugated by the conquistadors, but capitalism and wind power are doing what the first invaders never could.[79] In recent years, extortion, torture, and murder from government and both right-wing and Marxist paramilitaries have left the community near collapse. Forty thousand people in the community are hungry, with many of them starving to death.[80] The 19.5 MW World Bank financed Jepírachi industrial wind-energy-harvesting facility stands on a tract of stolen Wayuu land, sending electricity and money to Colombian cities and leaving behind damage to the habitat, wildlife, and semi-nomadic herding and fishing traditions of the region. While the developer talks about "community participation" and creates a "social management plan," the reality of the project is familiar: outsiders come with promises of material goods and leave with land and money. "To separate the Wayuu from their land is to destroy their identity as a people," says Juan Guillermo Sanchez, a professor of indigenous literature at the Universidad Javeriana. Many Wayuu fear that Jepírachi is just the beginning of a wave of industrial wind-energy development that might lead to the end of their traditional ways.[81]

---

[78] Soledad Mills et al., "Defining and Addressing Community Opposition to Wind Development in Oaxaca," Equitable Origin, January 2016.

[79] "Wayuu," *Intercontinental Cry Magazine*, Indigenous Peoples.

[80] "Humanitarian disaster in La Guajira," *Mama Tierra*, April 9, 2014.

[81] "Changes in the wind," *The City Paper Bogota*, April 23, 2013.

When industrial wind-energy-harvesting facilities are welcomed by local communities, or forced in despite their opposition, local human quality of life often suffers. There's light pollution from hundreds or thousands of powerful, blinking aircraft warning lights. Subsonic "infrasound" that flits at the edge of hearing can cause terrible headaches. Infrasound is not blocked by house walls or pillows over the head, and it can excite the nervous system and cause dizziness, headaches, elevated blood pressure, and other problems. Some studies have found major sleep disturbances (due to infrasound as well as louder, more audible frequencies such as gears grinding and other mechanical sounds) and impaired mental health in residents living within a mile of wind-energy-harvesting facilities. Other reported effects include hearing problems, tinnitus, anxiety, and depression.[82]

Why would we believe wind turbines wouldn't do the same to nonhumans, many of whom are far more sensitive to sound and vibration than are humans?

Or do we not care?

Energy harvested from wind turbines does not come from nowhere; it's extracted from energy in the wind. Leeward of an industrial wind energy generation facility, wind speeds are lower, because energy has been removed from the system. Research based on NASA satellite imaging has shown, in fact, that these facilities cause a local warming of the area where they're located. Other

---

[82] Roy D. Jeffry. et al., "Adverse health effects of industrial wind turbines," *Canadian Family Physician*, May 2013; 59(5): 473–475.

studies have shown these facilities cause precipitation, not only at the site but across the whole region.[83]

Some wind energy boosters acknowledge this effect, and even pretend it's a good thing. For example, Mark Jacobson wants to use this effect to, in his words, "tame" hurricanes. A 2014 paper he wrote, published in the journal *Nature Climate Change*, titled "Taming Hurricanes with Arrays of Offshore Wind Turbines," uses computer models to estimate that massive offshore wind energy harvesting facilities could reduce hurricane wind speeds by 56 mph to 92 mph and storm surge by 6 percent to 79 percent.[84]

What could possibly go wrong?

Here's a list of just a few of the benefits of hurricanes: They bring rain to dry areas like the U.S. Southwest, and East and Southeast Asia; they maintain global heat balance by distributing huge amounts of energy around the planet; they repair barrier islands and beaches by carrying sand from deeper waters to the shore; they drive upwelling of deep ocean water, which carries nutrients and maintains deepwater circulation currents; they contribute to natural succession and biodiversity by killing old and dying plants and contributing to the complexity of natural communities; they bring influxes of water and nutrients to coastal swamps and lagoons; and they distribute seeds (and even whole plants and animals) to new habitats. This is, of course, only a partial list.

Hubris is one of the worst traits of civilization, and hubris lies behind the plans of Mark Jacobson and every other booster who claims to be able to harness and control the power of the wind

---

[83] David Kirk-Davidoff, "Wind Power Found to Affect Local Climate," *The Conversation* (republished in *Scientific American*), February 14, 2014.

[84] Mark Z. Jacobson et al., "Taming hurricanes with arrays of offshore wind turbines," *Nature Climate Change* 4, 195–200 (2014); published online February 26, 2014.

without consequence. Have none of these people heard the story of Icarus?

Shiny fantasies of a clean, green future are being built on numbers that aren't real. Most of us don't have the time or the training to investigate past an article or two. We know there's an emergency; we believe the educated, earnest leaders; we read headlines that ease our fears, and isn't Germany doing it already? Someone has a plan—an engineer, a senator, an environmental group—and even if the details are difficult, surely the idea is basically sound? What we are asking you to consider is that the idea of "green energy" is not sound—neither in the broad strokes (continuing to fuel the destruction of the planet is in fact a bad idea) nor in the particulars (that nondestructive sources of industrial scale energy exist).

The numbers on wind energy don't add up. To put it bluntly, two Harvard University researchers, David Keith and Lee Miller, used data from over 57,000 wind turbines and found that the estimates used as a foundation by the U.S. Department of Energy, the Intergovernmental Panel on Climate Change, and green energy proponents like Mark Jacobson do not match reality.

For wind, "the average power density ... was up to 100 times lower" than common estimates.[85] The power density for solar energy was also much lower than in widely used estimates. Any meaningful transition to wind and solar electricity would demand five to 20 times more land than the plans on the table. Miller and Keith calculate that 12 percent of the continental United States would have to be covered in windfarms to meet current electricity demands. But electricity is only one-sixth of the nation's energy

[85] Leah Burrows, "Wind farms will cause more environmental impact than previously thought," *The Harvard Gazette*, October 4, 2018.

consumption. To provide for the U.S.A.'s total energy consumption, fully 72 percent of the continent would have to be devoted to wind farms. At the scale required, wind farms would be "an active player in the climate system."[86] They would change the climate.

Please read that again.

The turbines' action forces rising hot air back down to the ground; heat can't escape; temperatures rise. Wind turbines would warm surface temperatures by .43°F. The worst warming would be at night, when temperatures would increase by 2.7°F.[87] Reports David Keith, who led the development of Harvard's Solar Geoengineering Research Program, "If your perspective is the next 10 years, wind power actually has—in some respects—more climate impact than coal or gas."[88] Over 10 other studies have already established the warming effect of wind farms, yet there is utter silence from the people who claim to be fighting climate change.[89]

These so-called environmentalists are willing to sacrifice birds and bats, deserts and mountains, children in the Congo and entire regions like Baotou. They will also, as it turns out, be sacrificing the climate to save the climate, until the lone and level sands will indeed stretch far away.

Many well-meaning people call for small-scale, community-operated renewable energy. In *This Changes Everything*, Naomi Klein dedicates a whole chapter to defending "local power,"[90] citing Hamburg, Germany, along with Boulder, Colorado, and Austin,

[86] Ibid.

[87] Lee Miller and David Keith, "Climate impacts of wind power," *Joule* 2, no. 12 (December 19, 2018): 2618–2632.

[88] Miller and Keith, op. cit.

[89] Burrows, op. cit.

[90] Naomi Klein, op. cit.

Texas, as shiny green examples. The idea is that people should have a democratic voice in decisions about their energy systems. When left to corporate directors, profit will be the priority. That's the nature of corporations. If local communities make decisions, public interest can take precedence over private profits. When citizens are in control, they have been able to vote for "clean" energy.

But does the ownership of the technology change the nature of the technology? We raise this point because the argument for local control always arises when we critique solar and wind. The argument, however well meaning, has an unspoken premise: industrial civilization has to continue and the problem facing us is how to power it.

This is the continental divide facing environmentalists. Is industrial civilization the thing that has to be saved? Or is it the destruction that has to be stopped? Think long and hard. On one side of that divide are whole towns of lung disease, rain that burns, the exploded hearts of birds and bats, and mines from which the earth will only heal in geologic time. On the other side is our only planet, once lush with life and the promise of more, still, despite everything, calling us home.

Before you decide, think how a wind turbine is made, though it requires the grammar of heartbreak. Remember the verbs: explode, strip, batter, massacre, devastate. These are not words that should ever apply to living beings. Remember the nouns: forest, wetland, heron, wolf. Remember the adjectives: endangered, indigenous, displaced, extinct. And remember the scale: every mountain for 50 miles, 58,575 valleys, a billion tons of toxic materials, 30 percent of the fish. This is the promise of renewables: more of the same, endlessly more.

Wind turbines claim to be "better" than fossil fuels, but in practice, this has little meaning. Wind turbines generate less CO_2 than the equivalent generation from coal-fired power plants, but there's no evidence that wind power has displaced the burning of coal, oil, and gas. As wind power has expanded globally, fossil fuel burning hasn't gone down. In fact, the number of coal-fired and natural gas power plants is increasing. Research from Richard York at the University of Oregon has shown that for every unit of "green" power brought online, only one-tenth as much fossil fuel is taken offline.[91]

Solar booster Hermann Scheer says, "Our dependence on fossil fuels amounts to global pyromania, and the only fire extinguisher we have at our disposal is renewable energy."

No, that's just putting a different fuel on the fire.

There are plenty of ways to put out the inferno that is the fossil fuel economy; the simplest and most important would be to simply deny capitalists the ability to continue business as usual.

But that isn't a popular thing to say. It doesn't make for good headlines, it doesn't bring £60 to your organization for each new customer, it doesn't get you grants from foundations, and most important of all, it doesn't make the capitalists any money. And so, capitalists get what they want: they make profits, they get good PR, and they don't have to fight environmentalists (at least, not many). And the bright green groups get to walk away feeling they've won a victory for the planet. It's a win-win, so long as the planet doesn't do it for us. Meanwhile, the earth continues to be killed by the same old industrial processes.

---

[91] Richard York, "Do alternative energy sources displace fossil fuels," *Nature Climate Change*, 2, 441–443, March 18, 2012.

We started this chapter in Spring Valley, Nevada, and in Spring Valley we will end it. Do you remember those big turbines that required materials from around the world, with the attendant harm caused by mining, milling, refining, and shaping those materials? These turbines have an extended usable time of about 25 years. After that, the turbines will be demolished and resulting materials hauled away. According to a representative of the company, nothing will be recycled. The concrete foundations will be removed to four feet below present grade.[92]

This is how we save the planet?

[92] Julie Bundorf, "Notes on Spring Valley Wind Project Site Visit (Resource Advisory Committee for BLM)," July 20, 2012.

Chapter 6

THE LIE OF GREEN ENERGY STORAGE

Indian people stood in the way of progress, and progress is a
sort of madness that is a god to people. Decent people commit
horrible crimes that are acceptable because of progress.[1]

—LINDA HOGAN

[The United States has] about 50 percent of the world's wealth
but only 6.3 percent of its population.... Our real task in the
coming period is to devise a pattern of relationships, which will
permit us to maintain this position of disparity.[2]

**—GEORGE KENNAN, STATE DEPARTMENT
DIRECTOR OF POLICY PLANNING, 1948**

Energy storage is essential to technotopian fantasies. Remember,
alternating current electricity can't be stored. Power supplies need

---

[1] Derrick Jensen, *Listening to the Land: Conversations About Nature, Culture, and Eros* (San Francisco: Sierra Club Books, 1995), 126.
[2] George Kennan, "Review of Current Trends, U.S. Foreign Policy," Policy Planning Staff, PPS No. 23. Top Secret. Included in the U.S. Department of State, Foreign Relations of the United States, 1948, Volume 1, Part 2 (Washington, D.C., Government Printing Office, 1976), 524.

to be constant for industrial production; and wind and solar aren't nearly reliable enough to guarantee this: how do you power factories on dark and windless nights? And without oil, coal, or gas, vehicles like trains, ships, trucks, and cars must rely on energy stored in batteries, fuel cells, and compressors. The entire bright green scheme depends on energy storage.

The most important energy storage technologies already being used or in development include batteries, supercapacitors, hydrogen fuel cells, pumped hydro (where you pump water up a hill, then later release water to spin turbines), compressed air, and thermal. We'll look at each of these in turn.

At their most basic, batteries store chemical energy, and then, under certain conditions, release some of this energy as electrical current.

They're mainly used in transportation and small-scale energy storage (in everything from wristwatches to flashlights to cellphones to off-grid solar-powered houses to those horrible battery-powered motorbikes for five-year-olds that seem like nothing so much as lawsuits waiting to happen), but there's an increasing trend toward using batteries for grid-scale storage. There are only a handful of utility-scale battery-storage projects today, the largest around 100 MW.

The global market for batteries is a bit over $108 billion per year and rising fast, with the increase primarily driven by demand for automobile batteries and consumer (especially portable) electronics.[3]

---

[3] "Battery Market Size, Share & Trends Analysis Report By Product (Lead Acid, Li-ion, Nickle Metal Hydride, Ni-cd), By Application (Automotive, Industrial, Portable), By Region, And Segment Forecasts, 2020–2027," Grand View Research.

Two battery types dominate "green" technology: lithium-ion (including sub-types) and lead-acid. The primary advantage of lithium-ion over other batteries is that they store more energy for their mass: about one Megajoule per kilogram (MJ/kg). Some believe one day batteries may reach an energy density of 5 MJ/kg.

While that's a lot for a battery, it's not much compared to, say, gasoline, which stores about 46 MJ/kg. This is why electric cars have 1,000 pounds of batteries and yet a shorter driving range than a gas-powered car with less than a hundred-pound fuel tank. Or here's another number: Jet fuel is 43 times more energy dense than the best batteries available today.[4] The brutal truth is that oil is functionally irreplaceable for an industrial economy.

More than 50 percent of lithium extraction is from high desert basins in places like Nevada, Tibet, Bolivia, and Chile, where evaporation has concentrated lithium salts in (often dry) lake beds. Another 25 percent comes from hard rock mining, 7 percent from clays, and the rest from other sources.

Let's get hard rock and clay mining out of the way first. The harms they cause mirror those of copper mining. You've got land clearance; explosives; fleets of heavy machinery; truckloads of industrial solvents like sulfuric acid; water contamination; and high energy use for furnaces.

The major form of lithium extraction, a process called "brining," involves leaching lithium salts into water, then evaporating the water to concentrate the salts. In dry climates where salt flats are found, water use is one of the major harms. Understand the scale of this: 500,000 gallons of water are needed to produce one

---

[4] Andrew J. Hawkins, "Electric flight is coming, but the batteries aren't ready," *The Verge*, August 14, 2018.

ton of lithium.[5] Another major harm is direct land destruction. For example, in the salt flats of the Salar de Uyuni in Bolivia and Chile, a great wilderness—more than 5,000 square miles of salt flats and isolated "islands" of raised land with unique cacti and other plant and animal species—is under threat from lithium mining.

This account, from the U.K.'s *Daily Mail*, of a visit to a lithium mine in the Atacama Desert in Chile is worth quoting at length: "In the parched hills of Chile's northern region the damage caused by lithium mining is immediately clear. As you approach one of the country's largest lithium mines the white landscape gives way to what appears to be an endless ploughed field. Huge mountains of discarded bright white salt rise out of the plain. The cracked brown earth of the site crumbles in your hands. There is no sign of animal life anywhere. The scarce water has all been poisoned by chemicals leaked from the mine. Huge channels and tracts have been cut into the desert, each running with heavily polluted water. The blue glow of chlorine makes the water look almost magical, but these glistening pools are highly toxic. The chlorine [is] used to water down the potentially carcinogenic lithium and magnesium compounds that are commonly found in the water table around lithium deposits. A Chilean delegation recently visited Salar De Uyuni [in Bolivia] to warn locals of the problems of lithium mining. According to the delegation's leader, Guillen Mo Gonzalez, the unique landscape of the salt plateau would be destroyed within two decades. The increasing water scarcity around the Chilean mines has also accelerated the decline of the region's subsistence agriculture. An entire way of life is disappearing as families leave their near impossible existence in the mountains and head for the cities."

Gonzalez goes on: "Like any mining process it is invasive, it

---

[5] Amit Katwala, "The spiraling environmental cost of our lithium battery addiction," *Wired*, August 5, 2018.

scars the landscape, it destroys the water table and it pollutes the earth and the local wells. This isn't a green solution—it's not a solution at all."[6]

High up on the Tibetan plateau, a peaceable people have fished and herded for thousands of years. They call the mountains holy, the grasslands sacred, and they are now in "anguish."[7] Their land, their animals, and their existence are being destroyed by lithium mines.

The Liqi River was once full of fish: Almost none are left. Chemical spills from the Ganzizhou Rongda lithium mine have killed many. "The whole river stank, and it was full of dead yaks and dead fish," said one villager.[8] "Masses" of dead fish have covered the river.[9] The people got the mine shut down three times, only to have the government reopen it.

One of the elders said, "Old people, we see the mines and we cry. What are the future generations going to do? How are they going to survive?"

A local activist surveyed people in the area. Even if mining companies split the profits and promised to repair the land after the mines are exhausted, the Tibetans wanted no part of it.

"God is in the mountains and the rivers, these are the places that spirits live," he explained.[10]

Bright green technology offers everything: every luxury, every whim, available at the touch of a carbon-free button. But this is

[6] Dan McDougall, "In search of Lithium: the battle for the 3rd element," *The Daily Mail*, April 5, 2009.

[7] Simon Denyer, "Tibetans in anguish as Chinese mines pollute their sacred grasslands," *Washington Post*, December 29, 2016.

[8] Ibid.

[9] Katwala, op. cit., August 5, 2018.

[10] Denyer, op. cit.

the world that these technologies provide: rotting, desecrated, and, finally, dead, while the elders mourn.

Even if all the lithium reserves in the world are exploited, there isn't enough easily extractible lithium to meet likely demand for electric-vehicle batteries. It's a concern that has been brought up by Mark Jacobson himself. "More than half the world's lithium reserves lie in Bolivia and Chile," he writes. "That concentration, combined with rapidly growing demand, could raise prices significantly. More problematic [than pricing] is the claim by Meridian International Research that not enough economically recoverable lithium exists to build anywhere near the number of batteries needed in a global electric-vehicle economy. Recycling could change the equation, but the economics of recycling depend in part on whether batteries are made with easy recyclability in mind, an issue the industry is aware of."

Please note that Jacobson's concern is how to provide industry with raw materials, not the effects this provision has on the living world.

Lithium prices roughly doubled between late 2014 and late 2016, then slumped in recent years due to overproduction as electric car sales flagged well behind early projections. Yet analysts still project exponential demand increases into the late 2020s and 2030s. The main driver of this growth is batteries for electric and hybrid cars, demand for which could easily grow 50 times. Daimler is investing $550 million into tripling battery production in Germany. Volkswagen is partnering with LG and Panasonic to build several $2 billion battery factories. GM sources batteries from a $350

million battery factory in Holland, Michigan that is expanding rapidly. According to one mining company CEO, "The future demand
for lithium is truly staggering.... Battery demand is rising at the
rate of one to two new lithium mines per year, growing to two to
three mines per year by 2020."[11]

And indeed, more than 8,000 lithium mining claims were
staked in Nevada between January 2015 and September 2016.[12]

Because these batteries can only be created by a complex global network of industrial production, they're linked to almost every other
industrial process on the planet. As John Weber has written, all
green technologies are predicated on "machines making machines
making machines."[13] This is literally true; batteries are made by
machines, and the machines that make batteries are themselves
made by other machines, and so on. Each of these connections has
its own industrial supply chain, reliant on materials and energy
inputs from all around the world.

In concentration, lithium is harmful to living beings. It can interfere with sperm viability, cause birth defects, memory problems,
kidney failure, movement disorders, and so on.[14] But the other
materials in an electric-car battery cause about six times more

---

[11] James Stafford, "Why lithium will see another price spike this fall," Oilprice.com, July 18, 2016.

[12] "RE: Lithium exploration wells, production wells, and brine extraction," State of Nevada Department of Conservation and Natural Resources, Division of Water Resources, September 27, 2016.

[13] John Weber, "Machines Making Machines Making Machines," sunweber.blogspot.com, December 3, 2011.

[14] John Laumer, "Living with the Side Effects of Lithium-Ion Batteries," *Treehugger*, February 21, 2010; and "Lithium toxicity," Medline Plus.

harm than lithium,[15] with nickel and cobalt electrodes being the most destructive component.[16]

About half of the cobalt used in lithium batteries comes from the Democratic Republic of the Congo, where 40,000 children as young as seven are essentially enslaved in mines, carrying back-breaking loads in conditions of intense heat, with no safety equipment, under abusive managers and guards, for a wage of a dollar a day.

Companies that make batteries using cobalt from this area include Apple, Microsoft, and Vodaphone.[17]

The maximum federal subsidy for an electric car in the U.S. is $7,500, with additional subsidies from many states. In California, a Tesla Model S sportscar receives about $10,000 in taxpayer subsidies (in the form of tax credits and rebates). In Germany, a 2016 policy would put $1 billion into direct purchasing.[18]

And that, really, is what the bright green movement is about. Capturing subsidies for specific sectors of the industrial economy.

To the dedicated young people marching to save the planet, we offer our solidarity. But the demands of this movement boil down to public money for sectors of the industrial economy. What that money pays for, very directly, is the bright white salt and the cracked brown earth, masses of dead fish and no sign of animal life,

[15] Dominic A. Notter et al., "Contribution of Li-Ion Batteries to the Environmental Impact of Electric Vehicles," *Environmental Science & Technology*, 44(17), (August 2010): 6550-6556.

[16] "Study Identifies Benefits and Potential Environmental/Health Impacts of Lithium-ion Batteries for Electric Vehicles," Abt Associates, May 28, 2013.

[17] Annie Kelly, "Children as young as seven mining cobalt used in smartphones, says Amnesty," *The Guardian*, January 18, 2016.

[18] Samantha Page, "Germany Just Announced a Major Push to Increase Electric Car Sales," *Climate Progress*, April 28, 2016.

the destruction of the last wilderness and the places that spirits live, while the elders cry for future generations, because there is no future in any of this.

One case study in the moral bankruptcy of bright green environmentalism is billionaire Elon Musk. Musk has become a cult figure among both bright greens and businesspeople. Searching for Elon Musk on Google returns headlines like: "Tesla CEO Elon Musk's Plan to Save the World." "How Tesla Will Change the World." "Tesla and SolarCity Join Forces to Save the World." "Tesla's Brilliant—and Generous—Move to Help Save the Planet." Here's a favorite: "Elon Musk: The World's Raddest Man." The top comment on a Tesla video on *YouTube* shows the prevailing opinion on Musk: "We really need more people with minds like Elon Musk's, creating technology that actually helps people without having to destroy or harm something else."

If some see Musk as a messiah, then his miracles are his machines. One of Tesla's latest products is the Powerwall: a lithium-ion battery system designed for the home. Basically, it's an energy-storage device for houses with solar energy generation systems, that shuffles energy back and forth from grid to house. The debut video on *YouTube* is a bit like a rock concert, with Musk continually getting interrupted by cheering and shouting.

Tesla also has a version of the "Powerwall" for use by commercial consumers and energy providers, called the "Powerpack." Musk claims that 2 billion Powerpacks would be enough to provide battery storage for a worldwide "renewable" energy economy. Sounds great, right? Totally doable. The "green" economy is just around the corner.

Each Powerpack weighs 3,575 pounds. Two billion Powerpacks

equals 7.175 trillion pounds equals 3.575 billion tons. In comparison, the mass of all cars produced annually is a little under 200 million tons, so purely on a mass basis, the material in the batteries required for Musk's scheme would be equal to almost 18 years of global car production. The energy required to produce cars is much less than what's required for a proportional mass of lithium-ion batteries (which are by far the most energy intensive portion of a Tesla electric car), so in reality the impact of building 2 billion Powerpacks would be equivalent to many decades of global car production.

It's painful that we have to explicitly state that this would not be a good thing for the planet.

An article titled "Tesla's Model 3 Could Take 300,000 bpd [barrels per day] Off U.S. Gasoline Demand" notes that the release of Tesla's first affordable electric car could have this effect by 2035.[19] In 2019, the U.S. consumed about 20.46 million barrels of petroleum per day; this headline is acclaiming the fact that Tesla cars may, in 20 years, reduce oil demand by a jaw-dropping 1.4 percent.

Here's an irony: The same website that hosts the Tesla article links to other articles on similar topics, with the first result being "Tesla, Apple and Uber push lithium prices even higher." The article explains that lithium demand is rising fast and is poised to "explode." Lithium-battery production is set to double by 2027. So, at the same time that 20 years of Model 3 electric car production will slightly reduce oil demand, it's also dramatically increasing

---

[19] Irina Slav, "Tesla's Model 3 could take 300,000 BPD off U.S. gasoline demand," Oilprice.com, September 27, 2016.

lithium demand. This is expected to trigger a "feeding frenzy"—
their words, not mine—of new lithium mining.[20]

One reason Musk is so popular is that he appeals to a broad set of
deeply held beliefs. For business-oriented people, Musk represents
the classic rags-to-riches story (never mind that his mother was a
model and his father an engineer, so it's more of a short-sleeved-
button-down-shirt-with-a-pocket-protector-to-riches story). He's
a billionaire who has shaken up well-established industries with
innovative risk-taking (and massive public subsidies). For people
whose loyalty is to the high-energy, high-consumption lifestyle of
modern civilization, Musk represents a savior working to deliver
them from the threat climate change poses to the continuation of
their lifestyle. And for bright green environmentalists—whose loyalty also is to this way of life—he represents a chance to make a
perverse form of environmentalism popular by packaging it with
exquisite marketing, shiny gadgetry, a big budget, and no disruption at all to the industrial system that is killing the planet.

Tesla is building a new lithium-ion battery production facility outside of Reno, Nevada. Called a "Gigafactory," it will be one of the
largest factories in the world, at 10 million square feet. Apparently,
when they're producing batteries, enormous factories somehow
become something for environmentalists to applaud. Nevada politicians are certainly applauding; the state has given tax breaks and
other incentives to Tesla that are worth about $1.3 billion.

Musk says, "What we're really designing in the Gigafactory is

---

[20] James Stafford, "Tesla, Apple and Uber push lithium prices even higher,"
Oilprice.com, October 17, 2016.

a giant machine. There will need to be many Gigafactories in the future."

Musk has also stated, "Where the great potential is, is building the machine that makes the machine. In other words, it's building the factory. I'm really thinking of the factory like a product."

Machines making machines making machines.

Meanwhile the 10,000 humans who oversee the machines making machines at a Tesla manufacturing facility often work long hours: Until recently, many worked 12 hours per day, six days a week, and they still work in "a culture of long hours under intense pressure, sometimes through pain and injury, in order to fulfill the CEO's ambitious production goals." As one production technician stated, "I've seen people pass out, hit the floor like a pancake and smash their face open. They just send us to work around him while he's still lying on the floor." Workers who speak of their pain are told, "We all hurt. You can't man up?" by supervisors who "put the production numbers ahead of the safety and wellbeing of the employees." Workers who can't "man up" are put on "light duty" and have their pay reduced by more than 50 percent, down to $10/hour. As one employee states, "No one wants to get a pay cut because they're injured, so everyone just forces themselves to work through it."

Musk's rationale for working people so hard? "We're doing this because we believe in a sustainable energy future, trying to accelerate the advent of clean transport and clean energy production, not because we think this is a way to get rich."[21]

So says the multibillionaire. This is the man *Time* says will "save

[21] Julia Carrie Wong, "Tesla factory workers reveal pain, injury and stress: 'Everything feels like the future but us,'" *The Guardian*, May 18, 2017.

the world," and to whom some people wish to give the Nobel Prize in economics.

In November 2019, Bolivian President Evo Morales was forced out of office and into exile in what Morales and others described as a "lithium coup." Bolivia and neighboring Argentina and Chile contain half of the world's known lithium reserves, and the ouster of Morales replaced a socialist government committed to local control of resource extraction (not, we must note, to protection of the land) with a right-wing government led by Jeanine Añez. The Añez administration has already announced plans to invite multinational corporations into the salt flats at Salar de Uyuni to extract billions of dollars' worth of lithium.[22]

Much of this lithium may end up inside Tesla vehicles. Shortly before the November 2019 coup, it was revealed that Elon Musk and Tesla were in talks with Brazilian president Jair Bolsonaro and Brazilian businesspeople to build a new Tesla Gigafactory in the southern state of Santa Catarina, where BMW and GM already have factories, which would likely require lithium from the Salar de Uyuni. Jeanine Añez's running mate, the Bolivian businessman Samuel Dorina Medina, has called publicly for Tesla to build a Gigafactory in Salar de Uyuni itself. In light of this, Elon Musk was questioned in July 2020 about his support for the Bolivian coup. His response: "We will coup whoever we want! Deal with it."[23]

And so goes the Salar de Uyuni.

[22] "Elon Musk Confesses to Lithium Coup in Bolivia," *TeleSUR English*, July 25, 2020.
[23] Vijay Prashad and Alejandro Bejarano, "'We Will Coup Whoever We Want': Elon Musk and the Overthrow of Democracy in Bolivia," *CounterPunch*, July 29, 2020.

Lead-acid is the second major type of battery in wide use. Much cheaper than lithium-ion batteries, lead-acid batteries' most common use is in cars. They're also often used to store energy for solar power systems in homes. Sometimes they're used in utility-scale energy storage, but rarely and on a small scale, primarily because they're not very energy dense: .17 MJ/kg (if you recall, lithium-ion batteries are about 1 MJ/kg, and gasoline is about 46 MJ/kg). This low-energy density means you need a large mass of batteries to make them useful for storage.

Most of the mass of these batteries comes from the two main components: lead (in the form of thick plates) and sulfuric acid.[24]

Lead is usually locked into rocks unless removed by human activity. Even in tiny doses, lead is extremely toxic. According to the World Health Organization, "There is no known level of lead exposure that is considered safe." The WHO estimates at least 143,000 human beings are killed by lead poisoning every year.

In 2011, lead smelting and lead-acid battery recycling were separately ranked in the top 10 worst toxic pollution problems globally. The issue is most severe in Africa, Central and South America, and Southeast Asia.[25] One recent report found that nearly 50 percent of children in Mexico are at risk of developmental disabilities due to lead poisoning.[26]

In the bloodstream, lead mimics zinc and iron, metals we need to be healthy and that are naturally present in foods. Enzymes are attracted to the lead and bond to it, interfering with critical life

---

[24] Minor components include plastics and barium sulfate, which, interestingly enough, is one of the ingredients in fracking fluid.

[25] Jessica Harris, Andrew McCartor et al., "The World's Worst Toxic Pollution Problems Report 2011," the Blacksmith Institute and Green Cross Switzerland.

[26] Leonor C. Acosta-Saavedra et al., "Environmental exposure to lead and mercury in Mexican children: a real health problem," *Toxicology Mechanisms and Methods*, November 21, 2011.

processes all over the body. Lead also impairs the body's ability to create new hemoglobin—the miracle protein that carries oxygen from the lungs around the body and returns carbon dioxide to be exhaled—by interfering with enzymes that enable the process. And it attacks the walls of red blood cells, weakening them and reducing their lifespan. These effects undermine cellular respiration, our most basic metabolic process, leading to symptoms of anemia: shortness of breath, exhaustion, confusion, and feeling like you're going to black out.

In the brain, lead scrambles the release of neurotransmitters, releasing some for no beneficial reason and preventing others from being released at all. Lead also causes cell walls between the brain and the bloodstream to break down. Children's brains are particularly sensitive. Even at low levels, lead exposure can cause inattention, hyperactivity, reduced intelligence, and irritability in children. Higher levels of exposure can cause brain damage, memory and hearing loss, delayed growth, and death. One doctor described the effect of lead on the brain as "progressive degeneration of all brain function."

In the peripheral nervous system, lead strips the myelin sheath from nerves, damaging their ability to transmit electrical signals and causing muscular weakness, fatigue, and difficulty with coordination.

In the kidneys, lead molecules attach to proteins and move into the nuclei of healthy kidney cells. Normal kidney function begins to break down, and compounds critical to health (like glucose, phosphates, and amino acids) begin to be urinated out rather than absorbed. This causes rising acidity, rickets, rising blood pressure, severe dehydration, and acute inflammatory arthritis.

In the heart, lead can cause abnormal heart rhythms, heart attack, and sudden coronary death. In the reproductive system, it can damage chromosomes, interfere with hormones, and lead to a variety of childbearing problems from premature delivery to miscarriage. Lead also affects the developing fetus in the womb, causing the majority of the same effects we've already mentioned.[27]

These effects aren't limited to humans: Lead has equivalent effects on the majority of multicellular plants and animals.[28]

The main source of lead contamination is lead mining, smelting, manufacturing, and recycling—although leaded gasoline and lead paint are still major issues in some areas. Altogether, more than three-quarters of all lead extracted globally is used for lead-acid batteries.[29]

Lead mining is similar to mining for copper and iron ore. Explosives are used to shatter stone, which is crushed and ground into fine powder. Sulphur is removed by roasting this powder together with superheated oxygen in the presence of coke (a fossil fuel input) or charcoal (an industrial logging input). Next comes reduction, a process in which the remaining ore is heated to thousands of degrees in a furnace using a series of settling areas to separate lead from other elements, which are lighter and float to the top. The heat for this furnace is generally supplied by the combustion of coke (fossil fuel). The final step is to refine the lead to make it pure enough for commercial use, a process requiring heating with natural gas

---

[27] Gagan Flora et al., "Toxicity of lead: a review with recent updates," *Journal of Interdisciplinary Toxicology*, June 2012.

[28] "Lead Exposure in Animals and Plants," University Library Wildlife Resources, Ramapo College of New Jersey, 2000.

[29] "Lead poisoning and health," World Health Organization factsheet, August 2015.

(fossil fuel) as well as the addition of wood chips (logging), coke (fossil fuel), and/or sulfur (industrial mining).

EPA notes that "emissions of lead ... occur in varying amounts from nearly every process ... within primary lead smelter/ refineries."[30]

Like other mining industries, the lead business is highly concentrated. One corporation—Doe Run Resources—was responsible for more than 10 percent of the lead extracted in 2005. The town of Herculaneum, Missouri, home to a Doe Run smelter, was in the news in 2003 after EPA found some of the highest lead levels ever seen—more than 240,000 ppm (with 40 ppm being considered unsafe). More than half the children living nearby had levels of lead in their blood far above the CDC limit for causing irreversible and serious harm. Isotope tests proved that the lead contamination came directly from the Herculaneum smelter, and EPA numbers showed the facility was emitting 101,000 tons of carbon dioxide, 42,000 tons of sulfur dioxide, 30 tons of lead, and 61 tons of other chemicals, particulates, and gases every year. But from 2003 to 2010, instead of shutting down the smelter, EPA and Doe Run shut down the town, putting up signs warning children against playing outside and residents against gardening, and buying out homeowners within a three-eighths-of-a-mile radius around the facility.[31]

Humans weren't (and aren't) the only ones harmed. A U.S. Geological Survey study found lead in songbirds at nearly 40 times

[30] "12.6: Primary Lead Smelting," AP 42, 5th ed., vol. 1, chap. 12: Metallurgical Industry, Technology Transfer Network, Clearinghouse for Inventories & Emissions Factors, United States Environmental Protection Agency, January 1995.
[31] Rebecca Leung, "A Diet of Lead: High Lead Levels in Missouri Town," *60 Minutes*, CBS News, July 9, 2003.

the average level. "More than half of the tested birds showed signs of lead poisoning," said the chief author of the study.[32]

Finally, in 2010, the company was fined $7 million for pollution and forced to put $65 million into cleanup projects for their Missouri facilities. It was one of the largest EPA fines in history. Instead of cleaning up the smelter in Herculaneum, Doe Run decided to close it down.[33]

When the externalities—the costs of poisoning everything—are integrated into the economics of an industrial activity (even partially), that activity turns out to be a very bad deal.

Of course, in the shell game that is the global economy, this closure probably won't prevent those emissions. Some other lead smelter, probably in a poor nation with lax environmental laws, will replace its production.

Now you see the pollution, now you don't.

Doe Run has mining and manufacturing facilities in La Oroya, Peru, where extraction has been underway for nearly a hundred years. La Oroya is one of the world's most polluted places. Ninety-nine percent of the town's children have lead levels in their blood that exceed World Health Organization guidelines. Levels of arsenic and cadmium are similarly elevated. Nonhuman life is even more devastated; the area around the town has been described as a moonscape.[34]

---

[32] Keith Lewis, "Elevated lead levels found in lead district songbirds," *Southeast Missourian*, June 26, 2013.

[33] Chad Garrison, "Doe Run Settles with EPA: Lead Company to Close Herculaneum Smelter, Spend Millions," *Riverfront Times*, October 8, 2010.

[34] "La Oroya, Peru," Top 10 Most Polluted Places, 2007, Blackstone Institute.

Doe Run is owned by RENCO Group CEO Ira Rennert, who controls—at a $5 billion valuation—one of the largest privately owned industrial empires in the United States. Rennert is, of course, a major political donor, because that's how the system works. He lives in one of the most expensive private homes in the United States, worth $200 million. The 110,000-square-foot house has 29 bedrooms and 39 bathrooms, and it sits on 63 oceanfront acres in the Hamptons on Long Island.[35]

At first glance, supercapacitors seem similar to batteries: Both are devices mostly used to store energy in electronics. However, supercapacitors can charge and discharge almost instantly. They're also more durable: able to withstand cycles of charge and discharge for decades. But their energy density is even lower than that of batteries, at .01 to .036 MJ/kg.

Supercapacitors are used in a variety of consumer products, from computers to cell phones, usually as a supplement to batteries or grid power and a way to stabilize fluctuations in the voltage delivered to sensitive electronics. Between 20 and 30 percent of wind turbines use supercapacitors to provide backup power to the motors that change the angle (pitch) of the blades. If a storm knocks out the power supply, these supercapacitors rotate the blades to shed the wind and prevent damage. One company, Maxwell, had, at the end of 2013, more than 7 million supercapacitor cells installed in wind turbines worldwide.[36] Supercapacitors are also widely used at transformer substations to stabilize the voltage coming out of

[35] "#108 Ira Rennert," 2015 Billionaire Ranking, *Forbes*.
[36] Stefan Werkstetter, "Ultracapacitor Usage in Wind Turbine Pitch Control Systems," Maxwell Technologies, January 2015.

wind and solar facilities, since voltage fluctuates wildly as the wind gusts or the sun goes behind clouds.[37]

Supercapacitors are made of two metal plates that store energy in the form of an electrostatic field, the same type of energy that pulls your hair upward when you rub a balloon on it. The plates are coated in a conductive, high-surface-area material, most commonly activated carbon.

People who promote supercapacitors often claim materials used in supercapacitors are nontoxic. This is not true. A partial list of harmful materials used in supercapacitors include acetonitrile (toxic), arsenic compounds (exceptionally toxic, causing multisystem organ failure), tetrafluoroborate (damages the lungs and causes severe chemical burns, ulcers, anemia, hair loss, kidney damage, thyroid dysfunction, and reproductive damage including "withering of the testicles"[38]), diethyl carbonate (highly irritating to human tissues; can cause vomiting, nausea, weakness, and loss of consciousness; also highly flammable, a possible carcinogen, and believed to cause reproductive damage[39]), and carbon nanotubes (a similar effect on animals' bodies to asbestos, entering through lungs and mucous membranes and causing cancer, damage to the respiratory system, and lesions throughout internal tissues of the body[40]).

The process of creating supercapacitors creates its own harms. Acetonitrile, for example, is a byproduct of making acrylonitrile and polyacrylonitrile, highly flammable and toxic chemicals that

---

[37] "The Role of Energy Storage for Mini-Grid Stabilization," International Energy Agency, Photovoltaic Power Systems Programme, July 2011.

[38] "Tetrafluoroborate Material Safety Data Sheet," Santa Cruz Biotechnology.

[39] "Diethyl carbonate hazardous substance fact sheet," New Jersey Department of Health and Senior Services, April 2006.

[40] Larry Greenemeier, "Study Says Carbon Nanotubes as Dangerous as Asbestos," *Scientific American*, May 20, 2008.

cause cancer and are especially damaging to aquatic life. Exposure in humans causes blisters, skin irritation, abdominal pain, vomiting, and convulsions.[41] Carbon aerogels are typically made using formaldehyde and resorcinol, both probable carcinogens that are dangerous to human health and widely used in industrial products. Tetrahydrofuran is derived from butane, which is itself refined from natural gas (and in the U.S., more than half of natural gas now comes from fracking). Barium titanate production requires a furnace temperature of more than 2000° F, and its particles (which are increasingly used in technology and medicine) are toxic to aquatic creatures.[42] The production of carbon nanotubes releases at least 15 different aromatic hydrocarbons, including four of the extremely toxic polycyclic variety (similar to those produced by internal combustion engines), some of which cause cancer and respiratory problems in humans.[43]

Nothing compares to the energy density of fossil fuel. Its 46 MJ/kg made industrial civilization possible. It takes energy to fight a war against life itself, because life wants to live. It takes energy to turn biotic communities into dead commodities and ship them across oceans and over continents, and the only way to do it at a profit is if the energy is essentially free. But $50 a barrel is pretty close to free.

The math is not complicated. The best lithium battery can only store 1 MJ/kg. Imagine life in an industrialized country at a mere

---

[41] "Acetonitrile," the National Institute for Occupational Safety and Health, March 13, 2001.

[42] Hudson C. Polonini et al., "Ecotoxicological studies of micro- and nanosized barium titanate on aquatic photosynthetic microorganisms," *Aquatic Toxicology* 154 (September 2014): 58–70.

[43] "Toxic byproducts of carbon nanotube manufacturing: are there green alternatives?" *ScienceDaily*, August 24, 2007.

46th of the amount of American consumption. You'd have just over 30 minutes of electricity a day. The average American drives 37 miles a day: divide that by 46. That's assuming your car would exist, which it wouldn't, not without the fossil fuel to mine the ores and make the steel. And your car would be mostly useless without the fossil fuel needed to carve out and pave roads. The infrastructure and consumer goods of industrial civilization require a level of extraction, transportation, manufacture, and distribution only possible with an easy flow of fossil fuel.

We are being sold a story, and we are buying it because we like it. We want it to be true. We want to believe that our lives can go on with all the ease and comfort we accept as our due. How painless to believe that a simple switch of wind for oil and solar for coal and we can go on with our air conditioning and cell phones and suburbs. Every time we hit a trip wire of unsettling facts or basic math, we soothe ourselves with our faith in technology. If all that stands between us and the end of the world is a battery that can store 46 MJ/kg, surely someone is working on it.

And indeed, they have been, for decades, and yet there is no new battery. The ubiquitous lithium-ion batteries are a refinement of technology that's 40 years old. Steve LeVine, author of *The Powerhouse: Inside the Invention of a Battery to Save the World*, understands how high the stakes are. He is also very honest: "When you get the really serious battery guys over a beer and ask them, off the record, 'Tell me the truth. Has anyone you know in any of the formulation[s] had a breakthrough?' The answer is 'No.' No one even has one on the horizon."[44]

---

[44] Michael Zelenko, "The US is losing the high-stakes global battery war," *The Verge*, August 13, 2018.

One of the biggest public health problems in cities of the 18th and 19th centuries was horse manure. The *Times of London*, for example, predicted in 1894 that by 1950 every street in London would be covered in nine feet of equine feces, while people in New York City believed that by 1930 horse manure would be piled even higher, up to third-story windows in Manhattan. "The stench," according to urban planning export Eric Morris,[45] "was omnipresent."[46]

At the time, the economy was dependent on horses. They dragged plows, skidded logs, pulled carts and carriages, and transported individuals. In the late 1800s, when urban horses were at their peak, about 15 million acres—an area the size of West Virginia—were needed to grow horse feed.

The introduction of railroads was widely hailed as a technological solution to the horse problem. But instead, rail made these issues worse. More efficient transit by rail allowed more trade to take place, and since every item shipped by rail needed to be picked up and delivered by horse-drawn wagon, overall demand for horse transport and thus the scale of the problem went up.

New technologies don't always displace older problems; sometimes they just pile on top.

What finally did replace horse transportation was the automobile, which by 1912 outnumbered horses in many American states. Aided by new regulations on urban horses, cars took over the streets and were proclaimed to be an environmental savior. According to Morris, "Neither draconian regulations nor disincentives for travel were necessary to fix the horse pollution problem.

---

[45] Eric Morris, "From horse power to horsepower," *Access*, 2007, Issue 30, 2–9.

[46] The horses weren't happy either, and they had more than bad smells to worry about. Healthy horses live for 25 or 30 years; the average streetcar horse lived barely two years due to crowding, disease, dangerous streets, and constant beatings and whippings.

Human ingenuity and technology did the job—and at the same time they brought a tremendous increase in mobility."[47]

But at what cost? Far from a triumphal tale about ingenuity and technology, the story of automobiles solving the problem of horse poop could be read as a cautionary tale on the perils of escalations in technology, and more fundamentally on the tendency within this culture to sidestep problems rather than solve them. In this case, the problem was not addressed; it was just transformed. Instead of feces-filled streets, we now have smog-filled skies and a greenhouse-gas filled climate. Trashing mountains, forests, wetlands, and prairies to provide food for horses was replaced with trashing mountains, forests, wetlands, and prairies to provide steel to Henry Ford's factories, and oil for the automobiles.

Now, in the face of a car culture that's ruining the climate, the response is to sidestep the issue again by developing technologies that will once more displace the destruction, not eliminate it.

The next bright green earth-saving energy storage technology is fuel cells. By now we should be able to predict the headlines: "The Perfect Energy Source for the Future," "Fuel Cells: Clean and Reliable Energy."

To most people who aren't chemists or engineers, fuel cells seem similar to batteries or supercapacitors.[48] But fuel cells differ in that they need an outside fuel source (usually hydrogen gas) and only make some of the energy stored in this fuel available for use.

---

[47] Morris, op. cit.

[48] "Deloitte's Electricity Storage Technologies, Impacts, and Prospects," Deloitte Center for Energy Solutions, September 2015. Hydrogen fuel cells are, along with supercapacitors, considered an early stage energy storage prospect. It likely will be many years—even decades—before fuel cells find full commercial implementation and maturity.

The byproducts of fuel cell discharge are water and heat, which is why many people say fuel cells are clean and renewable.

The two main types of fuel cells are polymer exchange membrane (PEM) and solid oxide (SO). The first is mostly used in transportation, the second for heavy industries and grid power storage.

PEM fuel cells are dependent on a catalyst applied to the inner surfaces of the fuel cell. The catalyst is usually made of platinum nanoparticles coated on a thin carbon-based material. Let's leave aside that platinum is mined, with attendant horrors, and just point out that platinum nanoparticles (like all nanoparticles) can be toxic to humans and other forms of life, causing lung inflammation, atherosclerosis, damage to cell growth mechanisms, and other harmful effects. One study notes: "The growing use of nanotechnology in high-tech industries is likely to become another way for humans to be exposed to intentionally generated engineered nanoparticles" and that "the smaller the particles are, the more the surface area they have per unit mass; this makes nanoparticles very reactive in the cellular environment [and enhances] intrinsic toxicity."[49]

The membrane itself is made of a type of polymer plastic, and the gas diffusion layer (which helps to transport fuel and water in and out of the catalyst layer) is made of carbon paper coated in the synthetic polymer polytetrafluoroethylene or PTFE,[50] commonly known as Teflon. PTFE is usually manufactured with a chemical called perfluorooctanoic acid; PTFE manufacturing has caused this substance to be released around the world. Some PTFE-treated products include pots and pans, carpets, toilet cleaners, clothing, rain gear, backpacks and other outdoor gear, pizza-slice

---

[49] Carlos Medina et al., "Nanoparticles: pharmacological and toxicological significance," *British Journal of Pharmacology* 150, no. 5, January 22, 2007: 552–558.
[50] Or sometimes other thermoplastics.

paper, ice cream cartons, and popcorn bags. When these products wear out, they release perfluorooctanoic acid. This acid is known to cause cancer, ulcerative colitis, thyroid disease, high cholesterol, and other health problems in humans, and it also bioaccumulates. More than 99 percent of humans in the U.S. have detectable levels of this chemical inside their body. The worldwide levels are similar, and thus far every animal species tested has PTFE-family chemicals in their bodies.[51] Surely, we are among them. You probably are as well.[52] Small creatures are also affected. Some of these chemicals were concentrated most significantly in zooplankton.[53]

Overheating PTFE (as sometimes happens with nonstick kitchen pans, and which may happen inside fuel cells) causes it to release 15 toxic gases and particles that cause "polymer fume fever," characterized by chills, headaches, and fevers. The production and the use of PTFE and other fluorinated polymers is causing rising levels of one of the volatile substances that make up these fumes, trifluoroacetic acid (TFA). There are no natural sources of TFA; it only comes from industry. In its concentrated form, TFA is extremely corrosive, causing severe injury or death in even small quantities. And even at low concentrations, it's toxic to aquatic life. Several studies have found TFA in water bodies at levels far beyond what was expected. As with many contaminants, the true scale of the problem is not fully known.[54]

---

[51] "DuPont vs. the World," *Democracy Now*, January 23, 2018.

[52] Wendee Nicole, "PFOA and cancer in a highly exposed community: new findings from the C8 science panel," *Environmental Health Perspectives* 121, no. 11–12 (November–December 2013).

[53] Gregg T. Tomy et al., "Fluorinated organic compounds in an eastern Artic marine food web," *Environmental Science and Technology* 38, no. 24 (December 15, 2004): 6475–81.

[54] Jean C. Boutonnet et al., "Environmental risk assessment of trifluoroacetic acid," *Human and Ecological Risk Assessment: An International Journal* 5, no. 1 (1999).

Take a deep, calming breath, and tell yourself that hydrogen fuel cells are clean and good for the planet.

PTFE chemicals also make up the core of the electrolyte in most PEM fuel cells, often a chemical called Nafion, manufactured by chemical giant Chemours, a DuPont spinoff,[55] made up of perfluoro vinyl, sulfonate, and tetrafluoroethylene combined into large polymer molecules. The properties of Nafion make it perfectly suited to use in fuel cells; they also make it nonbiodegradable. Once it's made, the only way to unmake Nafion is to incinerate it. Incinerating this chemical releases sulfur dioxide (which causes acid rain), hydrogen fluoride ("brief exposure to HF vapors at the parts per thousand level may be fatal," notes one textbook, going on to add that "fluorine is a cumulative poison in plants.... Fluorine produced by aluminum plants in Norway has destroyed forests of *Pinus sylvestris* up to 8 miles distant; trees were damaged at distances as great as 20 miles"[56]), and carbon dioxide.[57] And that's if incineration is done carefully.

A chemist friend of ours used to work at an incinerator. Her job was to ensure combustion occurs as cleanly as possible. When we asked her about Nafion, she said, "I'd worry most about the fluorine. In small quantities it's considered fine to burn (albeit ONLY in the few incinerators equipped with the best air pollution control equipment [of which there are two in the U.S.]), but fluorine is a problem chemical in incineration even with good equipment. It forms nasty toxins that if present in more than very small quantities go right through the equipment. This stuff should never ever

[55] Sossina M. Haile, "Fuel cell materials and components," *Acta Materialia* 51 (2003): 5981–6000.
[56] Stanley E. Manahan, "11.9: Fluorine, Chlorine, and their Gaseous Compounds," *Environmental Chemistry*, CRC Press, August 26, 2004, Eighth Edition.
[57] "Safe handling and use of perfluorosulfonic acid products," DuPont Fuel Cells division, 2009.

be incinerated in an average incinerator. Every living being around it would be poisoned for sure."

This sounds like a great new sustainable technology, right?

DuPont and Chemours corporations have been forced to pay more than $700 million in damages to people harmed by perfluorooctanoic acid (PFOA)/Teflon chemicals. In 2013, DuPont stopped making PFOA inside the United States. Most production moved to China. They've also created a chemical called GenX, which they market as a new sustainable replacement for Teflon. However, DuPont's own reports show that GenX has similar negative impacts, causing "organ growth, various forms of cancer, adverse changes in fat processing, birth defects, and more."[58] Despite existing for less than a decade, GenX has already been found in streams, lakes, and drinking water in North Carolina, Ohio, and West Virginia. In one case, the West Virginia Department of Environmental Protection gave a permit to DuPont allowing them to release GenX at a level 250 times the legal limit for PFOA into a stream near their plant.[59]

After the U.S. Army put its first experimental fuel-cell powered truck into service in 2005, Hillary Clinton said the project "was a critical step in the right direction." A spokesperson from General Motors added "fuel cell vehicles are a good match with U.S. Army goals…. [They are] both clean and quiet, and therefore can provide a battlefield advantage."[60]

---

[58] A.J. Rohn, "GenX and the Hazards of Teflon," *Geography Realm* March 3, 2016.

[59] Sharon Lerner, "New Teflon toxin found in North Carolina drinking water," *The Intercept,* June 17, 2017.

[60] Mike Hanlon, "US Army deploys first Fuel Cell truck," *New Atlas,* April 4, 2005.

Here's another headline: "Greening the military: It's not about saving the planet—it's about safer, cheaper fighting outfits." The article explains that the world's biggest militaries are increasing their effectiveness by using solar panels, wind turbines, and rechargeable batteries instead of relying on vulnerable fuel convoys.[61]

Bright green or four-star general, the point is not about saving the planet—it's about maintaining this way of life.

Bright greens often claim that "hydrogen-fuel-cell vehicles are zero emission," as in "Amazon's new zero emission forklift deal could be just the beginning of a new future for hydrogen-fuel-cell electric vehicles, off-street and on," or "Enjoy a clean, fun driving experience with a zero-emission vehicle.... Honda is paving the path to the future with new fuel cell technology." And on and on.

At the risk of stating the obvious, fuel cells—like other forms of energy storage—only store energy, they don't generate it. Their energy has to come from somewhere. Fuel cells are nearly always fueled either directly by natural gas or by hydrogen produced from natural gas through a process called steam hydrocarbon reforming. A study from the Tyndall Centre in the U.K. found that because of this fossil fuel input, carbon emissions from fuel cells might only be "marginally different" from combustion engines and fossil-fuel power plants.[62] And as we've mentioned, research has shown that natural gas, far from being "cleaner" is in fact even worse for

---

[61] Sara Stefanini, "Green the military. It's not about saving the planet—it's about safer, cheaper fighting outfits," *Politico*, December 31, 2015.
[62] J.C. Powell et al., "Fuel cells for a sustainable future?" Tyndall Centre for Climate Change Research, 2004.

climate change than coal because of the methane that leaks from natural gas wells, pipes, and processing facilities.[63]

The next cheapest method of extracting hydrogen involves gasification of low-sulfur coal in an industrial furnace, then using a device called a "scrubber" to extract hydrogen from the gas put off by this process.

Most expensive is the process environmentalists are rooting for: electrolysis. Through this process, hydrogen is extracted from water through chemical decomposition that uses electricity to split H_2O molecules. Electrolysis is very energy intensive—and much more expensive than using natural gas or coal gasification.[64] Aside from energy use, this method of generating hydrogen also uses water. This water isn't strictly lost; it will reappear when hydrogen bonds with atmospheric oxygen and drips from the tailpipes of a fuel cell vehicle. However, widespread use of fuel cells would certainly *redistribute* water. Most of this water will be pulled from local rivers, lakes, springs, and aquifers—places where it supports life—and will drip onto roadways, where most of it will evaporate. The net effect will be to remove more water from natural communities and shift it toward industrial use.[65] One estimate looked at private passenger vehicles in the U.S. and found that producing enough hydrogen for their operation would take 160 million gallons of purified water per day.[66] Running all the private passenger vehicles in the U.S. on water-powered fuel cells would be, in terms

---

[63] Joe Romm, "Natural Gas Bombshell: Switching from coal to gas increases warming for decades, has minimal benefit even in 2100," *Climate Progress*, September 9, 2011.

[64] "Hydrogen and Fuel Cells—Production," Alternative Energy Solutions for the 21st Century, altenergy.org.

[65] Ocean water can be used for fuel cells, but it first has to be desalinated, another energy-intensive industrial process.

[66] John R. Hoaglund III, "Chapter III, Section E: An Ultimate Resource Limitation for Hydrogen?" *Entropy Happens: An Energy Blueprint Toward Sustainability*, March 11, 2001.

of water consumption, like adding four new cities the size of Los Angeles.[67]

Pumped hydro storage (PHS) is a simple technology. First, you find a site where two sizable reservoirs (or natural water bodies) at significantly different elevations can be connected by pipes. When you want to store energy, you pump water from the lower to the upper reservoir, and when you want to use the stored energy, you let it run back down.

PHS is by far the most important form of energy storage used in electrical grids today. As of 2012, it accounted for more than 99 percent of bulk energy storage worldwide.[68] By 2018, total energy storage had grown by a factor of 12, but still only totaled around 8 GWh globally, with 96.2 percent of energy storage provided by pumped hydro.[69]

So, when bright greens talk about powering the economy, think big honkin' dams.

For the past few decades, there has been a lull in new projects because of high cost, slow permitting, and serious harm to the natural world. But now, thanks to the boom in the "green miracle" of wind and solar, new PHS projects are starting up all over the globe.

Despite this, most people have never heard of PHS, and fewer still have considered the costs.

---

[67] "Where is California water use decreasing? Water consumption for August 2015 in the Los Angeles Dept. of Water and Power," KPCC Southern California Public Radio.

[68] Elizabeth Ingram, "A (potentially) bright future for pumped storage in the U.S.," Hydro World, December 5, 2014.

[69] "Energy Storage Monitor: Latest trends in energy storage," World Energy Council, 2019.

Pumped hydro facilities are generally huge projects. The harms these projects cause to surrounding areas often lead to community opposition, which slows projects and raises costs. Permitting these projects inside the U.S. is difficult. So, proponents need to override or outlast the local opposition. Construction can take five to 10 years and can cost hundreds of millions or billions of dollars.

The largest pumped storage hydro facility in the world is the Bath County Station in northwestern Virginia, which can generate 3 GW of electricity at peak flow. The water source is Little Back Creek, which was dammed when the project was built in the late 1970s and early 1980s. The two dams on site have a volume of 22 million cubic yards, equivalent to about seven Hoover Dams. The two reservoirs created behind these dams cover more than 800 acres, with one about 1,200 feet higher than the other. The station manager calls it "one of the biggest engineering projects ever," adding "the machinery is huge." He's not exaggerating; each of the facility's six generators weighs 90 tons. During a single day, the upper reservoir can drop 105 feet and the lower reservoir can rise 60 feet as millions of gallons of water are exchanged through the system.[70]

In terms of harm to land, pumped hydro facilities are like dams; they rely on partially or fully damming a natural body of water, or on creating a completely artificial reservoir.[71] How this harms the land and associated waters should be obvious, but when you have an entire culture killing the planet and calling this destruction "saving the earth" we can never be too clear.

Dams block the movement of fish and other creatures up- and

---

[70] Ryan Koronowski, "The inside story of the world's biggest 'battery' and the future of renewable energy," *Climate Progress*, August 27, 2013.

[71] A completely artificial reservoir that has to be filled with water pumped in from somewhere else, and periodically topped off to counteract the loss of water that percolates into the soil or evaporates.

downstream. This not only harms these populations themselves, but also causes cascading harm to the whole of the local natural community. In some areas, nutrients essential for the natural community are delivered by anadromous fish like salmon, who hatch in fresh water, make their way to the ocean (at least they used to: these days, on their way downstream young fish are often killed by turbines, either by being pureed or killed by the rapid change in pressure), grow to adulthood, and return to spawn in the streams of their spawning (at least they used to: these days, dams often stand in their way).

Pumping water uphill can also introduce harmful species to new areas. For example, in South Africa, the Tugela-Vaal pumped storage pipeline introduced three new species of fish to the headwaters of the Tugela River. Now they're hybridizing and outcompeting species who (for now) live in the upper river.[72]

Reservoirs associated with PHS almost never develop healthy natural communities along their shorelines, because water levels fluctuate so much more (and so much more rapidly) than in natural lakes. Low water leaves plants and animals dry, while high water drowns them. This cycle occurs on a daily basis in pumped storage reservoirs, rather than on a monthly or yearly basis as it would in most natural ponds and lakes.

Reservoirs contribute to global warming; in temperate regions, they release about twice as much carbon dioxide and methane gas as does a natural lake, and in the tropics, reservoirs release four times the carbon dioxide and 10 times as much methane as do natural water bodies. This isn't a small contribution; reservoirs now make up more surface area than all the natural freshwater lakes on

---

[72] James Carlton and Gregory M. Ruiz, eds., *Invasive Species: Vectors and Management Strategies* (Washington, DC: Island Press, 2013), 322.

the planet combined, and they contribute about 4 percent of global carbon emissions and 20 percent of global methane emissions.[73]

Pumped storage projects also contribute to greenhouse gases during their construction. The Dinorwig Power Station in northern Wales, for example, built at the site of an abandoned slate quarry and inside tunnels and caverns of a mountain called Elidir Fawr, was, when it began in 1974, the largest governmental civil engineering project ever in the U.K. Construction involved digging 16 kilometers of underground tunnels and required 5,000 tons of steel and 1.1 million tons of concrete.[74] Producing that material generated over a million tons of carbon dioxide. That calculation doesn't count the emissions (let alone the other forms of pollution and land destruction) released when transporting materials to the site, blasting through rock, transporting rock back to the surface, driving workers to and from the site, constructing new roads, substations, and transmission lines, casting and assembling the turbines and other components, and so on.

Compared to natural streams and rivers, which are often partly or fully shaded by trees along the bank, reservoirs are wide open to sunlight. This increases water temperatures, which makes it hard or impossible for many native species to survive, and also tends to encourage introduced species instead. Pumping water back and forth stirs up sediments in the water, further decreasing water

[73] Vincent L. St. Louis et al., "Reservoir surfaces as sources of greenhouse gases to the atmosphere: a global estimate," *BioScience* 50 (2000): 766–775.
[74] "Dinowig Power Station," Mitsui & Co., Ltd.

quality. And, as alluded to earlier, turbines kill aquatic creatures directly.

The proposed Eagle Mountain pumped storage hydro project in Riverside County, California, is a good example of the devastation that comes with pumped hydro storage. To be located just outside Joshua Tree National Park, the facility will destroy habitat and disturb breeding and feeding for several sensitive bat species, including: the California leaf-nosed bat, the pallid bat, the pocketed free-tailed bat, the spotted bat, Townsend's big-eared bat, and the western mastiff bat. Other species to be harmed include: golden eagles, desert bighorn sheep, more than 100 species of plants, and 14 species of reptiles, including our friends the desert tortoises. Eagle Mountain would sprawl across 2,500 acres of sensitive Mojave Desert habitat and suck local groundwater at a rate of nearly 500 million gallons annually; this, in a place that gets barely four inches of rain per year.

When the Ludington plant in Michigan was brought online in 1973, it was, at 1.8 GW, the largest pumped storage facility in the world. The reservoir is 110 feet deep and covers 2.5 square miles. The pumping station has six tunnels, each 24 feet in diameter.

It kills fish.

In 1995, the owners of Ludington paid $175 million in fines for more than two decades of massive fish kills: the plant was killing nearly half a million salmon and trout, around 85,000 perch, and millions of smaller forage fish every year.[75] Today, more than two

---

[75] Karl Meyer, "The hidden costs of Northfield Mountain pumped storage," September 1, 2014.

decades after the settlement, the fish kills continue, despite a seasonal net stretched two and a half miles across the lake that's supposed to stop this. To "offset" these ongoing fish kills, some of the money from the 1995 settlement was placed in the *Great Lakes Fishery Trust Fund,* which finances hatcheries and habitat restoration along the shoreline of the lake.[76]

As of August 2015, about 75 percent of the energy used to pump water into the Ludington reservoir came from coal and natural gas, with the remainder split between nuclear and wind (there were 56 turbines nearby as of 2014). This isn't unusual. While bright greens hope that one day these reservoirs will exclusively store power from "renewable energy," that isn't the case now and has never been in the past.

A careful look at pumped storage shows that these facilities lead to more fossil fuels being burnt. For example, if a facility takes 1,000 MWh to fill its reservoir, and the facility is only 70 percent efficient, it will be able to deliver 700 MWh of energy. The rest of the energy is lost. At Ludington in 2013, fossil fuels burned to provide energy to pump water uphill and fill the reservoir produced nearly 3.5 million tons of carbon dioxide. Twenty-eight percent of that energy was lost to inefficiencies. The energy that was produced from the water flowing back through the generators would have released about 2.5 million tons of carbon dioxide *had it been generated directly by burning fossil fuels.* That means that operating the facility—not counting maintenance, construction, habitat destruction, reservoir greenhouse gases, fish kills, or any other impacts, but only the inefficiencies in the system—contributed

---

[76] Ron Meador, "Letter from Ludington: plant powers 1.4 million homes, and blends into scenery," *MinnPost,* July 2, 2014.

nearly 1 million more tons of carbon dioxide to the atmosphere that year than simply running a coal-fired power plant would have.[77]

No form of energy storage is 100 percent efficient. New lithium-ion batteries are about 80 to 90 percent efficient (meaning 10 to 20 percent of the energy is lost off the top), lead-acid batteries are 50 to 90 percent, and fuel cells are 40 to 60 percent (up to 85 percent with some designs). This means that as energy storage is added to the grid, the efficiency of the total system declines, often by quite a lot. The less power is produced "on-demand" and the more it must be stored for later use, the higher the inefficiencies. This means more energy has to be harvested, which means more infrastructure, more land disturbance, and so on. A 2013 paper in the journal *Energy* found that when the energy costs of storage were considered, energy return on energy investment for solar and wind power fell "remarkably"—a critical consideration when we remember that Mark Jacobson's plan relies on new efficiencies in the energy system for reducing total energy needs by 40 percent, and yet also calls for massive expansions in storage to cope with the variability inherent in renewable energy harvesting.[78]

Why aren't more people screaming at the absurdity of these bright green fantasies? The world is being killed before our eyes, and few people bother to sit down and do the fairly simple math.

---

[77] Andy Balaskovitz, "Is a Michigan hydro pumped storage facility clean and renewable? Lawmakers, experts disagree," *Midwest Energy News*, August 24, 2015.

[78] Daniel Weißbach et al., "Energy intensities, EROIs (energy returned on invested), and energy payback times of electricity generating power plants," *Energy* 52 (April 1, 2013): 210–221.

It can be fun thinking about "energy density," which, if you recall, is the amount of energy per unit mass you can store in some material. Here's what's funny about it: Bright greens are excited because lithium-ion batteries can store 1 MJ/kg, and they hope to someday reach 5 MJ/kg. But fat already can (and does, and will reliably) store 37 MJ/kg, and protein and carbohydrates store about 17 MJ/kg. We think we're so smart as we destroy the world so we can make a battery with less than one-third the energy density of a potato.[79] And maybe a 15th of the energy density of bacon.[80] Wood is about 16 MJ/kg, and cow chips are about 13 MJ/kg.

Yeah, we know, this is like comparing apples and oranges, or more accurately apples[81] (about 3 MJ/kg) and batteries (1MJ/kg or less). But the real point is that nature is really smart. It created these wonderful means to store and transfer energy, called, for example, "fish in the river," and we're destroying them.

One little word puts the lie to these bright green fantasies. This word is *trucks*. Look around you right now. What do you see? Perhaps a wooden table. A cloth-covered couch. A lamp. How many trucks were involved to bring each of these things to you? There were log trucks to move timber (and bulldozers to punch in the logging roads in the first place), flatbeds to haul the treated wood, various semis to move this wood to processing plants, warehouses, stores. There were trucks associated with agriculture and

---

[79] Potatoes are about 80 percent water, so 20 percent of 17 MJ/kg is 3.4 MJ/kg.

[80] Bacon is about 30 percent water, and we're presuming most of the rest is fat, then being conservative.

[81] Apples are about 84 percent water. Interestingly enough, grapes have a lower percentage of water than apples.

petrochemicals for the couch, trucks associated with mining for the lamp. I'm guessing that if you're reading this book indoors, you'll be hard pressed to find a single item that was never carried on a truck. Most of them were probably on at least a dozen.

And these trucks cannot feasibly be replaced by trains or ships. First, in the United States there are only 95,000 route miles of railroad tracks, and about 25,000 miles of navigable waterways. On the other hand, there are over 4 million miles of roads. When every act in an industrial economy harms the planet, it doesn't make ecological (or economic) sense to reproduce the road infrastructure in rail and canal. And good luck economically building a rail line to a logging site.

Even more important than this, however, is the question of energy density. Diesel fuel is remarkably dense, at about 48 MJ/kg. As Alice J. Friedeman, author of *When Trucks Stop Running: Energy and the Future of Transportation*, noted in an interview for this book, "A diesel semi-tractor can haul 60,000 pounds of freight 600 miles before refueling. To get a similar range, that tractor would have to have about 55,000 pounds of batteries." Subtract the weight of batteries from the 60,000-pound total capacity and you're left with 5,000 pounds of freight.

It just won't work.

Let's do one more cautionary tale about the perils of pumped hydro. It comes from Greece, where the Thisavros pumped storage facility was built on the Nestos River in the 1990s. Drily summarizing the damage, one European consortium concluded the project has "high negative impacts" on biodiversity, fish, climate, water, soils, and hydrology.[82]

The dam, the largest in Greece, directly destroyed habitat, and stands in the path of 20 species of fish who live in the Nestos River, preventing them from moving between different portions of their home. The technical term for this is "habitat isolation."

Among humans, the right to freedom of movement within one's home nation is recognized as critical. It's a foundation of the Universal Declaration of Human Rights. But these rights don't extend to nonhumans. Of course.

Changes in water temperatures because of the reservoirs have led to an influx of introduced species who are outcompeting native fish. Downstream of Thisavros, sediment no longer reaches the beaches of the river delta. Without natural replenishment, important habitat erodes.

This isn't a problem only at Thisavros. It's true all over. Large rivers naturally provide sediment to replenish beaches for dozens and often hundreds of miles in either direction of the river mouth. Dams prevent this from happening. Dams around the world are causing beaches downstream from them to shrink and disappear, and the overlooking bluffs to erode.

And if salmon don't do it for you, but your lovely vacation home with the beautiful ocean view on a (dangerously eroding) bluff *does* do it for you, then *maybe* there's a reason for you to care about dams.

Here's the thing: pumped storage, even while accounting for the vast majority of grid-scale energy storage, hasn't been that

[82] Annicka Wänn et al., "Environmental performance of existing energy storage installations," StoRE Project, February 2012.

common around the world. But that's beginning to change. One analyst writes that "in recent years, due to increasing concern for global warming and the call to decarbonize electricity, there has been increasing commercial interest in PHS. Developers are actively pursuing new PHS projects around the world. More than 100 new PHS plants with a total capacity of about 74 GW capacity are expected to be in operation by 2020."[83]

Debbie Mursch, chair of the National Hydropower Association Pumped Storage Development Council, adds more detail: "We can't continue to increase the amount of intermittent generation [such as wind and solar] while at the same time removing baseload nuclear and coal plants and not consider the need for grid-scale storage."[84]

She's right. From the perspective of industrialists, the basic issue is that there isn't nearly enough grid storage to cope with the fluctuations in power supply to which expansions in wind and solar energy inevitably lead. The result is a scramble to develop energy storage projects. Which means there are fortunes to be made. Which means forget the fish and mollusks and bats, and full speed ahead with industrialization. And never mind those "hypocritical and counterproductive" environmentalists who oppose these processes. Groups representing the pumped storage industry in the United States are working to, in their own words, remove "regulatory barriers." What this really means, of course, is that they're working to remove the threat posed by inconvenient obstacles like community opposition and protecting the land.[85]

---

[83] Chi-Jen Yang, "Pumped hydroelectric storage," Chapter 2 in Storing Energy by Elsevier.

[84] Elizabeth Ingram, "A (Potentially) Bright Future for Pumped Storage in the U.S.," *Hydro Review*, December 5, 2014.

[85] "Challenges and Opportunities for New Pumped Storage Development," National Hydropower Association, Pumped Storage Development Council, 2014.

An article in *Grist,* titled "Here's an idea for retired coal mines: Turn them into giant batteries," is the perfect distillation of the bright green history, future, ethos, and relationship to the earth. The article states, "It turns out the structure of coal mines is perfect for building these [pumped hydro] systems: Water can be cycled between reservoirs deep in the mine and holding ponds at the surface." The problem, the article continues, is that PHS is so expensive that a law had to be passed allowing the power companies to raise consumer rates. The article concludes, "As more solar is added to the grid—and the need for electricity storage ramps up—giant coal-mine batteries could just keep going and going right into the future."[86]

Here's the history and trajectory. First, you take the most easily accessible and usable energy, the energy for which you have to put out the least money or effort to attain, and that brings the greatest return on both energy and money. It's common sense. You access the oil you can scoop before you access the oil you drill for; the oil you drill for before the oil you drill for offshore; the oil you drill for offshore before the oil you drill for in deepwater; and so on. So, in this case, you first access the coal. And when the coal mine has played out, you move on to a less profitable (in terms of both energy and money) form of energy. In this case, it's solar, which requires storage, so it makes perfect sense to convert this spot from one form of industrial use to another.

This is the larger bright green process: Industrialists are moving from harming the earth through coal mining to harming the earth through industrial solar and consequent energy storage.

---

[86] Amelia Urry, "Here's an idea for retired coal mines: Turn them into giant batteries," *Grist,* May 26, 2017.

And who is the loser in all of this? The mountain, that's who. Every damn time.

Or, if the coal mine isn't used to store energy from windmills, it could be used to build the windmills themselves! There's an article in *Quartz* about this, with the headline: "The US coal industry's future could be to mine rare-earth metals for wind turbines." Subhead: "Renewed Digging."

The article states: "There are three known ways coal could be a source of rare-earth metals: Burning away hydrocarbons in coal leaves behind ash that is rich in metals, which can be extracted using chemical processes. Metal-rich parts of the total rock removed from the earth during coal mining can be manually separated out. Acid mine drainage can selectively remove rare-earth metals from coal. The process can occur naturally in mines that are rich in sulfur (which many coal mines tend to be) when water leaches out through the mines into rivers. If captured, the seepage can then be processed to separate metals. But right now, none of these techniques are economically feasible. In 2015, the US energy department set aside $20 million for projects to figure out how to lower the cost of recovering rare-earth metals from coal. Since then, the scientific community has already made some progress towards that goal."[87]

So, civilization destroys the land for coal, then it destroys the land for wind turbines, then it destroys the land to store the energy from wind turbines. Any questions?

---

[87] Akshat Rathi, "The US coal industry's future could be to mine rare-earth metals for wind turbines," *Quartz*, June 15, 2017.

We're not going to talk much about passive-solar thermal storage, where during the day you store heat in some medium, then release this heat at night to warm a building. That's an important form of energy storage used more or less forever by living beings, but it's not crucial to this discussion since it won't power an economy.

The concept behind the more active thermal-energy storage used for powering an economy is simple: when there's excess energy in the grid, use it to heat storage materials like molten salt or concrete blocks; then when you need energy, use the heat to boil water, then use the steam to spin a turbine and generate power.

The most common form of thermal-energy storage in "green" energy is molten salt, used in solar power "tower" facilities to store power for nighttime and cloudy periods. In these power plants, pipes carry salt to the top of the tower, where concentrated sunlight from mirrors heats it to about 1000°F. The salt is pumped down to a "hot tank," then stored. When power is needed, water is pumped through a heat exchanger alongside the hot salt till it boils, then used to drive a steam turbine to generate electricity. The salt cools to about 550 degrees and is pumped back up the tower to be reheated.[88]

Like most modern technologies, what sounds simple in theory requires in practice a complex industrial infrastructure. The molten salt method requires heavily insulated steel pipes and holding tanks, pumps, steam turbines, a water supply, and the salt mixture itself. At any commercial-scale power plant, these elements are massive. In southern Spain, for example, the 20 MW Gemasolar concentrated-solar power plant (the first commercial-scale power

---

[88] "How It Works: Molten Salt Plant," Power Generation, eSolar.

plant to use molten salt) uses two steel tanks, each 35 feet tall and 75 feet across, to hold 8,700 tons of molten salt.[89]

From an engineering standpoint, there's at least one major problem with molten salt as an energy storage medium: if it cools enough to begin solidifying, it gunks up the pipes. This means power plants using molten salt have to be outfitted with heating systems to reheat the salt in tanks and pipes if it gets too cool. The Gemasolar facility, for example, has 12 kilometers of mineral-insulated heating cable, probes, and insulation, with layers of redundancy.[90]

Let's follow the supply chain for these cables. Mineral-insulated heating cables are made of copper or kumanal (an alloy of copper, manganese, and aluminum) conductors in the center; a thick layer of magnesium oxide (MgO) insulation; a sheath made of copper or cupro-nickel; and sometimes an outer sheath of high-density polyethylene, an oil-derived thermoplastic.[91]

Magnesium is used in a wide variety of "green technologies" from prototype batteries to lightweight steel alloys.

Magnesium mining is conducted in typical strip-mining fashion, with massive machines chewing away at the land. Liaoning Province in northeastern China is the magnesium capital of the world, with about 85 percent of China's production (more than two thirds of world production). Hundreds of magnesium processing facilities have left the landscape devastated. One report found 70 percent of air pollution in the region came from magnesium production, which is surprising since this area is also a major center

---

[89] Gonzalo Azcarraga, "Evaluating the effectiveness of molten salt storage with solar plants," Torresol Energy.

[90] Jason Deign, "Molten salt: how to avoid the big freeze," *CSP Today*, December 21, 2012.

[91] "Mineral Insulated Heating Cable," KME.

for iron and steel, oil and gas, and a range of other heavy industries.[92] About 300 square miles of soils in Liaoning are completely covered with magnesium "crusts."[93]

MgO production is "extremely energy intensive," with MgO furnaces operating at 1300-3600°F, heated almost exclusively by natural gas, petroleum coke, and fuel oil.[94] Pollutants released by magnesium processing include sulfur hexafluoride (the potent greenhouse gas also released during solar panel production), hydrochloric acid, carbon monoxide, and dioxin.[95]

The magnesium industries in Liaoning have promised to clean up (and we all know we can trust industries when they make promises like that), but real-time pollution monitoring shows "unhealthy" or "very unhealthy" air quality across the province.[96]

The next green energy storage method is compressed air, where you pump air deep underground into a salt cavern, until it's highly pressurized, like in a SCUBA tank. Then, when you need energy, you release the air, which turns turbines.

As of fall 2015, there are only two major compressed air energy storage facilities operating in the world; one at McIntosh, Alabama, and the other in Huntorf, Germany. Both are located above salt

---

[92] "Factories changed for environment," China Education and Research Network, December 2001.

[93] Lei Wang et al., "Magnesium contamination in soil at a magnesite mining region of Liaoning province, China," *Bulletin of Environmental Contamination and Toxicology* 95, no. 1 (July 2015), 90–96.

[94] "Reference document on the best available techniques in the cement, lime, and magnesium oxide manufacturing industries," Joint Research Center/Institute for Prospective Technological Studies, May 2010.

[95] "It's Elemental: Magnesium," Environmental Literacy Council.

[96] "Air pollution in Liaoning: Real-time air quality index visual map," *World Air Quality Index*.

caverns more than 1,000 feet underground, and larger than 10 million cubic feet.

Here's where the narrative starts to fall apart: Both of these facilities are powered partially by natural gas, because the compressed air alone isn't enough to get the turbines spinning to regenerate power. Instead of turning the turbines directly, the compressed air coming out of the salt cavern is fed into a combustion chamber and natural gas is added. When the mixture is burnt, it creates superheated air that drives turbines to generate power.

Like other energy storage facilities, these facilities are inefficient. The McIntosh plant, which was brought online in 1991, uses 0.82 kWh of electricity to store one kWh worth of air in the salt cavern, then also requires natural gas equivalent to about 1.2 kWh. In total, this brings the facilities efficiency to less than 50 percent; more than half of the energy input is lost.[97]

The Department of Energy (DOE) website about the McIntosh facility has more of the creative accounting we've all come to expect. "Compared to conventional combustion turbines, the CAES-fed system ... uses only 30 percent to 40 percent of the natural gas." This, of course, is a remarkably dishonest comparison, since McIntosh is an energy-*storage* facility, not an energy-*generation* facility.

In any case, the main purpose of McIntosh (and all energy storage facilities) isn't to reduce carbon emissions or reduce the amount of fossil fuels that are burnt, but rather to balance the load on the utility companies.

Here's another way to describe it: utilities build energy storage facilities to save costs and keep the price of electricity down by avoiding having to build whole new power plants to meet peak power demands; this is called "peak shaving." The DOE couldn't

---

[97] "History of first U.S. compressed-air energy storage (CAES) plant (110 MW 26h): Volume 2: Construction," Electric Power Research Institute, April 1994.

be more explicit about this: "The key function of the [McIntosh] facility is for peak shaving."[98]

The Huntorf plant in Germany is a similar design, also based on natural gas and with a peak-shaving function, but was built earlier, in 1978, and has an even lower efficiency at only 42 percent.[99]

All of this has, as usual, a great big nothing whatsoever to do with saving the planet.

To be fair, green technology enthusiasts argue that CAES will improve; that the electricity required to pump air into salt caverns (which, at Huntorf and McIntosh is mostly from nuclear power and coal) will be replaced by wind and solar, and that new technologies will increase the efficiency of CAES. Adiabatic compressed air energy storage, for example, captures the waste heat generated when air is compressed and uses that heat to replace natural gas during the energy recovery phase. Isothermal CAES is another more efficient method that eliminates the need for natural gas. Both of these methods are unproven at commercial scales, although the first major adiabatic system was scheduled to come online in Germany in 2019 (courtesy of RWE Power, operator of 12 gas and coal-fired power plants). Other compressed-air energy-storage technologies are in the works too; LightSail Energy corporation, for example, is developing a method that uses modular and mobile storage tanks made out of carbon fiber to store compressed air rather than relying on underground caverns. A new CAES facility came online in 2019 in Ontario, Canada. This facility is smaller, more efficient— only losing about a third of its power through inefficiencies—and it doesn't require natural gas. But it's still just the third CAES project

---

[98] "McIntosh CAES Plant," Department of Energy Global Energy Storage Database, October 27, 2014.

[99] "Kraftwerk Huntorf," Department of Energy Global Energy Storage Database, February 17, 2014.

in the world, and it is tiny in the scale of energy storage. It only stores enough power for 2,000 homes for five hours.[100]

These new technologies won't offset the fundamentally destructive nature of this process. Like pumped hydropower, compressed-air energy storage is dependent on huge infrastructure projects. Utility scale projects that can deliver tens or hundreds of megawatts are generally $100 million projects. When it comes to infrastructure, more cost means more energy use, more complex engineering, and more material inputs. The infrastructure for compressed air of any sort is complex and polluting; you can't make a carbon-fiber storage tank without a global economy, and without fossil fuels. Building the McIntosh facility, for example, required drilling to the salt cavern 2,650 feet underground—using methods and equipment borrowed from the oil and gas industry—then pumping in fresh water to dissolve the salt, and finally pumping out the resulting saline brine (that has to be disposed of somewhere). About 50 gallons of fresh water are required to clear out each cubic foot in a salt cavern, which means that nearly 1 billion gallons of water were required to clear the 19.8 million-cubic-foot chamber at McIntosh. Aboveground, construction for the facility included a fuel oil unloading station and storage tank, a lubricant/hydraulic oil storage area, a transformer, a cooling tower, a gas compressor shed, an electrical building, a substation for electricity and another for natural gas, a 148-ton motor/generator unit, a diesel tank, and some two dozen other buildings, towers, and major components.

That's sustainable, right?

Pumped air energy storage doesn't make sense without being connected to a regional grid. The components can't be created (or maintained) without a global economy, which means they can't be

---

[100] Colin Butler, "How an old Goderich salt mine could one day save you money on your hydro bill," *CBC News*, November 24, 2019.

created (or maintained) without mining, which means that they can't be created (or maintained) without destroying the planet. Like every other form of industrial-energy storage, compressed air is a reasonable social decision only if you accept the fundamental bright green lie: that the health of the natural world is less important than maintaining industrial civilization.

There's no circumventing the fact that these energy-storage technologies are fundamentally destructive. And they're dependent on a global supply chain and advanced manufacturing technologies that, themselves, are fundamentally destructive.

Machines making machines making machines; and while more and more hyperbolic green headlines are written, the planet is being killed. The green economy envisioned by the likes of Mark Jacobson is impossible without a major expansion in energy storage. And industrial-energy storage is impossible without further destroying the planet. Again and again, the policies and technologies promoted by bright greens do the opposite of their purported goal.

Chapter 7

EFFICIENCY

In the past man has been first.

In the future the system must be first.[1]

—FREDERICK WINSLOW TAYLOR

Through the green economy an attempt is being made to tech-
nologize, financialize, privatize, and commodify all of the earth's
resources and living processes.[2]

—VANDANA SHIVA

In 2007, Google began to invest heavily in "renewable" energy technology, especially in startups and research. Their goal was to generate electricity more cheaply than could a coal-fired power plant, and to do so within a few years.

In 2011, the project was shut down.

Two Google renewable energy engineers who worked on the project, Ross Koningstein and David Fork (each of whom holds

---

[1] Frederick Winslow Taylor, *Principles of Scientific Management* (New York: Harper & Brothers, 1911), 7.

[2] *Earth at Risk* press release. Fertile Ground Institute for Social and Environmental Justice, 2014.

a PhD from Stanford), later stated they "came to the conclusion that even if Google and others had led the way toward a wholesale adoption of renewable energy, that switch would not have resulted in significant reductions of carbon dioxide emissions."

In other words, they'd realized that the premise of their work—that cheap green energy would significantly reduce emissions—was false.

They explained further: "Trying to combat climate change exclusively with today's renewable energy technologies simply won't work.... Our study's best-case scenario modeled our most optimistic assumptions about cost reductions in solar power, wind power, energy storage, and electric vehicles. In this scenario, the United States would cut greenhouse gas emissions dramatically: Emissions could be 55 percent below the business-as-usual projection for 2050. While a large cut in emissions sure sounded good, this scenario still showed substantial use of natural gas in the electricity sector. That's because today's renewable energy sources are limited by suitable geography and their own intermittent power production. Wind farms, for example, make economic sense only in parts of the country with strong and steady winds. The study also showed continued fossil fuel use in transportation, agriculture, and construction. Even if our best-case scenario were achievable, we wondered: Would it really be a climate victory?"

They continued, "Even if every renewable energy technology advanced as quickly as imagined and they were all applied globally, atmospheric CO_2 levels wouldn't just remain above 350 ppm; they would continue to rise exponentially due to continued fossil fuel use.... Those calculations cast our work at Google's RE<C program in a sobering new light. Suppose for a moment that it had achieved the most extraordinary success possible, and that we had found cheap renewable energy technologies that could gradually replace

all the world's coal plants—a situation roughly equivalent to the energy innovation study's best-case scenario. Even if that dream had come to pass, it still wouldn't have solved climate change. This realization was frankly shocking: Not only had RE<C failed to reach its goal of creating energy cheaper than coal, but that goal had not been ambitious enough to reverse climate change."[3]

And yet bright green energy enthusiasts, liberal politicians, business leaders, and major nonprofits, along with the millions of ordinary people they've duped, continue to promote green energy as the solution to global warming.

While the Google engineers do suggest reforestation as a partial answer to global warming, their primary hope seems to be the technological equivalent of wishing upon a star: "technologies [that] haven't been invented yet."

Part of the foundation of any plan for a green economy is "efficiency." Again, we could have predicted these headlines: "EVs Will Save the World (With Help From Energy Efficiency & Renewables),"[4] "Save

---

[3] Ross Koningstein and David Fork, "What It Would Really Take to Reverse Climate Change: Today's renewable energy technologies won't save us. So what will?" *IEEE Spectrum*, November 18, 2014.
[4] James Fenton, "EVs Will Save the World (With Help From Energy Efficiency & Renewables)," *Clean Technica*, November 28, 2016.

Energy, Save the World,"[5] and "Save the World by Saving Energy in Your Home."[6]

As part of his "100 percent clean energy transition," Mark Jacobson calls for a 40 percent improvement in overall energy efficiency in the global economy. The word *efficiency* appears 33 times in his widely applauded 16-page Energy Policy article from 2010.[7] The word *nature* appears not at all. We've seen some of the problems with other parts of his plan. What about efficiency?

Here's a question that gets to the heart of the efficiency question: Which scenario would cause less harm to the planet: all cars traveling 100 miles per gallon of gasoline or all cars traveling one mile per gallon?

Jacobson rests comfortably (in the driver's seat of his $100,000 Tesla Roadster) in the more-miles-per-unit-of-energy club. Most mainstream environmentalists, bright greens, and indeed most people in general, have by now joined him in this not-very-exclusive club. A car that gets 100 mpg is more efficient, more cost effective, more advanced. It's clearly so much better for the planet that the question seems absurd.

From the perspective of a salmon, however, or an old-growth forest, things look much different. A car that gets only one mpg would probably be far less harmful to the planet, because low efficiency creates a disincentive for driving, and indeed for the existence of cars at all.

---

[5] Kristen Brown, "Save Energy, Save the World," *Envirobites*, October 2, 2019.

[6] "Save the World by Saving Energy in Your Home," *Community Infographics*, visually by Rock Content.

[7] Mark Z. Jacobson and Mark A. Delucchi, "Providing all global energy with wind, water, and solar power, Part I: Technologies, energy resources, quantities and areas of infrastructure, and materials," *Energy Policy* 39, no. 2011 (December 2010): 1154–1169.

If you get one mpg, and gas costs $3 per gallon, you're paying three bucks a mile. Suddenly, walking starts to look a lot more attractive. For example, recently I (Derrick) drove five miles each way to eat at a wonderful taqueria, but there's no way I would have paid an extra $30 for the admittedly delicious tacos.

If every car got one mile per gallon, why would any of us buy a car in the first place? Why pay thousands of dollars for what essentially amounts to a pricey motorized wheelbarrow?

If cars are that inefficient, why build them?

Building highly efficient cars, on the other hand, reduces the cost of driving and lowers barriers to commerce. More cars will be built, and with economies of scale, the cost of each car will fall. This makes the technology accessible to more people, accelerating the cycle of production and consumption. More car sales drive car culture as a whole by creating greater need for asphalt, roads, parking lots, and so on. Suburban sprawl becomes not only feasible but inevitable. Politics follows this momentum. Government budgets shift, adding trillions of dollars in road construction to the subsidies for car manufacturers. More land is bulldozed, more factories are built, and more concrete, steel, and plastics produced. Toxins and global warming increase, and biodiversity declines.

If you value technological escalation and human mobility for those who can afford it, then 100 mpg sounds great. If, on the other hand, you value the millions of animals (more than a trillion, including insects) killed by cars each year, the mountains destroyed for mineral extraction, the habitat fragmented by roads, or the air polluted by the manufacture, distribution, operation, and disposal of cars, then one mpg—a level of efficiency that disincentivizes car culture itself—might seem a better option.

Earlier, we cited Richard York saying that for every unit of green energy brought online, only a tenth as much fossil-fuel generated electricity is taken offline. He's a sociologist and co-author of *The Ecological Rift: Capitalism's War on the Earth*, and author of articles with titles like, "Do Alternative Energy Sources Displace Fossil Fuels?" (spoiler: no) and "Choking on Modernity: A Human Ecology of Air Pollution" (spoiler: yes, we are). In an interview, he told us: "Efficiency sets in motion certain models of development that can have unintended consequences.... Look at whaling. It was the main source of oil for lamps for a long time. But whaling expanded after the rise of petroleum oil, not because there was a demand for whale oil but because fossil fuels expanded the reach and effectiveness of the whaling fleets. Then the whalers found markets in which to sell their whale oil. Production drove demand."

A core reason technological efficiency is harmful to the land is that low efficiency limits growth. For example, in desert regions such as Las Vegas, there isn't enough water to keep building new homes and businesses indefinitely, and real estate without water is monetarily almost worthless. As long as the number of households remains the same, efficiency might be good for the land, since greater efficiency means less water taken for use by humans. But that isn't what happens. Instead of reducing overall water demand, efficiency in arid areas frees up water for new subdivisions, leading to more urban sprawl and habitat destruction. As before, all the water is stolen for human use, only now the situation is worse than it would have been otherwise.

The efficiency of American homes tells the same story. Between 1970 and 2014, American homes became almost a third more energy efficient, but average house size grew by 28 percent. The average home today uses the same amount of energy it did 40 years ago, but the extra size also means more embodied energy, greater material demands for construction, and more rooms to be filled with cheap Ikea furniture.[8] Did efficiency advances—in production of raw materials, labor, construction, and so on—enable the size increases, or did size increases drive a greater need for efficiency? The truth is that growth and efficiency are all wrapped together. And through all of this, the earth loses.

Productivity and efficiency go together outside of individual home construction, too. In business, increased efficiency lowers costs and raises profits. Since businesses in capitalism have a growth imperative, a portion of the profits or savings from any efficiency increase will be reinvested in growth. On a macroeconomic scale, increased efficiency *leads directly* to growth.

Economists have understood this since at least 1865, when William Stanley Jevons, a British mathematician and pioneer in economic theory, published his book *The Coal Question*. This was in the midst of the industrial revolution, and the U.K.'s economy depended on coal. Coal-fired steam engines pumped water, ground grain, propelled trains and boats, excavated canals, powered factories, and dug more coal. Jevons wrote, "[Coal] is the material energy of the country—the universal aid—the factor in everything we do."[9]

Prior to the publication of *The Coal Question*, several new steam engine designs and improvements, starting with Boulton's

---

[8] Drew DeSilver, "As American homes get bigger, energy efficiency gains are wiped out," Pew Research Center, November 9, 2015.

[9] William Stanley Jevons, *The Coal Question* (London: Macmillan & Co., 1866), 14.

and Watt's improvements in the 1790s, had boosted efficiency. A key section of *The Coal Question* examined the impact of this increased efficiency on coal consumption. Jevons concluded, "The economical use of coal [will not] reduce its consumption. On the contrary, economy renders the employment of coal more profitable, and thus the present demand for coal is increased."

This is crucial: *Increased efficiency not only doesn't generally reduce demand, but instead increases it.* This is called "the rebound effect," and we see it all the time.

Total global energy use by human beings has been increasing for at least the several hundred years for which data is available, and almost certainly for 10,000 years, since the beginning of civilization. During this time, the efficiency with which human civilizations use both energy and materials has also risen more or less steadily. Today, farms feed 10 times as many people per acre as in early agricultural societies. Has that increase in efficiency meant less land under cultivation or, instead, greater population? Of course, it's the latter. Likewise, has the increase in water-use efficiency meant more water left in rivers, or more land under irrigation? Of course, once again, it's the latter. Has the near doubling in automobile fuel efficiency standards over the last 40 years meant less gasoline is burned? Of course not.

Efficiency has risen in production, too. Early factories were powered by mills or steam engines, with this power then transmitted through mechanical straps, gears, and shafts that were only about 25 percent efficient: three-quarters of the energy was lost to friction.[10] Later, these mechanical systems were replaced by DC electric lines powering motors, then the more efficient AC. Today, electrical transmission and distribution in the U.S. results in only

---

[10] Kris De Decker, "The mechanical transmission of power: endless rope drives," *Low Tech Magazine*, March 2013.

about a 10 percent loss in energy.[11] New high-voltage direct current (HVDC) cables are being used to carry power long distances with even greater efficiency. In the near future, superconducting power lines may reduce transmission losses to almost zero. Has that increase in electrical transmission efficiency meant less electrical generation? Of course not.

The trend has remained constant for hundreds (and probably thousands) of years. As efficiency has increased, so has total energy use.[12]

One reason that efficiency gains are regularly wiped out by growth is capitalism's constant creation of new markets. For example, look at marijuana. Since legalization in Colorado, Oregon, and Washington, indoor pot growing—which is remarkably energy intensive—has become a major consumer of energy. An indoor grow system for just four plants uses as much electricity as 29 refrigerators. In Colorado, half of all growth in electricity demand between 2012 and 2014 was from grow-ops. In Portland, Oregon, new projects coming online in 2015 caused seven power outages. The industry's energy use can be expected to continue rising, as California, Massachusetts, Nevada, and Maine all legalized marijuana in November 2016. Analysts predict that within a few years

---

[11] Jordan Wirfs-Brock, "Lost in transmission: how much electricity disappears between a power plant and your plug?" *Inside Energy*, November 6, 2015. Site visited 07/26/2016.

[12] Many bright greens pretend the Jevons Paradox is bunk, but their refutations rely on vast oversimplifications—essentially looking at small parts of the global economy in isolation. By separating a single minor portion of the global economy (such as air conditioners) for their analysis, they distort the focus of the Jevons Paradox. In the 1860s, coal was core to the British economy. In an increasingly globalized, integrated world, the Jevons Paradox can't be applied in isolation. Its lessons are systemic. Yes; in isolation, energy efficiency can lead to lower proximal energy use. But there is no isolation in today's economy.

the indoor weed industry will use as much electricity as data centers (neither of which existed as significant industries just 50 years ago).[13] It already uses 1 percent of electricity across the entire United States.

This is where energy from efficiency, wind farms, and solar panels will be going: to new and expanding industries like growing marijuana.

Here's the Jevons Paradox at work. Let's say you're a small grower in northern California, home to the best marijuana in the world. Let's say your lights cost you $1,000 per month in electricity; and your other expenses (e.g. fertilizers, pots, soil, and so on) run another $1,000 a month, not including your own labor. Let's say you grow three pounds of marijuana per month, which you sell for $2,000 per lb.[14] Income: $6,000. Expenses: $2,000. You make a decent living at $4,000 a month. But now the new Miracle-Brite™ Light, which will provide the same lumens for $500 a month, comes on the market. You have a choice. One option is that you put that $500 a month toward purchasing second-growth forest to allow it to regrow, become habitat for nonhumans, and sequester carbon. Or you could be a capitalist, double the size of your scene, grow six pounds per month at a cost of $3,000, and make $9,000 a month. You could even use all that extra money as a down payment on a Tesla.

Thus, an increase in lighting efficiency leads to an increase in fossil fuel use to make fertilizers and other associated items. And

---

[13] Melanie Sevcenko, "Pot is power hungry: why the marijuana industry's energy footprint is growing," *The Guardian*, February 27, 2016.
[14] With legalization, the wholesale price has dropped dramatically, but the point remains.

since the marginal cost of growing marijuana has decreased, you may as well triple or quadruple your grow scene and really rake in the money, thus increasing use of electricity as well.

The Jevons Paradox obviously applies not just to energy use. A 2017 article in *MIT News,* entitled "Study: Technological progress alone won't stem resource use: Researchers find no evidence of an overall reduction in the world's consumption of materials," discussed a Massachusetts Institute of Technology-led study that "gathered data for 57 common goods and services, including widely used chemical components such as ammonia, formaldehyde, polyester fiber, and styrene, along with hardware and energy technologies such as transistors, laser diodes, crude oil, photovoltaics, and wind energy. They worked the data for each product into their equation, and, despite seeing technological improvements in almost all cases, they failed to find a single case in which dematerialization—an overall reduction in materials—was taking place. In follow-up work, the researchers were eventually able to identify six cases in which an absolute decline in materials usage has occurred. However, these cases mostly include toxic chemicals such as asbestos and thallium, whose dematerialization was due not to technological advances, but to government intervention. There was one other case in which researchers observed dematerialization: wool. The material's usage has significantly fallen, due to innovations in synthetic alternatives, such as nylon and polyester fabrics. In this case, Magee argues that substitution, and not dematerialization, has occurred. In other words, wool has simply been replaced by another material to fill the same function."

One of the lead authors notes, "There is a techno-optimist's position that says technological change will fix the environment. This [study] says, probably not."[15]

I (Max) am walking in a forest, near the coast of Washington. I come to a broad meadow. Endangered Makah copper butterflies live here. Labrador tea grows in acidic boggy soil. Cedar waxwings gather huckleberries from tall shrubs. Many threatened and sensitive plant species, including Alaska plantain, Vancouver groundcone, swamp gentian, and goldthread live here, too.

The land begins to slope down, and the forest closes back in. The soil is moist, even now in the heart of summer. Skunk cabbages and beargrass grow on either side of the path. I smell the ocean. I hear sea lions barking. The trail is steeper now. After passing through thickets of salal and nettle, I step out of the forest and onto the beach. Rocky, forested islands rise in the offshore mist. The water is still. A heron wades in the tide. Seaweed lies in great mounds, where winter storms piled it.

This place is still rich in life, even in the midst of the biotic cleansing that has been underway for centuries here, millennia around the world. I cannot imagine how fecund it was in the past.

This is Makah land; the word Makah means "generous with food."

I turn north, and after a time come to the site of an old Makah village. According to their histories, the Makah lived here since the beginning of time. Scientists can carbon-date their existence here to at least 2,500 years ago, and likely 8,000 or more. And if you believe Vine Deloria Jr. and some new archeology, human

---

[15] Jennifer Chu, "Study: Technological progress alone won't stem resource use: Researchers find no evidence of an overall reduction in the world's consumption of materials," *MIT News*, January 19, 2017.

habitation of the West Coast may be much, much older. Whatever you believe, the Makah lived here a long time.

A slow mudslide destroyed the village around 275 years ago; the people survived, but most families moved elsewhere. The village was finally abandoned in the 1930s when it became illegal to keep children out of school, and the last Makah occupants were forced to move to Neah Bay.

Now, the bluff where the village stood is mostly overgrown. A cedar longhouse built in the 1980s stands as a memorial to the site. Winter storms are slowly eroding the soil of the bluff, exposing layers of history.

I pick my way across driftwood toward the hillside. Shells and small bones are exposed here and there. I spot two whale bones, barely visible, caked in dirt. I look closer and see a vertebra three feet across, and a fin bone with a triangular cross-section.

The Makah were one of a few nations in this region to hunt whales, rowing in cedar canoes to harpoon Gray and Humpback whales, then attaching seal-skin floats and towing their bodies to the village through cold Pacific swells. A single hunt could feed the village for weeks.

The Makah used each part of a whale: oil for rendering, meat for food, bone and sinew for tools, gut for storage containers. Even "trash" served a purpose; bones discarded nearby fed minerals to the trees and served as chews for mammals.

You could call this "efficiency," but the term doesn't fit. A better alternative might be "diversity."

In the natural world, diversity is a functional counterpoint to the industrial idea of efficiency. Most natural communities, looked at in parts, are not efficient at all. Grizzly bears, for example, often eat only the fattiest parts of salmon, leaving behind the rest. But because natural communities have evolved around diversity and not efficiency, there are thousands of other beings—trees, shrubs, mosses, beetles, slugs, coyotes, wolves, eagles, ravens, and so on—who eat the remainder of the salmon. The strength of the community comes not from its efficiency—its ability, to use the dictionary definition, to "achieve maximum productivity with minimum wasted effort or expense"—but from its diversity.

If we're going to talk about capitalism's obsession with efficiency and productivity, we need to talk about Frederick Winslow Taylor.

Born to a wealthy Philadelphia family in 1856, Taylor was from childhood fixated on efficiency. A boyhood friend noted that Taylor would "endeavor to discover the step which would cover the greatest distance with the least expenditure of energy; or the easiest method of vaulting a fence; the right length and proportions of a walking staff." At 17, Taylor went to work at Enterprise Hydraulic Works, a factory that made steam-powered pumps and machinery. He became obsessed with the contrast between the efficient precision of machinery and the wasteful fallibility of human beings. As one history notes, "The industrial revolution had ushered in a new era of technology [, but] the management structures that held everything in place had not changed since the days of artisans, small shops, and guilds: knowledge was largely rule of thumb, acquired through tips and tricks that would trickle down to aspiring craftsmen over the course of long apprenticeships." As Taylor wrote, this was highly inefficient; "It had no scientific basis."

Taylor didn't hide his contempt for workers. In his 1911 book *The Principles of Scientific Management*, he describes the average laborer as "so stupid and phlegmatic that he more nearly resembles in his mental make-up the ox than any other type.... He is so stupid that the word 'percentage' has no meaning to him, and he must consequently be trained by a man more intelligent than himself into the habit of working in accordance with the laws of this science before he can be successful."[16]

And Taylor saw himself as that more intelligent man. For the next 25 years, he worked relentlessly to "train" the "oxen." "Armed with a pen, a ledger, and a stopwatch, Taylor hovered over workers on the shop floor, timing every procedure, tweaking their actions, and timing again. He hired an assistant to catalogue the duration of every variant of every procedure. Determined to be as 'scientific' as possible in his optimizing, he followed the reductionist impulses of classical mechanics, breaking every job down to its most granular elements."[17] Based on these measurements, Taylor would prescribe a new set of procedures for each worker, laying out the most efficient actions they should take to carry out their job and time requirements that must be met. Employees who didn't meet the required speed would be fired.

The results were, for the capitalists, astonishing. "The cost of overhauling boilers dropped from $62 (around $2,000 today) to $11; machining a tire could now be done in one-fifth of the previous time; making a cannon projectile now took just ninety minutes instead of ten hours; 1,200 could now do work that would have taken 2,000 people at any other company."[18]

Taylor put in place similar procedures in hundreds of businesses. Scientific management overran the nation, then the world, moving from factories into government, schools, and private homes. "Best practices" for everything—from the best way to lay brick, to the

---

[16] Frederick Winslow Taylor, *Principles of Scientific Management* (New York: Harper & Bros., 1911).

[17] Stanley McChrystal, *Team of Teams: New Rules of Engagement for a Complex World* (New York: Penguin, 2015).

[18] Ibid.

correct way to insert paper into a typewriter, to the most efficient way to sit at a desk—became standardized.

Please note that these increases in productivity did not lead to increases in leisure (which Jevons could have predicted)—as in the laborers doing their jobs in less time and then going home to have fun with their families—but rather to increases in profits and production. For bosses, it was a revelation. But for workers and for the planet, it was a disaster.

Workers who had been trained in a more human workplace, where attitude and experience were valued more highly than raw productivity, went on strike. Managers fired them en masse, since the new standardized procedures meant even skilled workers could be replaced by a smaller force of cheaper unskilled laborers.

It's hard to overstate the influence of Taylor and his "disciples." Scientific management deeply influenced American capitalism and shaped Lenin's economic approach in Soviet Russia. Management expert Peter Drucker ranked Taylor with Freud and Darwin as some of the most influential people who have ever lived. Journalist Ida Tarbell called him "one of the few creative geniuses of our time."[19]

Historian Robert Kanigel wrote, "It could seem that all of modern society had [by the late 1920s] come under the sway of a single commanding idea: that waste was wrong and efficiency the highest good."[20]

Taylor, a devout Quaker, believed that his efficiency programs would abolish class divisions by raising wages and enabling more efficient production of goods that could be distributed fairly and cheaply. He was, of course, dead wrong. Just like efficiency doesn't reduce overall consumption, it doesn't abolish class divisions.

---

[19] Ibid.
[20] Ibid.

"In my judgement," Taylor wrote, "the best possible measure of the height in the scale of civilization to which any people has arisen is its productivity."[21]

When you're working for the most powerful businesses in the world, it makes sense to say this. Productivity is what leads nations and corporations to power. Productivity is what manufactures guns, drives factories, enables more resource-extraction from more colonies.

Whether they admit it or not, most bright greens—and others who value production over life on the planet, those who are trying to save civilization and its industrial production even as it grinds away at life—agree with Taylor's comment above. Productivity does lead to further "progress," and "progress" defines civilization.

Taylor's conceit is a common failing. As the great Chickasaw writer Linda Hogan said, "Progress is a sort of madness that is a god to people. Decent people commit horrible crimes that are acceptable because of progress."

Including, clearly, the murder of the planet.

The results of Taylorism are entirely predictable: efficiency leads to profit, profit leads to growth, and more money goes to managers, owners, and stockholders, not to the poor. Industries expand. The middle class grows, but only in the heart of empire. More forests fall, more mountains are mined, more products are manufactured.

---

[21] Ibid.

Let's talk about lightbulbs, which have, like many other technologies, followed a trend of increasing efficiency, complexity, and embodied energy.

Until recently, most lightbulbs were incandescent and worked by running electricity through a small wire filament that heats and glows.

Incandescent light bulbs are remarkably destructive, in part because the wire filaments are made of tungsten. Most ores contain less than 1.5 percent tungsten, so a huge amount of rock must be mined for a small amount of tungsten.[22] Tungsten mines produce pollution containing arsenic[23], mercury[24], thallium[25], and other heavy metals.[26] Tungsten itself is a poison. Until 2009, it was thought to be almost entirely benign. But new research has found that tungsten reacts with other compounds and moves through bodies quite readily, interfering with basic processes of metabolism shared by all life.[27]

---

[22] "Tungsten mining and beneficiation," International Tungsten Industry Association, 2011.

[23] Chuan-ping Liu et al., "Arsenic contamination and potential health risk implications at an abandoned tungsten mine, southern China," *Environmental Pollution* 158, no. 3 (March 2010): 820–826.

[24] Wenjie Lin et al., "Heavy metal contamination and environmental concerns on orchard at abandoned tungsten mine, southern China," *Applied Mechanics and Materials*, vols. 295–298 (2013), 1609–1614.

[25] Hongguang Cheng et al., "Thallium, arsenic, and mercury contamination of soil near the World's largest and longest-operating tungsten mine," *Polish Journal of Environmental Studies* 22, no. 1 (2013), 301–305.

[26] Myung Chae Jung and Iain Thornton, "Heavy metal contamination in soils and plants around a copper-tungsten mine in South Korea," *Environmental Geochemistry and Health* (1994) 16:92.

[27] "Surprising new health and environmental concerns about tungsten," *ScienceDaily*, January 19, 2009.

In 1995, Compact Fluorescent Lamp (CFL) lightbulbs were introduced as the successor to incandescent bulbs. Although they're more energy efficient than incandescent bulbs, they're still artifacts of the same extractive paradigm.

CFL bulbs have two main parts. The first is an electronic "ballast," a small circuit board that includes a capacitor, transistors, and a diode bridge. These components regulate the flow of electricity through the second main part of the lamp, which is a gas-filled tube. When you flick the switch, electricity flows through this gas, causing it to glow.

CFLs, like any new industrial technology, have created a whole new class of problems. Perhaps the most serious is that the bulbs contain between two and five milligrams of mercury. Even in small amounts, mercury is extremely toxic. If a CFL lightbulb breaks, the Environmental Protection Agency recommends a multistep cleaning process that includes treating the materials as toxic waste.

Years ago, when I (Max) lived in Bellingham, Washington, my friends and I attended Toastmasters—a sort of training club for public speaking—to practice speaking about political resistance. Most of the attendees were aspiring politicians or businesspeople wearing secondhand blazers. With our political t-shirts and youthful faces, we were the oddballs of the group. For several months we'd rise at 6:00 a.m.—a nearly impossible task for people in their early 20s—to attend the meetings held on the north side of town. Each week, a few members would stand and give brief speeches in front of the group, and we'd grade them and provide feedback. One week, a woman in her early 30s stood to make her speech. She told us how she'd wanted to save money on electricity and "go green," so she bought CFL bulbs for her house. One day, she came home to find that a lamp in her infant son's room had fallen to the floor and the bulb had shattered. She found him playing on the carpet among the fragments of the bulb. He wasn't cut, so she didn't think much of it. She cleaned up the broken glass, threw it out, and replaced the bulb. In the weeks after the accident, her son began to behave strangely, so she took him to the doctor, who told her that her son had mercury poisoning. There was no treatment. Her son had developed serious brain damage. As she told the story all those years later, she was shaking with grief and anger.

Vaporized mercury can cause mood swings, nervousness, irritability, emotional changes, insomnia, headaches, muscle twitches and atrophy, tremors, weakness, and, to use the distancing language of toxicology, "decreased cognitive functions." Higher levels of exposure cause kidney and respiratory damage and death.[28] Mercury is especially toxic to pregnant mothers and infants.

Mercury is also found in various other lightbulbs, including most fluorescent bulbs, black lights, cold-cathode bulbs, metal and ceramic metal halide bulbs, high pressure sodium bulbs, mercury short-arc bulbs, and neon bulbs.

In response to critiques of CFL lightbulbs because of their mercury content, some environmentalists have made the reasonable argument that using CFL lightbulbs reduces overall mercury pollution, most of which comes from burning coal for electricity. According to some estimates, the average incandescent bulb in the U.S. creates about 10 milligrams of mercury pollution over five years via burning coal. A CFL, because of higher efficiency, is responsible for only about six milligrams, even when you include the mercury in the bulb.[29]

Would you prefer six milligrams of deadly poison, or 10 milligrams?

---

[28] Charles Patrick Davis, "Mercury Poisoning," *eMedicineHealth*, December 17, 2015.
[29] Michael Graham Richard, "What about mercury from compact fluorescents?" *Treehugger*, June 17, 2005.

Apparently, there's no other option.

Critiques of CFL lightbulbs are largely moot, because the bulbs are rapidly being superseded by the next-generation lighting technology: LEDs, or Light Emitting Diodes. The average LED requires one-tenth the electricity of an incandescent bulb for a given brightness, and perhaps a third of a CFL bulb. They're also much more durable than incandescent bulbs or CFLs. So, LEDs are considered the "holy grail" of sustainable lighting technology. The U.S. Department of Energy says LED lighting "has the potential to fundamentally change the future of lighting in the United States."[30] The editors of the website *Treehugger* describe LED bulbs as one of their "obsessions."[31] Some bright greens have suggested that LEDs are "the" solution to global warming. As if putting LED headlights on a diesel semi-tractor is really going to stop the murder of the planet. (The notion that LEDS are "the" solution to global warming is misleading anyway: only about 7 percent of U.S. electricity (which means 1.4 percent of energy is used for lighting).

LEDs work because of electroluminescence: some substances emit light when electricity passes through them. The basic principle has been understood since 1927, but early LED designs emitted only infrared. These found their way into, among other applications, remote controls, which means that the technology now lauded by the mainstream environmental movement first found commercial use in allowing people to change the channel without getting off the couch.

In 1968, Monsanto became the first company to mass produce

---

[30] "LED Lighting," U.S. Department of Energy.
[31] Lloyd Alter, "Cree revamps entire LED line of better bulbs," *Treehugger*, September 13, 2016.

LEDs. It wasn't until the early 2000s that white LEDs became available, making standard lighting applications possible. Today, they're taking over the industry. Cities and businesses are investing millions to switch to LEDs to save money on their electricity bills. Utilities are pushing for individual renters and homeowners to make the switch by offering free or discounted LEDs. It's billed as a win-win; you get lower electric bills, the utilities save money since they don't have to generate as much power, and less fossil fuels have to be burnt, reducing the acceleration of global warming.

But as always, it's not a win for the planet. One of the things we're trying to do in this book is model the process of asking where products come from, and who is harmed by their production.

The production of LEDs is much more complex than that of incandescent and CFL bulbs. LEDs are built around a silicon chip called a "die." Each die consists of layers of high-purity crystalline semiconductor usually made from gallium arsenide, gallium phosphide, or gallium arsenide phosphide. As the name implies, two of these elemental combinations contain arsenic, a known carcinogen and environmental toxin.

These semiconductor crystals are created in much the same way as silicon wafers for solar panels. First, a high-pressure, high-temperature chamber is used to mix the ingredients of the die, turning them from solid to liquid. Liquid boron oxide is added to seal the materials together. A rod is dipped into the solution and withdrawn slowly, and the solution solidifies into a pure crystal on its surface. After the crystal is formed, the rod is sliced into thin wafers which are polished until the surface has a roughness of less than one nanometer, and it is cleaned using a variety of chemical solvents and high-frequency sound waves. At this stage, impurities must be added to produce layers with different mechanisms of conductivity. These additives include zinc, nitrogen, silicon, germanium, indium, selenium, and tellurium, each of which has its own supply chain leading back to destructive, polluting mines.

A common method of adding impurities (or doping) is called "liquid phase epitaxy." In this process, the semiconductor wafers are drawn underneath reservoirs containing the same molten base material used to form the original crystal, but with impurities added. Each time a wafer is drawn through, an additional layer of the molten material is deposited on top by a nozzle. With each pass, a different doping agent is added to achieve the desired electronic effects. The final doping step involves placing the wafers back in a high-temperature furnace and immersing them in a gas containing the final agent. This final agent is known as the "phosphor." The most common phosphor is YAG, or yttrium aluminum garnet ($Y_3Al_5O_{12}$), which is sometimes mixed with cerium or gadolinium. This is the key step in the process, since it results in LEDs that emit white light.

But we're not quite done. The final step in the creation of LED dies involves applying gold and silver compounds to the surface of the chip for attaching wires, a multistep process involving a photosensitive liquid called "photoresist" which is applied to each chip in a pattern and then baked into place in another furnace. Ultraviolet light further hardens the substance, and then the unhardened material is washed away. Next, "contact metal" can be applied. The chips are placed in a vacuum-sealed chamber, where a "chunk of [gold or silver] is heated to temperatures that cause it to vaporize." This vapor sticks to the exposed semiconductor. Now, acetone can be used to remove the photoresist, and the metal contacts which remain behind are further bonded by baking in a hydrogen/nitrogen atmosphere furnace at several hundred degrees for several hours.

The LED dies are now complete. Each wafer created in this

process may contain many individual LEDs, which now must be cut apart. Then the LEDs move to assembly, where they're heated and plasma-cleaned again to prevent them from delaminating later in the process. The chips are bonded onto metal leads, connected with tiny gold wires, and soldered in place. The final step (for real this time) involves sealing all this inside a plastic or epoxy package for durability.[32]

When manufacturing something this small and precise, a single speck of dust can ruin an entire batch of chips. Therefore, LED manufacturing takes place in "clean" facilities with sophisticated air filters and circulation systems. Production is mostly automated, with machines controlling nearly every operation. The fewer humans present, the better.

Seeing a plant, animal, fungus, or any other living being inside an LED production facility means a grievous error has taken place. A single LED production factory can also cost $100 million or more. So much for community-scale implementation.

Can you spot the environmental problems inherent in this process? Reread this description, and this time consider the supply chain of every material, and its costs to the natural world.

The bright green future is a corporate future, a centralized future, a robotic, mechanized future emerging from factories like new LED bulbs in plastic blister cases. What appears to be a simple lightbulb—flick the switch and it turns on—is the result of a long chain of industrial technologies and processes involving mining, factories, complex chemistry, robotics, research laboratories at corporate and government facilities around the world, and billions of dollars in investment. It's all tied together. LEDs would be impossible to create without globalization, imperialism, resource theft, and war.

---

[32] "Light-Emitting Diode (LED)," How Products Are Made, vol. 1, Madehow.com.

Components of LEDs are easily traced to atrocities. Yttrium, cerium, and gadolinium are rare-earth elements which naturally occur together, and they are mined in aggregate. As you may recall, the massive open-pit Bayan Obo mine near Baotou, China, is the single-largest source of rare-earth metals, and it has ruined everything nearby. Local fields can no longer grow crops, and livestock grow sick and die. One local resident told journalists that "all the families are affected by illness ... diabetes, osteoporosis, and chest problems." Many have been reduced to such poverty that selling sludge from tailings ponds to reprocessing plants is their only income.[33]

Purified yttrium, besides being used in LEDs, is also used in spark plugs, lasers, televisions, superconductors, medical devices, missile defense systems, fighter-jet engines, and fake diamonds. In the environment, yttrium is exceptionally toxic to humans and other animals. Low levels of exposure cause lung disease, while large amounts cause cyanosis—your extremities turn blue from lack of oxygenated blood—chest pain, breathing problems, and death.[34]

Cerium is known for being easy to produce. But the standards of the mining industry are probably different from yours and mine. Cerium processing begins by using hydrochloric acid to remove impurities. Then the ore is roasted in a furnace to oxidize it before a further acid treatment isolates the cerium. The process is supposedly simple, but "simple" in this case means only a few tens of millions of dollars of equipment are required, not hundreds of

---

[33] Cécile Bontron, "Rare-earth mining in China comes at a heavy cost for local villages," *The Guardian*, August 7, 2012.

[34] "Yttrium, Pocket Guide to Chemical Hazards," National Institute for Occupational Safety and Health.

millions—unless you're starting with the monazite variety of ore, which is more complex. Monazite processing involves hot concentrated sulfuric acid, sodium hydroxide (which can readily decompose proteins, lipids and living tissues), and ammonium oxalate. Further heat treatment is applied to increase the hardness of the metal, and then nitric acid can be applied to precipitate cerium oxide.

Monazite is also a common source rock for gadolinium, which besides being used for LEDs, is used in nuclear reactors (especially nuclear submarines), in fuel cells, and for nuclear medicine.

As for the LEDs themselves, their levels of copper, lead, nickel, and silver have gotten California to declare all but the low-intensity yellow diodes "hazardous."[35]

Whatever the starting ore, cerium processing produces radioactive waste containing isotopes of radium that release gamma radiation, which strikes directly at the genetic material of living beings.

Here's an excerpt from an article in *Quartz* by reporter Akshat Rathi about using algae to capture carbon from a cement factory. It begins, "Degerhamn, Sweden. As far as the eye can see, the only thing polluting our pristine environment is the gas-guzzling car I'm riding in. It's a chilly April morning in Kalmar county in southern Sweden, and as we drive past pastel-colored wooden houses separated by acres of farmland, Martin Olofsson, a researcher at Linnaeus University, tells me that only 5 percent of the electricity

---

[35] Seong-Rin Lim et al., "Potential environmental impacts of light-emitting diodes (LEDs): metallic resources, toxicity, and hazardous waste classification," *Environmental Science and Technology*, 2011, 45, 1, 320–327, December 7, 2010.

Swedes consume comes from burning fossil fuels. That's nothing compared to, say, the U.S., where two-thirds of electricity are fossil-fuel derived."

Of course, electricity is only 20 percent of total energy usage. It's not where the real action is. And keep in mind that much electricity in Sweden comes from hydro and biomass—including burning trash—which are dreadfully harmful and certainly not carbon neutral.

But there's more tomfoolery here. The only polluting thing Rathi says he can see is his car, and he mentions gas guzzling. He also calls the landscape "pristine." First, in many cases, the manufacture of cars causes more pollution than does their gasoline use, so his emphasis shouldn't be on the gas-guzzling—as if an electric car would be good for the world—but rather on the existence of the car itself. And are we co-authors the only people who can see the absurdity of saying houses and farmland crossed by roads are a "pristine environment"? I don't think the nonhumans who used to live on those farmlands would agree they're "pristine." And does this journalist really not understand embodied pollution: the pollution that comes from the fabrication of materials for the houses, and their construction and maintenance, as well as everything in those houses? And does runoff from the farms not count as pollution? Only one harm—pollution from the tailpipe—seems to count.

But we haven't even gotten to the real tomfoolery. Rathi is all excited because they're going to use algae to capture carbon dioxide from the smokestacks of a cement factory. The cement is made of limestone which comes from a local quarry. He writes, "Over the past 130 years, the cement factory has consumed huge amounts of limestone, leaving behind a flat piece of land, about 1 km (0.6 miles) in each direction, without a single tree in the expanse. As we approach the quarry, I spot a large excavator filling a haul truck—a vehicle engineered for heavy-duty mining and construction—with rubble. Every few months, Urban says, a team comes with explosives and blasts a large portion of the 10-meter-high limestone wall standing tall in front of us. The trucks then go back and forth between the quarry and the cement plant all day, almost nonstop, feeding the plant with limestone."

This is what they're excited about?

The low concentrations of sodium and potassium in this particular limestone means the cement can withstand the corrosive effects of saltwater and therefore lasts longer in the ocean. So, the cement in this environmental victory—where the only polluting thing the journalist can see is his car—is used for underwater construction.[36]

It's often said that Taylor "rationalized" the workplace. Certainly, the common definition of *rationalization*—the attempt to justify inappropriate behavior—is true, but another definition is meant here, which is to ignore or remove all considerations extraneous to the stated goal.

This is what bright greens are doing. In their quest for a (fraudulently accounted) carbon-neutrality, they ignore horrors perpetrated along the way. So, a cement factory that destroys a biome to facilitate the destruction of undersea biomes is suddenly an environmental success story. How? Simple. Ignore everything but the fact that algae are going to scrub carbon dioxide from the smokestacks. Ignore even that the algae will presumably be fed to cows or turned into fuel and burned, releasing the carbon anyway. Ignore the real world. Then the only polluting thing you'll remark is exhaust from the car you drove up in.

---

[36] Akshat Rathi, "The revolutionary technology pushing Sweden toward the seemingly impossible goal of zero emissions," *Quartz*, June 21, 2017.

That's the story we're debunking over and over in this book. That's the story of bright green lies.

What happens to LED manufacturers when everyone's sockets are full of LEDs that last 30 years? If you're in the business of making lightbulbs, this is a problem that has come up before. In 1924, several lightbulb manufacturers, including General Electric, Osram, and Philips, formed a trade cartel called Phoebus (side note: great secret cabal name). In a series of clandestine meetings, members of Phoebus decided to reduce the operational duration of their incandescent bulbs to a uniform 1,000-hour average to ensure continued healthy sales. Their scheme worked for 15 profitable years before competition forced them to improve the operational duration of their products.

Today, some LED manufacturers are moving in the same direction, deliberately reducing the operational duration of bulbs, but now it's in the open. These manufacturers are offering cheaper LEDs with substantially reduced operational duration in order to spark sales.[37]

There are other problems with LEDs. A June 2016 report from the American Medical Association found that high-brightness LED streetlights (already 10 percent of U.S. streetlights at the time the report was released) create a driving hazard. They found that LEDs emitting blue-rich light "have a five times greater impact on circadian sleep rhythms than conventional lamps" and that outdoor

---

[37] Lloyd Alter, "Cree revamps entire LED line of better bulbs," *Treehugger*, September 13, 2016.

LEDs disrupt nonhuman species who need a dark environment, including birds, insects, turtles, and fish.[38]

We're not the first to say technology doesn't solve problems created by technology. At best it displaces them.

Even leaving aside the toxic components and processes involved in the manufacture of LEDs, LEDs are a great example of what happens when you attempt to ignore the Jevons Paradox. Here's a headline: "The Switch to Outdoor LED Lighting Has Completely Backfired." The article begins, "To reduce energy consumption, many jurisdictions around the world are transitioning to outdoor LED lighting. But as new research shows, this solid-state solution hasn't yielded the expected energy savings, and potentially worse, it's resulted in more light pollution than ever before." And, "With the introduction of solid-state lighting—such as LEDs … —it was thought (and hoped) that the transition to it from conventional lighting—like electrical filaments, gas, and plasma—would result in big energy savings. According to the latest research, however, the use of LEDs has resulted in a 'rebound' effect whereby many jurisdictions have opted to use even *more* light owing to the associated energy savings."[39]

That's the Jevons Paradox.

Why is anyone surprised?

---

[38] "AMA adopts community guidance to reduce the harmful human and environmental effects of high intensity street lighting," *American Medical Association*," June 14, 2016.

[39] George Dvorsky, "The Switch to Outdoor LED Lighting Has Completely Backfired," *Gizmodo*, November 22, 2017.

What comes after LEDs? Experts say it's a technology called "laser diodes." According to some predictions, this technology could replace LEDs entirely by about 2025—which leads to this question: What's the point of making bulbs that last 30 years if they're going to be obsolete in 10?[40]

Nearly all bright greens speak of economic growth as positive, or at the very least don't speak against it. And the case for "greening the global economy" is made every day by many of these same people.

There's a book with that very title, *Greening the Global Economy*, by economist Robert Pollin. He claims economic contraction would be a disaster for the planet, because it undercuts the "necessary investments" in "green energy." Never mind the evidence that the only significant drops in greenhouse gas emissions have occurred during major depressions,[41] or that the cutting of the Amazon rainforest has declined only during recessions,[42] or that the only oceanic dead zone to recover—in the Black Sea—disappeared because of the collapse of the Soviet Union.

Given that the global economy is killing the planet, "growing the economy" will not help the planet.

Bright greens and the corporate press like to claim the economy can grow without a corresponding increase in energy usage. Joe Romm, for example, who has done important work advancing public understanding of global warming, has also written approvingly

---

[40] Christopher Mims, "Forget LED bulbs—the future of interior lighting is lasers," *Quartz*, November 13, 2013.

[41] Ben Geman, "EPA: Greenhouse gas emissions fell during recession," *The Hill*, February 23, 2011.

[42] "The economy booms, the trees vanish," *The Economist*, May 19, 2005.

that "electricity sales in [the U.S.] have been flat for nearly a decade even as the economy has kept growing."

Electricity consumption may be flat in the United States, but in the same period—2004 to 2014—annual electricity generation in China more than doubled, from 2.2 billion GWh to more than 5.6 billion GWh. Coal-fired power plants were responsible for about 75 percent of that increase.[43] Given that the U.S. annually imports about $500 billion worth of products from China, it's not a stretch to call this "pollution outsourcing." And it's not just an issue with China. Take a look at U.S. imports from Indonesia (clothing and shoes, rubber, electronics), South Korea (cars, electronics, machinery, oil, steel), Taiwan (electronics, machinery, cars, steel, plastic), and Singapore (chemicals, machinery, electronics).[44] All these nations export billions of dollars of goods to the United States, and the responsible industries are a roll call of despoilers. From 1990 to 2010, East Asian carbon emissions rose 142 percent while Southeast Asia's emissions rose 227 percent.[45] Combined emissions from Asia-Pacific nations rose another 18 percent between 2010 and 2019.[46]

Pollution outsourcing is an open secret. One article notes that "Britain, for instance, slashed domestic emissions within its own borders by one-third between 1990 and 2015. But it has done so as energy-intensive industries have migrated abroad. If you included all the global emissions produced in the course of making things like the imported steel used in London's skyscrapers and cars, then

[43] "China, People's Republic of: Electricity and Heat for 2004," *International Energy Agency*.

[44] "Countries and Regions," Office of the United States Trade Representative.

[45] Karl Lester M. Yap, "Southeast Asia burns up the ranks of global polluters," *Bloomberg*, January 13, 2016.

[46] "World carbon dioxide emissions from 2009 to 2019, by region (in million metric tons of carbon dioxide)," Statista Research & Analysis, 2020.

Britain's total carbon footprint has actually increased slightly over that time."[47] Green think-tank Heinrich Böll Foundation names "a move away from energy-intensive manufacturing towards less energy-intensive service sector work"—with the manufacturing moved elsewhere (if manufacturing is going to happen, it has to happen *somewhere*)—as one of the primary factors underlying decreasing greenhouse gas emissions in rich nations.[48]

The assumption of the bright green paradigm is that renewable energy production displaces fossil fuels energy production. This assumption underlies just about every calculation used to promote green energy.

The failure of displacement was recently quantified by Richard York, whom we've met twice so far in this book. After analyzing data from 128 nations, York found that "the average pattern ... is one where each unit of total national energy from nonfossil-fuel sources displaced less than one-quarter of a unit of fossil-fuel energy use and, focusing specifically on electricity, each unit of electricity generated by nonfossil-fuel sources displaced less than one-tenth of a unit of fossil-fuel generated electricity."[49]

Given that expansion is essential to the system, believing that new solar energy facilities can lead to the closure of coal power plants on a wide scale is a tragic misperception.

With all the world at stake, we need to be as clear as possible: new energy sources usually don't displace old; instead, new energy piles on top of the old energy sources. That extra energy is used

[47] Brad Plumer, "You've Heard of Outsourced Jobs, But Outsourced Pollution? It's Real, and Tough to Tally Up," *New York Times*, September 4, 2018.

[48] Bruce Watson, "Cutting greenhouse gas emissions won't slow global economic growth – report," *The Guardian*, September 26, 2015.

[49] Richard York, op. cit.

to "grow the system," and any opportunity for growth is not to be missed.[50]

It's not like any of this is unexpected. Below is a graph of primary (human) world energy consumption—separated by fuel type. Until about 1850, essentially all of (human) world energy consumption—excluding human and nonhuman slavery—came from burning wood. Coal use rose around that time, and total energy consumption climbed higher. Oil came next, becoming a significant energy source starting in the early 1900s, followed by natural gas and hydropower in the mid-20th century. Nuclear power was added in the 1960s.

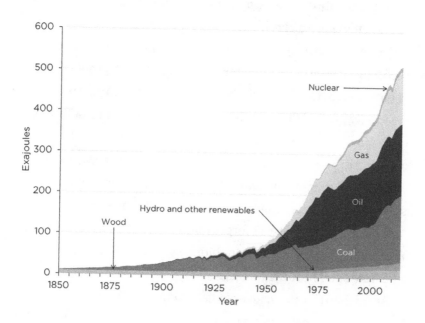

Two things about this graph are particularly important. First and most obvious is that total world energy consumption has

---

[50] Even if renewable energy displaced fossil fuels at a one-to-one ratio, something that is possible through government restrictions, the killing of the planet would still not be stopped.

risen steeply from about 15 exajoules/year in 1850 to more than 500 exajoules/year today. We are living in gluttonous times; this level of energy consumption could never be sustainable. The second important point is that despite the addition of new sources of energy throughout this period, none of the previous energy sources have ever declined significantly in total consumption. Even wood as an energy source is burned at nearly double the rate today as in 1850. And "renewables"? There has certainly been no displacement because of them. For 170 years, each new energy source has simply been added on top of the others.[51]

Adding more energy to the mix, no matter where it comes from, is not a solution. We've appropriated too much of the world's energy; it's time to give back.

In Europe, even a record increase in "renewable" energy, which you'd think would overwhelm the displacement problem, hasn't been enough to lower carbon emissions. In 2015, "renewable" electricity grew 2.5 percent to supply 29 percent of total European electricity. However, "a fall in nuclear and hydro levels, and an increase in total electricity demand, meant that fossil [fuel] generation was roughly unchanged in 2015.... German and Italian fossil generation barely moved, despite record renewables growth."[52] And of course, we mustn't forget that much of Europe's 29 percent "renewable" power comes from biomass, in part the practice of cutting down and burning forests entire.

As Richard York writes of displacement, "These results challenge conventional thinking ... they indicate that suppressing the use of fossil fuel will require changes other than simply technical

---

[51] Richard Heinberg, "Our Renewable Future: Introduction," *Museletter* #289, June 2016.
[52] "Record increase renewables in Europe, but emissions stay level," *Energy Post*, January 29, 2016.

ones, such as expanding nonfossil-fuel energy production." In other words, strategies based on providing cheap, plentiful green energy won't work. We have to stop fossil fuels directly.

We cannot count on efficiency to reduce the rate at which the planet is being destroyed, nor can we depend on green energy. Our only hope is to directly stop the burning of fossil fuels and all the other destructive activities of the industrial economy, from industrial logging to mining to international trade.

This is hard because, among other reasons, the legal system is set up to protect corporate interests at all cost. Back when I (Max) lived in Bellingham, Washington, a friend told me about an oil pipeline running underneath the city that carries crude oil from the Tar Sands in Alberta, Canada, to nearby refineries. We researched and found out the pipeline was up for renewal with the city. The previous agreement was $10,000 for a 10-year lease.

The people of Bellingham know how dangerous pipelines can be. On June 10, 1999, a gasoline pipeline running across Whatcom Falls Park ruptured. Downstream, an 18-year-old boy was overcome by the vapors while fishing and drowned. Ninety-seven minutes after the leak began, the vapors ignited, causing a massive explosion and sending towering plumes of flames and black smoke into the sky. A pair of 10-year-old boys playing in the creek were severely burned in the explosion, and both died in the hospital the next day.

A group of us began educating local residents on the issue and lobbying the city council. We held public forums, gathered allies, and spoke to hundreds of people about the destructiveness of the tar sands. The city council started to come around. But the city attorney told council members that if they failed to renew the pipeline lease, the pipeline company, Trans Mountain, would sue the city, and the law would be on their side. "It comes down to the Commerce Clause," the council told us, referencing a section in the U.S. Constitution that reserves to the Federal government the power to regulate interstate and international trade. Because the pipeline crossed an international border, local governments cannot legally stop the pipeline from continuing to operate when the gas was already flowing.

Every person in Bellingham voting on our side wouldn't have stopped the pipeline.

After more than a hundred years of Supreme Court rulings, corporations have protection under the First, Fourth, Fifth, Sixth, and Fourteenth Amendments to the Constitution, as well as under the Contracts Clause. As corporate anthropologist Jane Anne Morris writes, "Corporate persons have constitutional rights to due process and equal protection that human persons, affected citizens, don't have. For noncorporate human citizens there's a democracy theme park where we can pull levers on voting machines and talk into microphones at hearings. But don't worry, they're not connected to anything and nobody is listening except for us. What regulatory law regulates is citizen input, not corporate behavior."[53]

We already knew this when we started organizing against the pipeline.[54] But we organized anyway, partly because we wanted to experience failure for ourselves. We wanted to test the democratic process and see if we could use the system to make the change we wanted. And we couldn't, despite the fact that Bellingham had already at that time passed one of the most progressive municipal climate action plans in the nation, demonstrating some level

---

[53] Jane Anne Morris, "Help! I've Been Colonized and I Can't Get Up," *Rachel's Newsletter*.
[54] With gratitude to Paul Cienfuegos and Thomas Linzey.

of community commitment to sustainability, and also despite the fact that the population and the city council were both on our side.

In the end, the council passed two symbolic, nonbinding resolutions with tepid language saying that "Bellingham doesn't approve of the Tar Sands project in Alberta and would like to avoid burning these fuels in our city."[55] The local business journal described the resolutions as being intended to "gently steer" the city away from tar sands oil.[56]

This leads to two points. First, the legal system will not save us. It's certainly an important battleground, but alone it's likely to be a largely defensive battleground. Second, in the midst of a mass extinction event, "gently steering" isn't good enough.

Environmentalists have often championed two other economic approaches to stopping climate change. The first is called "cap and trade," and the second is a carbon tax. Both approaches impose costs on companies for releasing greenhouse gas emissions, but in different ways.

Cap-and-trade laws impose a gradually declining upper limit—a cap—on the allowable rate of carbon emissions from a given industry or nation as a whole, then give "credits" based on how much a given entity is polluting at the beginning of the program. Moving forward, these corporations and other large polluters can buy and sell these "pollution credits" among themselves. The idea is that the free market will determine the appropriate "cost" of pollution, creating an economic incentive to reduce greenhouse gas emissions.

---

[55] "Bellingham Municipal Code 2010–18 and 2010–19."

[56] Ryan Wynne, "City of Bellingham steers away from tar sands oil," *Bellingham Business Journal*, June 9, 2010.

The first problem with this is pollution outsourcing. Absent other changes, introducing these costs for polluting industries may simply cause businesses to move to more lenient jurisdictions. This dovetails with the second problem, carbon-laundering. Consider, for example, the Volkswagen scandal a few years ago involving covering up the true emissions from their cars. Hell, consider the bogus accounting that characterizes biomass and dams. This is undoubtedly taking place in many other businesses, and a cap-and-trade model would further incentivize this behavior.

The carbon tax method is simpler. It establishes a fixed tax on carbon dioxide and other greenhouse gas emissions and requires polluters to pay for what they emit. That money is then often earmarked for "climate-related" spending (usually subsidies for industrial technologies like electric cars, wind, and solar, none of which of course help the planet) or used to reduce taxes on individuals. Both the pollution outsourcing problem and the carbon laundering problem apply here as well, for the same reasons and by the same mechanisms as under cap and trade.

Some regions have already put in place carbon tax or cap-and-trade schemes. How have these projects worked? The European Union (which, ironically, evolved from an organization called the "European Coal and Steel Community") runs the largest cap-and-trade system in the world. These regulations have, according to their own calculations, reduced total EU greenhouse gas emissions by about 2.25 percent from 2013 to 2015.[57] But even these underwhelming reductions are questionable. For example, Facebook announced plans in January 2017 to open a major new data center in Denmark, where data centers consume about 15 percent of the national electricity supply. Facebook promoted the new project as

---

[57] "The EU Emissions Trading System," *European Commission Climate Action*, July 22, 2016.

being "powered by 100 percent clean and renewable energy." But this is a lie; as one article notes, "[the data center will] actually be substantially boosting the country's carbon output. Under the European Union's carbon emissions quota system, the server-powered increase in Denmark's emissions is supposed to be balanced by reductions in other countries' emissions. But that won't happen.... Peter Birch Sørensen, chair of the Danish government's Climate Council, explains, 'There is still a huge surplus of allowances, so increased emissions from Denmark will not cause lower emissions from other EU countries.'"

The market is flooded with allowances, making the whole system worthless.

Overall, efforts to slow global warming via economic means aren't working. And one September 2015 analysis predicted that even fully meeting the existing emissions reductions targets would be inadequate—leading, in fact, to "catastrophic" warming.[58] And here's a truth most bright greens won't acknowledge: one reason these efforts aren't working is that they aren't disrupting the overall business model of industrial capitalism.

After the Paris Climate Accord was reached in late 2015, a lobbyist representing the largest industries in Britain called it "an exciting opportunity for business." Some analysts predict that if carbon prices become too high for the market to bear, regulators may be pressured into releasing more "emissions credits," driving down the price and making the whole system, again, essentially worthless in terms of stopping carbon emissions.

Even anti-capitalists seem mostly unwilling to question

---

[58] Brian Merchant, "Even if every nation meets its pledge to fight climate change, we're still fried," *Vice*, September 28, 2015.

industrialism. For the most part, they don't even question continued dependence on fossil fuels. Oil financed the socialist governments of Gaddafi and Chavez, and Norway, for that matter. In most socialist nations, as well as capitalist ones, neither indigenous sovereignty nor the health of the land have been allowed to stand in the way of industrialization.

When anti-capitalists do oppose fossil fuels, "green energy" is a mainstay of their political platforms—especially in rich nations. There are only a few who acknowledge green technology's problems, and even fewer who oppose economic growth.

Degrowth socialists are one example of this sort of rare intellectual. The idea of "degrowth" as a serious economic approach has existed since at least the 1970s, when the economist Nicholas Georgescu-Roegen proposed it. After years of dormancy, these ideas surfaced again in 2001 and began to gain credence among French activists. The degrowth model calls for a planned economic contraction, mainly in rich nations, to a steady-state sustainable way of life.

It's a saner proposal than the ideas put forth by the likes of Mark Z. Jacobson, but even within socialist thought, it's a fringe idea.

Danny Chivers, an activist from the U.K., is another example of a leftist activist grappling with the impacts of green technology. Writing in *New Internationalist*, Chivers asks: "How much material would we need to transition to a 100-percent renewable world? ... It's irresponsible to advocate a renewably powered planet without being open and honest about what the real-world impacts of such a transition might be."

To answer his question, Chivers makes a number of calculations. To create a renewable electricity generation infrastructure, he estimates that 160 million metric tonnes[59] of aluminum, 110 million tonnes of copper, nearly 3 billion of iron, and 840 million tonnes of cement would be needed. Those are net material figures, so total extraction before refining would be more like 50 billion tonnes. Another 10 billion tonnes of extraction would be required for passive solar and other needs, and electric vehicle production would add another 20 billion metric tonnes of raw material demand. In total, Chivers's ballpark calculations are that about 80 billion metric tonnes of extraction would be required for this transition.

In Chivers's view, this economic transition could prevent around 1.8 trillion metric tons of fossil fuel extraction. When that's the comparison, it sounds like a great deal. But there are a number of problems with these calculations. First, the idea that 9 billion people can sustainably live "an eco-efficient version of the modern lifestyle" is nuts. Most human ecologists believe a population an order of magnitude lower than that still might be unsustainable. Second, Chivers makes a number of false assumptions about recycling—for example, the idea that 100 percent materials reclamation is possible (let alone desirable). The biggest problem with his vision, however, is that it presupposes governments being willing to cooperate in reducing the standard of living in rich nations and transitioning away from a capitalist model. That's not happening voluntarily in the real world, at least not on a meaningful timeline. Whatever movement we're seeing toward "renewable" energy is driven mostly by desires for profit and new sources of energy, not a real (or, for that matter, bogus) commitment to scaling down our current way of life. As we've learned, new energy sources are mostly stacked on top of old rather than replacing them.

---

[59] A metric tonne equals 1,000 kilograms; a North American ton equals approximately 2,000 pounds or 907 kilos.

At the end of his article, Chivers writes that mining "is one of the most notoriously destructive, poisonous and corrupt industries in the world," and notes "another serious issue here. This is one of those moments where it's easy to slip accidentally into a colonialist mindset, when referring casually to 'reserves' of minerals 'available' to the world. Whether or not those materials are dug out of the ground should not be a decision for someone like me, a white guy typing on a computer in Europe; it should be up to the communities that live in the area concerned and would be affected by the extraction." He concludes, "Will it be possible to obtain enough lithium for an electrified world without trampling over the rights of local communities? If not, then we'll need to find a different path to our renewably powered future."[60]

The moral calculus here is straightforward. Calling for 80 billion metric tons of extraction and locking in society to a future requiring an ongoing mining infrastructure to maintain the resulting machines is an atrocity of its own. Regardless of whether local communities give their permission for extraction to take place, destroying the land is a crime. If we democratically decide to destroy the planet, is it somehow a better decision? Is it worth laying waste to a certain landbase if it will provide one species— ours—with an "eco-efficient version of the modern lifestyle?" On such calculations are the lives of entire species, entire watersheds, entire mountain ranges balanced.

A recent report from the United Nations Environment Program states that "consumption of earth's natural resources has more

[60] Danny Chivers, "COPPRO: 'The stuff problem,'" *New Internationalist*, September 15, 2015.

than tripled in 40 years."[61] The report looks at "primary resources:" metals, fossil fuels, forests, grains, fish, and so on. In 1970, primary extraction accounted for 22 billion tons of material per year. By 2010, it was 70 billion tons per year and by 2019 had reached 92 billion tons.[62] By 2050, the rate is forecast to grow to 180 billion tons. That represents a staggering increase in the speed of the destruction of the planet. According to the report, the solution is to "significantly improve resource efficiency" and "decouple economic growth ... from ever-increasing use of natural resources."[63]

Even if this decoupling were possible, which of course it's not, it's not happening. The latest report from the U.S. Energy Information Administration, called the Annual Energy Outlook, shows this. It models the energy future of the United States through 2050. Even with a wide range of assumptions about economic growth and energy prices, "energy consumption varies minimally" across their range of projections, and greenhouse gas emissions look unlikely to decline significantly.[64]

Decoupling economic growth from "natural resource consumption"—the destruction of the planet—isn't possible, and the sooner we face that, the better. A 2018 analysis compared the GDP of every nation in the world to annual corporate revenues, and from the list calculated the largest economies in the world. Of the top 100, 69 were corporations.[65] Walmart is currently the biggest corporation on the planet. Next is State Grid, the government-owned

---

[61] Dominique Mosbergen, "Our consumption of Earth's natural resources has more than tripled in 40 years," *Huffington Post*, August 2, 2016.

[62] "Global Resources Outlook 2019," United Nations Environment Programme, 2019.

[63] "Global Material Flows and Resource Productivity," United Nations Environment Programme, International Resource Panel, July 2016.

[64] Bobby Magill, "U.S. on track to become net energy exporter by 2026," *Climate Central*, January 5, 2017.

[65] Nicholas Freudenberg, "The 100 largest governments and corporations by revenue," *Corporations and Health*, August 27, 2015.

electric utility in China. Five of the 20 largest corporations are oil and gas conglomerates. Four more are car manufacturers. Two are tech giants. Several are banks. And one (Glencore) is a commodities trader, specializing in zinc, copper, grain, and oil.[66] Each of these businesses makes its fortune by either directly destroying the planet through extraction and "development," or by facilitating these processes. "Decoupling" these businesses from the destruction of the planet would mean dismantling them whole.

The best way to estimate how much greenhouse gases are being released by a nation or a corporation is to use GDP as a proxy. Some, however, believe this linkage between GDP and greenhouse gas emissions is changing. The relevant term is "carbon intensity," which is a measure of the amount of greenhouse gases released per unit of economic activity. Late 2015 brought headlines such as "Global emissions to fall for first time during a period of economic growth."[67] The authors of the study explained that this delinkage was likely to be temporary. And indeed, it was. A March 2016 news release from NOAA showed that carbon levels jumped by their highest amount ever in 2015. The head researcher said that "carbon dioxide levels are increasing faster than they have in hundreds of thousands of years."[68] A paper in *Nature Geoscience* stated that carbon emissions were at their highest level not only in history, but in the past 66 million years.[69]

In 2018, carbon emissions climbed by 2 percent, faster than any

---

[66] "Global 500," *Fortune*, 2016.

[67] Adam Vaughan, "Global emissions to fall for first time during a period of economic growth," *The Guardian*, December 7, 2015.

[68] "Record annual increase of carbon dioxide observed at Mauna Loa for 2015," NOAA Climate Research, March 9, 2016.

[69] "Climate: carbon emissions highest in 66 million years," *Al Jazeera*, March 2016.

year since 2011.[70] And for 2019, carbon emissions hit an all-time high, smashing the previous record of 2018.[71]

There was no decline and there was no delinking.

Remember that it's possible to have a carbon-neutral civilization and still destroy the planet. Remember this as if your life depends on it, because it does. Global warming plays a role in only a small percentage of the two hundred species driven extinct every day. Salmon were nearly exterminated before climate change became significant. So were bison. So were old-growth forests and ancient grasslands and so many rivers. Fossil fuel is an accelerant, but it's not the reason. The catastrophe is civilization itself.

The roll is so long and so grim. The Syrian elephant was hunted to death for its ivory before 100 BCE. The Roman Empire sent the Atlas bear into decline, capturing them by the thousands so their deaths could be enjoyed in the Coliseum. The Mauritius blue pigeon was rare by 1755 and extinct by the 1830s when its island was deforested; its scientific name, *Columba nitidissima*, means "most brilliant pigeon" for its metallic blue feathers, and three taxidermic specimens are all that remain. The casualty list of species taken with the Mauritius blue pigeon is harrowing: an owl, a parrot, a duck, a heron, two giant tortoises, a small flying fox—the list goes on, an utterly senseless requiem. The Japanese Hokkaido white wolf was exterminated in 1889, killed en masse with strychnine, which is "an atrocious death."[72] It wasn't always thus. The indigenous Ainu called the wolf *Horkew Kamuy*, or "howling god."

[70] Jillian Ambrose, "Carbon emissions from energy industry rise at fastest rate since 2011," *The Guardian*, June 11, 2019.

[71] Chelsea Harvey and Nathanial Gronewold, "CO$_2$ Emissions Will Break Another Record in 2019," *Scientific American*, December 4, 2019.

[72] Gustav Schenk, *The Book of Poisons* (New York: Rhinehart & Company, 1955).

Many Ainu believe the wolves were the descendants of a goddess who mated with a wolf, and their culture requires respect and care for wolves. In case it needs saying, you care for your family; you don't torture them to death.

The choice before us is stark. We can try to find more fuel sources to devour the last of the living, or we can fight to save our wild and blessed kin.

Chapter 8

RECYCLING

The only superpower you need to singlehandedly save the earth
is to walk to the recycling bin.

—SIGN SEEN ON THE SIDE OF A DUMP TRUCK

IN EUGENE, OREGON

Without economics—without supply and demand of raw materials, recycling is nothing more than a meaningless exercise in
glorifying garbage.[1]

—ADAM MINTER, *JUNKYARD PLANET: TRAVELS IN THE*

BILLION-DOLLAR TRASH TRADE

According to bright green mythology, recycling provides a ready-
made response to any criticism of green technologies and associated demands for raw materials and consequent mining and pollution. Recycling, this mythology holds, can solve every materials
shortage, overcome every consumption and waste problem, and
indefinitely extend the operational duration of every component of
every solar panel and electric car.

---

[1] Adam Minter, *Junkyard Planet: Travels in the Billion-Dollar Trash Trade* (London:
Bloomsbury Press, 2013).

But bright green mythology doesn't correspond to physical reality. Here's what we've learned about metals recycling.

Let's start with aluminum. First, aluminum use essentially doubled between 2005 and 2019 (with the only decline coming from 2008 to 2009, of course because of the recession), which means new aluminum has to come into use every year, which means even if this culture already had 100 percent recycling, it would still need bauxite mines.

Second, some aluminum is used in paint, explosives, and other consumables.

Third, some aluminum is used in electronics. These are the horrors of electronics "recycling": 10-year-olds working in toxic conditions prying apart and melting down old cell phones, because their parents have been forced off their land by soldiers so the land can be used for export crops to make money for the global elites.

Fourth, to be recycled, aluminum must be heated to 1350°F. How is that to be done sustainably? And up to 15 percent of the material to be recycled is lost as dross. You can extract some aluminum from this dross, but the process also yields a highly complex and difficult-to manage waste material which, on contact with water, can release hydrogen, acetylene, and ammonia, among other gases. It can also spontaneously ignite on contact with air.

Aluminum recycling also requires chlorine, and it produces dioxins.

Now let's talk about steel. Here's a headline from a publication in Washington State: "August 4, 2010, Steel recycling leftovers turn Kent site toxic." The article begins: "It seemed like a good idea at the time—dumping leftovers from a steel-recycling process on an empty site in Kent. But now the groundwater has turned as toxic as drain cleaner."

The first sentence of another article, this one from Delaware: "At least 80 Claymont residents have joined a damage and personal-injury lawsuit targeting a long-troubled steel recycling plant there, in a case that claims owners failed for years to control 'poisonous clouds' of toxic dust."[2]

Eighty-three percent of all steel is already recycled in the U.S. So even ignoring the ecological effects and pretending that somehow recycling steel can be nontoxic and sustainable, only 17 percent more can be recycled before you reach 100 percent recycling; and given that world iron ore extraction more than doubled between 2000 and 2015,[3] 100 percent recycling would still require mines and smelters. And it would require slaves in Brazil living unutterably miserable lives making charcoal (in a process that contributes directly to Amazon deforestation) for the Brazilian pig iron industry, with a principal buyer being the U.S. steel industry.

Recycling scrap metal into steel requires arc furnaces heated to 3200°F. Where do we get the energy for that? And where do we get the energy to transport these metals to these furnaces? How does any of that happen sustainably?

Let's move on to copper. From a copper industry website: "Although copper's virtually infinite recyclability makes it environmentally advantageous for use in a variety of products, worldwide demand cannot be met exclusively by secondary copper.

[2] Jeff Montgomery, "80 Nearby Residents Sue Delaware Steel Recycling Plant," *Insurance Journal*, August 20, 2010.

[3] "Global iron ore production data; Clarification of reporting from the USGS," National Minerals Information Center, U.S. Geological Survey.

Continued production of new copper is also required to meet human needs. Fortunately, ample reserves have been identified to last for generations."[4]

So, once again, even, 100 percent recycling will not eliminate the "need" for mines or dispossession or unsustainability.

One final mineral: zinc. Let's do some math. One: today, "over 80 percent of the zinc available for recycling is indeed recycled"; and two: "At present, approximately 70 percent of the zinc produced originates from mined ores and 30 percent from recycled or secondary zinc."[5] Now for the not-very-tricky math: if recycling zinc went from 80 percent to 100 percent, that would mean the amount of recycled zinc and the share percentage of recycled zinc would increase by 25 percent, in other words, from 30 to about 37 percent, meaning about 63 percent would still be mined.

As environmental crises worsen, and as it becomes ever more obvious that industrial civilization is killing the planet, people will search for false solutions to these crises. And it won't matter how counterfactual these false solutions are: The point is maintaining this way of living, not stopping the destruction.

Bright green environmentalism has gained as much attention as it has in great measure because it tells a lot of people what they want to hear: that you can have industrialism and a planet too, or put another way, that you can have a planet and consume it too. But we can't. And so bright green environmentalism does great harm by wasting time we don't have on "solutions" that cannot work.

---

[4] "Copper Africa," Copper Africa Teacher Resource Centre, 2018.
[5] John Lee, "Zinc to Shine from 2-Year Doldrums," *Kitco*, October 20, 2008.

A slogan that emerged in the 1970s as part of rising environmental awareness was the three Rs: "Reduce, Reuse, Recycle." The point was to encourage people to act more responsibly with their consumption and waste through each of these actions.

There's a big difference between *reuse* and *recycle*. To reuse something is simply to, well, reuse it. This can be anything from riding your older sibling's hand-me-down bicycle to repurposing wood from a collapsing barn.

Recycling, on the other hand, is defined as "returning material to a previous stage in a cyclic process," and usually means an industrial operation is required to turn used material into a more basic form, and then further industrial operations are required to turn that more basic form into something else useful.[6]

So, old glass milk and pop bottles were returned, washed, and *reused*. Modern plastic bottles, on the other hand, must be melted down in order to be *recycled*, and likewise, paper must be turned into pulp before it can be *recycled*.

Downcycling, or converting a used material into a less useful or degraded version of the original, is also, for accounting purposes, considered recycling. This is great for those who promote recycling as a solution to the murder of the planet, since most "recycled" plastics, for example, aren't "recycled" but "downcycled."

We asked a recycling professional how the first two Rs got deemphasized. He said, "The city where I work has no official reducing/reusing program; and has in fact green-lighted the construction of an impressive number of big box stores over the past thirty years.

---

[6] We inserted the modifier about industrial capitalism because in a living natural community, dead beings are recycled all the time, reduced through digestion to more basic forms, then turned into something useful.

There are no signs at the doors to these airplane-hangar-sized buildings reminding people to buy less or make do with what they already own. Recycling is the only permissible activity of the original three, because it's the only option that doesn't impede capitalism."

Modern recycling is complex, and the recycling industry is a vast and profit-driven enterprise. In 2015, the global recycling industry made more than $23 billion in profits. In the U.S., scrap recycling generates more than $105 billion in economic activity per year and employs 500,000 people.[7]

It begins with collection by fleets of diesel- or natural gas-powered garbage trucks (140,000 of these trucks in the U.S. alone).[8] These trucks weigh, on average, 64,000 pounds,[9] and get about two to three miles per gallon; natural gas powered trucks get even worse mileage.[10] The trucks also produce about three dozen (currently known) airborne toxins.

At the materials recovery facility, the load is dumped onto a conveyor belt and the stream is either hand- or machine-sorted by type: paper and cardboard, plastics, glass, aluminum cans, and other metals.

About 50 percent of what is thrown in recycling bins ends up in

---

[7] Jessica Lyons Hardcastle, "US Recycling Industry Generates $105bn Annually," *Environmental Leader*, May 27, 2015.

[8] Gurdas S. Sandhu et al., "Real-World Activity and Fuel Use of Diesel and CNG Refuse Trucks," *Atmospheric Environment* 129 (March 2016): 98–104. DOI: 10.1016/j.atmosenv.2016.01.014.

[9] "Garbage Trucks and Your Roads," Titan Recycle and Trash.

[10] These trucks often have messages on their side panels like "This vehicle runs on clean natural gas," as though that somehow makes them better for the environment. Worse, this natural gas often comes from fracking, which does even more harm to the world than does the production of diesel fuel.

landfills, mostly because someone tossed the wrong thing in the bin. But in many areas even items marked with recycling symbols can't be recycled. For example, plastics #3 through #7 often have the recycling symbol, but in the U.S., they're almost always sent to a landfill.

After sorting, recycled materials are crushed or shredded, compacted into bales, then sold on the commodities marketplace to wholesale buyers. For most of the past few decades, the majority of U.S. bales have been sent to China, where expanding industry and short supply of raw materials drove demand. In 2012, the value of waste and scrap sent to China was $10 billion.[11] A significant portion of what arrived, however, was not in fact recyclable, but rather just trash China was then forced to deal with (or not). So, in 2013, China announced a new policy, called "Operation Green Fence," meant to prevent the importation of contaminated recycling bales. This was bad for U.S. "recycling" (read, "scrap and garbage exportation") businesses, which had come to rely on China's processing (and dumping).

When a bale of plastic goes to a recycling factory, white and clear plastics are sorted from colored (clear is the most valuable, since it can be dyed any color).[12] Next, bits of label or paper attached to the plastic are removed in a caustic bath of soda. The plastic is chipped, bathed again, then dried for 10 hours in large, heated, rotating drums.

Recycled chips aren't strong or stable enough to create new

---

[11] Benjamin Carlson, "Good news: US exports to China soar, setting new record," *Global Post*, January 20, 2014.
[12] Not infrequently, plastics are improperly sorted, leading to pollutants like BPA being present in recycled products claimed to be BPA free.

plastic bottles, so they must be combined with new plastic. Generally, the proportion of recycled content can't exceed about 10 percent. So, a recycled bottle contains 90 percent new plastic.

Recycled chips and new pellets are mixed, then heated to 550°F. The molten plastic is extruded at high pressure into molds to create what are called preforms: small plastic bulbs that are heated and stretched to form full-size plastic bottles.

The process of downcycling plastic drinking bottles into polyester clothing begins with sorting, cleaning, and shredding, then moves to a furnace, where the plastic is melted, then extruded through a sieve-like metal plate to yield polyester threads. These threads are collected, but they aren't yet strong enough for clothing; they have to be combined, heated, and stretched several times to bond the fibers together. These fibers are shredded—resulting in finer, longer fibers—then carded (brushed together) to align them. Finally, the fibers are turned into thread, which is woven on massive looms into sheets of polyester cloth. To create a smooth face on the fabric, another machine creates tiny loops on the surface, and then rotating rollers catch and tear those loops, giving the fabric a soft feeling. It takes an industrial factory to produce polyester clothing.

Polyester clothes are a major source of micro-plastic particles in oceans, rivers, and lakes: Each time you wash a polyester garment, millions of tiny fragments enter the wastewater stream and end up as pollution.[13]

Leaving aside that most plastic isn't recycled anyway, the process of recycling plastic uses "mind-boggling" amounts of energy. One

---

[13] "How Plastic Bottles Are Recycled into Polyester," *National Geographic Channel*, YouTube, December 13, 2009.

commenter says, "The amount of steps—not to mention electricity, water and manpower—that need to be taken to go from a bale of plastic bottles into safe, useable material is pretty staggering."[14]

Industrial humans produce roughly as much plastic each year as the weight of all humans combined. Half of the 8.3 billion—yes, billion—metric tons of plastic this culture has fabricated since 1950 was made in the past 13 years. Like all the other harms to the planet, plastic production is "rapidly accelerating."[15]

Plastic doesn't rot. It accumulates. And no matter whether this plastic is (for now) recycled as part of the 10 percent recycled contribution for a water bottle, or downcycled into a pair of polyester pants, eventually it's going to end up in the wild, and probably in the oceans, where it will contribute to their killing.

The threats to the world from plastic are real. The concern expressed by this culture about these threats is for the most part phony. If we were really concerned about these threats, we'd stop making plastic.

Here's a thought experiment to make clear how insincere is our culture's concern over plastic pollution. Remember, plastic doesn't decay. In fact, it was invented *specifically* because it doesn't decay. Another way to say *doesn't decay* is that *no one eats it*. That's what decay is: *someone eating you*. After you die, everyone from crows to ants to worms to fungi to bacteria eats you. That's *how* you decay. The wood in your home decays because fungi and other beings eat the wood. And people wanted to create materials that wouldn't decay, in other words, that no one could eat.

Now here's the thought experiment: Let's pretend some strain

[14] Jaymi Heimbuch, "Why Recycling Plastic Bottles Doesn't Help the Problem," *Treehugger*, June 2011.
[15] Sarah Zhang, "Half of All Plastic That Has Ever Existed Was Made in the Past Thirteen Years," *The Atlantic*, July 19, 2017.

of bacteria develops the ability to rapidly digest plastic. Yay! Everyone's happy! The oceans won't be suffocated by plastic! All the plastic trash disappears! (And let's ignore the fact that this would release a lot of carbon into the atmosphere, and instead deal with one problem at a time.)

But then we discover that these miraculous life-saving bacteria don't just eat *bad* plastic—plastic we throw away—but also *good* plastic, the plastic we're still using. And then we think things like: "Yikes! They're eating the plastic pots from the marijuana grow scene that the Jevons Paradox has allowed me to expand. Oh, no! I *bought* those damn containers because they wouldn't decay! And now those bacteria are eating the steering wheel in my car! The insulation on my electrical wires! My waterbed mattress! My alarm clock! My cell phone! My laptop! My polyester pants! It's a freaking emergency!"

If a strain of bacteria evolves to eat plastic as fast as is necessary to help the earth, this culture will work around the quickly decaying plastic alarm clock to develop new substances that won't decay. And we all know that's true.

Here's another illustration of the deceptions embedded in bright green storytelling. Burning plastic to generate electricity is sometimes considered a form of recycling. In fact, a major portion of "recycled" plastics globally is simply incinerated. Sweden is a great example. The nation boasts that less than 1 percent of its waste ends up in landfills, but more than half of Sweden's trash stream goes to incinerators to generate power (and to pollute the air).[16]

---

[16] "The Swedish Recycling Revolution," Sweden.se, September 24, 2015.

Worse, Sweden doesn't just burn its own trash, it imports garbage from neighboring countries to fuel the incinerators, too.

The Swedish officials promote this as a good thing.

Let's do another thought experiment: Let's say you take your oil supply and sell it to people. Then you have your buyers "throw it away." At this point, you collect it, fill up your power station, and burn it to generate power. Whaddya know! You're a genius with a sky-high recycling rate and some new eco-awards to put on your wall.

And recall that when alternative (that is, nonfossil fuel) energy sources are introduced, they generally don't displace the fossil fuel sources.

So, what is Sweden's incineration of garbage doing for the world?

Next, let's talk about glass. Glass recycling starts much like plastic, with collection, trucking, then a conveyor belt carrying it into a materials recovery facility. There, rotating magnets remove metal lids from the stream of incoming glass and an eddy current generated by more electromagnets removes nonferrous (nonmagnetic) metals. Next, the stream passes into an optical scanner that determines the color of the glass and sorts clear glass from colored. Finally, the glass is crushed into "cullet" (small fragments) and sent to glass manufacturers. There, the crushed glass is heated to 2700°F. The glass is cured, then while still molten cut into bottle-sized portions. Another large machine injects the molten glass into molds for bottles and other containers.[17]

When transportation costs are factored in, producing one ton of glass produces about 2 tons of carbon dioxide.[18] Producing recycled glass uses about 40 percent less energy in the melting stage—which, especially when transportation and other processing is factored in, means that making one ton of recycled glass still produces well over one ton of carbon dioxide.[19] Overall, "little energy is saved by recycling glass bottles." One study looking at the full "lifecycle" of glass containers found that products with 50 percent recycled glass content had only a 28 percent lower greenhouse gas impact.[20] An industry group gives similar numbers, stating that each 10 percent of cullet from recycled glass reduces energy needed for new glass by only 2 to 3 percent.[21]

Between 2006 and 2011, one glass recycling plant in Seattle was fined nearly $1 million (trivial compared to the corporation's profits of more than $1 billion per year) for violations of the Clean Air Act, making it the most-fined air polluter in the Northwest during that time. EPA calls the Saint-Gobain recycling facility a "high-priority violator" and has put it on a special watch list.

The company seems proud of its record, even pointing out that

---

[17] "Glass Recycling—Recycling to New Bottles," *WIH Resource Group*, YouTube, September 3, 2014.

[18] Warren McLaren, "Ecotip: Glass—What's the Environmental Impact?" *Treehugger*, November 22, 2004.

[19] Larry West, "Benefits of Glass Recycling: Why Recycle Glass," *About.com*, January 27, 2016.

[20] "Environmental Overview: Complete Life Cycle Assessment of North American Container Glass," *Glass Packaging Institute*, 2010.

[21] Milton Kazmeyer, "Energy to Recycle Glass Bottles vs. Aluminum Cans vs. Plastic," *SFGate*.

the Seattle glass facility is a national pilot project for pollution control technology. Meanwhile, it released 400 pounds of lead into the air in 2010. More than 100,000 people, most of them poor and/or people of color, live within a few miles of the factory.[22]

Remember, too, that glass is necessary for solar photovoltaics. And not just any glass. Over time, low-quality glass can cloud, reducing the efficiency of a solar panel. A shortage of high-quality tempered glass is a serious problem for the solar industry.

Solar panels—and this is true for windows as well, underscoring again how unsustainable this whole culture is—require what is called "float glass," made by floating molten glass atop a molten metal, usually tin, sometimes lead. This process results in a very flat panel. What this means in practice is that solar panels don't just require the heating of glass to 2,700 degrees, but also of metal.

Float glass production is highly concentrated, with just four companies controlling the bulk of global production. Each of the factories for producing this glass costs $200 million. Again, this is not a community-scale proposition.

A typical float-glass production facility only uses 15-30 percent recycled cullet as a raw source material.[23]

Bright greens keep telling us that glass is 100 percent recyclable and can be recycled endlessly without loss in quality or purity. But this, like so many other of their claims, isn't true. Window glass is

---

[22] Lisa Stiffler, "Recycling Plant Among Top Northwest Polluters," Oregon Public Broadcasting, November 7, 2011.

[23] Keith Burrows and Vasilis Fthenakis, "Glass Needs for a Growing Photovoltaics Industry," *Center for Lifecycle Analysis*, Columbia University.

not generally accepted for recycling. Nor are most other flat pieces of glass. Nor are drinking glasses. Nor mirrors. Nor vases. Nor any forms of leaded glass. Nor many other types of glass.

Remind us again how recycling will save the planet.

In the introduction to this chapter, we briefly debunked the bright green claim that somehow mining can be eliminated through 100 percent metals recycling. It's worth discussing metals recycling in greater depth, however, since steel, aluminum, and copper underlie every major green technology we've looked at. You cannot have wind turbines or solar panels on any scale without millions of tons of these metals.

Unlike plastic, however, steel and most other metals can be recycled almost indefinitely: there's no inherent degradation to the material from the recycling process, giving rise to the bright green claims of the possibility of "sustainable" industrial metals recycling.

So, is 100 percent recycling possible? Steel, aluminum, and copper are already recycled at relatively high rates. Depending on whom you ask, between 69[24] and 88[25] percent of steel is recycled, which adds up to about 80 million tons per year in North America (and also means that somewhere between 11 and 36 million tons of steel are discarded per year on this continent; that's how far we are from 100 percent recycling). The rate is slightly higher for copper and aluminum. We'll focus on steel recycling here, since it's the most important of these metals, and the process for recycling other metals is similar.

The main sources of steel for recycling are old cars and trucks,

---

[24] "50 Fun Facts About Steel," World Steel Association.
[25] "Steel is the World's Most Recycled Material," World Steel Association.

appliances, construction debris, rail tracks, shipping containers, machinery, and scraps from industry. These raw materials, millions of tons of them annually, are gathered by small recycling businesses using diesel powered forklifts, trucks, crushers, and ships. This scrap is taken to factories and sorted by alloy.

Some materials, like tin cans, require extra processing. Tin cans are made mostly of steel, coated with tin to prevent rust. Tin is removed from steel cans through reverse electroplating, which involves immersion in a bath of heated sodium hydroxide solution with an electric current flowing through it. Despite the fact that modern tin cans contain only a fraction of the tin they used to (making this detinning process dubiously profitable), tin is considered a major contaminant in scrap steel—so the process continues.[26]

Next, the iron and steel scrap are shredded. In the case of thick beams, plates, and cables, strong tools may be needed, such as hydraulic shearing machines or gas and plasma cutting torches. Many of these torches are inherently polluting, releasing nitrogen oxides, toxic metal particles, and other substances in the form of a harmful dust.

The shredders themselves are machines—many of them the size of large buildings—that use massive rotating drums to crush steel scraps. Often, entire vehicles are fed into these machines. Metal-on-metal friction generates high temperatures inside shredders, and fire is a concern since rubber, gasoline, and other flammable materials may be present. To reduce this risk, water is injected as the shredder drums rotate. An average steel scrap shredder may use 50 gallons of water per minute. This water, along with the dust produced by shredders, emerges highly contaminated. One study found that areas "nearby and downwind [of recycling facilities with

[26] Scott Sibley, "Flow studies for recycling metal commodities in the United States," U.S. Geological Survey, K6, 2004.

shredders] contained lead, copper, iron, zinc, cadmium, mercury, and arsenic, among many other pollutants."[27]

Scrapyards are a major source of pollution around the world: According to a 1983 report, scrapyards ranked "among the most commonly encountered examples of contaminated land."[28] Since the early 1980s, global recycling rates have risen dramatically, and with them the number of contaminated scrapyards. Stormwater coming off scrapyards is especially polluted, containing the metals already mentioned as well as PCBs and other toxic chemicals released from old industrial products.[29] One facility in Providence, Rhode Island, was described as "a mess" by the assistant attorney general after decades of fuel spills, toxic runoff, and growing accumulation of piles of unsellable scrap.[30] A 2014 study in Nigeria found "considerable metal contamination" in soils and groundwater at a series of scrap yards.[31] An investigation of five Houston-area recycling facilities found high levels of hexavalent chromium, one of the most potent known carcinogens, and an ongoing problem with explosions, fires, and smoke releases into the community.[32]

[27] "Curbing Pollution from an Oakland Auto Shredder," *San Francisco Baykeeper,* April 16, 2013.

[28] Andre Meunier, "Notes on the redevelopment of scrap yards and similar sites," Interdepartmental Committee on the Redevelopment of Contaminated Land, October 1983.

[29] Andre Meunier, "Environmentalists have Schnitzer Steel scrap yard in their sights," *The Oregonian,* December 5, 2008.

[30] Tim Faulker, "Concerns Metals Recycler Could Leave Behind Mess," *Eco Rhode Island News,* April 8, 2015.

[31] Oludare H. Adedeji, Olufunmilayo O. Olayinka, and Franklin C. Nwanya, "Soil and Water Pollution Levels in and around Urban Scrapyards," *IOSR Journal of Environmental Science, Toxicology, and Food Technology* 8, no. 5 (May 2014): 60–68.

[32] Ingrid Lobet, "Danger in air near metal recyclers," *Houston Chronicle,* December 29, 2012.

Interestingly, increasing standards for low-polluting vehicles and efficient appliances are driving pollution associated with scrapyards and recycling. In China, for example, where air pollution is a major health concern, changes in the law have made some highly polluting, but still relatively new, vehicles illegal. This has led to cars and trucks "piling up in huge numbers" in scrapyards across the country; more than 6 million additional vehicles were scrapped in China in 2014 in response to air pollution.[33]

Once the scrap from iron and steel is broken into manageable sizes, it's baled, sold to steel manufacturers, and transported to steel production mills. Steel recyclers tend to be relatively small businesses, but most steel producers are massive multinational corporations—ArcelorMittal, Nippon Steel, Baosteel, Nucor, and others. These companies purchase scrap (which is significantly cheaper than buying purified iron ore) and turn it once again into steel. Because what are known as basic oxygen furnaces are mostly used for producing primary (or new) steel and can only take small amounts of recycled scrap, most recycled steel is instead produced inside electric arc furnaces (EAF)—massive, highly complex machines that are key to modern metallurgy. (A third process, known as direct reduced iron, or DRI, is used only rarely.)

An EAF is essentially a vessel lined with refractory materials (such as magnesium-carbon bricks) that can withstand extreme temperatures without melting. At the top of the vessel are graphite electrodes to produce an electric arc that melts the steel scrap in the vessel. Along the side of the vessel is a tapping point where molten steel can be removed.

---

[33] Kaushik Patowary, "China's Air Pollution and Scrapped Vehicles," *Amusing Planet*, June 15, 2015.

Steel scrap is first lifted into the vessel by a large crane. A given furnace can melt around 150 metric tons of steel and iron in a single heat. Once the scrap is loaded, the furnace is sealed, and the heating begins. Electricity is fed through the graphite electrodes, producing electric arcs that heat scrap metal to more than 3000°F. Some furnaces burn a gas-oxygen-enriched-air mixture to further increase temperatures. During this heating, samples are taken to determine the chemical composition of the molten steel. Slag, composed of impurities such as nonferrous metals and oxides, rises to the top of the mixture and is poured off. This slag is cooled, crushed to a fine powder, and sold to other industries (most often, it's used in high-performance concrete and as a filler in road construction, but some slag is used in fertilizers).

Every time iron and steel are resmelted, chemical reactions taking place in the furnace remove some of the original target metals from the mixture, locking them up in complex chemical structures unusable in steel. A typical EAF loses around 250 pounds of slag for each ton of steel that's smelted.[34] Besides iron, other common components of slag from EAFs include calcium oxide, silicon dioxide, and magnesium oxide.[35]

Technically, this slag could be resmelted and the valuable components removed, but the process is uneconomical; the energy input relative to the amount of raw material gained is massive.[36] These slag losses are but one reason 100 percent metals recycling can never happen.

---

[34] "Generation of iron and steel slag," *Nippon Slag Association.*

[35] Jeremey A. T. Jones, "Electric Arc Furnace Steelmaking," Steelworks, Nupro Corporation.

[36] "Steel slag recycling," Harsco Metals & Minerals. Note: Some slag is recycled for the purposes of extracting metals, but these are small-scale operations and mostly operate cross-industry. For example, the slag from smelting copper often contains quantities of iron, which can be extracted economically. But it's not cost-effective to recover all the iron from the slag leftover from purifying any metal.

After the slag is poured off the top, other materials are added to the mixture to give the steel certain desired properties. For example, chromium and nickel may be added to form corrosion-resistant stainless steel or oxygen may be added to bond with impurities and thereby purify the steel.

Two other additives (put in before pouring off the slag) are lime and fluorspar. More than 300 pounds of limestone and lime can be required for a ton of steel. Mining limestone and producing lime (a crushed and refined type of limestone that requires heating) necessitates its own major mining operations as well as transportation networks.

Fluorspar comes from the mineral fluorite, which is mined for numerous industries. In steel production, it's used as a flux to decrease the temperatures necessary to melt steel and iron scrap. The toxicity of fluorides has been a major issue for decades. Elevated rates of lung cancers were found in fluorspar miners in the 1950s and '60s.[37] A 2004 summary of the effects of fluoride compounds on plants and animals noted that "the use of fluoride as a flux [and in other industries] ... has led to widespread air pollution and environmental damage.... Inorganic fluoride emissions damage crops, forests, and natural vegetation, and causes fluorosis in factory workers, livestock and wild mammals.... Over a million organofluorides are known.... They are a vital part of modern society but their effects on the environment are still largely unexplored."[38]

So long as civilization continues to ravage the earth—and for a time after—fluorspar is here to stay. A paper titled "Can Fluorspar

---

[37] A. J. de Villiers and J. P. Windish, "Lung Cancer in a Fluorspar Mining Community," *British Journal of Industrial Medicine* (April 1964).

[38] Leonard H. Weinstein and Alan Davison, *Fluorides in the Environment* (Wallingford: CABI Publishing, 2003), vi.

be replaced in steelmaking?" concludes that, while alternatives are available, "Fluorspar is by far the most convenient component to use as a fluxing precursor and additive."[39]

Another reason 100 percent recycling is impossible is that various types of metals and alloys are mixed in the waste stream. When these alloys are melted together, the metal that results is less useful than the original alloys. As one paper notes, "Metals can in theory be infinitely recycled ... however ... mixing of different metal species results in scrap quality that no longer matches the originals. Further losses occur when meeting the quality requirement of the target product requires dilution ... by adding high purity materials."[40]

Graphite electrodes are essential for steel recycling. As one report puts it, "Graphite electrodes are currently the only known commercially available products that have the high levels of electrical conductivity and the capability of sustaining the high levels of heat generated in an electric arc furnace producing steel."[41]

To make electrodes, premium-quality calcined coking coal is crushed, screened, heated, blended with pitch, then extruded into a mold and water-cooled at a precise temperature. Next, the proto-electrodes are baked at more than 1400°F in computer-controlled furnaces for one to two weeks to carbonize the pitch.

---

[39] Eugene Pretorius, "Can Fluorspar be replaced in steelmaking?" *Baker Refractories*.

[40] Shinichiro Nakamura et al., "Quality and dilution losses in the recycling of ferrous materials from end-of-life passenger cars: input-output analysis under explicit consideration of scrap quality," *Environmental Science and Technology* 46, 17 (September 4, 2012): 9266–73.

[41] "GrafTech International 10-K," *Wikilnvest*, March 16, 2007.

Another special pitch is applied to the electrodes, which are then rebaked at nearly 1300°F to set the second pitch application and remove impurities. Next, the carbon electrodes have to be turned into graphite. This requires that they be heated to more than 5000°F in a narrow electric resistance furnace to crystallize the carbon into the graphite electrode.

How are you going to do this without harming the planet?

These electrodes can be huge: some are more than 4,000 pounds and 30 inches in diameter.[42] And they don't last forever. During the heating process inside an electric arc furnace, the electrodes are partially consumed,[43] to the tune of about two to five pounds of electrode lost per ton of steel produced.[44] In fact, the cost of replacing electrodes—each one is expensive—is a significant portion of the cost of operating an EAF steel mill.

Also, the refractory lining of an EAF lasts several thousand "heatings" before it breaks down and must be replaced as well.[45]

A single steel production factory using electric arc furnaces can use as much electricity as a city of 100,000 people.[46]

Despite steel being recyclable, most new steel has only a portion of recycled content. In 2008, for example, total steel production

---

[42] "UCAR® Graphite Electrodes," *GrafTech International*.

[43] Through a variety of methods from simple breakage to oxidation and slow, progressive vaporization.

[44] Piotr Migas and Miroslaw Karbowniczek, "Selected Aspects of Graphite Applications in Ferrous Metallurgy," AGH University of Science and Technology, October 16, 2013.

[45] "Steel Foundry Refractory Lining Optimization: Electric Arc Furnaces," Missouri University of Science & Technology.

[46] "Electric Arc Furnace," Carmeuse.

was 1.3 billion metric tons, of which an estimated 500 million tons was made from scrap.[47] That's less than 40 percent (and we know this is a different number from earlier, which highlights that many of these statistics are ballpark estimates). Production has risen sharply since 2008, rising to 1.8 billion metric tons in 2018, but the proportion of secondary steel has remained similar.[48]

Even worse, recycling is, according to the Energy Information Administration, "the primary energy efficiency technology" available for the production of steel and aluminum. In other words, there's really no way to make steel production more efficient beyond using recycled scrap.[49]

This is the "environmentally friendly" way to make steel, since making steel from recycled scrap uses 75 percent less energy compared to making it from raw iron ore. That's good, right? Even better, according to one industry group, recycling one metric ton of steel offsets the need for 2,500 pounds of iron ore, 1,400 pounds of coal, and 120 pounds of limestone.[50] Another industry source adds 642 kWh of energy and 1.8 barrels of oil to these savings, then goes on to note that producing steel from scrap instead of ore reduces carbon emissions (by 58 percent), water use (by 40 percent), air pollution (by 86 percent), and water pollution (by 76 percent) compared to producing "virgin" steel.[51]

So, despite all the pollution, despite all the energy use, steel recycling is great, right? A lot of bright greens and some big

[47] "Ferrous Metals," Bureau of International Recycling.
[48] "World Steel in Figures 2019," World Steel Association.
[49] "Recycling is the primary energy efficiency technology for aluminum and steel manufacturing," U.S. Energy Information Administration, May 9, 2014.
[50] "Ore Conservation is a Major Benefit When Scrap Metal Gets Recycled," GLE Scrap Metal.
[51] Bureau of International Recycling, op. cit.

environmental groups (but more often, industry trade groups and governmental agencies) advertise it as such.

But this is inverted logic. Fifty-eight percent of a load of waste is still too much, especially when we're talking about a substance (carbon emissions) that's killing the planet, and an industry (secondary steel production) that's a major global source of emissions, pollution, and toxified water.

Aluminum recycling shares many issues with other metal recycling processes, but there are two additional issues: First, recycled aluminum doesn't provide a high-quality end product; and second, the use of chlorine compounds for cleaning results in inevitable production and emission of dioxins.

Like other metals, aluminum is produced in many different grades, based on slightly different compositions and treatments to produce different characteristics like strength, flexibility, brittleness or ductility, and so on.

Some aluminum uses (e.g., for aircraft, or for electronic circuits) require high grades of metal with a precise set of qualities. These metals are nearly impossible to produce with recycled feedstock, and so are almost entirely dependent on new bauxite extraction.

All of this means that when bright greens tell you that it's possible to have something resembling this way of life without mining, they're not telling the truth.

When paper is recycled, it's shredded and suspended in liquids to create a pulp. Sulfur-based compounds are used to break down the materials, leading to the release of sulfur dioxide and other compounds that lead to acid rain. Paper pulp production also releases other pollutants, including benzene, nitrates, mercury, carbon monoxide, ammonia, and chlorinated dioxins (which, to remind you, are among the most toxic known compounds and are considered "persistent" pollutants; they don't go away).

After recycled pulp is liquefied, it's cleaned and pressed into new sheets of paper, but during the process, a lot of waste is generated in the form of paper sludge. Paper sludge is the mixture of inks (many of which are petroleum based), cleaning chemicals like chlorine, dyes, heavy metals, and other contaminants. In most cases, this sludge is simply mixed with sand and sent to local landfills.

Other types of recycling are much more complex and hazardous than those we've mentioned. One example is lithium-ion batteries (which, as you recall, are critical for modern electric vehicles and play a small but increasing role in energy storage). Recycling lithium-ion batteries is theoretically possible but in practice is almost never done. As of 2011, only one company in the world (Umicore in Belgium) recycled lithium ion-batteries, because the process makes no economic sense: it's complex, hazardous, and expensive, and the end result isn't cost competitive with mining new lithium. Newer lithium-ion battery designs, which substitute iron, manganese, and titanium for cobalt and nickel to further cut costs, are even less economical to recycle.[52] As of 2019, recycling rates have barely increased. In Australia, about 2 to 3 percent of lithium-ion batteries are even collected for (overseas) recycling,

---

[52] John Petersen, "Why Advanced Lithium-Ion Batteries Won't Be Recycled," *Alt Energy Stocks*, May 2011.

and rates in the United States and the EU are less than 5 percent.[53] One analysis looking at car battery recycling concluded that "each recycling [process] will create its own impacts, often but not always lower [than primary production]." That same study stated recycling lithium-ion and other modern batteries faces another challenge: "the material being recovered [may] in 10 to 15 years be obsolete and might not be able to find a market."[54]

Hello, landfill! And once there, lithium-ion batteries continue to cause problems and possibly deaths. They are particularly volatile because the separator between the positive and negative components is extremely thin and easily breached, while lithium itself is "highly reactive."[55] If the device is crushed, punctured, or even just dropped, it can result in a "thermal event," a.k.a. a fire. One survey found that "83 percent of waste management facilities had at least one fire over the last two years of which 40 percent were caused by lithium-ion batteries."[56] The results can be "catastrophic."[57] In 2017 alone, there were 289 waste facility fires in the United States and Canada, resulting in three deaths.[58] This is only going to get worse as the electronic junk piles up.

[53] Mitch Jacoby, "It's time to get serious about recycling lithium-ion batteries," *Chemical & Engineering News (C&EN)*, July 14, 2019.

[54] Linda Gaines, "To recycle, or not to recycle, that is the question: Insights from life-cycle analysis," *Materials Research Society Bulletin* 37, April 2012.

[55] "Is your trash causing fires? Common batteries lead to facility fires," Dalton-Whitfield Solid Waste Authority, November 26, 2018.

[56] Ibid.

[57] Geoffrey A. Fowler, "The explosive problem with recycling iPads, iPhones and other gadgets: They literally catch fire," *The Washington Post*, September 11, 2018.

[58] "Is your trash causing fires? Common batteries lead to facility fires," Dalton-Whitfield Solid Waste Authority, November 26, 2018.

Electric cars (along with nearly all the other green technologies, especially solar panels) also contain electronics, circuit boards, and other computer components. When this material is thrown away, it's known as e-waste. Recycling e-waste is one of the most hazardous known industries, releasing lead, PBDEs (Polybrominated Diphenyl Ethers), dioxins and furans, and other toxins. E-waste has been called bluntly "a serious environmental and human health threat."[59]

Agbogbloshie is "Ghana's vast dumping site for electronic waste, where everything is smeared and stained with mucky hues of brown and sooty black," Afua Hirsch reported in *The Guardian* in 2013. Here are the realities of e-waste recycling: "Old VHS players, cassette recorders, sewing machines, computers from the 1980s and every period since lie haphazardly on large mounds in the dump, which stretches as far as the eye can see. 'Electric waste comes here from all over the world—but especially from Europe,' says Karim, 29, who, like almost all the scrap dealers at Agbogbloshie, originally comes from northern Ghana but has been salvaging, buying and selling at the dump for 10 years. 'We get a lot of health problems here, but we manage, because we need the money.'" And, Hirsch adds, "Deeper into the heart of Agbogbloshie, huge plumes of foul-smelling smoke rise up from three large fires, where the dismantled items are burned to remove traces of plastic, leaving the metal behind. The fumes are head-pounding, but the men, women

---

[59] Alejandra Sepúlveda et al., "A review of the environmental fate and effects of hazardous substances released from electrical and electronic equipment during recycling: Examples from China and India," *Environmental Impact Assessment Review* 30, no. 1 (January 2010): 28–41.

and children weaving in and out of the fires seem oblivious." The once fecund river now looks like used oil.[60]

We could also talk about the tens of thousands of tons of e-waste dumped—sorry, recycled—in Pakistan, where the country's poor pull apart or burn old electronics to "recycle" the metals, living day and night with the acrid smoke.

Or we could talk about the 63 million cell phones that have ended up in Bangladesh in just the last three years. This waste is, as the *Daily Star* delicately puts it, "handled by the informal sector," which is code language for these electronics being collected and dismantled, then the metals removed and sorted, by those living in, again to use the words of the *Daily Star*, "urban slums."[61]

A photograph from Asia shows great mounds of e-waste (sorry, electronic products waiting to be recycled) stretching from horizon to horizon. And here's another picture, this one showing a small, naked, African child toddling amidst the waste. Still another image reveals e-waste covering a beach, from ocean to cliff. Yet another photograph shows small children pulling apart the casing on a computer. And yet another picture displays small children standing in front of mounds of burning computers—the plastic is being burned so they can get at the metals. And now another, a Chinese infant surrounded by stripped wires from computers and telephones.

This is all madness.

---

[60] Afua Hirsch, "'This is not a good place to live': inside Ghana's dump for electronic waste," *The Guardian*, December 14, 2013.

[61] Rashna Raya Rahman and Naureen Shafinaz Mahboob, "Electronic Waste: The Story of Bangladesh," *Daily Star*, August 5, 2015.

For every statistic we provide in this book, for every time we mention environmental or health hazards, there are stories and pictures like these.

David Suzuki can talk about the beauty of windmills, but those windmills necessitate moonscaped mines as nightmarish as the miles of discarded computers, and they devastate those who live on the ground beneath, and those who fly in the air above. And we can fantasize all we want about electric cars revolutionizing the way we drive, but they require rare-earth metals ripped from the ground, and they prompt wars and the exploitation of humans and the extirpation of nonhumans that accompany these mines. And we can fantasize all we want about "design[ing] things for disassembly so that minerals are easily pulled from objects as they cease to be of use and ... turn[ing] those metals into parts for new things," but computers and cell phones still lead to the horrors that are e-waste "recycling."

Recycling solar panels is similar to other recycling. First, the panels are shredded, then put through a hammermill to crush the pieces. The semiconductor film is removed by the addition of acid and peroxide to a slowly rotating stainless steel drum. Liquids are separated from solids via a sorting machine, and then metals are precipitated from the liquid solution using a three-stage, increasing pH process. The resulting material is thickened in a dewatering tank, then packaged and shipped to another recycling facility for further sorting. This process recycles about 95 percent of the semiconductor material, and 90 percent of the glass.[62]

This process, like the process of producing solar panels in the

---

[62] Lisa Krueger, "Overview of First Solar's Module Collection and Recycling Program," *First Solar*.

first place, is highly industrial; it requires factories, globalized supply chains, rare and toxic materials, and massive energy inputs.

The most difficult part of a solar panel to recycle is the backsheet,
usually made of polyvinyl fluoride and possibly containing lead,
chromium, cadmium, selenium, arsenic, and antimony. One article notes that producing solar panels requires "a witch's brew of
toxic chemicals," which seems unfair, since none of the practicing
witches we know use materials that turn into persistent pollutants.

One company's "solution" to the problem of backsheet pollution
is a great example of what Russian-American researcher Evgeny
Morozov calls technological solutionism. They're formulating new
plant-based plastics that can withstand high temperatures and
high humidity, but which supposedly are still capable of being bio-
degraded, and which can be used as backsheets for solar panels.
Sounds great again, right? But of course, like other "bioplastics,"
these will require an industrial "composting" factory to make the
degradation process possible. You can't just throw them into a forest and expect them to disappear.

It's another example of how an industrial mindset, even with a
"green" veneer, leads to the inevitable results of industrial culture:
more factories, more production, more garbage.[63]

Here's a headline from an article in a 2017 edition of the *South
China Morning Post*: "China's ageing solar panels are going to
be a big environmental problem." Its subhead states: "The issue
of how to dispose of hazardous waste from ageing panels casts a

---

[63] Todd Woody, "Solar energy's dirty little secret," *Grist*, January 7, 2010.

shadow over the drive towards renewable energy and away from fossil fuels." The pull quote reads: "China will have the world's worst problem with ageing solar panels in less than two decades, according to a recent industry estimate."[64]

What sort of problem are we talking about? Globally, journalist Stephen Chen reports, 78 million tons worth of waste panels by 2050.[65] Tian Min, general manager of the recycling company Nanjing Fangrun Materials, called this "a ticking time bomb" that "will explode with full force in two or three decades and wreck the environment, if the estimate is correct." He also commented, "This is a huge amount of waste and they are not easy to recycle." And further, "If a recycling plant carries out every step by the book to achieve low pollutant emission, their products can end up being more expensive than new raw materials."[66]

Solar panels can't be sent to regular landfills. Lead and carcinogenic cadmium are just two of the persistent pollutants that rainwater can leach out of solar modules. It's worth noting the scale of the problem: a proposed solar harvesting facility that would partly power Microsoft data centers would contain 100,000 pounds of cadmium alone.[67] Also worth noting: These panels are made of glass and, as any four-year-old can tell you, glass breaks. Solar panels only work outside and hence can be damaged by the things that predictably happen outside: hail, hurricanes, tornadoes, and earthquakes. This has already happened at industrial solar harvesting facilities around the globe. A tornado destroyed 200,000

[64] Stephen Chen, "China's ageing solar panels are going to be a big environmental problem," *South China Morning Post*, July 30, 2017.
[65] Michael Shellenberger, "If Solar Panels Are So Clean, Why Do They Produce So Much Toxic Waste?" *Forbes*, May 23, 2018.
[66] Stephen Chen, op. cit.
[67] Shellenberger, op. cit.

panels in the Mojave Desert,[68] hail damaged 18,000 panels in San Antonio, Texas,[69] and Hurricane Maria took out a majority of the panels at Puerto Rico's second-largest solar installation.[70]

According to wind turbine manufacturer Vestas, globally about 90 percent of the steel from wind turbines can be recovered for recycling.[71] Note the word *can*. The portion that actually *is* recycled is probably more like the average steel recycling rate, about 70 percent. This means that at the end of its functionality, an average 5 MW wind turbine sends between 1,000 and 3,000 pounds of steel to the landfill. Most rotor blades in wind turbines aren't recycled, but rather sent to incinerators. The same happens to most of the plastic. Concrete used in wind turbines is usually downcycled and used as a filler material, often for road construction.[72]

You may remember the rare earth elements about which we've talked so much. Well, it's time to talk about them again.

A single electric car may contain cerium (found in glass, mirrors, LCD screens, batteries, catalytic converters, and polishing powder), neodymium (used in the motor), lanthanum (used in the catalytic converter and the battery), europium and yttrium (used in LCD screens), and dysprosium and terbium (used in the motor).

---

[68] Ibid.

[69] Kelly Pickerel, "How the Solar Industry Is Responding to the Increasing Intensity of Natural Disasters," *Solar Power World*, January 29, 2018.

[70] Dakota Smith, "Puerto Rican Solar Farms Heavily Damaged by Hurricane Maria." *The Weather Junkies*, September 27, 2017.

[71] "Environmental Case Study: Wind Energy," World Steel Association.

[72] Till Zimmerman, Max Rehberger, and Stefan Gößling-Reisemann, "Material Flows Resulting from Large Scale Deployment of Wind Energy in Germany," *Resources*, August 27, 2013.

"There are innumerable ways these metals make our technology faster, lighter, more durable, and more efficient," says one article.[73] "Take europium, used as a red phosphor in cathode ray tubes and LCD displays. It costs $2,000 a kilo, and there are no substitutes. Or erbium, which acts as a laser amplifier in fiber optic cables. It costs $1,000 a kilo, and there are no substitutes. Yttrium is sprinkled in the thermal coatings of jet aircraft engines to shield other metals from intense heat. Neodymium is the workhorse behind the high-performance magnets found in nearly every hard disk drive, audio speaker, wind turbine generator, cordless tool, and electric vehicle motor. The list goes on. Cancer treatment drugs. MRI machines. Nuclear control rods. Camera lenses. Superconductors. Rare earths are essential to such a bevy of technologies that a shortage would, according to the Natural Resources Council, 'have a major negative impact on our quality of life.'"[74]

Of course, we can't allow anything that would "have a major negative impact on our quality of life." Much better to destroy great swaths of the living earth.

Recycling rare earth minerals is a complex process. The rare earths in solar panels, such as tellurium or indium, are sometimes recycled. But in wind turbines, rare-earth metals used in the generator are rarely—if ever—extracted. That's because recycling rare-earth elements present "challenges at nearly every level."

As one article explains, "The elements are present in small amounts in things like cell phones. As parts get smaller, so do the amounts of material used. In a touch screen, for example, the elements are distributed throughout the material at the molecular scale. 'It's actually getting much harder to recycle electronics,' says

---

[73] Maddie Stone, "The Future of Technology is Hiding on the Ocean Floor," *Gizmodo*, April 5, 2016.
[74] Ibid.

Alex King of the Critical Materials Institute, a U.S. Department of Energy-funded 'Innovation Hub' focused on strategies for ensuring the supply of five rare earth metals identified by the government as critical. 'We used to have cell phones where you could snap out the battery, which is probably the biggest single target for recycling. With smartphones, those things are built so you can't get the battery out, at least not easily.'"

The article continues: "Cell phones are typically recycled by smashing, shredding and grinding them into powder. The powder can then be separated into component materials for disposal or recycling. But new cell phones incorporate more elements than ever—some around 65 in total. This makes the powder a more complicated mixture to separate than it was with older phones. 'It's easier to separate rare earth elements from rocks than from cell phones,' King says. To separate these materials often means 'very aggressive solvents or very high temperature molten metal processing. It's not simple,' says Yale University industrial ecologist Thomas Graedel. Because of the nasty materials or large amounts of energy needed, in some cases recycling could create greater environmental harm than mining for the metals in the first place."

The article explains that in some cases, recycling processes result in a huge loss of material. One study, for example, found that shredding hard drives to recycle the neodymium they contain resulted in 90 percent of the material being lost. "The large losses of material incurred while shredding the material puts serious doubts on the usefulness of this type of recycling as a solution for scarcity," says one of the researchers quoted in the article.[75]

---

[75] Jessica Marshall, "Why Rare-Earth Recycling is Rare (And What We Can Do About It)," *Ensia Magazine*, April 7, 2014.

In 2011, less than 1 percent of rare-earth minerals were recycled. By 2019, rates were still less than 5 percent.[76]

All of which is why, as Alex King puts it, "In an economy where the use of rare earths is growing, you cannot recycle your way out of trouble. Eventually, there will have to be new mines."

Perhaps the most toxic of all recycling industries is that of lead. Lead is found in large quantities in lead-acid batteries, which are used in many home solar systems and utility-scale energy storage facilities. Lead can be found in glass, ceramics, solder, explosives, insecticides, bullets, pipes, sheet lead for radiation protection, plastics, pigments, and even in cosmetics (e.g., the FDA allows lipsticks to have up to 7 ppm).

Lead recovery is a big business. Most new lead-acid batteries contain more than 75 percent recycled lead (100 percent recycling isn't cost effective). Because recycling is expensive in rich nations, many lead-acid batteries are shipped to low-cost recyclers in Africa, Central and South America, and Southeast Asia, where environmental regulations are unenforced or nonexistent. In small workshops and homes, people crack open these batteries and smelt

---

[76] Kristin Linnenkoper, "Is it now or never for rare earth recycling?" *Recycling International*, May 10, 2019.

The situation is similar with CFLs, which are legally required to be recycled because they contain highly toxic mercury. More than 65 percent of them end up in landfills and trash piles. If rates of rare-earth recycling ever go up, it will not be out of care for the planet, but rather care for money: "When small amounts of rare earths are part of complex mixtures, separation can be too expensive to justify for these elements alone, leading some to suggest that the even more valuable elements within electronics, such as gold, palladium and iridium, may make recycling economically worthwhile. 'It might be that the rare earths will pay for the price of doing the processing and the gold, platinum and palladium will be the cash flow,' says Eric Peterson of Idaho National Laboratory, who leads the rare-earth reuse and recycling research program for the Critical Materials Institute."

lead over open stoves without any safety equipment, resulting in horrific pollution. The Blacksmith Institute, which lists lead-acid battery recycling as one of the top 10 worst pollution problems, estimates that more than 1 million people at nearly 70 sites around the world are seriously harmed by this industry. Many of them can expect a lifespan 20 years below average for their area. And of course, nonhumans are probably worse off, as the soil, air, and waterways in these areas are poisoned.[77]

Workers at recycling facilities are commonly paid minimum wage for the exhausting, mind-numbing tasks required, including sorting a stream of incoming recyclables on a conveyor belt into chutes. Efficiency being the rallying cry of modern capitalism, these conveyor belts move fast, and if you can't keep up, you obviously don't deserve the minimum wage salary; out the door with you.

One article notes: "Recycling cannot be completely systematized because it deals with an ever-changing flow of materials in all manner of shapes and sizes. Workers may have to personally handle most of the scrap passing through recycling facilities, potentially exposing them to sharp objects, toxics, carcinogens, or explosives."[78]

Here's something else that's just nuts—and unsustainable—about recycling: the distances involved. Currently, almost every plastic soda bottle recycled in the U.S. is baled and shipped to Los Angeles, where it can be melted down and reformed into new bottles. A

---

[77] "Lead-Acid Battery Recycling," Blacksmith Institute, 2011.
[78] Brian Joseph, "Recycling Work: Low pay, poor training, hazardous tasks," *Oregon Live*, April 12, 2016.

sizable portion of U.S. scrap metal is shipped to Turkey; the majority of plastic scrap (still) goes to China. Other major export markets for U.S. scrap include Vietnam, Thailand, and Malaysia. The European Union exports even more scrap and waste to China than does the U.S. And most lead-acid batteries are shipped around the world for recycling, too.

The shipping distance between major East Coast ports and Turkey is more than 5,000 miles.

That's a lot of bunker fuel.

We're not saying you shouldn't recycle. We ourselves recycle, not because it will save the planet but because it's generally the right thing to do, and all other things being equal it's not more harmful to the planet to recycle than to send stuff to the dump. We're just saying that the fundamental lie of recycling is that it can lead to a green industrial economy that's self-sustaining. The lie is that with efficient recycling, no new raw material inputs would be required, and forests, mountains, rivers, and prairies could be left intact while industry continues happily along, endlessly recycling the same raw materials it started with. We have to set aside our false hopes and turn to face the facts. In the words of James Howard Kunstler, author of such books as *The Long Emergency* and *The Geography of Nowhere: A History of American Suburbia and Urban Development*, the planet needs us to be "reality-based adults,"[79] and the planet is out of time.

A much larger problem than that of materials lost or degraded

---

[79] James Howard Kunstler, *Too Much Magic: Wishful Thinking, Technology, and the Fate of the Nation* (New York: Grove Press, 2013), 198.

through recycling is that of growth. Increased demand for steel around the world means that mining iron ore has to expand globally. Recycling just can't keep up with industries, militaries, and the demand for consumer goods made out of steel. The story is the same when it comes to rare earth minerals. As science journalist Jessica Marshall writes, "Jelle Rademaker of the Green Academy in the Netherlands and colleagues calculated the potential for rare earth recycling from magnets in computer hard drives, hybrid cars and wind turbines, assuming 100 percent recovery in each case. They found that the amount available for recycling could be at most 10 to 15 percent of the demand between [2014] and 2015. The percentage dips even further toward 2020, as demand takes off but only computer hard drives are available for recycling."[80]

And, here we are, as this book goes to publication in 2020, with a tiny fraction of rare-earth metals being recycled.

This is true across the board with recycling: Demand is rising too fast, and recycling can't keep up, which means that more raw source materials need to be extracted. That means more mountains blown up, more forests turned into open-pit mines, more rivers poisoned. As long as the global economy is expanding, steel recycling (and all recycling) will never be enough to keep up with demand. And since 100 percent recycling is functionally impossible, even a steady-state (or zero-growth) economy can't be sustained by recycling. For recycling to eliminate the need for mining, the global economy would need to constantly shrink. And the initial shrinking would have to be dramatic: remember that less than 40 percent of steel comes from recycled sources. And since steel consumption is often used as a proxy for the "health" and growth of an economy (one book notes that "high energy societies could

[80] Jessica Marshall, "Why Rare-Earth Recycling Is Rare (And What We Can Do About It)," *Ensia Magazine*, April 7, 2014.

thrive without microchips, etc., but, by contrast, could not exist
without steel")[81], we could make a ballpark estimate that more than
60 percent of the global economy would need to disappear to reach
a "steel" steady state (with more disappearing each year after that).
And that's if 100 percent recycling were possible. More realistically,
we're talking about something like 80 percent of the global economy having to be shut down before achievable rates of steel recycling could match the (temporary) demand.

Because recycling is dependent on (and supports) the economic
system as a whole, it's also vulnerable to changing markets.

First, you must have enough supply—you have to get people to
recycle. In some cases, this is, with the right sort of education, possible. In the United States, about 34 percent of waste is recycled;
the top nations in the world are Austria (64 percent), Germany (62
percent), and Singapore (59 percent).

After this, you must have proper sorting facilities.

And you must have a bulk commodities market for the sorted
recyclable material (no one buys one used plastic bottle at a time).
The commodities market in turn depends on the market for the
recycled product itself—plastic pellets, ingots of aluminum or steel
or copper, paper pulp, and the other final products of recycling. In
other words, someone has to need thousands of tons of recycled
raw material.

Plus, the recycled raw material itself has to be competitive in
terms of quality and price.

And all this has to work geographically as well, factoring in

---

[81] Vaclav Smil, *Still the Iron Age: Iron and Steel in the Modern World* (Oxford: Butterworth-
Heinemann, 2016), 198.

transportation costs, storage, warehousing, and everything else that goes into an industrial supply chain.

If it's cheaper to extract a raw material, recycling depends on law, custom, or subsidy.

All of that means modern recycling is an unstable, fluctuating industry. In 2015, the U.S. was described as "awash in a glut" of scrap and recyclables because of a slow Chinese economy (a slower economy means less production, and less need for scrap materials). Recycling businesses were threatened by the saturated market driving down prices they received for their recycled product. One paper recycler said that "prices get so low that you can't even cover your own costs."[82]

We noted a moment ago that a main problem with the possibility of 100 percent steel recycling is growth. While this is true, it's even more important to say that steel production at any scale isn't sustainable. Steel production, or even recycling, is impossible at scale without industrial electricity which requires dams, coal power plants, nuclear power, or massive wind or solar energy harvesting facilities. It's impossible without factories to produce refractory materials, without other factories to produce electrodes, and without still other factories to create cranes and crucibles and oxygen injection equipment. In other words, it's impossible without an entire industrial infrastructure to support it.

Recycling as an industry is dependent on continued mass consumption. Anything that threatens the system of consumption will also threaten the recycling industry, since the recycling industry directly depends on the waste stream of the capitalist process. As

---

[82] James R. Hagerty and Bob Tita, "U.S. Is Awash in Glut of Scrap Materials," the *Wall Street Journal*, June 7, 2015.

usual, any threat to the system must be discouraged. This helps explain why "reduce" and "reuse" have been more or less eliminated from the program: the system is in charge, and anything that gets in the way of expanding the economy will be shunted aside or destroyed.

Steel recycling is at base a cost-reduction measure for industry. And remember, the steel industry includes every other industry that depends on steel in its products: aerospace, cars and trucks, ships, drills, mining equipment, construction, appliances, military. One article notes: "What once was a sideline industry—recycling—is becoming central to manufacturing."[83]

And here we find—as with industrial solar and improvements in efficiency—the true purpose of recycling: not saving the planet, but instead helping industry.

Physically, recycling benefits industry in at least two ways. First, it reduces energy costs for the industries involved in production. This savings doesn't go toward reducing harm to the planet or keeping growth in check; instead, it goes toward profits which are almost always reinvested in these or other industries. It's the Jevons paradox yet again. The result is further growth of the economy, which directly leads to more clearcuts, more "developments," more cars, more factories, more trawlers: in short, the death of the planet.

Second, recycling benefits industry by reducing materials costs for the industries involved, which leads to the same consequences as above.

---

[83] Ingrid Lobet, op. cit.

Recycling is a tonic for industrial civilization: more strength, longer life. Can't you already see the late-night TV advertisements?

Of course, some types of recycling aren't inherently profitable, so they have to be encouraged by law. The European Union, for example, dictates that manufacturers are responsible for costs associated with the end of their products' utility. Laws like this are good, in that they slow industry by imposing costs, but they're also insufficient, since, as we've seen, recycling itself can be energy intensive, toxic, and highly destructive.

The European mandate (indeed, any laws to encourage recycling) may result in slowdowns in some industries and reductions in pollution and toxins. But it will result in the growth of new dirty industries, too. And recycling industries will build chains of businesses dependent on the continued flow of scrap material; creating their own demand for raw materials. That can mean extra waste is generated on purpose, just so it can go to recycling providers, who can then make a profit—and everyone in the supply chain gets some new green street cred.

Sweden, for example, has become dependent on garbage for energy. What happens if their sources of garbage are cut off? This would be considered a disaster.

Recycling can't be successful without a market for the recycled product; the stuff has to be valuable to someone. But because recycling (and reuse) begins with used and degraded materials, there isn't always enough demand. The clothing industry is a great example. Even though most trashed textiles could be recycled (or better, reused), about 85 percent of them in the U.S. go directly to landfills.[84] Thrift stores and recyclers are overwhelmed. As of 2012, the average person in the United States purchased 64 items of clothing per year, which corresponds to the throwaway rate: more than 60 pounds of textiles per person, per year.[85] The 15 percent of this flood that does end up at thrift stores doesn't all get sold, either. A single Salvation Army store in New York City yields six tons of excess clothing per day. The majority of this is compressed into bales and exported, mostly to sub-Saharan Africa; clothing that won't sell there goes to industrial rag-production facilities.[86]

In 1901, the average American household spent about 14 percent of its income on clothing; today, the number is closer to 3 percent. As that proportion has declined, so has the average person's skill in sewing and so has the ability of tailors to make a living.

We live in a throwaway culture, a throwaway economy, and recycling does nothing to challenge this.

The natural decay process is one of the most fascinating and important cycles on earth. When people die, we become food for other creatures. Fungi grow through our bodies. Bacteria feast on our soft tissues. Our bones become calcium sources for deer, squirrels, and bears. Nothing is wasted; every part of our bodies becomes part of some other being, whether soil or tree or river or insect or anyone else. This is how life ends, and in so doing feeds further life (unless your corpse is buried by standard means, that is, embalmed by being pumped full of highly carcinogenic and toxic compounds, encased in concrete, and buried six feet deep).

[84] Sara Boboltz, "We Buy an Obscene Amount of Clothes. Here's What It's Doing to Secondhand Stores," *Huffington Post*, November 20, 2014.

[85] Luz Claudio, "Waste Couture: Environmental Impact of the Clothing Industry," *Environmental Health Perspectives* 115, no. 9 (September 2007): A449–A454.

[86] Elizabeth L. Cline, "The Afterlife of Cheap Clothes," *Slate*, June 2012.

The beautiful process of life feeding life is the same for everyone on this planet. I (Max) am eating the eggs of the chickens who are, as I type this, sitting next to me. In time, I may eat their bodies. Or maybe a hawk or fox will eat them, or perhaps they'll live to old age and receive a burial, but even then, they'll be eaten by the earthworms and soil who eat us all in the end. For now, the chickens enjoy their blessed experience here on earth, eating grass and insects, foraging between blooms of camas and daffodil. It's the same for the oak tree curving over my head: for now, it breathes the warm, rich, spring-scented air; it eats chicken and worm poop and the remains of old leaves and grass and camas and daffodil. But eventually (though I hope not for a long time) it too will die and be eaten by insects and bacteria and fungi, who will themselves become meals for someone else. Of course, the same will happen with me. I will die, and chickens will eat me. Or bears. Or vultures. Or mice, rats, insects, worms, or bacteria.

Industrial recycling is a toxic mimic of this process. It shares some broad characteristics, but perverts the actual function. Natural decay takes bodies, born or hatched or sprouted or otherwise formed into being, and turns them into nourishment for others. Industrial recycling starts with products ripped from the earth and maintains that destructive imperative throughout; every step of the way, more destruction. Instead of feeding nourishment to other living beings, industrial recycling feeds materials to machines, to industries, to empire.

We've been trained to believe that giving back to the land is impossible, that nature is based on everyone exploiting everyone else, that nature is "red in tooth and claw" and that natural selection itself is based on survival of the most exploitative, really the most capitalist. We've been taught that this culture is overrunning the earth because we're number one, but in reality, we're just better at this exploitation thing than everyone else.

It's not surprising, then, that so many people mistakenly interpret recycling not as a process that at best reduces the rate at which harm is occurring, but as something positive. After all, if all life involves destruction, then destroying a bit less is good, right?

But if all life involves harming the planet, how did the planet get so rich and fecund and alive and diverse in the first place? The earth became so rich by every being making the world better by their very existence, by their lives and deaths. Salmon make forests better by their lives and deaths. So do oak trees, eel grass, actinomycetes, and oyster mushrooms.

It's not surprising that so many people believe humans are inherently destructive. Most of us have grown up surrounded by the products of this culture: plastics, cars, airplanes, cheap clothes, bottled water, televisions, computers, parking garages, freeways, cell towers, skyscrapers, big box stores, power lines, dams, roadcuts, clearcuts, hardware stores, fences, ports, train tracks. Progress. We know what we see, and what we see is industrial civilization. And what we see is destruction. We see a world being killed before our eyes. How many of us speak nostalgically of forests or meadows where we played as children, in places we are now too heartbroken to visit, because those forests or meadows are gone, replaced by subdivisions, strip malls, and highways; the sounds of frogs and meadowlarks replaced by those of cars and trucks? It's not a surprise that so many, then, would attempt to convince themselves—to forestall going mad with a grief no being should have to bear—that such a loss is somehow natural or inevitable or, god help us all, acceptable.

But while it may not be a surprise, it's also not forgivable.

Ultimately, the important question for sustainability is not whether a society can be based on 100 percent recycling; it's whether a society can be based on improving the health of the world. In other words, does your society give back as much or more than it takes? Is your community good for the planet, or is it not? Recall that the Makah lived in place for thousands of years, as have many other indigenous peoples.

Industrial recycling doesn't help the planet. It doesn't even substantially reduce the rate at which the planet is harmed.

I (Derrick) have spent a lot of time thinking about mealworms, the larvae of darkling beetles. A couple of years ago I read an article about how bacteria in the guts of mealworms allow them to digest polystyrene (what we commonly and not-quite-correctly call Styrofoam). This excited me, in part because I love insects, and in part because I hate what plastics (and the rest of this culture) are doing to the planet.

So, I bought some mealworms online, presumably saving them from being eaten by someone's pet lizards, and I installed them in a nice bed of oats and cornmeal. Then, whenever I ended up with some Styrofoam waste, I'd toss that into the mealworm container too.

And they ate it!

Admittedly it wasn't particularly fast. It could take months for a standard polystyrene cup to disappear. But it was happening.

And the mealworms seemed happy. And fecund. Soon enough, I had a dozen breadbox-sized containers of mealworms as well as two containers of pupae I nightly removed from the mealworm containers, and one container of beetles I removed from the pupae containers. Every month or so I'd move the beetles to a container from which all the mealworms had graduated. And fairly often I'd remove dead beetles and put them in the forest. They always disappeared quickly. I felt good about converting polystyrene into food for birds and bears and rats and foxes and slugs.

I still had a question, though. The reason polystyrene isn't digestible by, say, humans, is that we don't have bacteria in our guts capable of breaking polystyrene's molecular bonds. If you swallowed a little polystyrene pill, it would probably pass right through you, and if later you checked your poop, you'd find it more or less intact. I knew the mealworms weren't simply chewing the polystyrene into smaller pieces and passing them through with nothing absorbed, but I didn't know if they were perhaps breaking those chemical bonds, absorbing what they could, and then pooping out something that was still indigestible by anyone else.

Finally came the big day when I got to harvest a bunch of "frass," the official name for insect larvae excrement. I sifted the few remaining mealworms from the frass, then put half the frass outside in tiny piles, and the other half around the stems of my houseplants. The piles outside disappeared overnight. I don't know who ate them. I'm guessing bears, since there was too much for slugs and maybe even rats. But what really excited me was that within a couple of days the inside frass was covered with mold, which meant that someone—in this case a mold—was able to digest the poop. Which means the normally unbreakable bonds of the polystyrene had well and truly been broken, the carbon been made available as food for others.

I immediately began daydreaming of setting up entire rooms full of mealworms who were happily eating everyone's to-go cups and packing peanuts—that's a great idea, right? Mealworms will save the planet from our stupidity! And even better, I learned they can also digest some polyethylene![87]

Enter the Jevons paradox. I (Derrick) needed a cooler, so I went to a Fred Meyer grocery store. I'm aware that "needed" is the wrong word. Humans don't *need* coolers. We've survived for scores of thousands of years without them, after all. That's one of the reasons this culture is killing the planet: we believe we *need* coolers—and more broadly, plastics, and still more broadly, the products of industrial civilization—and we don't seem to believe we *need* a living planet. In any case, there I was in Fred Meyer, facing probably 40 yards of linear shelf space packed with scores of different metal and polystyrene coolers. Who says diversity is disappearing from the planet? I decided, and this is where a strange variant of the Jevons paradox comes into play, to purchase a polystyrene container, specifically because I knew that when I was done with it, I could feed it to the mealworms. The fact that mealworms can digest polystyrene—and, I must admit, the cooler's $3.99 price—appealed to me.

But that's okay, isn't it? We can view this as me indirectly purchasing food to give to the forest, right? Mealworms eat the cooler, fungi eat the frass, slugs eat the fungi, ants eat the slug slime, spiders eat the ants, varied thrushes eat the spiders. Everybody wins.

But here's the problem. Only about 20 percent of the carbon in the polystyrene ends up either as mealworm mass or frass. The vast majority of it actually ends up in the air. As with other animals, mealworms expire carbon dioxide. So, while it's great that this little project is converting polystyrene into bears and fungi and everybody else, it's mainly converting polystyrene into atmospheric carbon.

---

[87] And gypsy wax moth larvae love, love, love to eat polyethylene.

And here's the point: Even a nonindustrial recycling of this industrial pollutant into nutrients *still* harms the planet.

But here's the real point: Prior to being converted into polystyrene, this carbon was stored safely under the ground. It never should have been brought up. The answer to the problem of polystyrene pollution isn't mealworms. The answer to the problem of polystyrene pollution is to not make it in the first place.

There's a fourth R that's far more important than the three in Reduce, Reuse, Recycle. This R stands for *Refuse*, as in: We must refuse to maintain our allegiance to this culture, and we must refuse to follow along with those who are more interested in protecting this culture than protecting the planet. We must refuse to settle for any solutions that do not materially help the real, physical world on which the lives of every being on this planet depend. We must refuse to allow this culture to kill the planet, whether this killing is powered by oil or wind.

There's certainly a fifth R as well: *Resist*, as in we must resist the dominant culture's destruction of the natural world with every cell and every breath. We must resist for the polar bears and salmon, hoary bats and golden eagles, sage grouse and desert tortoises.

And there's even a sixth R: *Restore*. As well as stopping this culture's murder of the planet we must align ourselves with the natural world to help restore it to whatever health it can achieve. We must restore grasslands and wetlands and rivers and streams and forests and seagrass beds and soil. The living earth will do most of that work. We just need to help out along the way.

Chapter 9

THE GREEN CITY LIE

Surely it is obvious enough, if one looks at the whole world, that it is becoming daily better cultivated and more fully peopled than anciently. All places are now accessible, all are well known, all open to commerce; most pleasant farms have obliterated all traces of what were once dreary and dangerous wastes; cultivated fields have subdued forests; flocks and herds have expelled wild beasts; sandy deserts are sown; rocks are planted; marshes are drained; and where once were hardly solitary cottages, there are now large cities. No longer are (savage) islands dreaded, nor their rocky shores feared; every-where are houses, and inhabitants, and settled government, and civilized life. What most frequently meets our view (and occasions complaint), is our teeming population: our numbers are burdensome to the world, which can hardly supply us from its natural elements; our wants grow more and more keen, and our complaints more bitter in all mouths, while Nature fails in affording us her usual sustenance.

—TERTULLIAN, 200 CE[1]

---

[1] Tertullian, also known as Quintus Septimus Florens Tertullianus, *A Treatise on the Soul*.

Sustainable urban planning is a booming field at universities around the world. Nearly every major city on the planet has a sustainable planning department. And it's common to see articles like "America's 50 Greenest Cities;" and to see books titled *Green Metropolis: Why Living Smaller, Living Closer, and Driving Less Are the Keys to Sustainability*; or *Triumph of the City: How Our Greatest Invention Makes Us Richer, Smarter, Greener, Healthier, and Happier*. Hundreds of billions of dollars are spent on "green city" projects every year. So-called "eco-cities" are being built from the ground up in coastal China, South Korea, and the United Arab Emirates (UAE).

Outside of popular imagination, however, green cities remain not just elusive but physically impossible. In fact, cities around the world function essentially the same as they have for thousands of years, as centers of consumption, control, and power. Modern cities are not just linked to the destruction of the planet; they're central to it.

The C40 Cities Climate Leadership Group is a network of "megacities" (originally 40 but now more than 90 and rising) "committed to addressing climate change" with "meaningful, measurable, and sustainable action on climate change."

On the group's website, the first question is: "Why cities?" Their answer is that since urban growth shows no sign of slowing, cities consume 75 percent of the world's energy, and cities are responsible for more than 80 percent of CO_2 emissions, it's clear that cities must be at the core of addressing the destruction of the planet.

In statistics clearly pointing toward one inevitable conclusion—that cities aren't sustainable—the group members see hope: "In the heart of the city lies an opportunity," they write. "Urban density presents a greener way to live."[2]

They're not alone in this belief. Greenpeace supports what they call the "compact city model," as does the Organization for Economic Cooperation and Development, which notes on its website that "compact cities lessen the impact on the environment."[3] The Urban Land Institute, American Planning Association, and European Environment Agency have all made statements in support of compact cities. The United Nations has a "Global Compact Cities Program." Elizabeth Farrelly, in her popular book *Blubberland*, writes, "If we were to design a green settlement-pattern from scratch, it would not be suburbia, or urban villages, or Greek fishing towns, or even say, Barcelona. It would be Manhattan. Manhattan—or something like it—is the greenest city on earth."

(And why Barcelona? Why not Tallahassee? Or Kinshasa, capital of the Democratic Republic of the Congo? Or more to the point, why not a community of indigenous people living traditionally, the only "green settlement-pattern" humans have ever "designed," a design that worked for all of humanity's existence prior to the metastasization of cities? Oh, yeah, it doesn't provide us with computers or televisions, or a level of prosperity that most people would accept as reasonable.)

The idea that a compact, dense city can reduce energy use and emissions, protect wildlands and water quality, save biodiversity, and provide a better quality of life is at the heart of the mythology of the sustainable city, and "mythology" is the operative word.

---

[2] "Why Cities?" C40 Group of Cities, 2015.
[3] "Compact City Policies: A Comparative Assessment," Organization for Economic Cooperation and Development.

Since they first emerged 8,000 to 10,000 years ago, cities have grown in a similar way. Cities are reliant on totalitarian agriculture, in which more or less all of the energy of a landscape is diverted to human use. This leads to an increase in human population. It also leads to the destruction of the land: to plant annual crops for humans, forests have to be cut down and grasslands plowed under.

For people who live in cities, this is a good news/bad news thing.

The good news for the city is that by converting the landbase into humans, the city can build great armies with which to conquer other peoples and take their resources. That's how empires grow.

The bad news is that they *have* to conquer other peoples, because they've overshot and harmed the carrying capacity of their homeland.

This is the history of cities.

Here's an example. Recent research has found that the expansion of the 6,000-year-old city of Akko, in modern-day Israel, led to the collapse of the local landbase. The researchers write that, "Urban growth involves one of the most extreme forms of ecological stress and land alteration.... The spatial concentration of agricultural, industrial and commercial activities led to increased demands on local ecosystems, and to an encroachment on and a loss of natural biotopes in and around the [ancient city]. Fragmented proto-urban ecosystems only persisted as small patches within a matrix of urban and agricultural expansion, or even disappeared. This human-induced ecological imbalance has prevailed throughout the last ~4,000 years, as the coastal vegetation became dominated by a dry and urban-adapted woodland in association with a shrub-steppe.... The lack of resilience of coastal ecosystems following the abandonment of the town may result from 3,500 years of continuous human pressure, leading to an ecological erosion marked by nonregenerating stands of forested communities."

The researchers go on to say that "the long-held belief of a 'golden age' of sustainable early urban development" is probably false. "The same mechanisms that degrade or overexploit the ecosystems nowadays were already at work [6,000 years ago].... Accepting large urban concentrations might [mean] an intrinsic impossibility to produce locally sustainable development."[4]

Urban sprawl is rightfully recognized as a major cause of environmental destruction. Between 1945 and 2000, 45 million acres in the United States (an area larger than Washington State) was converted to urbanized land.[5]

The word "converted" sanitizes what urban sprawl entails. When cities expand, forests, meadows, and grasslands are destroyed. Wetlands and rivers are drained. By chainsaw and bulldozer and plow, habitat for wild creatures is eliminated. Almost all native plants are killed. The animals who remain are forced to run a gauntlet of devastated habitat, roads, traps, bullets, poison, and booted feet. Sprawl, or urban "development," may be responsible for the endangerment of more species in the United States than any other human activity.[6]

It's no wonder most people—at least most sane people—recognize that suburban sprawl is an atrocity. Of course, this hasn't stopped "developers" from continuing to build more sprawl.

---

[4] David Kaniewski et al., "Early urban impact on Mediterranean coastal environments," *Scientific Reports* 3, no. 3450 (2013).

[5] Ruben N. Lubowski et al., "Major Uses of Land in the United States, 2002," United States Department of Agriculture, Economic Research Service, May 2006.

[6] Brian Czech et al., "Economic Associations among Causes of Species Endangerment in the United States," *BioScience Journal* 50, no. 7 (2000): 593–601.

But we can't include these people among the sane.

When it comes to mainstream thinking on environmentalism, recognizing the worst destruction usually isn't a problem. Most people understand that a clearcut or an oil spill is a disaster, and most people understand that suburban sprawl is, too. But recognizing the problem is one thing; recognizing a false solution is much more difficult. This is one reason there has been so little opposition to the "environmental" movement's focus on dense, "green" cities as a solution for a world in environmental collapse.

Dense urbanization does make superficial sense. Instead of metastasizing across the landscape, population growth and construction are contained within a small space. Public transit, bicycling, and walking can replace private vehicles. Homes tend to be smaller and more energy efficient, and shops and services can be located in the neighborhoods they serve. Theoretically, all this reduces habitat destruction and energy use. That sounds great, right? What sort of crazy people could be against compact "green" cities?

But the benefits of "green cities" are illusory. One urban planning professor, Michael Neuman, reviewed the literature and found that "the relation between compactness and sustainability can be negatively correlated, weakly related, or correlated in limited ways."[7] In a later interview, Neuman stated, "Since 1960, while human population has doubled, the global economy has quadrupled, and resource consumption quintupled. Thus, we are getting less efficient and less sustainable as we move to cities, not more,

---

[7] Michael Neuman, "Compact City Fallacy," *Journal of Planning Education and Research* 25 (2005): 11–26.

contrary to popular belief and professional dogma." Later in the same article, he comments about those "green" cities being built by the UAE and others: "Any high-tech and high-density city in a desert is folly, no matter who designs it. The overall costs, including embodied energy costs, if calculated comprehensively, will likely turn out to belie its supposed sustainability."[8]

Neuman isn't the only researcher to describe the failure of the compact city model. A Taiwanese study looked at increased urban density and found that, far from being any sort of benefit to the natural word, in truth it had a negative impact on environmental sustainability.[9] A Dutch researcher wrote that "the potential of the compact city policy to contribute significantly to the solution of environmental problems ... is limited."[10] And in Iran, another pair of researchers found that "where compact city policies had been implemented, follow-up studies ... show the predicted benefits did not happen."[11]

Other, more specific studies have looked at the link between urban density and energy used for travel and have found essentially no connection between the two. For example, one study in the Netherlands found less than 1 percent difference in personal travel energy use between rural and heavily urbanized areas. And this in a country known for high bicycle usage, which you'd think

---

[8] Alan Oakes, "Revisiting Neuman's 'Compact City Fallacy,'" gb&d [green building and design magazine], September/October 2013.

[9] Jen-Jia Lin and An-Tsei Yang, "Does the compact-city paradigm foster sustainability? An empirical study in Taiwan," Environment and Planning B: Planning and Design 33 (2006): 365–380.

[10] Jochem van der Waals, "The compact city and the environment: a review," Tijdschrift voor Economische en Sociale Geografie 91, no. 2 (May 2000): 111–121.

[11] Abdolhadi Daneshpour and Amir Shakibamanesh, "Compact city: does it create an obligatory context for urban sustainability?" International Journal of Architectural Engineering & Urban Planning, (October 2010).

would drive down travel-related urban energy use.[12] Another urban planner observed that "travel is much more strongly linked to fuel prices and income" than to urban density.[13]

Clearly, the compact city model is not supported by evidence. So why has it gained so much traction? Neuman's conclusion is that city planners, "environmentalists," and politicians have fallen back on the compact city model since they "do not know what [else] to do to be sustainable."

That's what happens when you try to pretend you can make a functionally unsustainable way of living sustainable.

If they want to know what to do to be sustainable, they could ask the land. If they can hear it beneath all the concrete.

Every summer since I (Max) was young, I've spent time on the coast of what is now called Washington State, where the Makah people have lived for at least 3,800 years. During much of that time, the Makah lived in five permanent villages with a combined population of about 4,000.

Makah traditional homes are cedar longhouses in which several families live protected from the almost perpetual damp and wind. In many cases, this wood was taken without having to kill the tree. As one source notes, "Few cedar trees were actually felled before European contact."[14] With a combination of stone axes, fire,

---

[12] Mirjan E. Bouwman, "Changing Mobility Patterns in a Compact City: Environmental Impacts," *Compact Cities and Sustainable Urban Development: A Critical Assessment of Policies and Plans from an International Perspective*, eds. Gert de Roo and Donald Miller (Aldershot, U.K.: Ashgate Publishing, 2000).

[13] Peter Hall, "Sustainable Cities or Town Cramming?" *Planning for a Sustainable Future*, eds. Antonia Layard, Simin Davoudi, and Susan Batty (Abingdon, U.K.: Routledge, 2001).

[14] Jim Pojar and Andy Mackinnon, *Plants of the Pacific Northwest Coast* (Auburn, WA: Lone Pine Publishing, 2004), 42.

and rock-hard yew wedges, planks three feet wide and 40 feet long could be split from standing old-growth western red cedar trees, or from those who had fallen naturally. These planks were then shaped to provide overlapping tile-like drainage and complete protection from rain. Since cedar is rot-resistant, each set of planks could last well over 100 years, and since cedar is lightweight, the planks could be carried to seasonal camps for salmon fishing, berry harvesting, and other activities, reducing overall demand for this building material. This is an example of how to build comfortable, snug homes without destroying the planet. There are thousands of such natural building techniques, from the adobe cliff dwellings of the Southwest desert to the round, portable, yurtlike Mongolian ger, which are similarly comfortable and sustainable homes.

In what is now downtown Seattle; thick old-growth forest once blanketed the hillsides. There were 400-foot-tall Douglas fir and 30-foot-thick red cedar trees, some 3,000 years old. The trees have been replaced by skyscrapers, concrete, and condominiums—each ingredient of which was extracted from a highly destructive strip mine, shipped hundreds or thousands of miles to the construction site, and assembled using heavy machinery. This is an example of how to build monumental architecture while destroying the planet you rely on for life.

Several years ago, I (Max) spent an afternoon with a basket weaver named Betty from the Makah nation. We walked through the forest and down to the beach, talking as the sun sank low and the spring chill sank through our optimistically thin jackets. As we walked through the young forest—the trees were about 50 years old—Betty told me stories of her relatives splitting cedar planks from the big, old trees, and how she herself harvests bark from cedars and takes the opportunity to trim the trees to help them grow stronger when she gathers materials.

"According to my teaching, I'm only allowed to take a piece this big," she said, holding her hand against a tree to show the width. "Or with grasses for basket weaving, I only take a piece this big for every area like this." She held out her hands, one with finger and thumb meeting in a circle the size of a quarter and the other spread flat. "In this way, I'm going to help the grasses to grow better. But sometimes the grasses don't want me to take even that, because they're going through a lot already. You have to listen."

This is a model of what some would call sustainable yield, and what others would call living in balance.

In many indigenous nations of the Pacific Northwest, western red cedar is considered a sacred tree, the source of not only building materials, but clothing, canoes, baskets, bowls, rope, boxes, blankets, cradles for children, paddles, combs, and countless other necessities of life. Cedar is central to these cultures to the point that some call themselves "people of the red cedar," and the Kwakwaka'wakw call cedar "the tree of life."

How's this for a measure of sustainability: If your way of life can last at least 3,800 years without trashing a place, that's sustainable. On the other hand, if your culture—largely driven by your dense cities—has managed to destroy 98 percent of a continent's old-growth forests within a few centuries, then your way of living is not sustainable.

There are more than 550 federally recognized American Indian nations in the United States today, and around 250 more which aren't federally recognized. That number, around 800, is smaller than the original number of indigenous nations; many were wiped out during colonization. Many of these cultures were living sustainably before they were wiped out by the urbanized dominant culture.

There's no shortage of models for sustainable living.

If urban planners don't know what to do to be sustainable, they're either not paying attention, or more likely, their assumptions don't allow them to consider other options for how to live.

The spoken question may be "How can we live sustainably?" but there are unstated premises at play. Most environmentalists assume we must maintain the high-energy modern lifestyle; we must at all costs avoid disturbing the "prosperity" so important to bright greens.

The real question they're asking is, "How can we have a sustainable industrial civilization?"

And of course, the real answer is that we can't.

This question is a model for all sorts of other questions that allow us to pretend we're "working on the problems" as we continue to kill the planet. We can ask, "How can we stop global warming?" when we really mean, "How can we stop global warming and maintain an industrial lifestyle?" And the answer is that we can't.

Similarly, we can ask, "How can we save the oceans?" but we really mean, "How can we save the oceans without stopping industrial fishing, global warming, and the production of plastics and other pollutants?" In other words, "How can we save the oceans and still have an industrial lifestyle?" And the answer is that we can't.

We can ask, "How can we save the salmon?" but we really mean,

"How can we save salmon without stopping industrial logging, industrial fishing, without removing dams, without stopping the murder of the oceans, and without stopping global warming?" In other words, "How can we save salmon and still have an industrial lifestyle?" And the answer is that we can't.

We can't stop atrocities without stopping the actions that functionally cause the atrocities.

While writing this chapter we received a note from someone saying that while he agreed cities are functionally and necessarily unsustainable, this inevitability is emotionally unacceptable to him, and therefore cities *must be* sustainable.

How does one respond to that—apart from perhaps pointing out that wishes do not reality make?

A few years ago, I (Derrick) got into a disagreement with a journalist who was interviewing me for the online version of *Nature*. He insisted it's possible to have an industrial city-based economy that's not exploitative of any human beings, but rather based completely on purely voluntary exchanges. I asked how people get around in his theoretical city. He said buses. I asked what the buses are made of. He said metal. I asked where the metals come from. He said they're from a mine owned and run by workers who receive such high wages they choose to spend their lives underground. I said we'd leave aside the difficulties raised by that proposition—mining is such a horrid existence that it was one of the first forms of human slavery—and merely discuss the harmful effects of mines on rivers. I got him to agree that mines are inherently toxic to rivers and groundwater. I then asked what happens to people who live along this river that is now going to be polluted. He said they would be paid to move.

I said, "What if they've lived on this river for 50 generations, and they love this river, and they love their way of life, and will not move?"

He said, "Pay them more."

I said, "Their ancestors are buried in this soil, and they will not move."

"How many are there?"

"What difference does it make?" I asked. "Let's say 400."

He said, "They have to move. We as a society would vote on what is best for society."

I said, "So the million people in the city would vote to dispossess the 400 people on the river? You've moved, in just a few sentences, from purely voluntary exchanges to reproducing democratic empire, conquest, genocide, and land theft from indigenous people. And of course, ecocide. All of that repression is functional in industrial civilization. All so you can have a city."

He didn't understand.

Things don't magically appear because it's convenient for you to think they do. Things come from somewhere. These things require materials. There are costs associated with extracting these materials. Those costs are paid by someone.

Even if you really want a groovy, solar-powered mass transit system, the materials still have to come from somewhere someone else lived until their home was destroyed so you can have what you want.

If we want to understand how and why a city—and by extension, an industrial civilization—can never be made sustainable, it would be nice to have a shared definition for *what a city is*. Not many people (including, ironically, urban planners) understand what a city is or how it functions.

We define a city as people living in high enough densities to require the routine importation of resources. This distinguishes cities from villages or towns which support their populations from nearby lands. (As an extension of this, a civilization is a way of life defined by the growth of cities, among other features such as agriculture, standing armies, bureaucracies, and hierarchies of unjust power.)

As soon as you require the routine importation of resources to survive, two things happen. The first is that your way of life can never be sustainable, because requiring the importation of resources means you've denuded the landscape of those particular resources, and any way of life that harms the landbase you need to survive is by definition not sustainable. As your city grows, you will denude an ever-larger area to sustain the city.

Let's get specific: Where do you get bricks for your city? Where do you get wood? Where do you get food? Where do you get copper for electric wires? Where does sewage go? (Well, in the case of New York City, it used to be dumped in the ocean, but when that was stopped by EPA, New York sent it to Colorado, and now it sends it to Alabama, where, "It greatly reduces the quality of life of anybody that this is around," according to Heather Hall, the mayor of Parrish, Alabama. "You cannot go outside, you can't sit on your porch, and this stuff, it's here in our town."[15]) Where does electronic waste go? Everything comes from somewhere and goes

---

[15] Oliver Milman, "'On a hot day, it's horrific': Alabama kicks up a stink over shipments of New York poo," *The Guardian*, March 11, 2018.

somewhere. Bright green fairies don't bring goodies in the night and simultaneously remove All Bad Things.

This is a pattern we've seen since the rise of the first city. The pattern is not an accident. Nor is it incidental. This is how cities function.

One sign of intelligence is the ability to recognize patterns. How many thousands of years of cities devastating landbases do we need before we recognize this pattern?

This is a real question.

The second thing that happens is that your way of life depends on conquest: if you need this resource and people in other communities won't trade you for it, you'll take it. If you can't take it, or you refuse to, your city will dwindle. This, again, is how cities have operated from the beginning.

A city may be small and dense in direct footprint, but a lot more land is needed to feed and provide for its occupants. This additional land, called "ghost acreage" by food systems expert Georg Borgstrom, author of *Hungry Planet*, allows a city to exist without its occupants coming into contact with the land they depend on, building, in essence, a "phantom carrying capacity" based on the consumption of soil, forests, grasslands, water, and so on from other locations.

So, for example, Bruce Mau, a prominent designer, is wrong when he says that "one side effect of urbanization is the liberation of vast depopulated territories for the efficient production of nature." In fact, the opposite is true; one primary effect of urbanization is the harnessing of vast territories of nature for the efficient production of goods for cities.

⊕

To provide an example, the 6 million occupants of the Seattle metro area require much more food than the nearby farms can provide. More than 60 percent of food in the region is imported not just from outside the specific landbase, but from other countries. That doesn't include domestic imports from major food-growing regions in California and the Great Plains, or even the eastern half of Washington State—which together make up more than 30 percent of the remainder.[16]

The transportation network that makes this possible consists of two elements: a maritime network of ports and ships, and a terrestrial network of depots, rail yards, rail lines, trains, roads, and semi-trucks.

The destruction caused by these transportation systems—and this is not to speak of the destruction caused by the extraction of the materials or the manufacture of the items to be transported—is hard to overstate. We talked earlier about some of the harms of bunker fuel, but we didn't mention that the 16 largest ships create more pollution than all the cars in the world. Globally, shipping causes about 25 percent of all of the nitrogen oxide pollution and just under 10 percent of the sulfur oxide pollution. It also emits more than 3 percent of this culture's greenhouse-causing gases.[17]

Put another way, in 2015 shipping emitted 932 million tons of CO_2. That's more than Germany emitted, and more than twice that

---

[16] "Agriculture, Food and Beverage Sector Profile – Seattle, Washington, United States," *Agriculture and Agri-Food Canada*, May 2010.
[17] John Vidal, "Health risks of shipping pollution have been 'underestimated,'" *The Guardian*, April 9, 2009.

emitted by the United Kingdom. It's more than would be emitted by 230 coal-fired power plants.[18]

Once you include this destruction, cities look a lot less green. One 2018 study found that when we account for imported products and services, cities are responsible for 60 percent higher carbon emissions than previously thought. As one article on the study puts it, "Wealthy 'consumer cities' such as London, Paris, New York, Toronto, or Sydney that no longer have large industrial sectors have significantly reduced their local emissions. However, when the emissions associated with their consumption of goods and services are included, these cities' emissions have grown substantially and are among the highest in the world on a per person basis, the report says. Meanwhile, 'producer' cities in India, Pakistan, or Bangladesh generate lots of industrial pollution and carbon emissions in the manufacture of products that will be sold and consumed in Europe and North America."[19]

The terrestrial shipping network isn't any greener than the maritime. Trains in the United States run on diesel fuel. While some nations have electric-powered freight trains, they're still uncommon, and there are compelling reasons the U.S. isn't moving in that direction. And of course, the production of electric train cars—like the production of every other industrial technology we've

---

[18] Megan Darby, "UN shipping climate talks 'captured' by industry lobbyists," *Climate Home News*, October 23, 2017.
[19] Stephen Leahy, "Cities Emit 60% More Carbon Than Thought," *National Geographic*, March 6, 2018.

discussed—causes its own share of harm. For now, rail in this country is completely dependent on fossil fuels.[20]

Semi-trucks are another critical element of the shipping network, and are estimated to be responsible for about 12.5 percent of all U.S. carbon emissions (and probably a similar percentage globally).[21] Electric semi-trucks are currently being developed that source their power from 5,000 pounds of lithium-ion batteries, but prototypes only travel 60 to 140 miles on a charge and require industrial-sized electric hookups only found at facilities like ports.

Truck range is dependent on the fuel's energy density, with diesel having far higher energy per mass than batteries; and on conveniently spaced refueling stations, which diesel provides but battery power does not. Semi-trucks are dependent on diesel—about a gallon of it every six miles.

Every city in the world imports huge volumes of material. This isn't just true for a modern city like Seattle bringing in supplies on container ships, trains, and semi-trucks; it has been the case since cities began. The stomachs of Rome were filled each year with 500,000 tons of grain imported from Sicily, North Africa, and Campania.[22] That these supplies were carried on wagon trains and wooden ships didn't eliminate the harm done by land clearance, road and ship building, growing fodder for draft animals, etc.

---

[20] Jean Paul Rodrigue and Claude Comtois, *The Geography of Transport Systems* (Abingdon, U.K.: Routledge, Third Edition, 2013), Chapter 8, Concept 2.

[21] Katie Valentine, "Big trucks emit huge amounts of carbon every year," *ThinkProgress*, June 2, 2015.

[22] Geoffrey E. Rickman, "The Grain Trade under the Roman Empire," *Memoirs of the American Academy in Rome*, vol. 36, the Seaborne Commerce of Ancient Rome: Studies in Archaeology and History, 1980.

Fundamentally, and functionally, cities take more than the land can support.

In land-based communities, people gather food and materials from the land around them. They don't take too much because there wouldn't be any left for the future; anyone can see that. From there, it's quite simple to develop protocols for avoiding overshoot, like the fish treaties that determined how many salmon could be taken each year by the various tribes along the Columbia River, or the Constitution of the Iroquois Confederacy that stated: "In all of your deliberations in the Confederate Council, in your efforts at law making, in all your official acts, self-interest shall be cast into oblivion. Cast not over your shoulder behind you the warnings of the nephews and nieces should they chide you for any error or wrong you may do, but return to the way of the Great Law which is just and right. Look and listen for the welfare of the whole people and have always in view not only the present but also the coming generations, even those whose faces are yet beneath the surface of the ground—the unborn of the future Nation."[23]

When our food and goods are imported from far away, however, we have less knowledge of how they were produced and less incentive to make changes. What matters most to us, then, are availability, quality, and price. Not the harm caused by the extraction, conversion, transportation, and later disposal of these materials.

And when our food and goods are delivered to us by the economic and social system, we can easily come to perceive the system as the source of the food and goods. The fish you just ate came from Safeway, not the ocean, and the materials in your house came from

---

[23] "Constitution of the Iroquois Nations," Constitution Society.

The Home Depot, not a forest. And when we perceive the system as the source of life, we can come to value the economic and social system over life on the planet. This is how an environmentalist can say that polar bears don't do it for her, and many others can strive to save industrial civilization over life on the planet.

Even when we understand in our heads that the earth is the source of all life, our *experience* will be that the system supplies us with what we need. And we will defend to the death—in this case the death of the planet—what we experience as supplying us with what we need.

In a city, there's no negative feedback loop for importing too much. Clearcutting a forest, for example, makes both dollars and sense. Deforesters profit from cutting corners (and trees), merchants profit as the volume of trade increases, and people in the city get cheap wood. Those people don't have to deal with destruction in their backyard. And when one watershed is trashed, suppliers just move to the next. No one will even notice—at least no one who matters.

Theoretically, at least, there are a couple of possible outcomes when through either resistance from the colonies or ecological collapse cities can no longer gain access to resources necessary to continue.

The first: people of the city recognize they've overwhelmed the carrying capacity of the land and so abandon their way of life. Humans have done this before. But in a city, gaining this understanding is difficult. Even as soil is destroyed, forests cut, and fish overharvested, urban people can comfortably maintain the illusion that everything is okay. The grocery stores are full, the markets are bustling; what could be wrong?

The second: the city and its leaders refuse to see they've

undermined the basis for their own survival, and their society collapses. This has been the fate of many civilizations. It's a common end to the societal choices that lead to drawdown. When you take too much, eventually you have to face the consequences of your actions.

The bright green movement is based on avoiding for a bit longer the consequences of our actions, life on the planet be damned. It's ignoring that this current way of life is and has always been unsustainable, ignoring that this particular party is over, and pretending we can keep this current orgy of planetary destruction going, only now powered by wind and solar. It's about rationalizing the despoliation of what remains of the planet—forget nonhumans (who don't really do it for us) and forget the future; we want to party on! It's a desperate attempt to stave off facing the consequences of our way of life, even though it will lead to an even more horrifying collapse at the end.

Here's yet another insane article that makes the sorts of insane claims to which by now we should be almost inured. The title: "The Surprising Ways Big Cities Are Good for The Environment." The article claims "that the very trends [of urbanization] that have resulted in 'unprecedented destruction of the environment' are now creating the necessary conditions for a possible renaissance of nature." And, "Counterintuitive as it may sound to anyone who's ever breathed in urban smog or looked out onto a natural landscape punctuated by buildings, cities are integral to this rosy vision of the future." Do you see the pattern? No, not the pattern of ubiquitous destruction of the natural world caused by every city throughout history. Instead, the pattern of these bright greens insisting that we ignore that pattern, ignore our senses, ignore our common sense, and believe their lies.

Here is the article's pull quote, which comes from the vice president of a big green environmental organization (and by "big green" we mean more than a billion dollars in total assets and more than $330 million in annual revenues, including, for crying out loud, over $27 million in "restaurant and merchandising sales and parking fees"[24]): "For the first time in the history of the modern man, we're heading to a point where we are laying the foundations for the sustained recovery of nature."[25]

It's not clear what planet these bright greens think they're talking about, but it sure isn't this one, where 200 species are being driven extinct each and every day, and this culture's omnicide is accelerating.

To look at some of the thought errors plaguing bright green attitudes toward what they would call green cities, let's consider the characteristics of a green city. According to the Natural Resources Defense Council (NRDC), a green city has nine elements:

1. Committing to green;
2. Green building;
3. Greening a city's supply chain (from paper and cleaning products to cars and trucks for the municipal fleet);
4. Green power;
5. Conserving nearby (and creating internal) green landscapes;

---

[24] "Wildlife Conservation Society and Subsidiaries: Consolidated Financial Statements and Schedules," June 30, 2018.
[25] Gloria Dickie, "The Surprising Ways Big Cities Are Good for the Environment," *HuffPost,* July 8, 2019.

6. Protecting water quality and quantity;

7. Creating compact mixed-use neighborhoods;

8. Green transport and increased accessibility; and

9. Getting to zero waste.[26]

Let's go through the NRDC's list of the essential elements for a green city one by one.

1. Committing to Green: This means setting clear goals under a guiding "green philosophy" at the level of city governments and using government power and influence to put into place new policies that change the way business and residents go about daily life. Overall, that sounds straightforward and positive. But since cities are based on drawdown and conquest, this "commitment" is in itself necessarily meaningless and abstract. Here's the NRDC's text itself: "First, a city needs to declare its intentions. Words matter. In particular, the city or county council needs to officially adopt a clear statement of green principles or guiding philosophy. It then needs to begin living by that statement in the face of inevitable obstacles and challenges. It needs to use its bully pulpit to move the private sector and residents, and go through planning processes, pass appropriate ordinances, and implement policies that will change the way everyone does business and makes everyday decisions."

But in the context of industrialism's inherent ecological destructiveness, "committing to green" is impossible without committing to deindustrialization.

---

[26] Lee Epstein, "The essential elements of green cities," *Natural Resources Defense Council*, April 3, 2013.

2. Green Building: By this, the NRDC means "officially requiring highly rated green buildings across all municipal functions and public spaces" as well as "some level of green building for all new private construction."

Unfortunately, and this won't surprise most of us, "green building" is more about branding than substantial change. The NRDC's author himself acknowledges this when he says that "even Platinum, the highest level of LEED [the most widespread green building certification] attainment, can be bestowed on places of low actual environmental achievement."

LEED is yet another case of greenwashing. This is well-illustrated by an article profiling "the New American Home" showcased at the 2013 American Builders Show in Las Vegas. This LEED-certified masterpiece is a monstrosity, almost 7,000 square feet (the average U.S. house is about 2,000 square feet, and the global average is closer to 750). Nearly every element of this "New American Home" requires advanced technology, from automatic sliding doors and UV air-purification system to heat pumps (electric powered, with natural gas backup) for heating and cooling. The house is located on the outskirts of Las Vegas, where "development" is pushing farther and farther into what used to be wildlands, destroying fragile Mojave Desert ecology. A series of outdoor pools and water features add to the harm caused by this house in a city already contributing to draining the Colorado River. And to top off the insanity, the house comes with a four-car garage for all your eco-friendly vehicles.[27]

And this building is certified LEED-platinum. The goal clearly isn't to live sustainably, but rather to maintain the illusion that the American Dream and all its consumption is sustainable.

---

[27] Lloyd Alter, "IBS Home Gets LEED Points, But Misses the Green Point," *Treehugger*, January 16, 2013.

On the checklist used for accrediting LEED buildings, points are awarded in a variety of categories and summed to determine whether the site is certified LEED silver, gold, or platinum. The closest the checklist comes to mentioning nature or nonhumans consists of two items: "sensitive land protection" (worth one point) and "open space" (one point). The same point value is given to "thermal comfort," "quality views," and working with a LEED-certified expert. Two points are given for "interior lighting," five points for "access to quality transit," and 18 points for "optimized energy performance."[28]

A friend told us about an elementary school he helped retrofit to LEED specifications. "They ended up using *more* energy," he said, "because the collective attitude of those working in the school was 'this building can run itself regardless of my action.'"

The recipe for a truly ecological building isn't hard to imagine. Here's *our* checklist.

1) Start within the context of a biophilic culture that isn't destroying the land.
2) Gather local building materials in quantities the land can sustain, without the use of any extractive industry. Transport these materials without using fossil fuels.
3) Choose a site that doesn't substantially harm the local nonhuman communities and that allows the human and

---

[28] "Checklist: LEED v4 for Building Design and Construction," U.S. Green Building Council, June 6, 2014.

nonhuman occupants of the site to live such that they enhance local ecology as much as (if not more than) they disturb or take.

4) Build your home in such a way that it's capable of decaying back into the landscape.

5) If all these elements are brought together in a way that could be repeated for centuries without causing a decline in the health of the land, then you've constructed a truly ecological building.

Otherwise, you're lying to yourself and others.

Modern eco-building regularly violates every one of those precepts. Not least important is that "green buildings" occur within the context of a culture destroying the planet. An eco-building in the heart of a metropolis filled with polluting industries, or an eco-building in which cars or other consumer goods are built (Intel, Volkswagen, and war-profiteer and mega-developer CH2M Hill all have LEED-certified factories[29]) is no eco-building at all.

If we apply the same definition of "local" as is commonly accepted in the local food movement—sourced within 100 miles—nearly all LEED-certified and other green buildings fail; they're mostly built with nonlocal materials, and a lot of them don't have a single local component. A solar hot water heater made on the other side of the planet is not "green" in any realistic sense. Nor are metals, concrete, gypsum, and other materials extracted and produced by polluting, highly destructive, and globalized industries.

The difference between the industrial model of green building and the model based on splitting planks from storm-felled

---

[29] Taimur Burki, "Myth #2: Factories can't be green," Intel Corp, U.S. Green Building Council, April 22, 2015.

old-growth trees in vast, unbroken forests is the difference between greenwashing and meaningful sustainability.

3. Greening a City's Supply Chain: This means switching to "green" alternatives for paper, cleaning products, cars and trucks, and all the other materials and goods a city government needs.

The desire to reduce harm is good. It's better for a city (or an individual) to use recycled paper, for example, than paper made from old-growth forests. But substituting a "greener" alternative isn't always a full solution. For example, almost all recycled paper is made using some nonrecycled pulp, often from heavily logged and degraded forests. Just because they're not old growth, is logging these forests somehow justifiable?

Here's the transcript of a current timber industry radio commercial running in Washington State: "Look closely at a working forest, and you'll see clean air; cool, clean water; and healthy salmon runs, thanks to scientific forest practices. You'll see renewable Northwest Wood, the most responsible building material on earth. And you'll see the green economy of the 21st century come to life in the innovative use of climate-friendly wood in modern building construction. See how working forests work for all of us at workingforestsareworking.org."[30]

The marketers behind this campaign packed a lot of fallacies and lies into 30 seconds.

First is the false cause fallacy, where one presumes a real or perceived relationship between things means one causes the other. In this case, a perceived relationship between clean air and water in the mountains and "working forests" (which means forests being

---

[30] "Responsible, Sustainable," Working Forests, *iSpot.tv.*

repeatedly logged) is used to promote the claim that logging leads to clean air and water. This is a lie. Logging not only causes air pollution, but also kills the plants who purify the air. And it hammers water quality by removing plants who keep soil intact, thereby increasing erosion, leading to the sedimentation of streams and rivers. One study showed that logging roads produce between 20 and 35 tons of sediment per acre of road surface per year.[31] One acre is about 0.6 miles of logging road. So that's about a ton per year every 100 feet. And there are at least 440,000 miles of logging roads in the U.S. on National Forest land alone.[32] In contrast, "Streams draining undisturbed forests in the Pacific Northwest usually have water of the highest quality."[33]

Here's another lie: that you'll see healthy salmon runs in "working" forests. Salmon are in a state of crisis. Nearly one-third of all Pacific salmon communities once found from British Columbia to California have been completely eliminated since European invasion, and nearly half of those remaining are listed under the Endangered Species Act. Forty percent of the habitat in this region has been completely destroyed.[34] Most of the salmon population that does still exist is sustained only by hatcheries, which decrease the genetic health of true wild salmon, compete for food with wild fish, falsely inflate population numbers, and provide the illusion

---

[31] Rodger B. Grayson et al., "Water quality in mountain ash forests—separating the impacts of roads from those of logging operations," *Journal of Hydrology* 150, no. 2–4 (October 1993): 459–480.

[32] Derrick Jensen and George Draffan, *Strangely Like War: The Global Assault on Forests* (White River Junction, VT: Chelsea Green Publishing, 2003), 3.

[33] R. Dennis Harr and Richard L. Frederiksen, "Water Quality after Logging Small Watersheds Within the Bull Run Watershed, Oregon," *Water Resources Bulletin* 24, no. 5 (October 1988).

[34] Richard G. Gustafson et al., "Pacific Salmon Extinctions: Quantifying Lost and Remaining Diversity," *Conservation Biology* 21, no. 4 (2007): 1009–1020.

Also: Philip Levin and Michael Schiewe, "Preserving Salmon Biodiversity," *American Scientist*, May–June 2001.

that some salmon populations are stable. As a 2011 NOAA study stated for watersheds draining into the Willamette Valley, "nearly all fish returning ... are hatchery origin."[35] In the Columbia drainage basin, between 97 and 99 percent of the salmon are gone.[36] Populations once numbering in the millions are now in the thousands, hundreds, or even just a few fish.

The main cause of the destruction of the great runs of salmon is, of course, dams—thousands of miles of rivers and streams are blocked. And industrial fishing is a terrible problem: the salmon on the Columbia, for example, were already in decline because of canning factories long before dams were erected. But logging is also responsible for salmon declines. Sediment released by logging roads and clearcuts clogs streams. Logging removes shade from rivers, increasing water temperature. Global warming adds to this threat. Many Pacific Northwest streams are for now cooled by melting snow, but by 2080, declining snowpack will cause half of Washington State streams to have average summer temperatures higher than 70°F.[37] Those temperatures kill salmon. And deforestation causes between 10 and 15 percent of all carbon emissions.[38]

The next fallacy (and implicit lie) is that "scientific forest management" is responsible for clear air, clean water, and healthy salmon. Again, this is not true. Scientific management had its origin in the theories of Frederick Taylor, who, if you recall, valued productivity above all else, and worked to develop processes that would allow factories to pump out more products. The one

[35] "Status Review Update for Pacific Salmon and Steelhead Listed under the Endangered Species Act: Pacific Northwest," NOAA Technical Memorandum NMFS-NWFSC-113, National Marine Fisheries Service, November 2011.

[36] Jim McDermott, "Endangered Salmon," November 2006.

[37] Katie Campbell and Saskia De Melker, "Northwest Salmon People Face Future with Less Fish," PBS Newshour, July 18, 2012.

[38] "Measuring the role of deforestation in global warming," Union of Concerned Scientists, December 9, 2013.

who was to be "scientifically managed" was the worker, and scientific management led factories (and soon, other businesses) to an ever more inhumane regimen of curtailed breaks, micromanaged actions, and enforced productivity.

Scientific management is no more life affirming when applied to forests. This culture's forest management—"scientific" or otherwise—has destroyed 98 percent of this continent's old-growth forests. Scientific forest management has ruined watershed after watershed. Scientific forest management has been and continues to be about maximizing profit, which means maximizing board-feet of timber while reducing costs, which means killing forests. It's not about maximizing the health of forests.

The most effective lies are those that contain and pervert truths. In this case, the lie is that because trees grow and contribute to the health of the planet (true), "managing" (read, cutting) forests creates "the most responsible building material on earth" (false).

The ad is produced by the Washington Forest Protection Association, which—and again this is no surprise—has nothing to do with forest protection and everything to do with forest destruction. Members of the WFPA include Weyerhaeuser (the largest timber company in the world), Sierra Pacific Industries (the second largest lumber producer in the U.S.), and 48 other companies, mostly logging businesses. Members of the "Forest Protection Association" are responsible for the majority of the following: in Southern Oregon, nearly 30 percent of the Coast Range forests around Roseburg was clearcut between 1971 and 2002; a similar percentage of the Olympic Peninsula was clearcut during the same period (and this in an area with nearly a third of the landmass protected in a National Park, meaning roughly half of the unprotected forests were cut); in the Central Cascades around Mount St. Helens, more than 1.7 million acres were clearcut; about 20 percent of the inland rainforest of southern British Columbia and the forests in the Williams Lake area was clearcut between 1976 and 2002.[39] These are just a few examples.

The next fallacy in the WFPA ad is that wood is a key element in the green economy of the 21st century. A major problem with this is that the "green economy" doesn't exist.

People don't like to admit—to themselves or others—that they're doing terrible things. As psychiatrist Robert Jay Lifton brilliantly laid out, before people can commit any mass atrocity, they must convince themselves and others that what they're doing is not, in fact, an atrocity, but instead that they're doing something beneficial. The Nazis were, in their own perspective, not committing mass murder and genocide, but rather purifying the Aryan Race. The United States wasn't (and isn't) perpetrating land theft and genocide against American Indians, but rather manifesting its destiny. Today, members of this culture aren't murdering the planet, but rather developing natural resources. Bright greens aren't providing the latest claim to virtue for murdering the planet—the planet that, according to them doesn't need to be saved, and that doesn't do it for them—they're saving industrial civilization. And in this case, these timber corporations aren't killing forests; they're participating in the "green economy."

"Sustainable forestry"—which, in most cases, is just traditional industrial forestry with a green veneer—and "eco-certification" are essential to most "green" building projects. But eco-certifications for logging operations like the Sustainable Forestry Initiative (SFI) and the Forest Stewardship Council (FSC) have been repeatedly debunked; even the founders of the FSC—now ousted—describe it as "captured by vested commercial interest."[40]

---

[39] "Map of the Cascadia Scorecard's Five Forest Study Areas," Sightline Institute, 2004.
[40] "About," FSC-Watch.

Do you remember our mention of the forests in the southeast-
ern U.S. being cut and ground into pellets for biomass energy?
Those cuts are certified as "sustainable harvests" by the Forest
Stewardship Council.[41]

By now readers should be able to perform similar analyses for other
materials imported into cities. Where does cement come from, and
what are the costs, and to whom? Where does steel come from, and
what are the costs, and to whom? Copper? Plastic? Every last consumer good?

Follow the supply chains. It's not hard to do.

Or let's talk about food. Bright greens like to claim that with intensive permaculture, "vertical farming," and a reduction in living
standards, cities could be made sustainable.

Norris Thomlinson is a longtime permaculturist. About a decade
ago, he and his then-partner bought a small house in Portland and
set the goal of using their small lot—a fifth of an acre, about half
taken up by the house—to produce enough food, water, and fuel
wood for two to four people.

For the next five years, they worked intensively, ripping out the
driveway to expand their garden, reshaping the whole plot to allow
more natural light, and planting. They barely used electricity. They
eliminated the lawn with sheet mulch, then experimented with
low-maintenance perennial vegetables until they found the best

---

[41] Almuth Ernsting, "Guest post: how FSC is helping to greenwash the destruction of
U.S. forests for European power stations," FSC-Watch/Biofuel Watch, August 2014.

crops for their microclimate. They started a food forest with edible fruits and nuts and a perennial understory. They raised small fish in a rainwater catchment pond, kept chickens and bees, and built a green roof on the house to grow garlic and other crops. They coppiced fast-growing woody shrubs and trees for firewood. And they documented the project exhaustively, weighing and cataloging every plant picked from the garden and every ounce of food.[42]

The results were sobering. After five years, they weren't close to their goal. The daily harvest averaged 700 calories, half of which came from animal products, mostly eggs and honey. (Norris estimates the chickens and especially the bees got half their food offsite, meaning perhaps only 500 calories were produced strictly on-site.)

"As far as our goal of self-sufficiency is concerned," Norris writes, "that means we could choose between feeding less than half of Tulsi [his then-partner] or one-third of me."

They had plenty of vegetables and enough water (though they considered the municipal water supply to be the equivalent of a creek, since Portland uses a gravity-fed rainwater system), but bulk calories and a balanced diet with enough quality protein and fat were lacking. As food forests go, theirs was young. More time for trees to get established would mean larger crops of fruits and nuts. But even in their best-case scenario, when everything was full-grown and their project well-established, Norris estimates their lot could only have fed one person.

So, what happens when you translate their experience to the city of Portland? According to Norris's calculations, "If everyone in the city does a better job of feeding themselves and fueling their houses from local resources than we expect to manage on our own site, the city could support about 280,000 people. In this best-case

---

[42] All of this information is available on Norris's blog, *FarmerScrub*.

scenario, the current population of 600,000 would have to kick out more than half the people to become sustainable."

Those are optimistic numbers. Much of the success their project did have was made possible by external inputs. At the beginning of the project, Norris and Tulsi brought in truckloads of wood-chips for mulch, along with six cubic yards of soil. The mulch came from an external source; trees the city cut and chipped using a die-sel-powered woodchipper. A limited supply of this organic matter in any one place guarantees not everyone will get this same boost of organic material. Other external inputs included stale bread and coffee grounds from a nearby bakery and food scraps from a grocery store, which provided important nitrogen to balance the wood chips. None of these scale up. In addition, modern, pollut-ing, high-energy materials made what success they did have pos-sible; their rooftop garden and home renovations couldn't have happened without modern plastics, glass, and other materials that have to be manufactured and delivered.

Even with steep reductions in our energy-intensive lifestyle, a return to subsistence living, and the best-known permaculture techniques, a city cannot be made sustainable. There are just too many people in too small an area. Resources will have to be imported.

Others have reached the same conclusion. One University of Washington analysis found that if all homeowners in Seattle replaced their lawns with crops (in this case, not a nutritionally balanced diet, but plants most suited to the climate) the result-ing harvest would provide 1 percent of the food needs of the city. Ripping out every street and planting on every rooftop with good sunlight would still provide only 21 percent of the city's food needs. The study estimated that leaving streets intact and simply ripping up all the grass in the city (not just yards but also parks, medians, and so on) would produce about 4 percent of the food requirement, a number they called a reasonable estimate of Seattle's "maximum food crop production capacity."[43]

We find ourselves filled with melancholy every time someone mentions "vertical farming." Sometimes the person mentioning it is smugly naïve, and the mention is thrown down as a gauntlet. "See, cities can be sustainable!" is the message. Our melancholy is born from the disjuncture between their unshakeable hubris—which will be the death of this planet—and their breezy ignorance of what life requires. Do they really not know that plants need light and food? Or that plants take up space? Since common sense clearly won't suffice, Stan Cox has run the numbers. The nation's vegetables would need 100,000 Empire State Buildings if grown indoors.[44] And vegetables use only 3 percent of our crop acreage. The lighting for those vegetables would require fully half of the total electrical output of the entire U.S. That's right: half. Just for the lighting. That doesn't include the heating, cooling, or nutrient manufacture and transport. An "LED-powered Caesar salad" would be an ecological nightmare. Could we put this idea down for good and take up reality?

A city's supply chain doesn't just encompass municipal purchases; it includes all the materials and energy inputs that support the city as a whole: water, oil, food, electricity, consumer products, cars,

---

[43] Sarah DeWeerdt, "This is why cities can't grow all their own food," *Conservation Magazine*, University of Washington, January 26, 2016.

[44] Stan Cox, "An engineer, an economist, and an ecomodernist walk into a bar and order a free lunch...," *CounterPunch*, August 1, 2018.

train cars, concrete, tires, paint, plastics, lumber, natural gas, electric cars, construction cranes, delivery trucks, nails, etc. Any assessment of the supply chain of a city that doesn't include "greening" these inputs (which of course, is impossible) is bunk. This means that making a city sustainable is impossible.

To change the nature of the whole, every link in the supply chain must be changed. To be sustainable, you must not merely reduce harm, but eliminate it. It's really straightforward: To stop killing the planet, you have to stop killing the planet.

4. Green Power: We've seen what "green power" means for the planet. We've also seen that reality doesn't stop overblown rhetoric.

In 2016, *Climate Progress* reported that Los Angeles is "on the verge" of using 100 percent "renewable energy." Here we go again. First, they mean "power," not "energy" which means we cut 80 percent off the top of their numbers. And second, in 2015, the city only got 20 percent of its power (i.e., 4 percent of its energy) from renewable—wink, wink—sources. Meanwhile, coal accounted for 40 percent of the power supply, and natural gas another 22 percent.[45] And this is, again, to speak only of "power" and not "energy." Only in the bright green world could 4 percent be seen as on the verge of 100 percent.

Meanwhile, the city grows and continues importing vast quantities of coal, oil, food, lumber, chemicals, concrete, and so on. Meanwhile, the planet comes a little closer to being killed.

---

[45] Samantha Page, "The second-largest city in the U.S. is on the verge of being 100 percent renewable," *Climate Progress,* June 10, 2016.

5. Conserving Nearby (and Creating Internal) Green Landscapes: Of course, there's nothing wrong with conserving land and creating green spaces in and around cities. All else being equal, it's a great thing to do.

But there are two major obstacles. The first is the verb *create*. Natural areas must, in this case, be created, not preserved, because the construction of cities destroys the original natural communities. Cities do not contain intact natural communities. Even in the few places where city parks protect old-growth and sometimes somewhat intact plant communities, most of the native animal species are missing. Some of them are extinct, some are threatened or endangered, and others have been driven far from cities, to *real* green spaces in the mountains.

This tells you pretty much everything you need to know about the relationship between cities and the real world.

These recreations only superficially resemble wild nature. You cannot create old growth forest communities, or mature plains communities, or fully developed wetlands. Nature can, over time.

A corollary to all of this is that these urban "green spaces" are, like everything else in the city, more for humans than nonhumans. They're a place for humans to walk, have picnics, and see the occasional butterfly, prairie dog, or red-winged blackbird during their lunchbreak.

That's not to say we shouldn't protect every bit—even the tiniest bit—of wild space. The empty lot behind the big box store on the strip mall? Frogs still sing their love songs there each spring. The roadside heading over the hill toward the community college? Those oaks were 200 years old, two centuries of spring buds and woodpeckers and bears and fall acorn bounties, before the natural gas company cut them down.

I (Derrick) was brought to do a talk in a small town in western

BRIGHT GREEN LIES

Illinois by someone whose love for prairies suffuses every cell of his body. He took me to the only remaining never-plowed prairie in his county. It was just a few acres, sandwiched between a parking lot and a factory. A mother goose hissed at me from her nest in this tiny haven. I couldn't stop crying, both at the beauty of this place and at all that has been lost. If the earth is to recover, the beginnings of this recovery will be from wild places big and small.

None of which changes the central truth of green spaces in cities: They're more for humans than nonhumans.

The second element worth noting is that "conserving nearby green landscapes" isn't necessarily possible, given the nature of cities. Cities develop according to the needs of commerce and power, and nearly always, as part of that development, nearby wetlands are drained, forests cleared, grasslands plowed, deserts irrigated. We've discussed this already; cities, by their nature, require the importation of resources, with much of that early destruction falling close to home.

Only here, in the wealthy nations, and especially now in this age of fossil fuels and globalized trade, can importation create the illusion of sustainable cities, cities that treasure green spaces. It's much easier to conserve nearby forests, meadows, and mountains when your primary source of timber, food, and minerals lies far away. You'll note that when David Suzuki got googly eyed over the possibility of windmills across the water from his vacation home, he didn't mention living next to one of the many mines those "beautiful" windmills require.

In response to our saying that the planet is being killed, someone once pointed out that there's more forest cover in Massachusetts now than there was 150 years ago. That is because people now get their food from Iowa and their wood from Maine, the Southeast, and South America. The harm has been exported.

The modern cities that are most often proclaimed as the green-est in the world—Vancouver, Bristol, Copenhagen, Stockholm, Portland, Oslo, San Francisco, Seattle—are the beneficiaries of global supply lines bringing them goods from exploited lands.

How "green" would cities appear if the industries that feed, clothe, and supply them were located next door? Strip mines, smokestacks, clearcuts, ocean trawlers, endless fields of corn and soybeans, and toxic waste are harder to ignore when they're in your backyard. But site them 100 miles away, or 1,000 or even 10,000 miles away, and the illusion of a clean green city becomes much easier to maintain.

John W. Day and Charles Hall, in their recent book on urban sus-tainability, write: "When economists claim that the U.S. economy as a whole has become less energy intense (defined as energy used per unit of gross domestic product or GDP), part of what they are really saying is that energy-intensive and highly polluting indus-tries such as aluminum- and steel-making have been outsourced to regions and countries where labor is cheaper and environmen-tal regulations are less stringent." However, our need to consume these imported products, often shipped over long distances, only increases, and particularly in densely populated urban areas with the sophisticated infrastructure of "The Efficient City."[46]

Conserving nearby land doesn't mean much when your econ-omy is killing the planet elsewhere.

6. Protecting Water Quality and Quantity: Like the others, this idea sounds great, but given that this culture is based on draw-down, the implementation within industrialism will inevitably fail.

---

[46] John W. Day, and Charles Hall, *America's Most Sustainable Cities and Regions: Surviving the 21st-Century Megatrends* (Göttingen, Germany: Copernicus Books, 2016).

The NRDC writes that, "Useable green space and green infra-structure that mimics natural areas' ability to infiltrate rainwater runoff can do double duty to help protect water quality."

The first problem, of course, is the verb *mimic*. There's no sub-stitute for intact native communities. Even with green landscap-ing, green buildings, and permeable surfaces, water quality in a city is going to be worse—a lot worse—than in an intact wetland or forest. Automobiles, chemicals, sewage, pets, fertilizers, pesticides, and the micro-detritus of a poisonous consumer culture guaran-tee this. Sure, some communities incorporate wetlands into their sewage treatment programs, and sometimes that's great; and sure reducing the harm done by water pollution to nearby streams is great too; but any time you're talking about hundreds of thousands or millions of people living in a dense settlement, water quality is going to be worse. The main question is, How much worse?

While less toxic water is preferable to more toxic water, the best option is clean water, which means not having a city there in the first place.

Cities destroy water quality. How many rivers, how many lakes, how many oceans, how many aquifers must be destroyed before we recognize a pattern that has been staring us in the face for sev-eral thousand years now?

Do we have the capacity to recognize patterns?

As always, putting the land at the center changes everything.

7. Creating Compact Mixed-Use Neighborhoods: We've already discussed the illusory benefits of compact cities. They're better than suburbs, but that's about it. Mixed-used neighbor-hoods are the same. Sure, it'd be nice to have a nearby park to take my morning power-walk, followed by a convenient trip to the

Happy Civet Café for a morning shot of the best tasting caffeine in the world, after which I could ride on bike trails to my wonderful earth-affirming job at SustainableSolarMiracle.com, with a break for lunch at ChiChi Chia Smoothies 'n Salads, then more earth-affirming work in the afternoon designing "solar farms" on what used to be desert tortoise habitat, and finally a trip to the Mangrove Lagoon Restaurant for a delicious shrimp dinner and drinks at The Groovy Granary Microbrewery and Pub, all within convenient walking distance.

Of course none of this matters a jot to the caged palm civets who excreted my delicious coffee[47]; the soon-to-be-extirpated desert tortoises on the site of my earth-saving solar facility; the now-devastated Central Valley of California, where once flocks of waterbirds darkened the sky, all gone to bring me and others in this sustainable city the greens for my salad and smoothies; the mangrove forests cut to put in shrimp farms for my creamy pesto shrimp; or the prairie dogs and buffalo ejected from the now-destroyed prairies for the grains in my favorite gourmet microbrew.

But maybe prairie dogs and buffalo never did it for me.

8. Green Transport and Increased Accessibility: Green transit is a core strategy of the bright green environmental movement: replacing gas-guzzling SUVs with electric cars and enhanced public transit. All the major green groups have initiatives focused on green transportation. Cities like Seattle and Los Angeles advertise themselves as "the best cities in the country to own an electric vehicle." The C40 group puts a major emphasis on transportation, with campaigns focused on promoting low emissions vehicles.

---

[47] See, for example, Rachael Bale, "The disturbing secret behind the world's most expensive coffee," *National Geographic*, April 29, 2016.

But Ozzie Zehner, author of *Green Illusions*, makes an apt comparison: the "benefits" of green automobiles are similar to the benefits of low-tar cigarettes. Only in a comparison with an atrocious alternative can they vaguely be considered "healthy" or "green."

As Zehner puts it, "Environmentalists generally stand against battery-powered devices and for good reason: batteries require mined minerals, involve manufacturing processes that leak toxins into local ecosystems, and leave behind an even worse trail of side effects upon disposal. Though when it comes to the largest mass-produced battery-powered electrical gadget ever created—the electric car—mainstream environmental groups cannot jump from their seats fast enough to applaud it."[48]

The central truth is that cars themselves—regardless of how "clean" they are, and regardless of their relative emissions—are an atrocity. After the BP oil spill, the satirical news site *The Onion* ran a great headline: "Millions of Barrels of Oil Safely Reach Port in Major Environmental Catastrophe."[49] The article captures the problem with the mainstream dialogue around oil spills. Spilled or burned, oil is a planetary disaster. To focus only on spills, or in the case of cars, emissions from the tailpipe, is to miss the point. Cars themselves harm the earth, whether they're made of steel, carbon fiber, or "eco-plastics"; and whether they're powered by gasoline, diesel, solar energy, or refined methane captured from unicorn farts.

Cars need roads, and roads are a disaster for the real world. Roads destroy the land in four major ways: habitat destruction; providing access for developers, loggers, and so on; habitat fragmentation; and killing of animals by cars and trucks.

---

[48] Zehner, op. cit., 144.
[49] "Millions of Barrels of Oil Safely Reach Port in Major Environmental Catastrophe," *The Onion*, August 11, 2010.

Direct habitat destruction is perhaps the largest threat to bio-diversity worldwide. Highway construction alone has directly destroyed 71 million acres of habitat in the United States.[50] That's an area the size of Nevada.

And then there's pollution from roads: asphalt, exhaust, toxic materials in tires, which release these toxins as you drive—that's what tire wear *is*: the slow release of those toxic materials into the landscape—and so on.

As we write, coho salmon are dying—being tortured to death, really—by pollution from roads. As a recent *Washington Post* arti-cle stated, "Adult coho have been seen thrashing in shallow fresh waters, males appear disoriented as they swim, and females are often rolled on their backs, their insides still plump with tiny red eggs that will never hatch.... A recent study traced a major coho salmon die-off to contaminants from roads and automobiles—brake dust, oil, fuel, chemical fluids—that hitch a ride on storm water and flow into watersheds. The contaminants are so deadly, they kill the salmon within 24 hours. 'Our findings are ... that contaminants in stormwater runoff from the regional transpor-tation grid likely caused these mortality events. Further, it will be difficult, if not impossible, to reverse historical coho declines without addressing the toxic pollution dimension of freshwater habitats,' said the study, published ... in the journal *Ecological Applications*.... The future for a species that experiences up to 40 percent mortality before spawning in Puget Sound is no mystery. 'The population will crash,' said Jay Davis, an environmental tox-icologist for the U.S. Fish and Wildlife Service who coordinated field research for the study. In separate interviews Thursday, Davis

---

[50] Mark L. Watson, "Habitat fragmentation and the effects of roads on wildlife and habitats," New Mexico Department of Game and Fish, January 2005.

and Scholz estimated that it could happen in as few as six years. 'We have to act now,' Davis said."[51]

That interview took place in 2017.

Roads also provide access. Once roads open a wild area, "development"—a euphemism for destruction—follows. Prospectors stake mining claims. Logging operations commence. Builders create new subdivisions. Waste managers find new options for trash and hazardous waste disposal. Hunters access areas that used to provide refuge for wild creatures.

Habitat fragmentation is one of the worst harms caused by roads. Animals accustomed to travelling across the land are interrupted by a dangerous physical barrier. They may attempt to cross it and be killed or injured, or they may avoid it entirely. Many smaller animals are unable to cross roads or other degraded habitat. Salamanders, for example, may become dehydrated crossing roads. Or crushed. I (Derrick) once saw an entire spring migration of tiger salamanders crushed by traffic on a busy road. Certain beetles will not cross any path wider than three feet. Roads isolate plant and animal communities, interrupting reproduction and access to sources of food and water. Roads can also fragment aquatic habitat, because when roads cross rivers and streams, they require culverts or bridges. Many culverts are not designed to allow fish passage, and so serve as total blockages. Those that are technically passable still serve as barricades, since many fish won't swim into small, dark tunnels.

Because many species can't tolerate noise, light, and pollution, members of those species avoid roads to distances of well over a

---

[51] Darryl Fears, "A huge salmon die-off is happening—and our cars might be responsible," *Washington Post*, October 20, 2017.

mile, even when areas nearer the road would otherwise be good habitat for them.[52] Further, many species of animals, plants, fungi, and bacteria have very specific temperature requirements, and forests, for example, modulate temperature, with their interiors being less hot, less cold, less dry, and less windy than just outside their limits. It may take well over a hundred feet from a clearcut (and roads are essentially long clearcuts) for the climate to be what it should. So, roads destroy even more habitat for those who require forest interiors. We can make similar arguments for those who require wetland interiors, desert interiors, prairie interiors, and so on.

We have to shift our perception of roads from narrow strips to a more accurate sense of their form: wide corridors of destruction and disruption.

Fragmentation is getting worse. A 2017 study reported that 7.2 percent of the world's remaining untouched wilderness areas have been compromised since the year 2000.[53]

Or, as *The Guardian* put it, "Rampant road building has shattered the earth's land into 600,000 fragments, most of which are too tiny to support significant wildlife, a new study has revealed.... Over half of the 600,000 fragments of land in between roads are very small—less than 1km². [Please note that this gravely understates the fragmentation, since the study included only 'roads between settlements.'] A mere 7 percent are bigger than 100km², equivalent to a square area just 10km by 10km. Furthermore, only

[52] "Noise Effect on Wildlife," Federal Highway Administration, Office of Planning, Environment, and Realty, July 14, 2011.
[53] Ellen Powell, "Development has affected 7 percent of virgin forests since 2000: study," *Christian Science Monitor*, January 14, 2017.

a third of the roadless areas were truly wild, with the rest affected by farming or people."[54]

Let's talk about roadkill.

Near my (Max's) home, a stretch of highway passes between a wetland on one side and a lake on the other. It's an important wildlife refuge. In the fall, when water levels begin to drop, many animals attempt to cross the road and are struck and killed by cars. The sides of the road are littered with flattened corpses: frog, snake, muskrat, raccoon, otter, deer.

Years ago, I bicycled along a stretch of coastal highway outside Arcata, California, where the coastal redwoods grow close on either side of the road. For miles, the edge of the highway was marked with the squashed bodies of thousands of slugs. First, some had attempted a crossing and been hit by cars. Their bodies had attracted more slugs looking for a meal, who were in turn hit, their bodies adding further to the smell wafting into the forest and drawing more slugs to their death.[55]

More than 1 million vertebrate animals per day are killed by vehicles just in the U.S.[56] Extrapolating from the network of U.S. roads (4 million miles) to the total world network (22.2 million miles, a conservative estimate based on old data) gives us a rough minimum of around 5.5 million vertebrates killed by cars per day,

---

[54] Damien Carrington, "New map reveals shattering effect of roads on nature," *The Guardian*, December 15, 2016.

[55] Some might see this as evidence of slugs being stupid. But slugs aren't stupid; they simply haven't experienced anything as deadly as roads before. Humans make the same mistake. Car accidents kill 1.3 million human beings per year, and yet we still flock to roadsides and highways.

[56] Mark Matthew Braunstein, "Driving animals to their graves: U.S. roads kill a million a day," *Culture Change*: 8.

worldwide. That's 38.5 million vertebrate animals per week, 165 million per month, and more than 2 billion per year.[57]

These numbers may be declining, but not because cars are getting less abundant or safer for animals; they're probably going down because in the last 40 years this culture has killed about half of all wildlife on earth.[58] And that estimate doesn't include those who were wiped out *more* than 40 years ago: bison, 60 million strong; passenger pigeons in the billions; great auks crowding North Atlantic islands, each living up to 25 years, killed and packed into ships by the thousands until they were driven extinct.

Overall, estimates of roadkill are probably almost universally low. A recent study shows harm to carnivores from roads have been seriously underestimated. Those most vulnerable include the Iberian lynx, who number less than 300, and Japanese badgers and martens, who may be driven extinct by roads within two decades. Even common species are in danger from the long-term effects of roads.[59]

The destruction that roads, trains, and automobiles visit on insects is even larger. A 2011 study conducted in the Netherlands estimated the nation's cars, about 7 million of them, kill around 1.6 trillion insects per year.[60] Applying that calculation to the United States predicts a yearly insect death toll of 32.5 trillion. Extending it around the world means that motor vehicles kill some 228 trillion insects per year.

When writing about the greatest mass extinction in the history

---

[57] "Country Comparison: Roadways," World Factbook, Central Intelligence Agency.

[58] Damian Carrington, "Earth has lost half its wildlife in the past 40 years, says WWF," *The Guardian*, September 30, 2014.

[59] "Carnivores more seriously threatened by roads than previously acknowledged," German Centre for Integrative Biodiversity Research, February 8, 2017.

[60] Stephen Messenger, "Trillions of insects killed by cars every year, says study," *Treehugger*, July 10, 2011.

of the planet, most journalists, it seems, can't keep from laughing. When writing about the decline of amphibians, for example, they'll consistently make feeble "jokes" like "The frogs are croaking." To most of these writers, mass extinction *is* a joke. This is especially true for the extirpation of insects, and more broadly roadkill. One car blog quipped that the killing of trillions of insects is a "buzz-kill" and ended their article with the smarmy phrase "total insect genocide."[61] Back around 2009 or 2010, 76-branded gas stations capitalized on this "joke" too, putting up posters at hundreds of gas stations across the country titled "A children's guide to splat-tered bugs," complete with images of actual bugs killed on cars and their taxonomic names. Search for the campaign: some of the first results call this "excellent signage," "part of a brilliant [advertising] campaign," "fun education to children during those long family road trips."

This is how you raise children to participate in an ecological apoca-lypse: through relentless propaganda starting at a young age.

Imagine you're a Fender's blue butterfly, pale turquoise flashing in the sun, wings ringed with stripes of white, then black. The egg from which you hatched was laid by your mother last May on the stem of a Kincaid's lupine, deep green topped with blue flowers; one of the few to be found. You need these flowers to survive, and they are a threatened species. Your own species is even more imper-iled than the flowers on whom you depend; there remains less than one-tenth of 1 percent of your original habitat—the upland prairies

---

[61] Jeremy Korzeniewski, "Buzzkill: cars murder trillions of insects each year," *Autoblog,* July 13, 2011.

of the Willamette Valley in Oregon—because the rest has been plowed or urbanized.[62]

You're drinking nectar. The sun feels good on your wings.

You take flight, following the scent of the next flower. Your flight pattern might look random or chaotic to an outsider, but in reality, it's based on precise measurements of scent concentrations in the shifting breeze.

Suddenly, a huge mass rushes past you. The wind spins you in circles. You're confused and dizzy. The day has only had light breezes so far; if it were stormy, you'd have taken shelter. You begin to orient yourself again, noticing the angle of the sun, the meadow ahead, and the stone beneath you. Another great mass approaches. You see it coming, but too late. In a sudden, final impact, you have become one of the trillions.

Studies have shown that 10 percent of butterflies in some communities are killed by cars.[63] And it's no exaggeration to say that threatened species like the Fender's blue butterfly are endangered by cars. One of their most important remaining habitats is surrounded on three sides by roads.

Species of all kinds are endangered by cars. The Federal Highway Administration estimates that roads present a serious danger to 21 threatened and endangered species in the United States. Given the source, the number is undoubtedly higher. The woodland caribou, a subspecies who used to live in the unique inland rainforest of North Idaho and southern British Columbia, is one example; being killed by autos is their biggest threat. In 2007, there were about 50 animals left in the Selkirk herd; by 2016, that was down to less

[62] "Blues: Fender's blue (Icaricia icarioides fenderi)," Xerces Society for Invertebrate Conservation.
[63] Paul M. Severns, "Road crossing behavior of an endangered grassland butterfly, Icaricia Icarioides Fenderi Macy (Lycaenidae), between a subdivided population," Journal of the Lepidopterists' Society (May 2008).

than 14.[64] Their situation may be terminal: the species has been declared "functionally extinct" in the United States.

In the early 1980s, nine Florida panthers, half of the population at the time, were killed by vehicles. In the '70s and '80s, at least 357 of the state's black bears were killed on roads. That was more than 25 percent of the population of the time. Another Florida species, the miniature Key deer, numbers less than 800 and are currently being killed by cars at the rate of about one per week. Other U.S. species on the hard-hit list include bighorn sheep, red wolves, desert tortoises, ocelot, and American crocodiles.[65]

Let's talk about pavement.

Most paved roads are made of either asphalt or concrete.

Asphalt (sometimes called blacktop or tarmac) is a combination of small gravel and bitumen. Bitumen is the same tarry fossil fuel mined at the Alberta Tar Sands, one of the most environmentally destructive projects on the planet. Besides the horrors of its mining, bitumen itself is toxic. Every inch of asphalt on the planet is leaching hydrocarbon toxins, heavy metals, and other contaminants into groundwater and soils. These pollutants cause cancer, birth defects, and genetic mutations.[66]

Asphalt is also a safety hazard when roads are being laid, since the bitumen has to be softened by heating before application.

[64] "What we do: Wildlife habitat: Woodland caribou," Conservation Northwest.

[65] Melissa Gaskill, "Rise in Roadkill Requires New Solutions," Scientific American, May 16, 2003.

[66] Ryan F. Shedivy et al., "Leaching characteristics of recycled asphalt pavement used as unbound road base," University of Wisconsin—Madison, May 2012.

You've probably driven past crews laying asphalt and can remember the horrible smells. Those smells cause cancer.[67]

Asphalt is often claimed to be 100 percent recyclable, but each time it's reused, more of the contaminants inside are released.[68]

Concrete is more durable than asphalt but more expensive. It's also responsible for more earth destruction than just about any other human-made substance. Only fossil fuels as a whole, lumber, and a few agricultural products could compare. By weight, the annual mass of concrete used worldwide is double that of steel, wood, plastics, and aluminum combined.[69]

Creating concrete is almost unbelievably energy intensive: as we saw earlier, concrete production (along with metallurgical coke, with which it is lumped for accounting purposes) makes up around 11 percent of all greenhouse gas emissions.

Extracting source rock for concrete is one of the largest mining industries in the world, with tens of thousands of mines dedicated to the global concrete industry, each an open scar on the land. These mines can be massive, as can be the equipment used. One standard truck, the mt5500, weighs over a million pounds and consumes over a gallon of diesel fuel every 30 seconds (137 gallons per hour).

Here's a classic example of bright green logic. Why don't we reduce the demand for clean water by using toxic wastewater to mix concrete, and then blend concrete using fly ash from coal fired power

[67] "Bitumens and Bitumen Emissions, and Some N- and S-Heterocyclic Polycyclic Aromatic Hydrocarbons," International Agency for Research on Cancer, World Health Organization, vol. 103 (2013).

[68] Andrew F. Nemeth et al., "The effect of asphalt pavement on stormwater contamination," Worcester Polytechnic Institute, May 28, 2010.

[69] "What is the development impact of concrete?" The Cement Trust, 2011.

plants and granulated slag left over from iron and steel production (both of which are already used sometimes in concrete)? According to bright greens, these actions "offer a holistic solution to reduce the environmental impact of several industries."[70]

No, these actions are a laundering scheme for environmental harm: feed in toxic processes and earth destruction on one end, and out comes clean, shiny holistic solutions and a nice phrase— they call it "industrial ecology"—to slip into press releases. Oh, and the toxic waste is still toxic waste, and still does what toxic waste does: it toxifies the landscape.

As coho salmon know all too well, another major environmental harm caused by roads and other paved surfaces is runoff. In contrast with natural soils that absorb water, pavement is impermeable. Runoff from paved surfaces often causes soil erosion, sewer overflows, and flooding, all of which carry toxins into rivers. In many urban areas, runoff from roads is the largest source of pollution into streams. And as soon as the impermeable surface area in a watershed increases to 10 percent, fish start to disappear, beginning with sensitive species who can't tolerate poison in their water.[71]

In an effort to address this problem, new types of porous concrete have been invented that allow water to pass through rather than puddling on the surface. These permeable concretes are being hailed as a solution to runoff problems, but celebration is premature. These surfaces aren't currently strong enough for use on roads

---

[70] Paulo J.M. Monteiro and P. Kumar Mehta, "Concrete and the Environment," University of California—Berkeley, Department of Civil and Environmental Engineering.
[71] "Paving Paradise: Sprawl and the Environment," Natural Resources Defense Council, April 14, 2000.

and so won't replace the majority of concrete surfaces. They're also even more energy-intensive (and expensive) than standard concrete. While they may reduce runoff problems, they certainly don't solve the fundamental destructiveness of the concrete industry.

In the U.S., about half of all urban space is paved, and more land is devoted to cars than to human housing. Pavement covers more than 2 percent of the surface area of this country.[72] Parking spaces alone, some 500 million of them in the United States, cover more than 1,700 square miles.[73]

The concrete, and especially the darker asphalt, absorbs energy from the sun and is one of the reasons (along with lack of tree cover and the destruction or capping of wetlands, creeks, and other water bodies) that cities are much hotter than rural areas. We've all experienced this when walking off a hot sunny blacktop street into a park under the shade of the trees. One study found that some city streets can be more than 25 degrees hotter than nearby rural areas.[74]

This urban heat island effect intensifies global warming by changing the albedo (reflectivity) of the planet's surface, and it contributes directly to the deaths of tens of thousands of people (mostly the elderly and sick) every year during heat waves.

If we agree roads and pavement are themselves destructive, then we probably agree this destructiveness doesn't depend on what

---

[72] Derrick Jensen, "Road to Ruin: An Interview with Jan Lundberg," *The Sun*, February 2001.
[73] Jared Green, "500 million reasons to rethink the parking lot," *Grist*, June 7, 2012.
[74] "Hot and getting hotter: heat islands cooking U.S. cities," *Climate Central*, August 20, 2014.

type of vehicle is driven on them. Green cars could be made of pure refined nonsense and fueled by bright green hot air combined with the broken and destroyed dreams of every nonhuman on earth, and they'd still be destructive.

We already mentioned that about 40 billion tons of sand are mined annually. Industrial civilization consumes more sand than any other material besides water. Most of this sand goes toward building cities and roads. Skyscrapers are essentially giant piles of sand held in place by cement and steel. Roads are almost entirely made of sand. The average American home requires more than 100 tons of sand, gravel, and crushed stone—and, if you include its portion of the street in front of it, more than 200 tons. Urban centers are consuming sand at an ever-increasing rate and are exploding in size. More than half of all humans now live in cities, and by 2050 the current urban population of 3.9 billion is expected to grow to 6.3 billion.[75]

Structural concrete requires sand of a certain quite rare grade and angularity. Dubai, located in the middle of a massive sandy desert, imports all of the sand it uses from Australia.

Sand extraction is, as we've discussed, very destructive. In Cambodia, sand miners in the Koh Kong province have "been ripping out the roots of mangroves, polluting rivers, collapsing riverbanks, destroying shallows where crabs breed, and ruining fish habitat…. Many people forced out of fishing had little choice but to leave their villages and seek low-paying, difficult jobs such

---

[75] Mark Swilling, "The curse of urban sprawl: how cities grow, and why this has to change," *The Guardian*, July 12, 2016.

as garment factory work in Phnom Penh."[76] This particular sand was shipped 700 miles to Singapore and dumped into the sea to expand the land base of this dictatorial nation with the world's highest per-capita rate of billionaires. Singapore's consumption of sand has been so rapacious that Malaysia, Vietnam, and Indonesia have restricted or banned sand exports to the nation. Activists and community members have been jailed or killed for fighting sand extraction in India, Cambodia, Indonesia, and Kenya.

At Poyang Lake in China, the world's largest sand mine is destroying the largest winter destination for migratory birds in all of Asia. As one investigative journalist reports, fishing villages on the lake are "dwarfed by a flotilla anchored just offshore, of colossal dredges and barges, hulking metal flatboats with cranes jutting from their decks.... Hundreds of dredgers may be on the lake on any given day, some the size of tipped-over apartment buildings. The biggest can haul in as much as 10,000 tonnes of sand an hour.... Poyang [is] the biggest sand mine on the planet, far bigger than the three largest sand mines in the U.S. combined."[77]

If you take a passenger train south from Seattle, you'll see that the track cuts through industrial yards much of its length. The heaviest, most polluting industries are always clustered around train tracks. Besides industry, there is poverty; tents and old RVs parked under overpasses. Then we break into "farm" country: massive industrial operations of thousands of acres of row crops, bare soil cleared of

---

[76] Jim Hightower, "Our ravenous appetite turns humble sand into an endangered natural treasure," *The Hightower Lowdown* 19, no. 8, August 2017.
[77] Vince Beiser, "Sand mining: the global environmental crisis you've probably never heard of," *The Guardian*, February 27, 2017.

every native plant and exposed to the elements, bleeding into the waterways on this gray January day.

The land near rail lines is a sacrifice zone—loud, polluted, fragmented. It's ironic, given the history and reality of railways as an accelerant of colonization and their importance to every major industry from logging to mining and beyond, that trains are now acclaimed as a solution to the destruction of the planet. But they are. The bright green movement has seized on efficient, high-speed rail as being key to a sustainable future, just as it has with solar, wind, electric cars, and compact cities. But the truth is that "green" trains are yet another bright green lie.

Years ago, I (Max) led a small group kayaking the bays and inlets south of Bellingham, Washington, where the main north-south rail line parallels the coast. The tide was low, and we looked down into the eelgrass waving in the gentle current. Eelgrass is both nursery and refuge for countless creatures, including young salmon recently emerged from nearby streams and becoming accustomed to the ocean. Little green crabs, camouflaged with algae and seaweed cultivated on their backs like oceanic bonsai, skittered across the bottom. Small fish darted among eelgrass leaves peppered with snails and fish eggs. Paddling south along the shoreline, my eyes kept being drawn to the rail line just above the rocky, artificial shore. Twice, trains passed, the first laden with lumber, chemicals, and oil, the second with car after car filled with low sulfur Powder River Basin coal.

Just ahead, the rail line crossed a small bridge, with a brackish estuary on the shoreward side of the tracks. The bridge's ties were solid timbers nine feet long, soaked in coal-tar creosote. I've walked those tracks on hot summer days, with the stench of creosote thick in the air.

There are more than 625,000 miles of rail line on the planet (a conservative number since it counts areas with multiple parallel tracks as a single rail line).[78] Each of these lines is supported by railroad ties, and 93 percent of these ties are made of wood (most of the rest are concrete, which, as we've covered, has its own problems). There are about 3,200 ties per mile of railroad in this country. This number varies around the world; England has around 2,600. A reasonable guess at a world average would be 3,000 ties per mile, which means there are somewhere around 1.85 billion railroad ties on the planet, of which about 1.7 billion are made of wood. Each of those ties was made from a living tree, usually a hardwood. In the U.S., red and white oaks from the Midwest are the main source of railroad ties. The average wooden railroad tie lasts between 33 and 50 years, which means between 2 and 3 percent of wooden ties have to be replaced every year. Worldwide, that means about 35 to 50 million wooden railroad ties must be replaced every year.[79] That means a hell of a lot of logging for a groovy green rail line.

Of course, the link between logging and railroads is much stronger than this. In the 1860s and 70s, the U.S. government granted scores of millions of acres to railroad companies, which often then spun off logging subsidiaries. Many of the worst logging companies in North America—including Weyerhaeuser, Potlatch, Boise Cascade, and Plum Creek—gained much of their holdings from the 40

---

[78] "Rail lines (total route-km)—Country Ranking," *IndexMundi*, Data from 1991-2012.
[79] "Frequently Asked Questions," Railway Tie Association.

million acres of federal land given to the Northern Pacific Railroad. This swathe, 100 miles wide and 2,000 miles long, ran from the Great Lakes to western Washington and much of that land—an area larger than Florida—still belongs to logging companies.

After they're cut and shaped from the trunk of a tree, each tie is treated to prevent rot. This involves placing ties in a large sealed cylinder, which is then filled with liquid creosote and raised to a pressure of 150 PSI for several hours.[80]

More than 300 chemical compounds in creosote have been identified thus far, many of them known carcinogens (causing cancer), teratogens (causing birth defects), and mutagens (causing genetic mutations). Beyond the known chemistry, there are thousands more substances in creosote that haven't been researched for health effects, or for that matter even chemically identified. A few drops of creosote on human skin irritates and burns the tissue. Larger doses (inhaled, eaten, or on the skin) cause excessive salivation, vomiting, dyspnea, headaches, dizziness, loss of pupillary reflexes, cyanosis, hypothermia, convulsions, coma, multiorgan system failure, shock, acidosis, respiratory depression, renal failure, and death. The American Wood Preservers Institute estimates that about 124 million gallons of creosote are used as a wood preservative each year in the U.S. alone; worldwide production is probably closer to 500 million gallons.[81]

Creosote doesn't remain where it's placed. Around 15 percent of the creosote in a given railroad tie is lost over its usable duration

---

[80] Salim Hiziroglu, "Basics of pressure treatment of wood," Oklahoma State University Cooperative Extension Service.

[81] "Petition for Suspension and Cancellation of Creosote," Beyond Pesticides, February 26, 2002.

(and of course, the rest either leaches out at landfills or is burned). Each of the 1.7 billion wooden railroad ties in the world is currently leaching toxins into the surrounding soil and water.[82]

To make matters worse, trains usually run through the flattest available land at the bottom of valleys, where water naturally gathers and wetlands form.

Beyond creosote, trains have many of the same issues we've seen with other technologies. They mostly run on diesel fuel, and those that don't, use energy-intensive, polluting battery systems. Rail lines contribute to habitat destruction and fragmentation and kill animals through impacts. Trains themselves are made of steel; the average unloaded rail car weighs 25 to 30 tons, and locomotives can weigh 200 tons. This isn't a low-impact, earth-friendly technology, and it never will be.

A prairie dog village in Colorado was recently poisoned to make way for a new light rail project. Prairie dogs are a keystone species, and more than 99 percent of them have been wiped out since the arrival of this culture.[83]

How's that for sustainable transportation?

9. Getting to Zero Waste: The only way to get to zero waste is to produce waste that is food for someone else, in quantities useful

---

[82] "Crossties (Railroad) Recycling and Disposal," Transportation Environmental Resource Center.
[83] Deanna Meyer, Prairie Protection Colorado, personal communication.

to the landbase. That's how nature works. That's how nature *is*. That's *what* nature is.

That's not how industry works. Slag is not food. Plastics are not foods. Nano-carbon materials are not food.

We asked before where the metals for your city come from, where the bricks come from. Likewise, where do these bright greens think the broken bricks go? Where do they think the hulks of cars go? The creosote-soaked railroad ties?

Even materials that in smaller quantities would be food—feces, for example, is food for detritivores and the soil itself—become toxic when there are too many people. The feces have to go somewhere.

Just as bright green fairies don't magically make our computers appear out of nowhere, they don't magically take away our broken computers and leave quarters under our pillows.

The point is not that efforts to reduce harm caused by cities are worthless. I have friends doing great work on that issue. The point is that this work isn't sufficient. And the real point is that for functional reasons it can never be sufficient.

Yes, people working in cities should work to green the supply chain and put in place better stormwater management. But we should never believe that these incremental reforms will change the fundamental nature of cities, replace earth-destroying industries, or threaten the system of power that is killing the planet. Instead, we should focus our energy on organized political resistance to that system, and on protecting wild beings and wild places.

Or maybe the thing to do is to collectively ignore all of this evidence, pretend the last 8,000 to 10,000 years of cities destroying landbases means nothing. Some people do this. Some even see evidence of the destructiveness of cities instead as evidence of their ability to cause positive change: "City growth has caused climate change," writes UCLA economist Matthew Kahn, "but that growth is also what's going to get us out of it."

Of course, he can't provide evidence for his claim that growth will solve climate change, because there isn't any. All the evidence points to the opposite conclusion. So much so, in fact, that climate scientists often use economic growth as a proxy for greenhouse gas emissions.

Kahn isn't alone in this insanity. Unfortunately for the planet, he has plenty of company. For example, "Growth is inevitable and desirable," says "smart growth" advocate Edward T. McMahon.

Contrast this with the words of radioecologist Robert Baker, who studies the recovery of nonhumans in exclusion zones around nuclear accidents: "Typical human activity [by which, of course, he means typical civilized, urbanized human activity] is more devastating to biodiversity and abundance of local flora and fauna than the worst nuclear power plant disaster."

And contrast the bright green insanity with this commentary by the degrowth economist Timothée Parrique, "The validity of the green growth discourse relies on the assumption of an absolute, permanent, global, large and fast enough decoupling of Gross Domestic Product from all critical environmental pressures. Problem is: There is no empirical evidence for such a decoupling having ever happened. This is the case for materials, energy, water, greenhouse gases, land, water pollutants, and biodiversity loss, for which decoupling is either only relative, and/or observed only temporarily, and/or only locally. In most cases, decoupling is relative. When absolute decoupling occurs, it is observed only during rather short periods of time, concerning only certain resources or forms of impacts, for specific locations, and with minuscule rates of mitigation."[84]

The entire mythology of Green Cities is contained in this quote. "When we build more densely, we use less transportation energy (and when we build densely, make places walkable and add effective transit, we use much less transportation energy).... We've already seen a set of profound lifestyle shifts, driven largely by good design, technological invention and changing cultural preferences. Car-free and 'car-light' living is the most obvious example, with urbanites getting rid of their cars (or going from two cars to one) by the millions over the last five years."[85]

Who are these urbanites getting rid of their cars? Every academic source we could find says the number of cars in use globally has been increasing steadily. Between 1950 and 1970, the number of cars in the world quadrupled. Then, by 1986, it rose to 500 million. By 2010, the number had reached 1 billion, and that number shows no signs of doing anything but rising.[86] The rate of new vehicle production has risen more or less steadily since at least 1961, reaching 56.4 million in 2014.[87] The International Energy Agency forecasts that there will be 1.7 billion cars globally by 2035.[88] Inside the United States, there has been talk of "peak car." A 2013 *New York Times* article titled "The End of Car Culture" suggested that car ownership and miles driven per person in the U.S. had both

---

[84] Timothée Parrique, "Decoupling is dead! Long live degrowth!" *Degrowth*, July 10, 2019.

[85] Alex Steffen, "Building to save the planet," BASF, May 2015.

[86] John Sousanis, "Word vehicle population tops 1 billion units," *WardsAuto*, August 15, 2011.

[87] "Table 1-23: World Motor Vehicle Production, Selected Countries (Thousands of vehicles)," Bureau of Transportation Statistics.

[88] Phil LeBeau, "Whoa! 1.7 billion cars on the road by 2035," *CNBC*, November 12, 2012.

peaked, perhaps as early as 2005.[89] But it isn't hard to find numbers suggesting the opposite is true. Car ownership rose from 133 million in 2000 to 137 million in 2008.[90] Including trucks and motorcycles, the number of registered highway-capable vehicles in the U.S. rose from 253.6 million in 2012 to 273.6 million in 2018.[91]

The number of licensed drivers in the US rose from 200 million in 2005 to 227.5 million in 2018.[92]

Where is this "profound lifestyle shift"? This seems to be a trend: green-growth advocates making stuff up. Shocking, isn't it?

According to archeologists, our species has existed for about 200,000 years. Our direct ancestors existed for 6 million years. Cities, on the other hand, have existed for between 8,000 and 10,000 years. This means cities have only existed for less than 5 percent of our time on this planet. And of course, even during the period that cities have existed, the vast majority of people lived outside cities and did just fine.

Obviously, we don't *need* cities.

The question of whether cities can be "green" is fundamental to our survival as a species, and indeed the survival of the earth. Modern industrial civilization is rapidly destroying the planet, and to stop this destruction people have to understand the fundamental reality of cities. But many well-intentioned people are misled by a culture that venerates technological progress and is contemptuous of nonhumans (whose extirpation is the source of jokes, and

---

[89] Elisabeth Rosenthal, "The End of Car Culture," *New York Times,* June 29, 2013.
[90] Kate Miller-Wilson, "Car Ownership Statistics," Love to Know.
[91] "Number of U.S. Aircraft, Vehicles, Vessels, and Other Conveyances," U.S. Department of Transportation, April 30, 2020.
[92] "Total number of licensed drivers in the U.S. in 2018, by state," Statista Research & Analysis, 2020.

who don't "do it for us"). Instead of doing the most effective work, work that can stop the destruction of the planet, countless people end up lending their energy to furthering one of the cultural patterns most responsible for killing the planet.

If we truly wish for a living planet, then the false mythology of the "green city" has to be abandoned along with, ultimately, cities themselves. Only then can the world in all its fullness be restored.

Chapter 10

THE GREEN GRID LIE

It's pretty obvious that Western lifestyles which rely on gigantic
amounts of electricity use up far more resources than a
subsistence-based life. A little more poverty would be a good
thing. The recession itself, in fact, has already slowed down
carbon emissions.

—TOM HODGKINSON[1]

The power grid is almost everywhere. Powerlines crisscross neighborhoods, follow streets, and spread along highways. They hang over fields, cut strips through forests. They're so commonplace that they're often ignored. They also play a key role in bright green lies.

"Alternative" energy—like all industrial electricity—is not useful without the ability to transmit electricity from centralized generation facilities to distributed consumption locations. Technically, it's possible to generate power from small-scale renewable electricity projects located on individual homes, small businesses, and

---

[1] Tom Hodgkinson, "Shakespeare had no Blackberry: let's have a technological Sabbath," *Ecologist*, November 9, 2009.

communities. But centralized electricity generation at large power plants is between two and five times more efficient.[2] Further, key "renewable" energy sources are variable. Windstorms cause spikes in power output from wind energy harvesting facilities, while calm weather can leave them generating no power at all. Solar energy, too, varies. Here in the Pacific Northwest, sunlight hitting the surface of the planet averages around 3 to 4 kilowatt hours per square meter per day. Those numbers double in the Mojave Desert, which explains the metastasization of solar energy harvesting facilities there.[3] And that's not even to account for seasonality; the sun shines all year in the Mojave, while in January the Northwest dips down to 0 kWh to 2 kWh/m² per day. Variability affects hydroelectric plants, too, as droughts and seasonally low summer and fall water levels reduce power output. Even biomass is dependent on grid distribution, because it's only reasonably efficient at a large scale.

All of this means you need a grid to distribute power from the places where it's generated to the places where it's not.

Further, there are major technical challenges to integrating intermittent renewables in the power grid when that power is coming from thousands of distributed sources. Fewer, larger power generation facilities make the intermittency problems easier to juggle for grid operators.[4]

For all of these reasons, the orderly distribution of power from "renewables" is even more dependent on the grid than are coal, oil, and gas.

---

[2] "Distributed vs. Centralized Generation. Battle of the CEOs," *T&D World Magazine*, July 14, 2014.

[3] Billy J. Roberts, "Photovoltaic solar resource of the United States," National Renewable Energy Laboratory, September 19, 2012.

[4] "Distributed vs. Centralized Power Generation," Large-Scale Solar Technology and Policy Forum, Woods Institute for the Environment, Stanford University, April 2010.

Green energy boosters recognize the need for an expanded power grid. Mark Z. Jacobson and Elaine Hart write that "reliable integration of renewable resources on to the electricity grid represents an important step ... [which] is complicated by both the variability and the uncertainty associated with power output from renewable resources, like wind and solar power."[5] Lester Brown also sees the need: "The U.S. electricity grid today resembles the roads and highways of the mid-20th century before the interstate highway system was built. What is needed today is the electricity equivalent of the interstate highway system."[6]

He might be understating the scale of grid expansions necessary for a "renewable" energy economy. A 2017 National Renewable Energy Laboratory report stated, "Transmission expansion will play a vital role in allowing for efficient usage of renewable resources.... If transmission is not built to support new wind generation in the western United States, significant renewable energy curtailment (15.5 percent) could be an issue."[7] According to the study, the modern power grid can only support 35 percent of power coming from wind, and 12 percent from solar, for a total of 47 percent. Remember, this is electricity, not energy. In 2016, U.S. electricity consumption totaled about 14 percent of total energy consumption.[8] That means the modern U.S. grid is only prepared to provide about 6.7 percent of total energy needs via renewable energy. To make good on the bright green myth, the grid requires major expansion.

[5] Elaine K. Hart and Mark Z. Jacobson, "The carbon abatement potential of high penetration intermittent renewables," *Energy Environ. Sci.* 5 (2012): 6592.

[6] Lester R. Brown, *Plan B. 4.0: Mobilizing to Save Civilization* (New York: W. W. Norton & Company, 2009), 103.

[7] Jennie Jorgenson et al., "Reducing wind curtailment through transmission expansion in a wind vision future," National Renewable Energy Laboratory, January 2017.

[8] "U.S. Energy Facts," Energy Information Administration. "What is U.S. electricity generation by energy source?" Energy Information Administration, April 18, 2017.

To talk about "the grid" is really a misnomer in more than one sense. First, it's more a network than a grid. Second, it's not a single grid, but hundreds of grids around the world, each carrying power around a specific region. In the United States and Canada, four major grids—the Western, Eastern, Quebec, and Texas interconnections—link to one another. (Perhaps the Québécois and Texan secessionists want to keep their options open.)

Within a given region, electricity flows freely between all parts of the system. The entire grid essentially functions as one large circuit, beginning and ending at power plants. Subcircuits lead to individual homes or businesses. When you flip a switch in Washington State, the electricity that brightens your bulb could be coming from hydroelectric dams on the Columbia River, coal-fired power plants in Utah, or concentrated solar power plants in the Mojave Desert. In truth, your power is coming from all of these sources.

Between regions, electricity still flows, but is carefully regulated. The North American power grid could be considered the largest machine in the world. It includes 2.7 million miles of transmission lines, at least 70,000 substations,[9] and more than 7,500 power plants larger than 1 MW.[10] It is run by more than 3,200 utility companies.[11] This grid is so complex even electrical engineers can't fully understand it. Computer models regularly fail to function; it's said in the industry that the grid works in practice, but not in theory.[12]

---

[9] "Transmission & Distribution Infrastructure," Harris Williams & Co., 2010.
[10] "How many power plants are there in the United States?" U.S. Energy Information Administration, December 1, 2016.
[11] Mark Chediak and Ken Wells, "Why the U.S. Power Grid's Days Are Numbered," *Bloomberg*, August 22, 2013.
[12] Of course. the complexity of the power grid is *nothing* compared to the complexity of, say, a forest, the weather, or the biochemistry of a carpenter ant.

Split-second changes in current aren't compatible with a functioning industrial electric grid. Most home appliances can function
fine with a 5 to 10 percent voltage fluctuation, but many industrial
users require precise, stable currents. Milliseconds of disruption or
undersupply can damage sensitive equipment.[13]

Because it's difficult to combine intermittent, inherently unpre-
dictable flows of power from dozens of energy generation sites
into a reliable grid voltage and because grid-scale energy storage
doesn't really exist, we hear people like Trieu Mai, a senior analyst at the National Renewable Energy Laboratory, say things like,
"The grid was not built for renewables."

Another reason grids can't handle a major influx of solar and
wind power has to do with geography. "Renewable" energy harvesting often occurs far from major cities. The strongest and steadiest
winds in the U.S. are found east of the continental divide, in a band
centered on the Dakotas, Nebraska, Kansas, Oklahoma, and north
Texas.[14] The strongest and steadiest sunlight falls in the Mojave
Desert. "Where the best renewables are, there are few customers,"
summarizes James Hoecker, a transmission industry advisor who
formerly worked for the Federal Energy Regulatory Commission.[15]

To get power from these remote areas to the centers of population and industry requires the grid be significantly expanded and
upgraded.[16] This will not be simple, cheap, or benign. A report from

---

[13] Catalina Schröder, "Grid instability has industry scrambling for solutions," *Der Spiegel*, August 16, 2012.

[14] "Wind Maps," National Renewable Energy Laboratory.

[15] Diane Cardwell, "Fight to keep alternative energy local stymies an industry," *The New York Times*, March 23, 2016.

[16] Evan Halper, "Power struggle: Green energy versus a grid that's not ready," *LA Times*, December 2, 2013.

CalTech says that making electric grids compatible with renewable energy "represents one of the greatest technological challenges industrial societies have ever undertaken."[17]

Since grid operation is a high-cost, low-margin business, the federal government provides guaranteed profit margins. For example, PacifiCorp's $6 billion "Energy Gateway" transmission project, which links six western states, and which at the time of writing is mostly complete, is guaranteed 10.3 percent profit. This subsidy promises to "generate a significant return on investment for [Warren] Buffett and other Berkshire Hathaway shareholders."[18]

Is it any wonder businesses are on board with this plan?

Power grids have been expanding since the introduction of industrial electricity, but that expansion has recently accelerated. In just 10 minutes of research, we came across hundreds of news stories about just completed or planned grid expansion projects. In the U.S., tens of thousands of miles of new high-voltage transmission lines are scheduled or under construction.[19] In Vermont, a proposed 154-mile high-voltage transmission line would include 98 miles buried under Lake Champlain (the power company will pay $300 million over 40 years for cleanup efforts as part of the deal).[20] In Iowa, a $2 billion, 500-mile line will carry wind power to Illinois. One local resident says: "They're packaging it as a 'green' project ...

---

[17] "Grid 2020: Towards a Policy of Renewable and Distributed Energy Resources," The Resnick Institute, California Institute of Technology, September 2012.

[18] Sammy Roth, "Who will profit from the grid of the future?" *The Desert Sun*, February 1, 2017.

[19] "Power line frenzy hits rural America," *The Daily Yonder*, June 29, 2009.

[20] "About the project," TDI New England.

but I'm not sure the bottom line is really good for the environment and good for everyone. I think the bottom line is making a profit."[21] Rocky Mountain Power and Idaho Power are building a 1,000-mile-high voltage line from Wyoming to Idaho.[22] In Montgomery County, Texas, a proposed 138 kV line to supply a new suburban development ("5,000 new homes, more than eight million square feet of commercial office space and 1.2 million square feet of retail space") threatens a 12,000-acre forest preserve.[23] In New Jersey, a proposed 230 kV transmission line would cross through sensitive areas of the Navesink watershed.[24] In New Mexico, a $1.6 billion high-voltage transmission system will soon carry wind power to California.[25] A proposed line would run 203 miles from Québec to New Hampshire, crossing through Bear Brook State Park on the way.[26] One company alone, Clean Line, is permitting or building five major high-voltage transmission lines ranging from 200 miles to 780 miles long at a cost of $9 billion.[27]

With guaranteed 10 percent profit, you'd have to be an idiot not to get in on the action.

---

[21] Dennis Magee, "Property owners trying to stop proposed transmission line across Iowa," *The Courier*, November 17, 2013.

[22] "Gateway West transmission line project," Rocky Mountain Power and Idaho Power Gateway West Project.

[23] Lindsay Peyton, "Power line route sparks protest," *The Chronicle*, November 15, 2011.

[24] Michael George, "NJ residents pack arena to voice concern over proposed power line project," *NBC New York*, March 29, 2017.

[25] Joe Cardillo, "Remember that $1.6B energy transmission line? It's quietly moving forward," *Albuquerque Business First*, August 3, 2016.

[26] "Northern Pass Transmission Line Project EIS," Project Overview and Public Comments, Northern Pass EIS.

[27] Brian Eckhouse and Joe Ryan, "Tapping the power of the Great Plains to light up faraway cities," *Bloomberg*, February 9, 2016.

This rapid grid expansion is happening globally as well. In British Columbia, a new 110-mile 550 MW HVDC line is planned to run under the Strait of Juan de Fuca to Washington State.[28] In Mexico, the state utility has proposed and built dozens of major grid expansion projects in the past decade, with many more proposed. A rapid increase in the number of wind energy harvesting facilities on the Isthmus of Tehuantepec has led to major transmission line expansions and prompted local protests, blockades, and in response, police violence.[29] In Germany, major grid expansions have been part of the "green energy revolution" from the beginning. In 2012, grid operators estimated that Germany would need 2,361 miles of new high-voltage transmission lines—and that's simply to achieve the phasing out of nuclear power, not fossil fuels.[30] The project was reduced to 1,740 miles and is under construction. Before this began, another 1,150 miles of high-voltage lines were already planned or under construction in Germany.[31] A 1,400 MW underwater cable to Norway and a 1,000 MW line to Belgium are being planned to further link Germany's grid.[32] Another source counts more than 5,150 miles of proposed, in-progress, or completed high-voltage power lines as part of the German *Energiewende*.[33] By 2020, China expects to have 994,000 miles of high-voltage transmission lines in operation. In fact, the Chinese State Grid Corporation has proposed a $50 trillion global power grid to go into operation by 2050,

---

[28] "Juan de Fuca Cable Project," JDF Cable.

[29] David LaGesse, "Mexico's robust wind energy prospects ruffle nearby villages," *National Geographic*, February 10, 2013.

[30] "German power grid expansion to cost billions," *Der Spiegel*, May 30, 2012.

[31] "German power grid expansion behind schedule," *Argus Media*, April 29, 2013.

[32] Kerstine Appunn, "Connecting up the Energiewende," *Clean Energy Wire*, January 26, 2015.

[33] R. Andreas Kraemer, "Why Germany has no need for north-to-south power lines," *Energy Transition*, February 2, 2015.

including massive wind energy harvesting facilities at the North Pole.[34]

Like other industrial projects, power grids destroy land. First, they do so through the creation and maintenance of required buffer zones along high-voltage transmission lines. These buffers vary from about 75 to 400 feet wide. Because plants taller than 10 or 15 feet can damage transmission towers or lines, the first step is to clear this land completely. The most visually striking transmission lines, those in forested areas, require wide clearcuts stretching across entire mountain ranges. Once cleared, these areas must be maintained. Herbicides, chainsaws, mowers, and grazing are used to keep plants down for as long as the transmission line is in use.[35]

Transmission line rights-of-way add up to more than 9 million acres in the U.S. That's an area larger than Rhode Island, Delaware, Connecticut, and New Jersey combined.[36] This number is rising as larger and more interconnected power grids are built to support coal, oil, and gas, as well as "renewable" energy distribution.

Mark Z. Jacobson's proposals for a renewable energy transition include estimates about the land that would be destroyed by the construction of new energy harvesting facilities. In Washington State, Jacobson estimates that new wind, hydro, and solar energy

---

[34] Brian Wang, "China proposes $50+ trillion Global UHV grid connecting all power generation including massive wind farm at the North Pole by 2050," *Next Big Future*, March 31, 2016.

[35] "Transmission System Vegetation Management Program. Record of Decision," Bonneville Power Administration, July 2000.

[36] Richard Conniff, "Electric power rights of way: a new frontier for conservation," *Yale Environment 360*, October 16, 2014.

harvesting facilities would require 0.08 percent of the state's land area (more than 36,000 acres) as footprint, and, including spacing, 1.97 percent (almost 900,000 acres). These numbers don't include land harmed by grid expansions. Jacobson attempts to justify this exclusion by saying, "The actual footprint area of a transmission tower is smaller than the footprint area of a wind turbine.... A transmission tower consists of four narrow metal support rods separated by distance, penetrating the soil to an underground foundation. Many photographs of transmission towers indicate more vegetation growing under the towers than around the towers since areas around the towers are often agricultural or otherwise-used land, whereas the area under the tower is vegetated soil. Since the land under transmission towers supports vegetation and wildlife, it is not considered footprint beyond the small area of the support access roads."[37]

That's a remarkable statement for a number of reasons. First is the simple lack of evidence. Jacobson's viewing of "many photographs" is considered enough reason to discount millions of acres of new transmission line clearance.

The second is that Jacobson is (inadvertently) right in pointing out how destructive agriculture is. It's true; land that isn't regularly plowed, sprayed with chemicals, and harvested supports more life than land that is.[38] But his comparison is between land in bad shape, and other land in even worse (agricultural land). "Less bad" isn't a justification.

The third reason Jacobson's justifications are nonsense is fragmentation. We went over this earlier, during our discussion about

---

[37] Mark Z. Jacobson and Mark A. Delucchi, "Providing all global energy with wind, water, and solar power, Part I: Technologies, energy resources, quantities and areas of infrastructure, and materials," *Energy Policy* 39 (2011): 1161.

[38] See, for instance, *The Vegetarian Myth: Food, Justice, and Sustainability* by Lierre Keith (Crescent City, CA: Flashpoint Publications, 2009), or any of Richard Manning's works.

roads. Habitat fragmentation makes life difficult or impossible for many creatures. Transmission corridors fragment habitat just like roads do, slicing the land into smaller, more isolated pieces. Ignoring this impact doesn't do Jacobson's cause any good. Oops. Actually, ignoring it does do his cause good. It just doesn't do the world any good. And that's our point.

Finally, the grid is three-dimensional. It extends into the sky, and like most tall, unnatural structures, transmission towers kill birds. A 2014 meta-analysis of 14 different studies found that power lines kill between 12 million and 64 million birds per year in the U.S. via collisions (85 percent of the death toll) and electrocution.[39] An earlier analysis put the number at 174 million per year.[40] While both studies have a relatively large margin of error, and habitat loss is considered by far the largest threat to birds, death from power lines is now one of the leading human-related ways birds are killed.

Rutgers researcher Clinton Andrews, in contrast to Jacobson, has concluded that transmission will do even more harm to the land than will solar and wind energy harvesting facilities, adding that "the siting challenges [of a renewable power system], especially for transmission, are ... daunting."[41]

[39] Scott R. Loss et al., "Refining estimates of bird collision and electrocution mortality at power lines in the United States," *PLOS One*, July 3, 2014.
[40] Leslie Kaufman, "Conspiracies don't kill birds. People, however, do," *New York Times*, January 17, 2011.
[41] Martin LaMonica, "Figuring land use into renewable-energy equations," *CNet*, May 29, 2010.

Of course, power grids aren't only made of transmission lines. They also require substations, staging areas, depots, access roads, and more. These also destroy land. As one report says, "Most of the community and environmental impacts [of substations] are permanent. The extensive land clearing and excavation required for the substation foundation creates permanent changes to the land cover of the site. In addition, a permanent access road is needed."[42] Remember, there are at least 70,000 of these substations—some covering many acres—across the United States. Even more are being planned and built to distribute power from "renewable" energy facilities.

Oil, coal, and gas are also essential to the manufacture, transportation, assembly, maintenance, and decommissioning, dismantling, and disposal of transmission lines and towers. For example, towers are usually built with the assistance of either helicopters or large cranes, which are fueled with fossil fuels. These towers are built of materials transported using oil, across asphalt, which is made of fossil-fuel tar. Machines making machines making machines.

Transmission towers themselves require steel, about six metric tons per typical medium-sized high-voltage transmission tower. And there may be between four and 10 towers per mile.[43] Even using the lower number—four towers per mile—at 6 metric tons of steel per tower, and with 2.7 million miles of high-voltage

---

[42] "Environmental Impacts of Substations," Public Service Commission of Wisconsin, August 2013.
[43] Juho Yli-Hannuksela, "The transmission line cost calculation" (PhD dissertation, Vasa Yrkeshögskola University of Applied Sciences, 2011).

transmission lines, there's on the order of 65 million metric tons of steel in the U.S. high-voltage power grid in the towers alone. That doesn't account for steel used in foundations, transformers, substations, and wires.

Concrete is also required for the foundation of every high-voltage transmission tower. One estimate is that between 45 and 65 cubic meters are required for each tower. That's between 96 and 138 metric tons, meaning the amount of concrete in transmission towers in the U.S.—again, using the low-end number—is perhaps 1 billion tons. This is not making the world a better place.

In bright green fantasies, next-generation power grids will be built around "superconductors," complex materials that reduce loss of electricity (in the U.S., about 10 percent of power is lost during transmission). These superconductors invariably require complex production using toxic materials. For example, many superconducting wires are constructed of yttrium barium copper oxide alloys. Another common formulation is bismuth-based oxide. In these fantasies, high-pressure helium gas or liquid nitrogen will be used as a cooling system.[44]

Just in the United States, the grid already has 2.7 million miles of transmission lines. And an expanded grid is going to be cooled by high-pressure helium gas and liquid nitrogen?

We have two questions. First, what would be required to construct and maintain an infrastructure that cools more than 2.7 million miles of superconducting wire? And second, what are these

---

[44] Christopher Rey, ed., *Superconductors in the Power Grid* (Sawston, U.K.: Woodhead Publishing Ltd., 2015).

people smoking? Again, superconductors are not going to make the world a better place.

Building a functional grid that integrates "renewable" energy is difficult, but with enough money from public subsidies and private investment, it's likely possible. But this is not a good thing. The new grid looks a lot like the old grid. It delivers electricity to factories and subdivisions (and now, cars). The power it delivers was generated in processes that are destroying the planet. The grid itself is destroying the planet, in its production, installation, operation, and maintenance. Instead of campaigning for more grids, we should be fighting them, indeed removing them.

People are resisting new grid expansions. From Mexico to Iowa, Afghanistan to New Jersey, communities are fighting back. Even people who aren't environmentalists don't want to live near high-voltage power lines. They're loud, ugly, and may cause health problems. Sane people recognize that destroying land for major infrastructure projects is not sustainable, no matter how it is branded.

Chapter 11

THE HYDROPOWER LIE

That anyone would try to destroy such a place seems
incredible; but sad experience shows that there are people
good enough and bad enough for anything. The proponents
of the dam scheme bring forward a lot of bad arguments to
prove that the only righteous thing to do with the people's
parks is to destroy them bit by bit as they are able.... These
temple destroyers, devotees of ravaging commercialism,
seem to have a perfect contempt for Nature, and, instead of
lifting their eyes to the God of the mountains, lift them to the
Almighty Dollar.... As well dam for water-tanks the people's
cathedrals and churches, for no holier temple has ever been
consecrated by the heart of man.

—JOHN MUIR[1]

The Columbia River is a dark body of water a quarter mile across.
On the far slope, forests rise thick and green, broken by black basalt
cliffs. A waterfall, made small by distance, cuts through these cliffs.

---

[1] John Muir, *The Yosemite* (New York: The Century Company, 1912), 262.

The scene would be beautiful if not for high-power transmission lines in the background.

There's something else wrong, too. The river. It's too slow. If you didn't know better, you'd think you were looking at a reservoir. That is not how it's supposed to be.

Just downriver, the half-mile-wide Bonneville dam chokes the Columbia to a halt. When the dam was built in 1937, Bonneville was the biggest dam in the world. Now, it's one of the smallest of 14 major dams just on the main stem of the Columbia, and one of more than 500 dams in the watershed.

The Columbia River was once as magnificent as other now-destroyed wonders, like the passenger pigeons who numbered perhaps 5 billion. The great naturalist John James Audubon described how "the air was literally filled with pigeons; the light of noon-day was obscured as by an eclipse."[2] This went on for three days. There are descriptions of bison herds that took four days to thunder past. Or descriptions of how, at any stream in the Pacific Northwest, there would reliably, predictably, be a grizzly bear every 15 minutes. They're all gone.

Salmon and other anadromous fish like lamprey and eulachon smelt lived in more than 13,000 miles of the Columbia and its tributaries. Conservative estimates put the number of salmon who used to swim up the Columbia each year at 10 million to 16 million.

Between 1890 and 1974, dam construction blocked about half of the Columbia River watershed from fish passage. Today, the Columbia is the most heavily dammed watershed in the world, with flooded forests, covered rapids, blocked fish, and trapped silt.

---

[2] Erin McCarthy, "Ten facts about extinct passenger pigeon," *Mental Floss*, September 2, 2014.

Dams, combined with logging, global warming, agriculture, and industrial fishing, are pushing salmon to extinction. Wild salmon in the Columbia River are now at about 2 percent of their historic numbers. Eulachon smelt have suffered a similar collapse, and lamprey numbers are even lower.[3] Only one free-flowing stretch of the Columbia River remains: Hanford Reach, 50 miles of river in eastern Washington State.

The Hanford Site is a military facility where, starting in the 1940s, plutonium for 60,000 nuclear weapons, including the bombs dropped on Hiroshima and Nagasaki, was produced. From the beginning till today, the site has leaked nuclear waste and radiation, turning Hanford into the most radioactive site in the U.S., and one of the most toxic places in the world. Most of the high-level radioactive waste at Hanford—54 million gallons of it—is stored in underground tanks. Correction: stored in underground tanks *that have been leaking for decades.* An estimated million gallons of radioactive waste is traveling via groundwater into the Columbia River.[4]

Paradoxically, because the rest of the river has been so devastated by dams, the Hanford Reach is currently the most important section of the Columbia River for fish. Forty-three fish species—including a major portion of the river's remaining salmon and steelhead—use this portion of the river for spawning or some other portion of their life.[5] This means the Hanford Reach—the most

---

[3] James B. MacKinnon, "'Salvation fish' that sustained native people now needs saving," *National Geographic,* July 2015.

[4] Bechtel—the multinational construction firm that built the Ivanpah Concentrated Solar Power Planet, and also builds coal and copper mines, airports, gas power plants, dams, and so on—is also in charge of multibillion-dollar contracts at Hanford.

[5] Fish: Hanford Reach. U.S. Fish and Wildlife Service. February 24, 2014.

contaminated radioactive zone in the United States—is also the section of the Columbia River most full of life; or more accurately, the section that is, compared to the rest of the Columbia, the least devoid of life.

This not a commentary on nuclear waste. This is a commentary on the destructiveness of dams.

Once upon a time, dams were recognized for the environmental atrocities they are. Human beings understood that dams kill rivers, from source to sea. They understood that dams kill forests, marshlands, grasslands.

In the 12th century, Richard the Lionhearted (King Richard I of England) put in place a law forbidding dams from preventing salmon passage. In the 14th century, Robert the Bruce did something similar for Scotland. His descendant Robert the III went even further, declaring that three convictions for killing salmon out of season would be a capital offense.

Fast-forward to today, when dams are claimed to provide "clean" and "green" energy.

Where's Robert the III when you need him?

As recently as three decades ago, at least environmentalists still consistently opposed dams. But the coup that turned so much environmentalism away from protecting the real world and into a lobbying arm of favored sectors of the industrial economy has rhetorically turned dams into environmental saviors. And climate change activists are among the most relentless missionaries for the gospel of the green dam.

This issue is urgent. While here in the United States, no new large dams have been built in many years (although many shovel-ready proposals are waiting for public funding), large hydropower dams are being built around the world as quickly as (in)humanly possible.

Once again, environmental engineer Mark Jacobson is an example, as he always seems to be, of someone working hard to kill the planet in order to save it. His 100 percent "renewable" transition plans—and remember, bright greens and many mainstream environmentalists love this guy—call for building about 270 new large hydroelectric dams globally, each at least the size of the Hoover or Glen Canyon dams.[6] He also calls for major expansions to existing dams by adding new turbines. His models rely heavily on hydro because solar and wind facilities are by their nature intermittent and unreliable.

Setting aside all the intrinsic harms of "renewables," his plan probably wouldn't even work. His proposals were challenged recently by a group of scientists who wrote that Jacobson's research "involves errors, inappropriate methods, and implausible assumptions"—especially regarding hydropower.[7] Jacobson's response has generally not been to prove his critics wrong, which of course he can't do, but rather to sue them and associated organizations for millions of dollars. (His lawsuit was dismissed as frivolous and he was ordered to pay attorney fees for those he sued.)

In one of Jacobson's models, hydro harvests 1,300 gigawatts of peak power in the U.S. by 2055. That's about 15 times the current national hydropower capacity. Critics of Jacobson's paper say that dam outflows of that magnitude would be disastrous for aquatic

---

[6] Mark Z. Jacobson and Mark A. Delucchi, "Providing all global energy with wind, water, and solar power, Part I: Technologies, energy resources, quantities and areas of infrastructure, and materials," *Energy Policy* 39 (2011): 1154–1169.
[7] Christopher T. Clack et al., "Evaluation of a proposal for reliable low-cost grid power with 100% wind, water, and solar," *PNAS*, June 19, 2017.

creatures who call those rivers home.[8] They also point out that the capacity Jacobson wants is "physically impossible."

One way that dams kill rivers is by killing insects who are food for dozens of other species. A 2016 study found that "hydropeaking"—the process of running more water through a hydroelectric dam during the high-demand workday hours—results in rapidly fluctuating water levels along the banks of reservoirs upstream of dams and rivers downstream. These dry periods are devastating for mayflies, caddisflies, and other insect species who lay their eggs in shallow water. Very few of their eggs are able to survive the fast wet/dry cycles. Their failure to survive affects how much food is available for fish and countless other species who depend on insects and their larvae.[9]

Costa Rica derives 80 percent of its electricity from hydropower. The media has been quick to label this a green miracle. *The Independent, Treehugger, Quartz, Science Alert, Time, Inhabitat, Fast Company*, and many other news sources routinely gush about Costa Rica supplying nearly all its electricity from hydro. As usual, the articles conflate electricity with energy, as when *Treehugger* writes of "99% renewable energy." *Inhabitat, The Independent*, and (ironically) *Science Alert* all make the same mistake. Meanwhile,

---

[8] Peter Fairley, "Can the U.S. grid work with 100% renewables? There's a scientific fight brewing," *IEEE Spectrum*, June 19, 2017.
[9] Nathan Collins, "How hydroelectric power kills insects, and why that matters," *Pacific Standard*, July 15, 2016.

Costa Rica's recent "explosive growth in private vehicles" drove up gasoline demand by 11 percent in 2016 alone.[10]

Left unsaid is the ecological harm caused by dams. Besides the significant carbon emissions caused by the concrete, steel, trucking, and land clearance necessary to build dams, the reservoirs created by dams are major sources of greenhouse gas emissions.

Reservoirs are responsible for, at the very least, between 1.3 and 4 percent of global greenhouse gas emissions.[11] A single dam in the Brazilian Amazon, Tucuruí, is estimated to release more emissions on its own than Sao Paolo, the fifth-largest city in the world.[12] The Brazilian National Institute of Space Research says reservoirs are "the largest single anthropogenic source of methane, being responsible for 23 percent of all methane emissions due to human activities." Philip Fearnside, a researcher at the Brazilian National Institute for Research in the Amazon, calls dams in the tropics "methane factories." Since he made that statement, research has shown that reservoirs in temperate regions could be described similarly: the conventional belief that reservoirs in temperate climates don't produce much methane is being overturned. Since the data is so new, and the emissions are "far higher than previously assumed," these emissions aren't counted in global inventories of greenhouse gas emissions. The primary author of some of the new

---

[10] Lindsay Fendt, "All that glitters is not green: Costa Rica's renewables conceal dependence on oil," *The Guardian*, January 5, 2017.

[11] Bridget B. Deemer et al., "Greenhouse gas emissions from reservoir water surfaces," *BioScience Journal* 66, 11 (2016): 949–964; and "Reservoir emissions," International Rivers.

[12] Philip M. Fearnside, "Greenhouse gas emissions from a hydroelectric reservoir (Brazil's Tucuruí dam) and the energy policy implications," *Water, Air, and Soil Pollution* 133, no 1–4 (January 2002): 69–96.

research says that even the revised emissions estimates are probably low.[13]

The 2013 book *Climate Governance in the Developing World* has this to say about Costa Rican dams: "These [reservoir methane] emissions, however, are neither measured nor taken into account in calculating Costa Rica's carbon balance. Given that the nation's electricity demand is projected to increase by 6 percent per year for the foreseeable future, and that the majority of this is to be met with increased hydroelectricity production, including such emissions in neutrality calculations would probably make it quite difficult for the country ever to achieve its goals [for reducing greenhouse gas emissions]."[14]

All of this is ignored as an inconvenient truth by utility companies, often by state regulators, and certainly by bright green environmentalists, who continue to promote Costa Rica as some sort of carbon/environmental success story.

Hydroelectricity as "carbon-free" energy has been codified into the Kyoto Protocol and United Nations agreements on climate change. Under this falsehood, the World Bank, the International Monetary Fund, and other major funding agencies are investing hundreds of billions of dollars in dam-building.

Across the world, about 3,700 large hydropower dams are either planned or under construction.[15] In Brazil alone, 60 planned or under-construction dams would flood 3 percent of the Amazon—an area of rainforest the size of Michigan.[16] Including the projects

[13] Matt Weiser, "The hydropower paradox: is this energy as clean as it seems?" *The Guardian*, November 6, 2016.

[14] Gary Wockner, "The false promise of hydropower," *Waterkeeper Alliance Magazine* 11, no. 2 (Summer 2015).

[15] Christiane Zarfl et al. "A global boom in hydropower dam construction," *Aquatic Sciences* 77, no. 1 (January 2015): 161–170.

[16] Simeon Tegel, "Brazil's hydro dams could make its greenhouse gas emissions soar," *GlobalPost*, July 1, 2013.

in Brazil, there are more than 500 planned, under construction, or finished dams in the Amazon basin. Construction of the planned dams would cause, in the words of one riverine scientist, "massive environmental damage all the way from the eastern slopes of the Andes to the Atlantic Ocean."[17]

Large dam projects not only destroy rivers, they also subvert or destroy indigenous rights. Indigenous Lenca activist Berta Cáceres said that megadams are "worse than colonization."[18] Violence against indigenous people fighting dams is common. In 2016, after years of organizing opposition, leading road blockades, and suffering death threats and attacks by private security, Berta Cáceres was murdered in her home by gunmen. A colleague, Nelson García, was gunned down 12 days later. They weren't the first deaths of this particular war. Three years before, Tómas Garcia was shot and killed by a soldier while protesting the same Agua Zarca dam. Other resisters have faced beatings, sexual assault, and other forms of torture. At least 124 Honduran activists fighting dams, logging, mines, and tourist resorts have been murdered since 2010.[19]

Subjugation of indigenous people in the service of "green" hydropower doesn't just occur in the global south. Despite decades of indigenous-led resistance, in 2015 in Canada, BC Hydro began preliminary construction on its latest large dam, the Site C "Clean Energy Project." The Site C dam is expected to flood 15,000 acres of the Peace River valley in Alberta, including thousands of cultural sites and hunting, fishing, and gathering places. It will also fragment one of the most important wildlife passageways in the Yellowstone to Yukon migration corridor. Okanagan Grand Chief

---

[17] "Amazonia's future will be jeopardized by dams," *Eureka Alert*, University of Arizona, June 14, 2017.

[18] Sian Cowman and Philippa de Boissiére, "For indigenous peoples, megadams are 'worse than colonization,'" *Common Dreams*, March 14, 2016.

[19] "Financiers of Agua Zarca's hydroelectric dam to pull-out," *TeleSUR*, June 6, 2017.

Stewart Phillip and Ben Parfitt write that the whole region looks "like one giant industrial sacrifice zone. Layer upon layer of environmentally devastating developments occur here. Nowhere else in B.C. do you see major hydroelectric, logging, mining and natural gas industry activities all happening simultaneously."[20] In recent years, indigenous people in Canada have also been fighting other major dam projects, including Muskrat Falls in Labrador and Keeyask Dam in Manitoba.

Dams are a major mechanism of land destruction and theft. Here are two examples from Costa Rica. Reventazón Dam, which was completed in late 2016, is the largest dam in Central America and was built along a critical wildlife corridor. Methane emissions from this reservoir of course haven't been considered at all and won't be accounted for in national calculations. Nearby, the proposed El Diquís dam would be built adjacent to the Osa Peninsula, which has been called "the most biodiverse location on earth."[21] This proposed dam, larger than Reventazón, has been protested by indigenous groups for years. It would flood nearly 15,000 acres of forests and indigenous lands of the Curré, Boruca, Guaymi, Bribri, Ujarrás, Cabagra, and Salitre people. To push the project, the Costa Rican government has "subjected the community to a propaganda campaign specifically meant to deceive them, which the [government] then referred to as formal consultations."[22] The power station for the Diquís dam would be located downstream of the dam in the Térraba-Sierpe wetlands, the most important mangrove site in Central America and a site protected under an international wetland conservation treaty (the Ramsar Convention). Despite the

---

[20] Grand Chief Stewart Phillip and Ben Parfitt, "Water usage in B.C.'s northeast requires indigenous consent," *DeSmog Canada*, July 6, 2017.
[21] "About the Osa," *Osa Conservation*.
[22] John Ahni Shertow, "Indigenous groups opposed to El Diquís hydro project," *Intercontinental Cry*, March 10, 2008.

Convention, the power station will destroy an estimated 750 acres of wetlands.[23] Rural communities in Costa Rica have also fought against the transmission lines necessary for the dam, part of the massive SIEPAC (Integración de sistemas eléctricos y de comunicación) project to link Central American energy and communication infrastructures, which would bulldoze hundreds of miles of native forest to construct electric lines.

The World Commission on Dams estimates that at least 40 million to 80 million people have been displaced by dams. The Yacyretá Dam on the border of Argentina and Paraguay displaced 68,000 people. The Sobradinho Dam in Brazil displaced 60,000. The Itaipu Dam between Brazil and Paraguay displaced 59,000. And so on.[24]

Itaipu Dam is one of the largest in the world. At nearly five miles long and more than 700 feet tall, Itaipu generates more electricity than any other hydroelectric dam (nearly 12 GW average in 2016). Two national parks—Sete Quedas in Brazil and Saltos del Guiará in Paraguay—were dissolved by the ruling Brazilian military government and Paraguayan regime in 1981 for this dam to be built. Itaipu flooded the world's most powerful waterfalls, the Sete Quedas or Seven Falls. Before their destruction, the roaring of the Seven Falls could be heard for nearly 20 miles. After the dam was built, the reservoir began to fill, inundating the forest and drowning countless millions of creatures. One video shows primates trapped in the tops of trees as the water rises, leaping from branch to branch, with

---

[23] Kendra Patterson et al., "The proposed PH Diquís and its compliance with international law," University of Florida Law School, Conservation Clinic, July 23, 2009.

[24] Bogumil Terminski, "Development-induced displacement and resettlement: Theoretical frameworks and current challenges," Library of the Commons, May 2013.

nowhere to go except into the water and into extinction.[25] It's hard to get that image out of your head.

Once the reservoir was filled, the submerged cliffs that made up the face of the Seven Falls were dynamited for the sake of shipping. With the removal of the natural barrier the falls presented, a "massive invasion" of nonnative fish moved into the upper Rio Paraná basin.[26]

The only remaining legacy of Sete Quedas today is cheap electricity for the industries of Brazil and Paraguay.

In Myanmar and China, there are at least 10 major proposed dams along the Salween River, until now the longest free-flowing river remaining in Southeast Asia, and one of the most biodiverse places on the planet. These dams would harm 194 endangered plant species and 42 endangered mammal species, as well as dozens of endemic fish species who migrate up and down the river. Indigenous Karen residents fear that the dams will destroy their source of food. They've proposed a 2,000-square-mile "peace park" of protected forests and rivers as an alternative to the dam projects.[27] The dams in Myanmar would export most of the electricity they generate to Thailand and China under deals signed by the military dictatorship that ended (kind of) in 2011. Other dams in Myanmar, such as the Upper Paunglaung Dam, have already displaced thousands of people and led to an epidemic of suicides among poor, dispossessed farmers. This particular dam supplies power to the capital city of

---

[25] Diogo Caleffi, "Fim das Sete Quedas," YouTube, November 26, 2012.

[26] Horácio Ferreira Júlio Júnior et al., "A massive invasion of fish species after eliminating a natural barrier in the upper rio Paraná basin," *Neotropical Ichthyology* 7, 4 (2009): 709–718.

[27] Demelza Stokes, "Damming the Salween: what next for Southeast Asia's last great free-flowing river?" *Mongabay*, November 23, 2016.

Napyidaw, a city built from scratch in the early 2000s at the behest of the military government.[28] Napyidaw is well-known as a ghost town, sprawling over 2,700 square miles crisscrossed with 10-lane highways and a very low population density.

In nearby Cambodia, Tonlé Sap, the largest lake in the region and one of the richest breeding grounds for fish in the world, is threatened by the construction of major dams on the Mekong River in Laos and China. Tonlé Sap is a unique 160-mile-long lake that floods seasonally during the monsoon, when the Tonlé Sap River reverses course. Then when the monsoon ends, the water and millions of fish drain back into the Mekong, leaving the freshwater mangroves and a much smaller water body behind. Tonlé Sap is home to around 150 species of fish, including the Mekong Giant Catfish, who can grow to 600 pounds. The dams proposed for the Mekong would end this seasonal flood and destroy the ability of the fish to reproduce there.

Prior to the erection of the dams that have already destroyed much of the Mekong River, the Mekong was home to the largest animal migration on the planet. Larger than flocks of passenger pigeons darkening east North American skies for days at a time. Larger than the great herds of ungulates on the Serengeti. Larger than the salmon so thick they turned huge rivers black and roiling with fish.

These were migrations of the Mekong Giant Catfish. Millions upon millions of these giant fish moved upstream to spawn.

---

[28] Connor Macdonald, "Myanmar: Hydropower and the cost of life," *Al Jazeera*, June 30, 2016.

Dams are wiping them out. But more dams are planned for the Mekong. And more after that. And more after that.

In the Cascade Mountains, in a national park, the trail winds alongside the clear water, and stone-flanked mountains rise on the far side of Ross Lake. But it's not a true lake; it's the uppermost of three reservoirs created by hydroelectric dams on the Skagit River between the 1920s and 1940s to provide power to Seattle. Before the dams were built, the Skagit Gorge was dense with old growth, mostly Douglas fir, western hemlock, and western red cedar. In 1945, Seattle City Light sold the trees to a logging company, which clearcut in and around the site of the future reservoir.[29] The thin forest and the stumps in the shallows are testament to "the most intensive logging that ever took place in the North Cascades."[30]

Dams in forested areas are always accompanied by logging, and often, logging leads to the construction of dams.

Before the widespread use of electricity, most sawmills were powered by waterwheels mounted in dams. Reservoirs also served as a convenient storage area for logs floated downstream, then towed to the mill. Today, this continues.

In the "scientific management" worldview, clearcutting the soon-to-be-flooded reservoir is efficient. Nothing is wasted. Hell, it even reduces future greenhouse gas emissions by reducing the load of organic material in the reservoir. It's a "green" approach, right?

[29] Scott Pattee, "A history of the Skagit River basin snow surveys and hydroelectric project," Western Snow Conference, 2004.
[30] "Loggers," North Cascades National Park, February 28, 2015.

The proposed Tapajos dam, in the heart of the Amazon, is a prime example of dams being linked to deforestation. A 2016 study found that dam builders are likely to reinvest their profits from the dams in soy farming and cattle ranching in the area, leading to a "wave of deforestation" in the rainforest.[31]

Dams are often linked to mining too. In Brazil, for example, many major hydroelectric dams have been built to supply power to large mining operations. Zoe Sullivan of *Mongabay* writes, "The Amazon basin, and Pará state in particular, offer several clear examples of mines associated with hydropower projects. Besides Tucuruí Dam and the foundries in Bacarena and São Luis, there is also the bauxite mine at Paragominas which the Norwegian firm Hydro acquired from Alcoa last year. [And] although not active yet, the Belo Sun gold mine would take advantage of the Belo Monte dam's power supply."[32]

Hydropower serves an important role in bright green propaganda in part because of confusion caused by the term "renewable." Hydropower is "renewable," in the sense that so long as rain continues, reservoirs will be replenished. But as we've seen, renewable does not equal carbon-free or benign. This confusion allows nations to claim that a higher proportion of their energy comes from what they call climate-friendly sources.

Nations that generate a good deal of their power from dams include Lesotho (100 percent), Paraguay, Bhutan, Albania, Mozambique, Democratic Republic of Congo, Nepal, Ethiopia,

---

[31] Chris Arsenault, "Proposed Amazon dam would fuel land speculation, deforestation, study says," Thomson Reuters Foundation, June 28, 2016.
[32] Zoe Sullivan, "Unexamined synergies: dam building and mining go together in the Amazon," *Mongabay*, June 22, 2017.

Burundi (greater than 99 percent), Norway (96 percent), Iceland (73 percent), North Korea (71 percent), Canada and Austria (60 percent), Switzerland (58 percent), New Zealand (55 percent), Sweden (46 percent), Chile (31 percent), Turkey (26 percent), and so on.[33]

Every dam is a disaster for the real world.

China is on a dam-building spree which opponents call a "love affair." The government has referred to hydro as a "key area of focus,"[34] and is now planning a series of large dams in Tibet (a not insignificant reason for China's occupation of Tibet is that Tibet forms the headwaters for rivers that flow throughout Asia). One of these dams, on the Yarlung Tsangpo River, would be three times bigger than the world's current largest dam, the Three Gorges Dam on the Yangtze.[35]

Explosives are a key element of dam construction. The construction of the Hoover Dam, for example, required about 8.5 million pounds of dynamite.[36]

Explosives can also be used *against* dams. Stories exist of outraged locals filling boats with explosives and floating them downstream to demolish dams that threatened their food supply. One example is the Cougar Creek Dam on the Washougal River, near Portland, which was built in the 1920s. The very night the construction was finished, a great noise was heard by the caretakers. In the morning, they found only mangled remnants of the dam

[33] "Electricity production from hydroelectric sources (% of total)," *IEA Statistics*, World Bank, 2015.
[34] Solidiance, "Hydro power in China," *Ecology.com*.
[35] Yong Yang, "World's largest hydropower project planned for Tibetan plateau," *China Dialogue*, May 3, 2014.
[36] "Hoover Dam," Ritchie Wiki.

(and a free-flowing river). The dam had been blown up, never to be rebuilt.

The Beni River in Bolivia, in the Amazon Basin, is threatened by a dam that would flood 500,000 acres, including a large portion of Madidi National Park. In Ecuador, the Jondachi River, which flows through a jungle and is part of the Sumaco Biosphere Reserve, is threatened by a dam. The Quijos River, near Ecuador's capitol, already has one dam, and several more hydroelectric dams and tunnels are now proposed. The government of Ecuador refers to this as "clean" and "sustainable." In Chile, the Maipo River, Santiago's main drinking water source, is being gradually dewatered by a hydropower tunnel project that is stealing water from tributaries upstream. Electricity from the project is mainly going to the mining industry. The Ñuble River, in southern Chile, is threatened by two hydroelectric dams. Like the dams on the Maipo, the electricity from these projects would go mainly to mining. The Rocín River, in Northern Chile, is the site of several proposed dams which would be private projects built to provide electricity to ... more mining companies. And the Marañón River in Peru, the largest tributary of the Amazon, is facing 20 dam projects.[37]

In the Democratic Republic of the Congo, the world's largest dam project—the $114 billion Inga project—is set to begin construction on the Congo River. The project would have a peak capacity of 40 GW, twice as much as the Three Gorges dam in China. Most of this

[37] Gary Wockner and Lydia Bleifuss, "7 wild rivers under attack by hydropower dams," *EcoWatch*, October 12, 2016.

power would go to heavy industry in South Africa, and to large mines in the DRC.

The lower Congo River is home to more than 300 fish species, 80 of which are found nowhere else—one of the highest rates of endemism in the world. These endemic species include the *mbenga* (goliath tigerfish), the blind and pigmentless *Lamprologus lethops*, and the *Nzonzi a mpofo* (Congo blind barb). There are also numerous endemic frogs and snails in the river, as well as turtles, African manatees, and three crocodile species. The dam would likely lead to the local or complete extirpation of many of these species.[38]

Around 60,000 humans would be displaced.[39] This project costs almost $2 million per displaced person in a country with a per capita income of about $730, which means that this costs about 2,600 years of income for every person displaced.

The people displaced, and the world, would be better off if they were each paid $7,300 per year—10 times per capita income—to protect and preserve local wildlife, with bonuses for those who helped their biomes the most. And it would save a hell of a lot of money. But there always seems to be enough money to destroy, but never enough to restore.

"Environmentalists" promoting hydroelectric dams show how far the movement to save the planet has been co-opted. It's like the promotion of nuclear energy by too many environmentalists. When your primary allegiance lies with industrial civilization and not with life on the planet, it's easy—and, more to the

---

[38] Britt Norlander, "Rough waters: one of the world's most turbulent rivers is home to wide array of fish species. Now, large dams are threatening their future," *Business Library*, April 20, 2009.
[39] John Vidal, "Construction of the world's largest dam in DR of Congo could begin within months," *The Guardian*, May 28, 2016.

point, necessary—to justify atrocities. Industrial civilization needs energy. Coal, oil, and gas are finite and are clearly warming the planet and (more importantly, for this mindset) threatening civilization in general. Therefore, the solution is so-called "carbon-free" electricity, including hydropower and nuclear.

As it turns out, rivers play a major role in global carbon cycles, carrying soil and plant matter into the ocean. Much of this material eventually sinks to the seabed, where it may be for all practical purposes sequestered. Dams destroy this cycle.

In the Columbia River watershed, dams block the movement of salmon and other keystone species that provide food to hundreds of other animals, plants, and fungi. Forests on salmon-bearing streams typically grow three times faster than forests without salmon, since so many oceanic nutrients are carried in the bodies of the fish, then distributed through the forest by bears, birds, and other predators and scavengers. When you build a dam, fish can't pass. Salmon (and other animals) suffer, and so does the forest. This is habitat fragmentation and habitat starvation.

Stagnant and warmed by the sun, reservoirs regularly reach temperatures fatal to native fish. Adult salmon headed upstream that are either able to navigate the "fish ladders" or get trapped and trucked around the dams, as well as young fish heading down to the ocean, simply can't survive the heat. Warm reservoir temperatures favor nonnative fish, such as bass, perch, bluegill, and walleye.

Dams also trap sediment behind them, depriving areas downstream of that material. This prevents beaches and banks from being replenished and harms wetlands, devastating downstream habitat. This means that in addition to destroying rivers and forests, dams also destroy riparian areas, seasonally flooded lands, estuaries, and beaches.

Dams concentrate mercury. The process begins when the slow water in reservoirs allows naturally occurring bacteria to flourish. Meanwhile, mercury—much of it originating from coal power plants, garbage and medical waste incinerators, landfills, mines, and dentistry—flows downstream and gathers in the reservoir. The newly abundant bacteria "methylate" the mercury flowing into the reservoir, making the mercury much more toxic and allowing it to pass from blood directly into the brain. This mercury then bioaccumulates, concentrating especially in larger fish.[40]

Years ago, an indigenous friend told Max a story about a man in her community who insisted on fishing in the local river, despite the fish being poisoned with mercury from a nearby coal power plant. When asked why he kept eating the poisoned fish, the man said, "I am part of this river. If the river is sick, I will be sick."

When dams are removed, rivers come back to life. One of the most dramatic examples is the Elwha River in Washington State. In a series of stages between 2012 and 2014, two dams on the Elwha were removed. Soon, 27 million cubic yards of sediment that had been trapped behind the dams began to flow downstream. Within months, what had been cobbles became sandy beach. Juvenile salmon, sardines, anchovies, sand lance, surf smelt, herring, shellfish, shrimp, and other species who prefer sand began to return.

40 "Poison in the Arctic the human cost of 'clean' energy," *EurekAlert!*, Harvard University—John. A. Paulson School of Engineering and Applied Sciences, September 7, 2015.

Eulachon and Dungeness crab were documented in the estuary for the first time in decades. Even before the second dam was removed, the 2013 chinook salmon run was the biggest in two decades. Three-quarters of the redds (nests where salmon lay eggs) were found upstream of the first dam removal. Within a week of the second dam coming down, chinook salmon and bull trout were seen in the upper river for the first time in 102 years. In 2016, salmon began to spawn above the upper dam site for the first time since dam construction. Lamprey are coming back. Birds are benefiting too; more eagles have been seen than in decades, and American dipper and spotted sandpipers are thriving in the new river channel. River otters are moving up and down the full length of the Elwha. Beavers are moving in, as are elk. Small mammals are thriving in the young forest of the former reservoir-bottom. Life is returning.

A 2017 letter to the Spokane, Washington, newspaper reads: "With record high electric usage as we all try to stay cool in the near or 100 degree temperatures, it got me to thinking about the folks who want to remove or breach the hydroelectric dams on the Snake River. On calm days as the windmills stand idle, please turn off your air conditioners, so you may experience what it would be like without the dams generating abundant electricity."[41]

Here's a counterproposal: On hot days, as dams pump methane into the atmosphere, turn off your air conditioning so you can experience the truth of global warming.

---

[41] "Hydro dams are cool," *Spokesman-Review*, August 19, 2017.

Another example of greenwashing related to dams would be fish hatcheries. Fish hatcheries were first built in the 1800s as a method of boosting fish populations decimated by dams, logging, and over-fishing. In many cases, hatcheries were built as part of "mitigation" for dam construction. The ultimate goal, of course, was to support commercial fishing. In recent decades, the stated mission of hatcheries has been expanded to include conservation and restoration. Visiting schoolchildren are taught that hatcheries play a key role in helping restore fish populations.

Fish hatcheries are aquatic versions of factory farms: crowded concrete pens, artificial food pellets, constant doses of antibiotics. It's hell on earth. They share almost nothing with natural rivers or streams except that all are wet. Predictably, fish from hatcheries are very different from their wild cousins. As one study put it, hatchery stocking leads to "clear signs of negative effects, including lower survival and reproductive fitness of hatchery fish in the wild and reduced genetic variation in the hatchery populations."[42] Another study found that hatchery-raised steelhead trout had more than 700 genetic changes compared to wild fish after only a single generation.[43]

Hatcheries directly harm wild fish populations in many different ways. One is that hatchery fish are often released in huge numbers at once, meaning hatchery fish may eat nearly all the food, leaving the much smaller number of wild fish with less. Next, hatchery fish are much more disease-prone than wild fish, and they can infect wild fish. And hatchery fish can interbreed with wild salmon, reducing the ability of the next generation of wild fish to survive.

---

[42] Hitoshi Araki and Corinne Schmid, "Is hatchery stocking a help or harm? Evidence, limitations and future directions in ecological and genetic surveys," *Aquaculture*, 308 (2010): S2–S11.

[43] Chad Shmukler, "Surprise, surprise: more proof that hatcheries harm wild steelhead," *Hatch Magazine*, February 18, 2016.

The outcome, as one friend put it, is that hatcheries "erase tens of thousands of years of adaptation just to pump out a few more fish in the short term."

A consequence of global warming is more droughts, and during droughts, hydroelectric dams don't function very well.

Let's say you're in charge of a nation's electricity supply, and your economy is dependent on hydropower that's suddenly unavailable because of drought. What do you do?

The answer, of course, is that you turn to coal, oil, or gas. That's exactly what's happened recently in Zimbabwe, where drought caused hydroelectricity to drop from 50 to 34 percent of national supply. Their response was to install a diesel power plant—and to build more dams on other rivers.[44] The equivalent happened in California in 2015, when a major drought forced the state to buy $1.4 billion of electricity generated from natural gas to make up the hydropower deficit.[45]

Dams are no "green" solution to any of the problems that the world faces.

---

[44] Jeffrey Gogo, "Zim turns to fossil energy, as drought bites," *The Herald* (Zimbabwe), January 4, 2016.
[45] James Wilt, "What's the future of hydroelectric power in Canada?" *DeSmog Canada*, July 5, 2017.

Chapter 12

OTHER LIES

For a successful technology, reality must take precedence over
public relations, for Nature cannot be fooled.

—RICHARD P. FEYNMAN[1]

We're only going to debunk a few more forms of bright green technology. It would be a waste of everyone's time to debunk every single bright green lie that comes down the turnpike (a turnpike made of photovoltaic cells that charge your electric car as you drive over them)! And besides, new bright green lies emerge every day. Our hope is that by this point you have the tools to debunk them on your own.

It doesn't, for example, take much searching to learn about geothermal energy harvesting taking place inside a national park in Kenya, turning wildlands into an industrial zone. More than 90 new geothermal wells were drilled between 2014 and 2017, meaning more roads were punched across the park and more habitat

---

[1] Richard P. Feynman, *"What Do You Care What Other People Think?" Further Adventures of a Curious Character* (New York: W.W. Norton & Company, Inc., 1988), 237.

was destroyed or fragmented. Maasai people have been violently evicted en masse.

The drilling releases mercury, arsenic, and boron into groundwater. And water for drilling wells—about 8 million gallons per month, a number expected to rise sharply—is taken from a local lake which is part of a wetland of international importance.[2]

Equipment used for geothermal power generation—steel pipes, brackets, and turbines; trucks for installation and maintenance; drilling equipment; and so on—are all made of materials produced at the expense of the planet.

Here's another example: Geothermal drilling in Nevada is threatening a newly discovered toad species, the Dixie Valley toad. Its habitat, which measures only about four square miles, would be obliterated by a proposed geothermal power expansion.[3]

Another example: Iceland is volcanically active, and the country has become a center of geothermal-energy-harvesting facility construction. This industrialization is pushed relentlessly by bright greens, corporate green organizations and foundations, mining interests, climate activists, and pretty much everyone else who cares more about industry than life on the planet.

This construction has been opposed by local environmentalists, who call it "geothermal ecocide." The group Saving Iceland writes that "the exploitation of the Reykjanes peninsula's geothermal areas spells the end of this magnificent nature of the peninsula as we know it. Test drilling and boreholes, endless roads and power lines, power plants and other infrastructure; all this would turn the Reykjanes peninsula—this unique land of natural volcanic wonders ... into a large industrial zone. But these are only the

---

[2] Robert C. Thornett, "Kenya's energy quandary," *Earth Island Journal*, Summer 2017.
[3] Maya L. Kapoor, "Recently discovered toad species already face threats," *High Country News*, July 26, 2017.

very visible impacts of the planned large-scale exploitation. Other environmental catastrophes are in fact inevitable with large-scale geothermal industry, becoming increasingly visible to the public as the green reputation of geothermal energy slowly decreases."[4]

Iceland is the site of three aluminum smelters, which in 2010 used 73 percent of all electricity generated in Iceland. Their power is supplied by geothermal-energy-harvesting facilities as well as a highly controversial hydroelectric dam that was opposed by environmental and community groups in the courts, via protest, and with direct action.[5] These smelters claim to be the "greenest" smelters in the world. But self-identification does not equal reality. The smelters are major polluters, and have been linked to birth defects, cancer, and bone deformations in nearby communities.

Geothermal facilities are also directly linked to pollution in Iceland. Between 1999 and 2012, levels of sulfur dioxide rose 71 percent in the Reykjavík area due mainly to geothermal plants. This is causing acid rain and respiratory conditions, and worsening heart problems. Elevated levels of hydrogen sulfide from geothermal-energy-harvesting facilities have also been linked to higher death rates. Geothermal waste fluid, which contains "high concentrations of heavy metals and other toxic elements including radon, arsenic, mercury, ammonia, and boron," has been released into groundwater.[6] Iceland is currently planning or building at least 21 major geothermal-energy-harvesting facilities, some of them in the highlands, the largest wilderness in Europe. Most of the energy they harvest will be exported via submarine cable to the U.K.[7]

---

4 "The geothermal ecocide of Reykjanes peninsula," Saving Iceland, May 11, 2012.
5 Michael Chapman, "Iceland's troubled environment," Saving Iceland, August 7, 2017.
6 "The geothermal ecocide of Reykjanes peninsula," Saving Iceland, May 11, 2012.
7 Helga Katrín Tryggvadóttir, "Does living next to a geothermal power plant increase your risk of dying?" Saving Iceland, July 28, 2015.

The technology for drilling geothermal wells was developed primarily by the oil and gas industry. Geothermal brine injection shares many techniques and problems with fracking. In fact, a relatively new technology called "enhanced geothermal systems" (EGS) borrows fracking technology directly, using the same method of injecting high-pressure slurries to fracture subterranean rock formations. The only difference is that fracking releases gas, while EGS releases superheated water and steam. Like fracking for gas, geothermal fracking poisons groundwater and causes earthquakes. And like fracking for gas, geothermal fracking typically uses a wide range of toxic chemicals. At one site in Oregon, these include naphthalene, safranin, rhodamine, lithium, cesium, rubidium, fluorescein, plastics, and any number of trade-secret compounds.[8] This technology is already used in Nevada, Oregon, Australia, Europe, and elsewhere.[9]

A new technology claims to capture 100 percent of the carbon emissions from burning natural gas. This is celebrated with headlines like, "This Power Plant Has Cracked Carbon Capture."[10] Common sense leads us to wonder: But where are they putting the carbon? In this case, they turn it into "plastics, chemicals and building materials."[11]

So, should we extract fossil fuel, burn it, capture the CO_2, and

---

[8] Cassandra Profita, "Geothermal features vs. hydraulic fracturing. What's the difference?" *OPB*, January 24, 2012.

[9] "Why geothermal energy is the new fracking," *The Economist/Business Insider*, August 15, 2014.

[10] Alan Jeffries, "This power plant has cracked carbon capture," *Bloomberg*, July 3, 2018.

[11] Ibid.

use it for a brief blip of geologic time? Of course not, because plastics, chemicals, and building materials will eventually degrade, releasing their carbon into our tattered atmosphere.

Of course, way more carbon would be captured than would ever be turned into plastics. What will the company do with this? They want to sell it for EOR—enhanced oil recovery. EOR is a common practice in which fluid is injected into the ground to force oil and gas upwards. Water accounts for 50 percent of the liquid used, but CO_2 is already injected for 5 percent of U.S. crude oil extraction.

It's morally exhausting to have to explain everything that's wrong with EOR. First is the oil, which should stay in the ground. Second is the practice of EOR, which is a terrible threat to groundwater, i.e., to life. Third, EOR can result in blowouts, where contaminated fluids and gases erupt to the surface "harming air, land, wildlife and water."[12] One report notes that "the resulting violence of the blowouts is astounding."[13] The speed of escaping flow can reach sonic velocity. A blowout in Tinsley Field, MI, lasted for 37 days, hurting workers and first responders and asphyxiating nonhumans. When it was finally over, 27,000 tons of contaminated soil and 32,000 barrels of toxic fluid had to be removed.

Removed to where? That's always the question. The earth is a bounded sphere. Where can the "contaminated" and the "toxic" go that isn't here?

This wasn't even an active well. It had been capped decades before. One of the problems with injecting CO_2 is that it reacts with water and becomes carbonic acid. The acid can then cause elements like barium, chromium, and strontium to be released into the water table. It also corrodes equipment like the pipe that failed in Tinsley Field. Blowouts are now increasing, as capped wells

---

[12] "Enhanced oil recovery: a threat to drinking water," Clean Water Action, 2018.
[13] Les Skinner, "CO_2 blowouts: an emerging problem," *Mississippi Coal*, January 2003.

are reaching an age where corrosion and pressure have done the inevitable.

Pumping oil and gas out of the earth destroys the planet. Burning that oil and gas destroys the atmosphere, a protective blanket 3.8 billion years in the making. No shiny, new machine can change the nature of this activity.

This technology is pointless. Our original question—where are they going to put the carbon? —doesn't have an answer. The sheer scale of fossil fuel consumption "far exceeds the ability of EOR to soak up carbon dioxide."[14]

As long as the earth has been a planet, it has held water. Water and rock were formed in concert some 4.6 billion years ago. The moon is almost as old, at 4.51 billion years. For all of that time, the moon has reached for water and the water has reached back. Some of us abandoned the oceans and learned to live on land, but we took the oceans with us when we left. We are a set of electrical impulses inside a watery environment, and our fluids still match the salinity of our original home. Blood has been called our "private ocean," as the liquid—the plasma—has salt and ions in proportions "remarkably similar" to the oceans.[15]

An estuary is where the river becomes the sea, where the force of current meets the pull of tide. Estuaries are some of the most fertile habitat on the planet. Their fecundity is born from the constant flow of nutrients carried in by the tides. Phototrophs—plants and algae—convert the sun's energy into the organic compounds that form their bodies. This has been named "primary production,"

---

[14] David Roberts, "That natural gas power plant with no carbon emissions or air pollution? It works," *Vox*, June 1, 2018.
[15] Natalie Angier, "The Wonders of Blood," *New York Times*, October 20, 2008.

and the rest of us depend on it because we can't do it. The constant transmutation of carbon into carbohydrate is the litany of life, and we should indeed worship with reverence and rejoice with trembling: it is the phototrophs from whom all blessings flow. And the phototrophs in estuaries have far and away the highest rate of primary production—higher than grasslands, higher than forests—because of the tides.[16]

The tides, with their 4 billion years and all the life they cradle, are now in danger, because the hungry ghosts of humanity have declared the tides theirs for the taking.

The principal technology to turn tides into electricity is called a barrage. It's a dam built across an estuary—words that should strike terror in every heart. The flow of water is the life of an estuary. It brings oxygen, nutrients, and creatures in, and takes wastes (which are someone's food), silt, and more creatures out.

Harvesting energy from the tides changes and weakens that ancient exchange. For those who are numb to the horror, start with "oxygen." All animals die without it. In an estuary, oxygen arrives every 12 hours on the tides. Without the full, rhythmic complement of oxygen, creatures both great and small will suffocate. Maybe not all of them, all at once, but their numbers would be reduced, and that link in the food chain—between the lush primary production of the plants and the microorganisms and invertebrates who eat them—would start to crumble. Without them, the next link is strained, and the next, until eventually species break. Even in oceans, humans can create deserts.

There are over 80 species of mud shrimp alone who live in estuaries, thousands of bird species, and more than 200 species of fish. The tiny miracle of copepods, so thin they are transparent. The pool-dwelling blenny, a fish who can change color like a chameleon.

---

[16] "Estuaries," Canadian Wildlife Federation, 2019.

The female blenny—the mother—protectively lays her eggs in crevices and under stones. The father stands guard until they hatch.

Or the limpets with their eldritch shells, who can find their way home to the exact spot of rock that is theirs. On hard rock, they grind down the edge of their shells to fit that precise location. On soft rock, they know when the tide is going out, somehow, and will return before their home is emersed, and neither "displacement experiments" nor "forced detours" will stop them.[17] How much like us do animals have to be before we give them standing or care? Or love? How can we not love a creature who loves its home so much?

Barrages increase silt deposits, which kill the plants and all their primary production with them. Without plants, there is nothing to eat. The silt also kills the snails, clams, crabs, starfish, and barnacles that are simply smothered. On the other side of the barrage, there is no silt, and dunes erode, changing the entire outline of the coast. Fish migration and spawning is disrupted. The water is too shallow, too hot, too muddy: without babies, there will be no more fish. Over 11,000 amphipods were counted in one square meter of mud in the Bay of Fundy, when a million sandpipers need food for their 2,500-mile flight to South America.[18] Put in enough barrages and the sandpipers will starve into extinction. With them will go the snow goose, the brant, the northern gannet.

Sea mammals, as well, need estuaries. Harbor seals give birth and raise their young on estuary land. Whales use the calm waters of estuaries for their nurseries. The list goes on. And if we have to explain that animals need oxygen and food, that their lives matter, and that this planet is the only home that we have, then it's a list of the damned.

---

[17] Anthony Cook et al., "A study of the homing habit of the limpet," *Animal Behaviour* 17, no. 2 (May 1969), 330–339.

[18] "Estuaries," Canadian Wildlife Federation.

The other form of tidal power is called tidal stream generation. Picture a wind turbine in the ocean: as the tide moves in and then out, the blades spin. It's those blades that are the problem. Porpoises, whales, seals, fish, and birds are all sliced apart by "blade kill." Biologist Mike Dadswell, who has been studying the issue for decades in the Bay of Fundy, states the obvious: "It's literally impossible to turn a blade in the water and not kill, maim, or harm some fish."[19] For any creature 10 feet or longer, strike is virtually 100 percent.

Blade strike is only one cause of death. Like wind turbines, tidal turbines also kill by the pressure changes—essentially small explosions—created by the spinning blades. The force ruptures animals. Some burst instantly while others hemorrhage slowly: either way, they die. Turbines also kill fish by shear generated when two velocities of current intersect. Shear "can literally tear their head off," explains Dadswell.[20] Animals are also deafened by the sound of pile driving as these devices are built.

Nova Scotia's "first tidal turbine is catastrophic," says fisherman-turned-activist Darren Porter.[21] A unique genetic strain of striped bass "has been wiped out." That last sentence is unspeakable, yet here we are. If 200 to 300 turbines go in as planned, the results will be "devastating." A brief listing of who is at risk: 360 bird species depend on the Bay of Fundy and 40 species of mammals, including 12 species of whales. The bay is the main breeding ground for the harbor porpoise. How will they have babies if they

---

[19] "Bay of Fundy turbines will produce 'Red Energy' not 'Green Energy'—Dadswell," *Fundy Tides*, November 2, 2009.
[20] Jerry Lockett, "Tidal Power ... Is It Really Green?" YouTube video clip.
[21] Ibid.

are ground up in turbines? The white shark, the blue whale, and the Inner Bay of Fundy salmon are already endangered. There are still northern right whales mating in the Bay, and there are only 350 of them left in all the world. How will they get past the turbines? How will they hear if their eardrums have ruptured? How will they call each other, lover to lover, mother to child? Why are we doing this to the world?

To save it, argue some who once called themselves environmentalists. Greenpeace claims that tidal power should "play a key role in supplying the world with clean, reliable, and completely renewable energy."[22] The Sierra Club says the same.[23] The World Wildlife Fund Scotland says, "Marine renewables—including tidal—will have a critical role to play" in reducing climate emissions.[24] WWF's *Energy Report* offers this tepid critique, "Tidal power installations could affect the local marine environment.... It is critical that appropriate sites are selected and technologies are developed that minimize any negative impacts."[25] How many more negative impacts are a species reduced to 350 members supposed to absorb?

"Tidal energy will not be 'Green Energy' but rather 'Red Energy' from the blood of its victims," writes marine biologist Mike Dadswell.[26] That list of the damned will go on, as will the destruction.[27] That includes the destruction of the humans who love this place. To the Mi'Kmaq, the Bay of Fundy is sacred. They are fighting

---

[22] "Wave and tidal power," Greenpeace U.K, 2019.

[23] "Maryland beyond coal," Sierra Club.

[24] Tyler Hill, "Tide is turning for a new source of green energy," *TakePart*, September 1, 2016.

[25] Steven Singer, ed., "The Energy Report: 100% renewable energy by 2050," World Wildlife Fund.

[26] "Bay of Fundy turbines will produce 'Red Energy' not 'Green Energy'—Dadswell," *Fundy Tides*, November 2, 2009.

[27] Art Mackay, "81 species of concern in the Bay of Fundy region, Maine and New Brunswick, 2010," *Scribd*.

the turbines in defense of the water and the life of the bay. Dorene Bernard, a Mi'Kmaq water protector, called the political process "broken."[28] Yes, the broken process of a broken people intent on breaking the world for reasons we will never understand.

Remember what is at issue and what is at stake. The desperate scramble for technological solutions may leave you confused. We have every reason to be confused when these solutions come shrouded in physics, chemistry, and math most of us find impenetrable, and boosted by organizations and political leaders we tend to trust. So, remember a few very clear things. Industrial civilization cannot be sustainable, based as it is on drawdown and overshoot. All civilizations collapse and this one will end no differently. More, industrial civilization requires industrial levels of energy, and fossil fuel is functionally irreplaceable. Anyone who tells you otherwise is lying. They may really believe the lie, but it is nevertheless a lie.

Which brings us to biofuels. A decade ago, researchers made grandiose and giddy promises. In an article with the title containing the words "biofuel obituary," Robert Rapier writes, "Technologies that were abandoned decades ago because the economics weren't viable were revived and received government funding to once again prove that the economics aren't viable."[29] They were going to turn straw, wood chips, and sugar beets into fuel for a dollar a gallon. They were going to produce 10,000 gallons of oil from an acre of algae. They were going to fuel the Navy with their Rumpelstiltskin skills. The only thing that came to pass was a colossal waste of

---

[28] Trina Roache, "Mi'kmaq, local fishers unite to fight Bay of Fundy energy project," *APTN News,* January 20, 2017.
[29] Robert Rapier, "An algal biofuel obituary," *Forbes,* October 22, 2018.

taxpayer money. "Many companies," writes Rapier, "made claims that weren't remotely credible"—a sentence that's true for every last bright green lie.

As confusing as the math may be, there are some simple equations before us. Wind power equals no Scottish wildcats and millions of dead songbirds. Solar means suffocated desert tortoises, chemical burns in people's throats, and the last sliver of prairie hauled away as sand. It doesn't get simpler. If you have one blanket of air, one cradle of soil, one place called home, and you destroy it: one minus one.

New bright green lies are told every day and we could keep debunking them until the end of the world—*literally* until the end of the world—and so long as there exist those who care more about their own comforts and elegancies than life on the planet, more lies would pop up to replace them.

For example, we wrote earlier about LEDs. But we didn't talk about how "the antique-style lamps that are fast becoming a design necessity for retro bars, hip restaurants and chic homes from New York to London are helping to save the earth—and keep people buying." These new LEDs—well, they're not actually new LEDs, but rather LEDs rearranged "onto a strip inside the bulb instead of in a clump"—are going to "save the earth" because "shifting fashions in lighting could help drive sales of LED bulbs," which means "the industry has found a way to make people pay more for lighting because it's cool," and "not because they need it."[30]

That will "save the earth" about as much as will huge banks of wind turbines.

---

[30] Jess Shankleman, "How Many Hipsters Does It Take to Change the Lightbulb?" *Bloomberg*, January 8, 2018.

Speaking of which, how 'bout them offshore wind-energy-harvesting facilities covering hundreds of thousands of deepwater ocean acres? The great thing about these facilities is that "advances in construction are allowing wind farms to be built in deeper water farther offshore, significantly lessening the public's concern about seeing turbines close to the coast."[31] Isn't it wonderful that the people using this electricity don't have to see the turbines, just like they don't have to see the mines required to make the turbines, and they don't have to see the seabirds killed by the turbines, and they don't have to see any of the destruction of the natural world caused by this technology that is saving the natural world?

Or how about saving the planet through building a 2,300-square-mile artificial island in the North Sea—yes, you read that correctly, 2,300 square miles[32]—to be used for a massive wind-energy-harvesting facility? That will surely save the planet.

The North Sea never did it for us anyway.

Or how about dams on the bottoms of oceans? Having already made great strides toward killing the oceans, let's mess up the sea bottom even more than we already have, by "building underwater walls at the mouth of the world's most unstable glaciers—huge piles of sand and stone, stretching for miles across the seafloor—[which] would change how those glaciers respond to the warming ocean and atmosphere."[33]

Another proposal is to harvest the energy from evaporating water. How it works: Bacterial spores are stuck to tape. They curl

[31] Roger Drouin, "After an Uncertain Start, U.S. Offshore Wind Is Powering Up," *Yale Environment 360*, January 11, 2018.

[32] Akshat Rathi, "The Dutch plan to build an artificial island to support the world's largest wind farm," *Quartz*, January 2, 2018.

[33] Robinson Meyer, "A Radical New Scheme to Prevent Catastrophic Sea-Level Rise: A Princeton glaciologist says a set of mega-engineering projects may be able to stabilize the world's most dangerous glaciers," *The Atlantic*, January 11, 2018.

as water evaporates, forcing the tape to contract. Tape and bacteria are housed in a floating structure with shutters that close as the tape contracts. This traps the water vapor, which condenses back to a liquid and then the process repeats. The force of the curling tape can be used to generate electricity. You might think that's a cute science project for a seventh grader, but that would be a gross misapprehension of the dreams of the Sociopocene: the Age of the Sociopath. They want to supply 70 percent of U.S. electricity by covering the surface of every lake bigger than .1 square kilometer with these contraptions.

That would, of course, be the death of every covered lake, as well as many rivers and probably the oceans. Phytoplankton will die without sunlight, followed, as phytoplankton are the beginning of the food chain, by everyone who calls a body of water home. All the plants in the littoral zone will die as well, so populations of species who depend on them for food and habitat will collapse. Would it make any difference to write a requiem of their thousand names? From the tiny crustaceans in the benthic zone to the soaring grace of the Trumpeter swans, every water creature will die.

Phytoplankton sequester carbon dioxide "on a scale equivalent to forests."[34] How is starving them to death in vast numbers a plan to stop climate change?

Finally, the researchers claim the U.S. would "save 95 trillion liters of water each year that is currently lost to evaporation."[35] Lost to evaporation? That's called "the water cycle." That's how rain happens. Remember rain, the thing that makes land life possible?

This is the mechanistic mind laid bare. A machine is the sum of

---

[34] Rebecca Lindsey and Michon Scott, "What are phytoplankton?" *NASA Earth Observatory*, July 13, 2010.

[35] Josh Lowe, "New energy source: scientists discover technology that could power 70 percent of U.S.," *Newsweek*, September 27, 2017.

its parts and no more. It can be dissembled and reassembled with no loss to the whole. A living creature cannot be so dissembled without the loss of everything. Likewise, every species is a part of the whole called *life*, and its dissembling is happening in earnest.

If lakes were parts of a machine, you could remove them, rewire the mechanism to work without them, or discard them for parts. But the world is not a machine, and neither lakes, their creatures, nor the water cycle can be removed without all of us—every last one—dying.

We can't go through and debunk every crackbrain plan put forward by members of an insane culture who will do anything to maintain this way of living. But we do need to describe one more, because this crackpot plan is where this culture has been heading for a long time, and this particular atrocity will kill the earth.

Geoengineering, sometimes called climate engineering, is the deliberate modification of weather/climate patterns by human intervention. The most popular geoengineering proposals involve using high-altitude airplanes to inject fine particles called aerosols into the upper atmosphere. These particles would, in theory, reflect some incoming solar radiation, thus cooling the planet.

It sounds like the plot of a comic book villain, but it's being seriously considered by national governments and scientific bodies.

It's being considered partly in response to the planet being on track for greater than 2°C rise in temperature, and continued expansions of the coal, oil, and gas industries. But mostly it's being considered because of this culture's absolute refusal to question the wisdom of open-air experiments on the living planet, and more to the point, its slavish devotion to a way of life that's killing the earth, our only home. It's the logical endpoint of a culture that values machines over life.

Many things can—and if history is our guide, will—go wrong with geoengineering. For example, aerosols only mask global warming; they don't address its causes. If, as we can expect, greenhouse gases continue to accumulate, aerosols would have to be released constantly and at ever greater concentrations to mitigate the strengthening greenhouse effect. This would be done via thousands of airplanes operating at high altitudes, which of course contributes more to global warming. As soon as the release of aerosols stops for any reason, warming will resume, very quickly. If greenhouse gas levels continue to rise, then governments will be left with essentially no choice but to intensify the geoengineering.

The second problem with aerosol geoengineering is that it changes sunlight intensity reaching the earth, which would have global repercussions. Plants, animals, bacteria, humans, and many other beings and processes are regulated and dependent on the sun. Hell, nearly all life on the planet is dependent on the sun. Reducing light would, at the very least, affect global plant growth, food production, quality of sleep, vitamin D and human and non-human health, and—ironically—solar-energy harvesting. Aerosols could also harm the ozone layer, potentially having a major impact on cancer rates.

The sun also drives global weather patterns, so blocking sunlight would alter weather—especially water cycles—potentially causing unusual patterns of flooding, drought, storms, and so on. Geoengineering via aerosols would affect the tropics much more than the poles—which are warming faster, and therefore are where the cooling effect is more needed. To chill the poles, "overcooling" would be necessary near the equator.

Some scientists believe aerosol injection could even end

seasonal monsoons across Africa and Eurasia. This would devastate the human and nonhuman communities over about half the planet's surface.

Hey, here's an idea: Why don't we try it and see what happens?

One of our heroes is the Indian habitat restorationist Suprabha Seshan, who works with a team at the Gurukula Botanical Sanctuary in the Western Ghat mountains in Kerala, India, rescuing individual plants (especially endangered species) from areas that are going to be destroyed, and cultivating them in hopes of reestablishing self-sustaining communities of these plants. Their sanctuary contains more than 2,000 species. Seshan describes the work as "a search-and-rescue mission, and we refer to these plants as refugees, similar to human refugees suffering the depredations of war, displacement, climate change, and general toxification of the environment."

These plants, and more broadly the human and nonhumans of India and much of the rest of Asia, are dependent on the monsoon. Seshan writes, "As gardeners and habitat-restorers we, of course, are dependent wholly on the timing and duration of the monsoon, on its intensity and quality—because our wards, namely the land and the plant species we conserve, are.... Most Indians believe that the monsoon is unassailable: a wind system 18 million years old, which has breathed life into the subcontinent since the rise of the Himalaya, whose formidable heights block it from traveling to Central Asia, condensing it instead into long hard rain. Its intensity varies from year to year, but we believe it will blow. But ever since I have been here, about 24 years now, I have heard people talking about how the monsoon has gone awry, that it is no longer what it used to be. We also know this from scientific data, but crucially for us, we know this from the behavior of the plants and animals in our sanctuary.... The monsoon is changing in fundamental ways.... But what if the monsoon fails?"[36]

Spraying aerosols from planes is only one of the lunatic ideas put forward under the name of geoengineering. Also floated are ideas like putting mirrors in space to deflect sunlight, or somehow changing the earth's orbit. Or dumping iron into the oceans to promote blooms of phytoplankton.

What could go wrong?

Scientists speaking in favor of geoengineering (and the governments and corporations they work for) are being forced to confront the reality that global warming could destroy civilization. Their turn towards geoengineering is predictable. Rex Tillerson, formerly the head of ExxonMobil, more recently President Trump's first Secretary of State, has said of global warming: "It's an engineering problem, and it has engineering solutions."[37] We can all get outraged at that, but how is this any different from those who promote solar, wind, and electric cars? If they're unwilling or unable to stop burning fossil fuels—and more broadly unwilling or unable to stop killing the planet—then their only option for (short-term) survival is to enslave the entire planet's climate. They've already taken flocks of pigeons that went on for three days and herds of bison that went on for four. They've emptied the rivers of water and the oceans of fish. They've taken the old-growth forests and the grasslands, too. Why not take the climate as well?

---

36 Suprabha Seshan, "Once, the Monsoon," *Deep Green Resistance News Service*, June 25, 2017.

37 Chris Mooney, "Rex Tillerson's view of climate change: It's just an 'engineering problem,'" *Washington Post*, December 14, 2016.

Here's a set of guiding questions or principles by which any bright green technology should be evaluated.

First, there is the technological thing itself, whether it's a photovoltaic cell, a windmill, a battery. What is it? What is it made of? Where do these materials come from, and how are they extracted from the earth? What harms do these extractions cause? Who suffers these harms? What infrastructures are required to support these extractions? What harms are caused by these infrastructures? Who suffers these harms?

Someone simply saying materials were "recycled" does not insulate the technology from being subject to these questions, no more than if someone said the materials came from Santa Claus. By what processes and at what costs were the metals removed from the electronics, the impurities removed from the metals?

Who lives in the places from which you want to extract the materials? Who calls those places home? What will happen to those places, those beings?

How are these materials transported and converted into their final products? How is iron ore transported, smelted? How is steel fabricated, transported, melted, turned into pieces to be used in your bright green windmill? How is the windmill itself assembled and transported?

What are the onsite effects of this bright green technology? How many birds will be killed by the solar- or wind-energy-harvesting facility? How many tortoises, how many bats?

For what will this bright green technology be used? If it's used to harvest energy, to what purpose? Does this use of the bright green technology help the real world? The physical world? The planet that is the source of all life? Or does it help industry? Those are not the same.

And when the piece of technology wears out, what happens to

the materials? How toxic are they? What happens to the site? Will it be habitat for sage grouse or hoary bats or whomever used to live there? Or will it damage their genes and their generative organs for thousands of years?

Is the point of the technology to help the earth, or is it to maintain this way of living at the expense of the earth?

All of which brings us to Aldo Leopold's reverent statement: "A thing is right when it tends to preserve the integrity, stability and beauty of the biotic community. It is wrong when it tends otherwise."

This is the measure by which we should judge bright green—and all—technologies. It's the measure by which we should judge our actions, and our lives.

Chapter 13

MORE SOLUTIONS THAT WON'T WORK

Eager to work with business, many environmentalists are moving from confrontation to the best kind of collaboration.

—DAVID KIRKPATRICK, *CNN MONEY*, FEBRUARY 1990[1]

Do I have to convince you of a utopia before you will take action against a tyranny? Have our spirits decayed to the point where the only actions we will take are in the pursuit of self-interest and self-preservation? What happened to the time when we willingly committed acts of self-sacrifice for generations we haven't even met yet? Does this not speak of the need to transform our way of being and thinking?

—MI'KMAQ WARRIOR SAKEJ WARD, COMMUNITY OF ESGENOOPETITJ (BURNT CHURCH FIRST NATION, NEW BRUNSWICK, CANADA[2]

---

[1] David Kirkpatrick, "Environmentalism: The New Crusade," *Fortune*, February 12, 1990.
[2] Sakej Ward, Facebook posting, May 5, 2015.

We've come a long way from the land ethic envisioned by Aldo Leopold. Instead of a movement to save the planet,[3] we have a movement to continue its destruction.

Around the world frontline activists are fighting not only big corporations but also the climate movement as wild beings and wild places now need protection from green energy projects.

A *Vox* headline reads, "Reckoning with climate change will demand ugly tradeoffs from environmentalists—and everyone else."[4] But as ever, the "tradeoffs" are demanded of wild nature. Industrialism's demands are nonnegotiable, and always rising. And the world must comply.

It shouldn't surprise us that the values of the environmental movement have degraded so much in the last 30 years. Now more than ever, people are immersed in technology instead of the real world. As one report states, "The average young American now spends practically every minute—except for time in school—using a smartphone, computer, television or electronic device."[5] A recent poll in Britain found that the average 18-to-25-year-old rated an internet connection as more important than daylight.[6]

We've come a long way from the naturalists we were born to be; from inhabiting a living world flush with kin to serving a society in thrall to machines.

It's no wonder, then, that so many people believe in nonsensical

---

[3] There are, of course, exceptions. We're thinking primarily of organizations like Patagonia and Wild Earth Guardians, and smaller organizations like Buffalo Field Campaign and Community Environmental Legal Defense Fund.

[4] David Roberts, "Reckoning with climate change will demand ugly tradeoffs from environmentalists—and everyone else," *Vox*, January 28, 2018.

[5] Timothy Egan, "Nature-deficit disorder," *New York Times*, March 29, 2012.

[6] Lucy Sheriff, "Young people would rather have an internet connection than daylight," *Huffington Post U.K.*, March 17, 2016.

technological solutions. Technology does it for them and the real world doesn't.

And so, the absurd becomes normal. We hear that green technology will stop global warming. We hear that cutting down forests and burning them is good for the planet. We hear that damming rivers is good for the planet. We hear that destroying the desert to put in solar panels is good for the planet. We hear that industrial recycling will save the world. We hear that commodifying nature is somehow significantly different than business as usual. We hear that we can invest our way to sustainable capitalism. We hear that capitalism can be sustainable.

A global growth rate of 3 percent, which is considered the minimum for capitalism to function, means the world economy doubles every 24 years. This is, of course, madness. If we can't even name capitalism as a problem, how are we to have any chance of saving the planet?

There's no doubt that global warming is apocalyptic. I (Max) have stood on thawing permafrost above the Arctic Circle and seen entire forests collapsing as soils lose integrity under their roots. This culture is *changing the composition of the planet's climate*. But this is not the only crisis the world is facing, and to pretend otherwise ignores the true roots of the problem.

The Sierra Club has a campaign called "Ready for 100." The campaign's goal is to "convince 50 college campuses, a dozen key cities and half a dozen key states to go 100 percent renewable.'" The executive director of the Sierra Club, Michael Brune, explains, "There are a few reasons why Ready for 100 is working—why it's such a powerful idea. People have agency, for one. People who are outraged, alarmed, depressed, filled with despair about climate change—they want to make a difference in ways they can see, so they're turning to their backyards. Turning to their city, their state, their university. And, it's exciting—it's a way to address this not just through dread, but with something that sparks your imagination."[7]

There are a lot of problems with that statement. First, is Ready for 100 really "working," like Brune says? That depends on the unspoken part of that statement: working to achieve what? He may mean that the campaign is working to mobilize a larger mainstream climate movement. He may mean that Ready for 100 is working in the sense that more "renewable" infrastructure is being built, in great measure because more subsidies are being given to the industry.

If he means Ready for 100 is working to reduce the burning of coal, oil, and gas—which is, in fact, what he means—he's dead wrong, as "fossil fuels continue to absolutely dominate global energy consumption."[8]

There's more about Brune's quote that's bothersome. He's explicitly turning people's "outrage, alarm, depression, and despair" into means that serve the ends of capital; through causing people to use these very real feelings to lobby for specific sectors of the industrial economy.

If a plan won't work, it doesn't matter if people have "agency." The ongoing destruction of the planet, and the continued dominance of coal, oil, and gas, seems to be less important than diverting people's rage—which, if left unchecked, might actually explode into something that would stop capitalism and industrialism from murdering the planet—into corporate-friendly ends.

---

[7] Bill McKibben, "Keep it 100," *In These Times*, August 22, 2017.

[8] Barry Saxifrage, "These 'missing charts' may change the way you think about fossil fuel addiction," *National Observer*, July 13, 2017.

Led by 350.org, the Fossil Free campaign aims to remove financial support for the coal, oil, and gas industries by pressuring institutions such as churches, cities, and universities to divest. It's modeled on the three-pronged boycott, divestment, and sanctions (BDS) resistance to South African apartheid (a model used today against Israel). The Fossil Free campaign has thus far pressured 800 institutions and 58,000 individuals to divest $6 trillion. Some of these are partial divestments, such as withdrawing from tar sands but continuing to fund fracking.[9]

Still, sounds great, right? Anyone fighting to stop coal, oil, and gas is doing a very good thing.

But given how little time we have, and how badly we're losing the fight for the planet, we have to ask if divestment is an effective strategy.

The answer, unfortunately, is not really. Jay Taber of *Intercontinental Cry* points out that "All this divestment does is make once publicly held shares available on Wall Street, which allows trading houses like Goldman Sachs to further consolidate their control of the industry. BDS, when applied against apartheid states by other states and international institutions, includes cutting off access to finance, as well as penalties for crimes against humanity." He states quite bluntly that divestment acts to "redirect activism away from effective work."[10]

Bill Gates—not usually someone we'd listen to—seems to agree. "If you think divestment alone is a solution," Gates writes, "I worry you're taking whatever desire people have to solve this problem and kind of using up their idealism and energy on something that

---

[9] "Divestment Commitments," Go Fossil Free, 2017.
[10] Jay Taber, "Social capitalists: Wall Street's progressive partners," *Intercontinental Cry*, February 24, 2015.

won't emit less carbon—because only a few people in society are the owners of the equity of coal or oil companies."[11]

If it occurs on a wide enough scale, divestment makes previously held stocks, bonds, and other investment products available for purchase. This glut drops prices, making it easier for less ethical investors to buy. This not only consolidates the industry, but it also makes fossil fuel stocks more profitable for those who snatch them up. As journalist Christian Parenti writes, "So how will dumping Exxon stock hurt its income, that is, its bottom line? It might, in fact, improve the company's price to earnings ratio thus making the stock more attractive to immoral buyers. Or it could allow the firm to more easily buy back stock (which it has been doing at a massive scale for the last five years) and thus retain more of its earnings for use to develop more oil fields."[12]

It's unlikely any divestment campaigner believes divestment alone will stop global warming. The Fossil Free website recognizes this, writing: "The campaign began in an effort to stigmatize the Fossil Fuel industry—the financial impact was secondary to the socio-political impact." But as the amount of money being divested continues to grow, *reinvestment* is becoming a more central part of the fossil fuel divestment campaign. The website continues: "We have a responsibility and an opportunity to ask ourselves how moving the money itself ... can help us usher forth our vision."

Great! So, they're suggesting these organizations take their money out of oil industry stocks, and use that money to set aside land as wilderness, for wild nature, right?

---

[11] Emma Howard, "Bill Gates calls fossil fuel divestment a 'false solution,'" *The Guardian*, October 14, 2015.

[12] Christian Parenti, "Problems with the math: is 350's carbon divestment campaign complete?" *Huffington Post*, November 29, 2012.

Well, no. They want the money to be used to fund "renewable energy." And they've slipped a premise past us: the idea that divestment and reinvestment can work to create a better world. It's an extraordinary claim, and not supported by evidence. As Anne Petermann of the Global Justice Ecology Project writes, "Can the very markets that have led us to the brink of the abyss now provide our parachute? ... Under this system, those with the money have all the power. Then why are we trying to reform this system? Why are we not transforming it?"[13]

Activist Keith Brunner writes, "Yes, the fossil fuel corporations are the big bad wolf, but just as problematic is the system of investment and returns which necessitates a growth economy (it's called capitalism)." His conclusion: "We aren't going to invest our way to a livable planet."[14]

Is it better to fight for "achievable, realistic" goals through reform, or address the fundamental issues at their root? Usually, we're in favor of both. If we wait for the great and glorious revolution and don't do any reform work (which we could also call defensive work), by the time the revolution comes, the world will have been consumed by this culture. And if we only do defensive work and don't address the causes of the problems, this culture will consume the world until there's nothing left.

But it's pretty clear that the real goal of the bright greens isn't defending the planet: Everyone from Lester Brown to Kumi Naidoo has been explicit about this. The real goal is to get money

---

[13] Cory Morningstar, "McKibben's divestment tour—brought to you by Wall Street," *Wrong Kind of Green*, May 17, 2013.
[14] Ibid.

into so-called green technology. A recent article notes, "Climate solutions need cold, hard cash ... about a trillion a year."

One of Naomi Klein's biggest contributions to discourse is her articulation of the "shock doctrine," which she defines as "how America's 'free market' policies have come to dominate the world—through the exploitation of disaster-shocked people and countries." In her book *The Shock Doctrine: The Rise of Disaster Capitalism*, Klein explains—brilliantly—how the same principles used to disorient and extract concessions from victims of torture can be leveraged to extract political concessions from entire nations in the wake of major disasters. She gives many examples, including the wave of austerity and privatization in Chile following the Pinochet coup in 1973, the massive expansion of industrialism and silencing of dissidents following the Tiananmen Square massacre in China in 1989, and the dismantling of low-income housing and replacement of public education with for-profit schools in New Orleans in the wake of Hurricane Katrina in 2005.

The shock doctrine also perfectly describes the entire bright green movement: Because of a terrible and very real disaster (in this case, climate change), you need to hand over huge subsidies to a sector of the industrial economy, and you need to let us destroy far more of the natural world, from Baotou to the Mojave Desert to the bottom of the ocean. If you don't give us lots of money and let us destroy far more of the natural world, you will lose the luxuries that are evidently more important to you than life on the planet.

Once you start looking for this trend, it's really clear. There's a 2016 article in *Renewable Energy World* magazine about the Desert Renewable Energy and Conservation Plan. The plan allows major solar energy harvesting facilities to be built in some areas of the California desert, but not other areas. Shannon Eddy, head of the Large-Scale Solar Association, considers protecting parts of the desert "a blow." She says, "The world is on fire—CO_2 levels just breached the 400-ppm threshold. We need to do everything we can right now to reduce emissions by getting renewable projects online."[15]

Everything including destroying the desert. This is reminiscent of a phrase from the Vietnam War era, which originated in 1968 with AP correspondent Peter Arnett: "'It became necessary to destroy the town to save it,' a United States major said today."

We need to return to the real world. This culture functions by converting wild land into commodity production zones. Over the past 20 years, about 10 percent of the world's remaining true wilderness has been lost.[16] According to one study, between now and 2050, solar and wind "development" threaten to destroy as much land as urban sprawl and expansion of oil and gas, coal, and mining *combined.* Solar "development" outranks agricultural expansion and wind (tied for second place) as the single largest "development" threat considered in the study.[17] Yet environmentalists continue to push solar, wind, and other bright green lies as *solutions.* This has become a movement that does not help the earth, but rather helps its destroyers.

---

[15] Susan Kraemer, "Final Plan for California Public Lands Devastating for Renewable Energy," *Renewable Energy World*, October 13, 2016.

[16] James E.M. Watson et al., "Catastrophic Declines in Wilderness Areas Undermine Global Environment Targets," *Current Biology* 26, no. 21 (November 7, 2016): 2929–2934.

[17] James R. Oakleaf et al., "A World at Risk: Aggregating Development Trends to Forecast Global Habitat Conversion," *PLOS One*, October 7, 2015.

We need to return to the real world. We need to return to being people who love the world—all its places and all its creatures—and who will fight to defend it.

Chapter 14

REAL SOLUTIONS

When the oppressors give me two choices,

I always take the third.

—MEIR BERLINER, A POLISH JEW AND CITIZEN OF

ARGENTINA WHO DIED RESISTING HIS NAZI CAPTORS AT

TREBLINKA CONCENTRATION CAMP

As we were working on this book, Derrick received a letter from a reader of some of his other books, who stated: "I live in Corsica. I used to believe 'Mediterranean landscapes' were naturally dry lands of rocks and maquis. Most people here believe that. But it's not true. Giant trees used to cover the land, and the rocks were where they belong: under the soil. The trees were cut to build cities, and the soil is long since washed away. It's the same in Sicily, Sardinia, North Africa, and so on. It was sad to learn these landscapes are the consequence of exploitation."

This reader's sadness over mankind's exploitation and destruction of our planet echoes the feelings of writers and environmentalists from throughout the ages, but perhaps it was the Shawnee warrior Chiksika Matthew (c. 1760-1792) who said it best: "The white man seeks to conquer nature, to bend it to his will and to use it wastefully until it is all gone and then he simply moves on, leaving the waste behind him and looking for new places to take. The whole white race is a monster who is always hungry and what he eats is land."[1]

Industrial civilization is incompatible with life on the planet. That makes the solution to our systematic planetary murder obvious, but let's say it anyway: Stop industrial civilization. Stop our way of life, which is based on extraction. No, that doesn't mean killing all humans. That means changing our lifestyle dramatically. The Tolowa lived just fine in Northern California, just south of the Oregon border, where Derrick and Lierre live now, and they did so without destroying the place. Industrial civilization has been here less than 200 years, and the place is trashed. So, yes, stop civilization.

You could argue that you don't want to give up on the luxuries our way of life brings you, but we would respond that we don't want to give up on life on this planet. Life is more important. Sure, we love our luxuries as much as the next person, but there are far greater things at stake than laptops and hot showers.

It's hard to overestimate the scale of the destruction that's being visited upon the planet. In 2017, a report was published showing that deforestation, agriculture, and other land-use changes have reduced the global biomass of plants by more than 50 percent.[2]

The numbers are equally stark for animals. One paper notes: "Even the largest species of wild terrestrial vertebrates now have aggregate zoomass that is only a small fraction of the global

---

[1] Cited in Allan W. Eckert, *A Sorrow in Our Heart: The Life of Tecumseh* (New York: Bantam Books, 1993), 176.
[2] Karl-Heinz Erb et al., "Unexpectedly large impact of forest management and grazing on global vegetation biomass," *Nature*, December 20, 2017.

anthropomass. Minuscule remnants of once-enormous herds of bison, America's largest surviving mega-herbivore, total only about 40,000 t C (tons of carbon). The latest continent-wide count of African elephants enumerated 470,000 individuals in 2006. With average body mass of 2.6 t, this equals about 0.5 percent of the global anthropomass. And even a liberal estimate of the total zoomass of wild terrestrial mammals at the beginning and the end of the twentieth century yields no more than about 50 Mt of live weight (about 10 Mt C) in 1900 and 25 Mt of live weight (about 5 Mt C) in 2000, a decline of 50 percent. In contrast, during the same time, the global anthropomass rose from roughly 13 to <55 Mt C. This means that the global anthropomass surpassed the wild mammalian terrestrial zoomass sometime during the second half of the nineteenth century, that by 1900 it was at least 30 percent higher, and that by 2000 the zoomass of all wild land mammals was only about a tenth of the global anthropomass."[3]

When you include the biomass of pets and domesticated live-stock, the gap between the numbers of wild land animals and human beings widens even further.

That lost animal biomass—which in reality was not "biomass" at all, but rather living beings—has, like plant biomass, been turned into greenhouse gases and material goods and been consumed by livestock and humans. It's no exaggeration to say that industrial civilization is consuming the planet.

When we talk about ending industrial civilization, one of the most common questions we hear is, "But what's the alternative?" Sometimes, what people are really saying is: "The story of

[3] Vaclav Smil, "Harvesting the Biosphere: The Human Impact," *Population and Development Review* 37, no. 4 (December 2011): 613–636.

alternative energy has allowed me to alleviate my feelings of fear or guilt about the murder of the planet. You've threatened my comfort, so I'm angry. I can't imagine life without widespread, cheap industrial electricity. I demand that you provide me with a solution that leaves industrial civilization in place."

But often people are so shocked by the idea of their lifestyle disappearing completely that they honestly can't imagine what could come next. They care deeply about the planet, but what they want to know is: "Can't we find a solution that leaves our way of life intact?"

Which is, of course, impossible. Large-scale electricity generation for a steadily increasing global population is unsustainable: this is physical reality. As Bill McKibben rightly says, "You can't argue with physics."

"How can we continue to harvest industrial quantities of energy without causing harm?" is the wrong question. The correct question is: "What can we do to help the earth repair the damage caused by this culture?"

Industrial technology will ultimately not be part of that repair. As Jeff Gibbs asks so poignantly in his film, *Planet of the Humans*, "Is it possible for machines built by industrial civilization to save us from industrial civilization?" Remember Chellis Glendinning, who declared: "All technologies are political." Remember Lewis Mumford, who pointed out how authoritarian technics "raised the ceiling of human achievement: the first in mass construction, the second in mass destruction, both on a scale hitherto inconceivable." Remember our guiding questions from Chapter 12 by which any green technology should be evaluated?

If we apply those questions to bright green technology—where its materials came from, how it impacts the Earth, and what happens when it wears out—and answer them honestly: not one bright green technology helps the planet. All of them destroy what's left of the living.

The first real solution, then, is to lay down our denial and face reality full-on. Facing reality requires an avalanche of grief right now: We know what we are asking. But if you love this planet, it has to be done.

The rest of what we should do is straightforward. First, we need to stop the ongoing destruction being caused by so-called green energy projects, by oil and gas extraction, by coal mining and ore mining, by urban sprawl, by industrial agriculture, and by all the other million assaults on this planet that are perpetrated by industrial civilization.

And second, we need to help the land heal.

The good news is that plants are already doing their part. In total, plants absorb about a quarter of the carbon emissions released by burning coal, oil, and gas. Over the last 30 years, and especially between 2002 and 2014, plants on land have begun to absorb more and more carbon dioxide—about 17 percent more. This "greening" has, according to climate scientists, "significantly slowed" the rise of greenhouse gas concentrations in the atmosphere. Plants are using less water than normal to do this, thus becoming both more effective and more efficient in their work of defending a livable climate.[4]

But there are limits to the amount of carbon plants can reabsorb. One study estimated that even if all the carbon that has been

[4] Lei Cheng et al., "Recent increases in terrestrial carbon uptake at little cost to the water cycle," *Nature Communications* 8, Article 110 (July 24, 2017).

emitted by deforestation and "land-use change" could be restored by regrowing forests, this would only reduce global CO_2 levels by 40 to 70 ppm.[5] That wouldn't even take us back to 350 ppm, let alone the 270-ppm preindustrial level.

A 2017 study found that deforestation has twice the previously suspected impact on global warming: Even if greenhouse gas emissions from coal, oil, and gas were completely eliminated, continuing deforestation would be enough to push global warming past 1.5 degrees Celsius above preindustrial levels, which is seen as the "safety limit."[6]

And even if solar, wind, and other green technologies were able to completely replace fossil fuels—an impossible scenario in itself, and one that doesn't curtail emissions—as long as deforestation continues, that's not enough to stop global warming.

Our original goal for this chapter was to do the math on exactly how much emissions reduction you get per dollar by switching from coal, oil, and gas to "renewable" energy, and then compare this to other ways that money could be spent (for example, to protect existing forests from logging). But as we started writing, the question broke down. Consider University of Oregon sociologist and environmental studies scholar Richard York's research, which we've already described, about how solar, wind, and other non-fossil fuels don't really displace that much coal, oil, and gas. As a

---

[5] Kate Dooley, "Misleading Numbers: The case for separating land and fossil-based carbon emissions," *Fern*, January 2014.

[6] Natalie M. Mahowald et al., "Are the impacts of land use on warming underestimated in climate policy?" *Environmental Research Letters* (September 18, 2017).

reminder, his research found that "Non-hydro renewable [energy] sources have a positive coefficient, indicating *the opposite of displacement* [emphasis ours], but this coefficient is not significantly different from 0, indicating that renewables tend to simply be added to the energy mix without displacing fossil fuels."

In other words, the amount of emissions reductions you get per dollar invested in "renewable" energy is essentially zero. In fact, the emissions actually increase, because the production, installation, maintenance, and disposal of these "renewable" energy forms release greenhouse gases; and because the extra power provided by these renewable sources is being used to power more electronics, more data centers, more marijuana grows, and more military installations, which all have their own associated greenhouse gas emissions, from destruction of forests and grasslands to production of cement, plastics, and other materials.

In terms of stopping the destruction of our planet, or at least stopping global warming, all the mainstream solutions are, at best, distractions. They're really responses to the recognition that a) world oil supply is finite; b) industrial energy demand will continue to rise; and c) the demands of the economy are not negotiable; which means d) these mainstream solutions are really about getting subsidies for new forms of industrial energy. None of them help the earth.

Stopping deforestation and restoring logged areas would remove more carbon dioxide from the air each year than is generated by all the cars on the planet.[7] A 2019 study found that, as a headline in *The Independent* put it, "Massive restoration of world's

---

[7] Mike Gaworecki, "Here's a great way to visualize the huge potential of forest conservation and restoration as 'natural climate solutions,'" *Mongabay*, December 6, 2017.

forests would cancel out a decade of CO_2 emissions."[8] Compared to solar, wind, and so on, with their net zero carbon reduction per dollar, any investment in protecting forests actually works.

Not only terrestrial plants are fighting for a livable planet. Per acre, salt marshes, mangroves, and seagrasses absorb and store 10 times more carbon dioxide than do many forests.[9] It is estimated that a 150-acre salt marsh restoration project in the inland Salish Sea, encompassing Seattle and Vancouver, will store between 6,000 and 14,000 tons of carbon dioxide over the next 75 to 100 years. Likewise, the annual global destruction of 2 million acres of coastal wetlands for "development" releases some 550 million tons of carbon dioxide per year.[10] Coastal seaweed has also recently been found to sequester huge amounts of carbon, at least 190 million tons per year.[11] We need to protect such places for their own sake, for the sake of biodiversity, and for their ability to save the climate from what this culture has done to it.

Grasslands are doing their part, too. One study in West Virginia revealed that grasslands store four tons of atmospheric carbon per acre per year.[12] In 1990, when the Soviet Union collapsed, 49 million acres of agricultural land were abandoned. Almost immediately,

---

[8] Josh Gabbatiss, "Massive restoration of world's forests would cancel out a decade of CO_2 emissions, analysis suggests," *The Independent*, February 18, 2019.

[9] "Coastal Blue Carbon," National Oceanic and Atmospheric Administration.

[10] Jeff Tollefson, "Climate scientists unlock secrets of 'blue carbon,'" *Nature*, January 9, 2018.

[11] Dorte Krause-Jensen and Carlos M. Duarte, "Substantial role of macroalgae in marine carbon sequestration," *Nature Geoscience* 9 (2016): 737–742.

[12] Martha Holdridge, "What grass farmers have known all along—research shows grass sequesters carbon," Soil Carbon Coalition, August 6, 2008.

the land began to recover.[13] Forests and grasslands began to return.[14] Over the next 10 years, that land captured 63 million tons of carbon—a globally significant amount.[15]

Again, the most important, and simplest, solution to the destruction of the planet is to stop the destruction of the planet.

Estonia was once home to thousands of peat bogs. In these bogs, layers of sphagnum moss and other plants die and are trapped underwater. Due to the particular chemistry of these bogs, the dead plants don't decay. Instead, layers accumulate over thousands of years. Eventually, these layers are compressed into dense peat, which stores vast amounts of carbon. Left alone for millions of years, many peat bogs become coal deposits. According to some accounts, peat bogs store carbon more efficiently than any other natural community on the planet.[16] When water is drained from peat bogs, however, they begin to decay and release greenhouse gases.

Peat has been burned as a small-scale fuel source for millennia. With industrialization came the inevitable conversion of this sustainable process into an ecological disaster. Russia, Finland, Ireland, Estonia, and the U.K. all burn peat today in large power plants as a significant source of energy (when burned, peat releases more carbon dioxide than coal or natural gas).

[13] Immo Kämpf et al., "Post-Soviet recovery of grassland vegetation on abandoned fields in the forest steppe zone of Western Siberia," *Biodiversity and Conservation* 25, no. 12 (November 2016): 2563–2580.

[14] Tobias Kuemmerle et al., "Post-Soviet farmland abandonment, forest recovery, and carbon sequestration in western Ukraine," *Global Change Biology* 17 (2011): 1335–1349.

[15] Nicolas Vuichard et al., "Carbon sequestration due to the abandonment of agriculture in the former USSR since 1990," *Global Biogeochemical Cycles* 22, GB4018 (2008).

[16] Sandrine Hugron et al., "Tree plantations within the context of ecological restoration of peatlands," Université Laval, Québec, September 2013.

Peat is exploited for other reasons too. Bogs are regularly drained to allow logging and agriculture, and mined peat is used in the potted plant and flower industries.

In Estonia, small-scale peat bog restoration projects have been underway for many years. The process is simple. First, fill in or dam artificial drainage ditches. This begins to restore the water table. Then, transplant a number of species from healthy bogs to the restoration area. Within three years, bogs begin to return to health, sequestering carbon dioxide and providing habitat for rare species.[17] It's not complicated.

We can all do the same. All it takes is choosing a place and starting work. In India, beginning in fall 2017, Gurukula residents formed a neighborhood conservation group to heal the Kallampuzha stream. They removed trash and chemical-saturated agricultural waste from the water, spoke to neighbors to discourage pollution and use of pesticides, got local children involved, and stopped the use of poisons and dynamite for fishing. The results were dramatic. The Kallampuzha's water became clearer. Fish began to recover.

Life *wants* to live.

Another example from India comes from Kerala. For decades, the Kuttemperoor River was used for illegal sand mining, sewage dumping, and worse. As more and more of the watershed became concrete, the river shrunk from 120 feet wide to barely 20. But then a group of 700 locals, mostly women, began cleaning up the river—primarily by physically wading into it, removing trash and plastic, and dredging out toxic silt. One of the participants, P. Viswambhara Panicker, wrote, "Initially many discouraged us

---

[17] Eric Niiler, "Tiny country cuts carbon emissions by planting bogs," *National Geographic*, August 4, 2017.

saying it was a mere waste of money and energy. But we proved them all wrong." Within 70 days of the effort starting, the river had been restored to full flow. Local wells began to fill, and the stench of sewage was gone.[18]

This is how you heal the planet. You begin with one river, then the next, and the next.

But you can't begin if your time and resources go toward false solutions. That's why the first step is to stop believing in bright green fairy tales that technology will save the planet. Instead, put your belief in soils, grasses, forests, seaweeds, and the billions of living beings who every moment are working to regenerate the conditions that support life and beauty on this planet.

That is why we've written this book.

Here are some meaningful goals for establishing a truly green community—although, since the world is at stake, these are not guidelines but rather absolute requirements:

> *1. There is consensus among members of the scientific community that in order to prevent catastrophic climate change beyond what the industrial economy has already set in motion, net carbon emissions must be reduced by 100 percent as soon as possible. Because we wish to continue to live on a habitable planet, we*

---

[18] Ramesh Babu, "How 700 Kerala villagers waded through a dead river, cleansed it and brought it back to life in 70 days," *Hindustan Times*, May 7, 2017.

must undertake a carbon reduction of 20 percent of current emissions per year over the next five years.

2. Dwayne Andreas, former CEO of Archer Daniels Midland, has said, "There isn't one grain of anything in the world that is sold in a free market. Not one! The only place you see a free market is in the speeches of politicians."[19] He's right. Much of capitalism is based on subsidies. For example, commercial fishing fleets worldwide receive more in subsidies than the entire value of their catch. Timber corporations, oil corporations, banks, the dairy and meat industries—all would collapse without government subsidies and bailouts. Therefore, governments need to stop subsidizing environmentally and socially destructive activities and shift those same subsidies to activities that restore biotic communities and that promote local self-sufficiency.

3. We must find nondestructive ways of becoming a sustainable society. This means an immediate and permanent halt to all extractive and destructive activities: fracking, mountaintop removal, tar sands production, nuclear power, and offshore drilling chief among them. The list of activities to be halted must also include the manufacture of photovoltaic panels, windmills, hybrid cars, and so on. We must find nondestructive ways of becoming a sustainable society. (We fully recognize the previous sentence is a tautology. People must understand this.)

---

[19] Don Carney, "Dwayne's World," *Mother Jones*, July/August 1995.

4. *All remaining native forests must be immediately and completely protected. We must end clearcutting, "leave tree," "seed tree," "shelter tree," and all other "even-aged management" techniques, no matter what they are called, and no matter what rationales are put forward by the timber industry and the government to justify them. All forests must each year have more volume in living and standing dead trees than the year before. Likewise, all remaining prairies and wetlands must be permanently protected.*

5. *Further, all damaged lands must be restored, from the redwood forest to the Gulf Stream waters. Because soil is the basis of terrestrial life, no activities shall be allowed that destroy topsoil. All properties over 60 acres must have soil surveys performed every 10 years, and if they have suffered any decrease in health or depth of topsoil, the lands shall be confiscated, and ownership transferred to those who will build soil.*

6. *No activities that draw down aquifers can be allowed, and all polluted or compromised rivers and wetlands must be restored. There are more than 2 million dams just in the United States, and more than 70,000 of these dams are over 6.5 feet tall. If we removed one of those 70,000 dams each day, it would take 200 years to get rid of them all. Salmon and sturgeon don't have that much time. Therefore, no more dams can be built, and the removal of dams must begin—at the rate of five per day over the next 40 years—starting no later than one year from today.*

Also, please note that bright greens want to build dams. We—and the salmon, sturgeon, and others who call rivers home—want them gone.

7. An immediate phase-out must begin from mono-crop agriculture, perhaps the most destructive activity humans have ever perpetrated.

8. The government must make an annual survey of all endangered species to ascertain whether they are increasing in number and range. If species are not increasing, steps must be taken to make sure they do. The government must be charged with the task of doing whatever is necessary to make sure there are more migratory songbirds every year than the year before, and there are more native fish every year than the year before, more native reptiles and amphibians, more native insects.

9. The government must immediately cease all funding for vast infrastructure projects such as new highways, dams, thermal power projects, and mines that disrupt or destroy biomes and dispossess and immiserate hundreds of thousands of people (in India alone, 50 million people have been displaced by large "development" projects).

In addition to these biocentric goals and requirements, we must recognize that there are underlying political and socioeconomic realities which must be confronted:

1. Foremost is the understanding that perpetual growth

is incompatible with life on a finite planet. Economic growth must stop, and economies must begin to contract. We need to understand and acknowledge that if we don't begin this contraction voluntarily, it will take place against our will, and it will cause untold misery.

2. Overconsumption and overpopulation must be addressed through bold and serious measures. Right now, more than 50 percent of children born are unplanned or unwanted. The single most effective strategy for making certain all children are wanted is the liberation of women. Therefore, all forms of reproductive control must become freely available to all, and women must be given absolute reproductive freedom and full political, economic, and sexual liberty.

3. The American government itself must undergo a significant transformation in recognition of the fact that it can only be of, by, and for the people if it is concurrently of, by, and for the earth. The fact that the animals and plants and natural communities don't speak English is not a valid excuse for failing to provide for their well-being. Those people and organizations whose economic activities cause great harm—including great harm to the real, physical world—should be punished. Environmental crimes must receive punishment commensurate with the harm caused to the public and to the planet.

4. Lastly, we must commence with the closure of all

*U.S. military bases on foreign soil. All military per-
sonnel should be brought home within two years. The
military budget must be reduced by 20 percent per
year, until it reaches 20 percent of its current size.
This will provide the "peace dividend" politicians used
to promise us back in the 1990s, and it will more than
pay for all necessary domestic programs, starting
with biome repair and including food, shelter, and
medical care for all.*

When we've shared these goals publicly, the response has been
widely split. Many people love them, but some say, "These demands
would destroy the economy." We always thank those people for
precisely making our point. When they complain that a demand
that the economy not destroy the planet would in fact destroy the
economy, they're implicitly acknowledging that the economy is
based on destroying the planet.

Any set of "green guidelines" that doesn't start from this understanding can never be "green" and should not be used as guidelines.

The story of Knepp Castle Estate, told by Isabella Tree in her book
Wilding: The Return of Nature to a British Farm, shows how simple the solution is.[20] Tree and her husband, Charlie Burrell, own
a 3,500-acre property located 44 miles south of London. After 15
years of farming with every possible efficiency added, they were
facing financial collapse. And indeed, collapse was evident everywhere Tree looked. In 1970, the U.K. had 20 million pairs of

[20] Isabella Tree, *Wilding: The Return of Nature to a British Farm* (London: Picador, 2018).

farmland birds. By 1990, half were gone, and by 2010, the population had been halved again.[21] That same halving also struck insects and invertebrates, and for some it was even worse. Butterflies dropped by 76 percent, moths by 88 percent.[22]

"Intensive farming," Tree writes, has "altered the landscape beyond anything our great-grandparents would recognize." The "disappearance of native flowers and grasses" is "almost total." The causes are obvious: "chemical fertilizers and weedkillers ... the wholesale clearance of wasteland and scrub ... the ploughing of wildflower meadows and the draining and pollution of watercourses and standing ponds has wiped out habitat."[23] Biotic cleansing of the British Isles is near complete.

Even as their finances were falling to ruin, Tree and her husband wanted to help the Knepp Oak, a 550-year-old tree on their property. The tree was clearly in distress. The expert they hired explained what had gone so terribly wrong for these last, ancient trees. "These oaks, which should be in their prime, were ailing, possibly fatally, and their condition was down to us. Intensive farming had been taking its toll, and not simply on the trees themselves but the very earth in which they stood. The soil of the park that, under permanent pasture five decades ago, would have been full of vegetal chatter as mycorrhizae fired off messages between trees like a chemical circuit board, was now, in all probability, as silent as the grave."[24]

So, they stopped farming. They laid down the weapons of the longest war ever, including human hubris. What happened next at Knepp—a series of miracles—occurred because Tree and Burrell

---

[21] Ibid., 5.
[22] Ibid., 6.
[23] Ibid., 3.
[24] Ibid., 30.

put their faith in the intelligence of "self-willed ecological process-es."[25] The humans helped in a few key ways, but they knew that those 500 quadrillion relationships we mentioned back in Chapter 1 could never be understood, let alone managed, by people.

Tree and Burrell gave the land a boost by reseeding native meadow species in the near-dead soil, and reintroduced browsing and grazing species. Frans Vera, the Dutch ecologist responsible for the rewilding Oostvaardersplassen project, explains, "Animals are drivers of habitat creation, the impetus behind biodiver-sity. Without them, you have impoverished, static, monotonous habitats with declining species. It's the reason so many of our efforts at conservation are failing."[26] Or as Tree writes, "The key to the Oostvaardersplassen's extraordinary dynamism is grazing animals."[27]

Vera learned this from the greylag goose. The Oostvaardersplassen was a wet parcel of land that had been zoned for industrial "devel-opment." The economic recession of 1973 gave the land a reprieve, and as the wetland plants came back, the birds followed—some of them so rare that environmentalists took note. In 1986, the land was officially protected as a nature preserve. But shallow ponds tend to seal up as reeds and silt fill in, followed by willows and other trees, until eventually the wetland is gone. In many nature preserves, human effort keeps the reeds and silt out, but the Oostvaardersplassen was too big for that to be feasible. Vera and his colleagues had accepted that the area would turn to woodland.

And then the geese arrived. Thousands of them discovered the wetland and took shelter in its isolation. Geese molt for about six weeks and need a safe haven while their feathers grow back. They

[25] Ibid., 8.
[26] Ibid., 59.
[27] Ibid., 58.

also need to eat. They ate so many marsh plants that the marsh and its string of ponds didn't close up. "This was the astonishing thing: the geese were leading vegetation succession—not the other way around. But more than that, their grazing was adding to the biodiversity."[28] Other species appeared as the geese diversified the marsh habitat. The geese were a keystone species, and no one had had any idea.

Back at Knepp, fallow deer were brought in, then Old English longhorns, followed by Exmoor ponies and Tamworth sows to replenish the suite of megafauna that the land needed to be whole. And it worked, at a speed that "astonished observers."[29] Tree lists species after species—birds, mammals, insects, and plants—that have returned, a liturgy of the living. A small sample: Knepp has 13 bird species on the International Union for Conservation of Nature's Red List and 19 on the Royal Society for the Protection of Bird's Amber List; all five of the U.K.'s owl species; 62 species of bees; 19 species of earthworms; and 13 of the U.K.'s 17 bat species. They have 60 invertebrate species of conservation importance, including the U.K.'s largest breeding population of endangered purple emperor butterflies. Nightingale territories have gone from zero to 34 in 10 years, and peregrine falcons have nested there. The rare water violet now blooms in the ponds, giving shelter to tadpoles and dragonfly nymphs—including the scarce chaser, who has been reduced to a dire six sites in the U.K. Twenty-three different species of dung beetles were counted in a single cow patty—one of them was the *Geotrupes mutator*, last seen in the area 50 years ago. A flock of thousands of pink-footed geese, migrating from Greenland, have spent the night at the lake. This is the multiplying

---

[28] Ibid., 60.
[29] Ibid., 8.

miracle of life's return, each species calling the others home. All people have to do is stop destroying.

Around 120 million years ago, a new kind of plant emerged. It would cocreate an entire entourage of animals to go with it, covering the drier biomes of the planet in abundant success. This plant was grass, and its growth point is at the base of the blade, not the tip. This is crucial because grass needs to be grazed and growing from the bottom up allows that.

Why does grass need to be grazed? Because in the dry climates where grasslands reign, there isn't enough microbial activity at the surface of the soil for much of the year for the basic work of life to continue. Plant matter piles up, the plants beneath die, bare patches appear and spread, and the downward spiral begins. Without plants, no roots. Without roots, no rain recharge. Until dry dust is all that's left.

Add a ruminant, which is what the grasses did, and the process is reversed. The surface bacteria may be dormant across the long, dry summer, but they are very much alive inside the multichambered stomach of a ruminant. Bison, for instance, don't actually eat grass: they feed it to their internal farm of bacteria. Bacteria, whether inside or outside of a ruminant, are one of the only creatures who can break down cellulose, and 98 percent of plants' bodies are cellulose—essentially everything but the seeds. The bacteria eat the grass, the bison eats the bacteria, and one day the bison will return to the soil, which in the end eats us all. And the nutrient cycle is complete.

When grass is grazed, it grows more roots. The tearing of its blades triggers the plant to release a surge of sugar through its roots, calling the microbes to it. The bacteria take the sugars in exchange for a packet of nutrients, which stimulates plant growth; being eaten makes grasses stronger. And the world is made richer. More roots mean more soil, more soil means more life.

The sheer abundance of animals who once lived on the Great Plains serves as extraordinary proof of that richness. Prior to European conquest, there were 30 to 40 million pronghorn antelopes, 10 million elk, 10 million mule deer, 2 million mountain sheep, 60 million bison, and maybe 5 billion prairie dogs. The largest recorded prairie dog colony stretched for 250 miles and contained an estimated 400 million of them.

There were also maybe 2 million wolves, because, without predators, the whole community collapses. Predators will reduce population, yes, but their impact goes way beyond numbers. Predators change the behavior of the herd as a whole. When 14 wolves were released at Yellowstone, the results were called "a near-miracle."[30] The elk stopped eating the riverbank to bare mud; willows, cottonwoods, and especially aspen returned. Aspen are in decline all over the west and "no new trees were found surviving animal browsing from the 1920s to the early 1990s, when wolf packs were absent in Yellowstone."[31] With the return of the trees, the riverbanks have stabilized. The understory has also repaired, and with more bushes came berries and then birds. Out of nowhere, beavers, long extinct from the region, appeared. They did what they do, and they made wetlands. Creature after creature cascaded into the park. The wolves also culled coyotes, which left more rabbits and mice, which brought foxes, weasels, and badgers back.

We are, none of us, our full selves without our community.

---

[30] "A wild anniversary: 25 years for Yellowstone Wolves," *Wolf Conservation Center*, January 12, 2020.
[31] Corey Binns, "Yellowstone wolves reintroduce 'ecology of fear,'" *Live Science*, July 27, 2007.

Never forget: Life as a whole is a series of relationships, not an assemblage of separate parts.

Without predators, the action of browsers and grazers will ultimately turn destructive. Without wolves or big cats or grizzly bears, ruminants have no reason to bunch or to move. Instead, they will engage in what's called "continuous grazing," and like the elk at Yellowstone, they will degrade the biotic community. Regenerative farmer Joel Salatin understands the creation of the grasslands' abundance: "the pulsing of the predator-prey-pruning cycle on perennial prairie polycultures."[32] Salatin is one of the people leading the charge in the battle to restore soil. On his farm in Virginia, Salatin has attempted to take up his human role as apex predator so that in this case, the cows and grasses can be their full selves. His experiments with "mob grazing," "holistic management," or "managed grazing" have produced extraordinary results. The soil organic matter has gone from 1.5 percent to 8 percent.[33] Those are numbers to make the angels sing. Increasing soil organic matter is another way of saying "sequestering carbon."

What follows is the final round of numbers in a book that certainly has its share. These last numbers, though, are not another catalogue of horrors but an arithmetic of hope.

Soil scientist Dr. Rattan Lal states, "A mere 2 percent increase in the carbon content of the planet's soils would offset 100 percent of all greenhouse gas emissions going into the atmosphere."[34] Remember that all tillage agriculture contributes to global warming—indeed, agriculture marks the beginning of it. Annual grains

---

[32] Joel Salatin, "Joel Salatin responds to *New York Times'* 'Myth of Sustainable Meat'," *Grist*, April 17, 2012.

[33] H. Brevy Cannon, "Farmer Joel Salatin puts 'nature's template' to work," *UVA Today*, September 21, 2009.

[34] Ronnie Cummins, *Grassroots Rising: A Call to Action on Climate, Farming, Food, and a Green New Deal* (White River Junction, VT: Chelsea Green Publishing, 2020), 33.

release about 1,000 pounds of carbon per acre. The carbon is released because the soil essentially vaporizes, breaking the bonds that hold the carbon in place. Our job now is to restore that soil. Growing soil, combined with stopping fossil fuels, is our one and only hope—and it's also not too late.

"Our living soils and forests," urges Ronnie Cummins, "have the capacity to sequester and safely store enough carbon to bring us back to the safe levels of CO_2 ... that we had before the advent of the industrial revolution."[35] Luke Smith of Terra Genesis International did the calculations for 5 billion acres of the earth's most degraded land: "Assuming a conservative average sequestration of 5T/ha/yr, it would take just 30 years to return our global climate to below pre-industrial levels."[36] British author-activist Graham Harvey writes, "Carbon capture by the world's farmlands could total as much as 10 billion tonnes of carbon dioxide a year.... Grassland production wouldn't merely help with the problem of global warming; it could solve it."[37]

There's a thriving community of people dedicated to restoring soil and all that flows from there. Scientists are measuring sequestration and declaring it good.[38] Biologists are helping rare species recover. A tiny, precious cadre of farmers and ranchers are converting degraded landscapes to sanctuaries using both domesticated and wild ruminants—over 9 million hectares are being restored globally using managed grazing. Advocates are educating consumers about the multilayered benefits of grass-based

[35] Ibid., 32.
[36] Ibid., 33.
[37] Graham Harvey, *The Carbon Fields: How Our Countryside Can Save Britain* (Somerset, U.K.: Grass Roots Press, 2008), 54.
[38] See, for instance: W.R. Teague et al., "The Role of Ruminants in Reducing Agriculture's Carbon Footprint in North America," *Journal of Soil and Water Conservation*.

farming and helping people find the good stuff.[39] And activists are doing their best to get these solutions before policy makers as well as the public. Australian scientist Christine Jones and her group Carbon for Life created a soil carbon accreditation scheme. Farmers are paid for every ton of carbon they sequester—finally, a subsidy for the living world. "Grazing animals and microbes" are the heavy lifters; humans are the movers. By Jones's calculations, increasing soil organic matter by 1 percent on 15 million hectares would sequester the total greenhouse gas emissions for the entire planet.[40]

We don't need technology that breaks the world while it continues to break us from the world. We need to let our planet repair while we repair our place within it. It really is that simple.

One final example of hope is the African Centre for Holistic Management. Founded as a learning site for restoring "land, water, and wildlife using livestock,"[41] particularly for subsistence farmers and herders,[42] the site is 3,200 hectares of dryland savanna, and a river runs through it, the Dimbangombe, for the first time in a long time. Seth Itzkan, cofounder of Soil4Climate, explains that after only a few years of restoration, of growing soil and repairing habitat, "new surface water is available in the dry season 1.5 kilometers upstream *from where it has ever been.*"[43] There is surface water now, year-round, which means everything to the animals.

That's what grasses do: provide channels for the rain to enter

---

[39] See: Jo Robinson's site, EatWild.com.

[40] Harvey, op. cit., 56.

[41] Africa Centre for Holistic Management, Dimbangombe Learning Site.

[42] The fact that they are subsistence farmers and herders is key to their sustainability: the biomass of plants and animals the farmers/herders encourage and eat will never leave their land.

[43] Seth Itzkan, "Reversing global warming with livestock?: Seth Itzkan at TEDXSomerville," May 24, 2012.

soil. That's what ruminants do: help the grasses build soil. And that's what soil does: It stores water. The site now supports four times the number of livestock as when they started, as well as a gloriously expanding population of "elephant, lion, buffalo, sable, giraffe, kudu, leopard, and more."[44] Livestock moves are planned very carefully, to avoid conflict or competition with the wild creatures for food, water, or shelter. And the final blessing: There are now more elephants at the site than at the nearby national park.

Anyone can take part in this work, no matter where you live or how little you have. Find something you love and defend it. A stream, a stand of trees, a struggling songbird: They need your protection and care. Even a tiny backyard is habitat. Even a city balcony can offer food and water. Everyone can do something for our straining world.

Prairie dogs are a keystone species of the North American grasslands, with over 140 other species directly dependent on them, from burrowing owls to black-footed ferrets. Once, prairie dogs were the most numerous mammals on the continent, but both their numbers and their habitat have been reduced by 99 percent. They are barely hanging on. For instance, when Deanna Meyer of Sedalia, Colorado, learned that a prairie dog colony was slated to be gassed in the service of a shopping mall, she fought and lost the zoning battle, but she was able to get some of the animals evacuated to safety. Five years later, the colony is thriving—and she has saved four more colonies.

---

[44] Africa Centre for Holistic Management, op. cit.

We do what we can, with our desperation entwined with the hope that somehow life will find a way. For instance, there was a devasted acre surrounding Lierre's house. Two hundred dollars of native seeds and a few loads of fresh manure—for the bacteria more than the nutrients—was all it took to bring it back to life. The grasses sprouted and stretched, the insects returned, then the birds. Rabbits are everywhere at dawn and dusk: A pair of Cooper's hawks arrived for the feast and stayed to raise chicks. Now the grasses are silently sequestering carbon, recharging the water table for the nearby creek and endangered Coho salmon who miraculously carry on. Life poured in, each species providing for the next, until the circle was full again. All Lierre had to do was set it in motion.

Max is helping trees migrate north in preparation for global warming. Fifty years from now, it may well be too hot for California black oaks in their current range. He carries the seedlings 300 miles north. Forests can only move about a mile a year—they won't make 300 miles in 50 years—but Max's seedlings may survive and populate the region if the worst climate chaos comes to pass, their DNA a fragile cache for the future.

Forests can regrow. Grasslands can reclaim vast portions of the planet. Oceanic dead zones can shrink rapidly, and ocean populations can rebound. There is still hope, but everything depends on our will to resist.

Restoration is essential, but on its own, it's not enough to save the planet. There's simply too much ancient carbon being released by the burning of coal, oil, and gas. And besides, this culture is still destroying forests, prairies, peat bogs, wetlands, salt marshes, mangrove swamps, seagrass beds—the world.

So, what do we need to do? We need to stop the burning of coal, oil, and gas. And we can't forget monocrop agriculture, which has released as much greenhouse gases through destroying soil over the past 6,000 years as has been released from burning coal, oil, and gas during the industrial era. This has to stop, too. So, too, does logging, urban expansion, road building, mining, nuclear power and weapons production, and all the other major industrial activities that are shredding the living flesh of our planet.

These industries won't voluntarily stop. They can't. In most countries, it's illegal for publicly held corporations to act against the profit motive, which means they're legally obligated to grow, which means they're legally obligated to destroy the planet. These industries are no longer meaningfully controlled by human beings. They have a momentum and logic all of their own. The planet will not survive as long as corporate personhood still stands. So, there's another task for your list.

Those of us who care about life have to be the resistance. We start by rejecting false solutions. We have to coalesce around goals that will save the planet. We need massive movements to relentlessly impede the functioning of industrial civilization, using every tactic: political pressure, legal challenges, economic boycotts, civil disobedience, and whatever else becomes necessary. Standards of living will have to decrease in rich nations, but with the weight of global capitalism lifted, they will rise dramatically for the global poor. Areas of India that now export dog food and tulips to Europe, like areas of Tanzania that now export lima beans, could return to their former role of supporting local populations.

And never forget that full human rights for women and girls is both ecologically necessary as well as the right thing to do.

Whatever happens is likely to be chaotic. We're already seeing food scarcity, extreme weather, climate refugees, increased and open violence (including sexual), rising surveillance, and a global pivot toward open fascism. One friend who comes from Pakistan often says that collapse is not a future state there (or in much of the world); it's an ongoing process. Collapse is not a fear but a daily reality in countless parts of the world. Look at Chicago and Flint, Michigan; look at Pine Ridge Indian Reservation in South Dakota. Look under the bridges in your town. Collapse is right here, among us.

The best way to prepare for this is also the best way to prepare to bring about just human societies after collapse: not by leaning even more into industry but by building communities based on self-sufficiency, biological integrity, and human rights. This is work anyone can support.

If you want a solution, here it is: Fight for the living. It's not too late.

Make no mistake, we are up against entrenched and global systems of power that have gone rabid with destruction. Environmental philosopher Kathleen Dean Moore often gets asked, "What can one person do?" Her answer: "Don't be one person." And she is exactly right. We need organized political resistance. The only thing that is going to bring those systems down is all of us rising up.

No matter how weary, your heart is still beating. Listen to it. Whatever work it is calling you to do—for democracy, for human rights, for animals and the earth, for the girls and the grasses—it is sacred work. Because life itself now hangs in the balance. When the call of your heart becomes the work of your hands, that may be what tips the balance back toward life. So never give up.

Whatever you love, it is under assault. But love is a verb. May that love call us to action.

Chapter 15

CONCLUSION

We can live on without electricity. It's a convenience.

—CHIEF CALEEN SISK, WINNEMEM WINTU

A false premise underlies this book. It's that people make choices based on the best available information, that when they're presented with accurate and compelling facts and analyses, these facts and analyses inform not only their personal but collective choices.

That is, of course, nonsense.

A 2016 article in the *Washington Post* runs under the headline, "Global warming could deplete the oceans' oxygen—with severe consequences."[1] The article was, given the headline, short on naming these consequences. Let's fill in. These severe consequences can include the death of all life in zones devoid of oxygen, something already happening across the world. It's entirely possible this could, along with agricultural runoff and industrial fishing, essentially end fish life in the oceans.

---

[1] Chris Mooney, "Global warming could deplete the oceans' oxygen—with severe consequences," *Washington Post*, April 28, 2016.

On a planet whose surface is primarily ocean, you'd think we'd act decisively to stop this from happening. But you'd be wrong.

How wrong? A 2018 article in *The Guardian* is titled: "Oceans suffocating as huge dead zones quadruple since 1950," scientists warn: "Areas starved of oxygen in open ocean and by coasts have soared in recent decades, risking dire consequences for marine life and humanity." Here's a key quote: "'Major extinction events in earth's history have been associated with warm climates and oxygen-deficient oceans.' Denise Breitburg, at the Smithsonian Environmental Research Center, who led the analysis, said: 'Under the current trajectory that is where we would be headed. But the consequences to humans of staying on that trajectory are so dire that it is hard to imagine we would go quite that far down that path.'"[2]

Hard to imagine? We don't even *need* to imagine. Just look around.

Another day, another headline: "Sea Level Rise Projections Double, Painting Terrifying Picture for Next Generation." The article's first three sentences: "In a consistent trend, future projections of an increase in the overall global temperature, as well as increases in sea level rise, continue to outpace previous worst-case scenarios. This is due to a simple equation: there is already enough CO_2 in the atmosphere and heat absorbed into the planet's oceans that even if we stopped emitting carbon completely right now, the planet would continue to experience and display dramatic impacts from anthropogenic climate disruption for thousands of years. The second part of that equation is this: there is simply nothing to indicate that national governments around the world are willing to

---

[2] Damien Carrington, "Oceans suffocating as huge dead zones quadruple since 1950, scientists warn," *The Guardian*, January 4, 2018.

take the immediate, radical steps that would be necessary to begin to seriously mitigate these impacts."[3]

And now, here's one that brings it all home. Headline: "As the Arctic Melts, Nations Race to Own What's Left Behind." A key sentence: "For the nations in the Arctic Council—Canada, Russia, Norway, Denmark, Finland, Iceland and the United States—climate change presents an opportunity for access to brand new waters, previously cloaked in ice, that are chock full of valuable resources." The article states, "The problem is there's a lot of overlap between each of the ... claims."

Yes, that's certainly the first problem that leaps to mind, except for that little one about murdering the planet.

The article continues, "A potential trove of resources hide in these contested waters, ranging from untapped fishing stocks of cod and snow crabs (in which even non-Arctic nations like China and South Korea have expressed interest), to rare minerals like manganese, uranium, copper and iron below the seafloor.

"Nations are also interested in drilling for energy resources in the Arctic, which the U.S. Geological Survey estimate contains 30 percent of the world's undiscovered natural gas and 13 percent of the world's oil."[4]

Pretty clear, right?

During my talks across the country, I (Derrick) have asked people, "Do you think this culture will undergo a voluntary transformation

---

[3] Dahr Jamail, "Sea Level Rise Projections Double, Painting Terrifying Picture for Next Generation," *Truthout*, January 2, 2018.

[4] Francis Flisiuk, "As the Arctic Melts, Nations Race to Own What's Left Behind," *The Revelator*, January 4, 2018.

to a sane and sustainable society?" and out of thousands of people at my talks, no one ever says *yes*.

I'm increasingly convinced that within this culture the primary use of human intelligence is to try to rationalize whatever behavior we already wanted to do. Much of our philosophy and religion—from Plato to the Bible to St. Augustine to Descartes to Adam Smith right up through today, including bright greens—can easily be seen as providing intellectual support for human supremacism and the conquest of the earth.

Recall Robert Jay Lifton's understanding that before you can commit any mass atrocity, you must have a claim to virtue. That is, you must attempt to convince yourself and others that what you're doing is not in fact an atrocity, but instead a good thing. So, you're not killing the planet; you're developing natural resources. You're not killing the planet; you're saving industrial civilization. You're not killing the planet; you're saving the planet.

But all the while you're killing the planet. All of those claims to virtue must be devised and maintained. And we as a culture can harness tremendous intellectual energy to this end.

The attitudes of our culture are well articulated by Jeff Bezos, the CEO of Amazon and the richest man in the world: "You don't want to live in a retrograde world. You don't want to live on an earth where we have to freeze population growth, reduce energy utilization. We all enjoy an extraordinary civilization, and it's powered by energy, and it's powered by population. That's why urban centers are so dynamic. We want the population to keep growing on this planet and we want to keep using more energy per capita."[5]

---

[5] Jeff Bezos, "Jeff Bezos vs. Peter Thiel and Donald Trump / Jeff Bezos, CEO Amazon / Code Conference 2016," *Recode*, YouTube, May 31, 2016.

All of which is why, throughout this book, we've repeated Naomi Klein's comments about polar bears not doing it for her. Not to be snarky, but instead because that's the single most important passage in this book.

Although we've spent hundreds of pages laying out facts, ultimately this book is about values. We value something different than do bright greens. And our loyalty is to something different. We are fighting for the living planet. The bright greens are fighting to continue this culture—the culture that is killing the planet. Seems like the planet doesn't do it for them.

Early in this book we quoted some of the bright greens, including Lester Brown: "The question is, can we save civilization? That's what's at stake now, and I don't think we've yet realized it."[6] And Peter Kareiva, chief scientist for The Nature Conservancy: "Instead of pursuing the protection of biodiversity for biodiversity's sake, a new conservation should seek to enhance those natural systems that benefit the widest number of people."[7] And climate scientist Wen Stephenson: "The terms 'environment' and 'environmentalism' carry baggage historically and culturally. It has been more about protecting the natural world, protecting other species, and conservation of wild places than it has been about the welfare of human beings. I come at it from the opposite direction. It's first and foremost about human beings."[8] And Bill McKibben: "We're

---

[6] Lester Brown, "The Race to Save Civilization," *Tikkun*, September/October 2010, 25(5): 58.

[7] Peter Kareiva, Michell Marvier, and Robert Lalasz, "Conservation in the Anthropocene: Beyond Solitude and Fragility," *The Breakthrough Institute*, Winter 2012.

[8] Gabrielle Gurley, "From journalist to climate crusader: Wen Stephenson moves to the front lines of climate movement," *Commonwealth: Politics, Ideas & Civic Life in Massachusetts*, November 10, 2015.

losing the fight, badly and quickly—losing it because, most of all, we remain in denial about the peril that human civilization is in."[9]

Do we yet see the pattern?

And no, we're not losing that fight because "we remain in denial about the peril that human civilization is in." We're losing that fight because we're trying to save industrial civilization, which is inherently unsustainable.

We, the authors of this book, also like the conveniences this culture brings to us. But we don't like them more than we like life on the planet.

We should be trying to save the planet—this beautiful, creative, unique planet—the planet that is the source of all life, the planet without whom we all die.

No, we shouldn't be *trying* to save the planet. We hate to quote Yoda, but "Do or do not, there is no try."

So many indigenous people have said that the first and most important thing we must do is decolonize our hearts and minds. We must grow, they've told me, to see the dominant culture for what it is: not as the most wonderful thing that has ever happened to human beings, but instead as a way of life that provides conveniences—luxuries—to one set of humans at the expense of everyone else—human and nonhuman. We must recognize that everything comes from somewhere, and that someone else already lived there. We must recognize that the dominant culture has always been based on taking land from indigenous peoples, and it has always been based on drawdown.

And we must recognize that because the earth is the source of all

---

[9] Bill McKibben, "Global Warming's Terrifying New Math," *Rolling Stone*, August 2, 2012.

life, the health of the earth must be the primary consideration in our decision-making processes.

This is the first and most important thing we must do. *This* changes everything. Because the truth is that we can debunk each and every piece of bright green technology, and ultimately it won't make a bit of difference to bright greens or anyone else whose loyalty is not to the earth but to the economic and social system that is dismantling the earth.

The murder of the planet has never been a question of facts. The facts are clear and obvious, and they have been since the beginning. The question has always been one of value. People protect what they value, and so long as they value this culture and the conveniences it brings to some humans over life on the planet, so long shall they try to save this culture and their own conveniences at the expense of the life that does not seem to do it for them.

If the planet—and ironically enough, if we ourselves—will survive, it will only be because enough of us begin to value life over these conveniences. The irony comes because the bright greens claim that their proposals are "all about us." But "us" clearly doesn't include those who will inherit the wreckage of a world their plans will leave behind.

When we change our values, previously insoluble problems become soluble. Instead of asking how we can meet insatiable industrial energy demands and still live on a planet at least minimally capable of supporting life, the question *must* be: How can we help the earth to be stronger and healthier while still meeting human needs (needs, not conveniences, not luxuries, not addictions, and further, *human* needs, not the needs of industry and commerce).

So long as we continue to ask the wrong questions, the world will continue to be destroyed, and we will continue to waste time we don't have on solutions that won't help the earth.

When, on the other hand, we start asking the right questions, and start acting in the best interests of the natural world, we will find ourselves beginning to live our way into the answers to these questions.

We will find ourselves no longer having to lie—to make up bright green lie after bright green lie—but we will find ourselves where we should have been all along, in alignment with the earth and with the powerful, wonderful, beautiful, creative processes that have made life on this planet what it is.

AFTERWORD

Derrick Jensen

The point of this book is simple. Industrial civilization is functionally and inherently unsustainable. It will not—indeed cannot—last
forever, and after this way of living is no longer tenable, we would
prefer—for the sake of both the humans and nonhumans who
come after—that more of the living planet remain, rather than less.

Current events have reinforced everything we wrote in this book.
The Green New Deal, which is being pushed so hard by mainstream
environmentalists, has far less to do with saving wild places and
wild beings than it does with generating subsidies for favored sec-
tions of the industrial economy, with estimates of the giveaways
running from hundreds of billions to trillions of dollars. As one
of its most well-known backers, U.S. Representative Alexandria
Ocasio-Cortez, has stated, "We must again invest in the development, manufacturing, deployment, and distribution of energy, but
this time green energy."[1]

Not that we'd mind that money being spent—in fact we'd be
delighted—if it helped the living planet. But by now we should all
know that solar-energy-harvesting facilities don't help waterfowl,
migratory songbirds, desert tortoises, Joshua trees, or deserts

---

[1] Alexander C. Kaufman, "Alexandria Ocasio-Cortez Will Be the Leading Democrat on
Climate Change," *Huffington Post*, June 27, 2018.

themselves. And wind energy harvesting facilities don't help meadowlarks, golden eagles, little brown bats, or ridgelines or grasslands.

Just as President Franklin D. Roosevelt's New Deal was aimed at subsidizing the U.S. economy out of the Great Depression, and President Obama's stimulus package was aimed at subsidizing the U.S. economy out of the 2008 recession, the Green New Deal is aimed at stimulating the economy, as Thomas Friedman put it, to "spur our economy into the 21st century."[2] And the massive infrastructure projects of the Green New Deal will no more help the planet than did the massive infrastructure projects of the original New Deal. Think: Grand Coulee Dam. Think: Hoover Dam. Think: 13 Hoover Dams per day.

What would the salmon want? What would North Atlantic right whales want? Would they want turbines in the Bay of Fundy? Would sage grouse want lithium mines or wind-energy-harvesting facilities in Nevada?

Global carbon emissions dropped dramatically in the first part of 2020. No, not in anticipation of an Earth-saving Green New Deal, but because of a pandemic-associated economic slowdown. As *Nature* magazine reported: "Government policies during the COVID-19 pandemic have drastically altered patterns of energy demand around the world. Many international borders were closed, and populations were confined to their homes, which reduced transport and changed consumption patterns.... Daily global CO2 emissions decreased by 17% ... by early April 2020 compared with the mean 2019 levels, just under half from changes in surface transport. At their peak, emissions in individual countries decreased by 26% on average."[3]

---

[2] Thomas L. Friedman, "A Warning from the Garden," *New York Times*, January 19, 2007.
[3] Corinne Le Quéré et al., "Temporary reduction in daily global CO_2 emissions during the COVID-19 forced confinement,' *Nature*, May 19, 2020.

And it's not just CO2. Through the 2020 economic downturn, nitrogen dioxide concentrations in many cities have decreased as much as 70 percent. The same is true for particulate matter in Los Angeles, Wuhan, Seoul. In some cities, people can see the horizon for the first time in recent memory. Water pollution is down as well. And any decrease in industrial ocean traffic dramatically increases the quality of life for those who live there.

If you reduce activities that are systematically destroying the planet, the planet is destroyed more slowly, and in some cases recovers. Funny, that.

There's an image I can't get out of my head that describes the mainstream environmentalist response to the murder of the planet. A patient is brought into the emergency room, bleeding out from scores of wounds. The doctors and nurses work frantically to close the wounds, stop the bleeding, infuse more blood. They use every high-tech machine and medicine they can, and they do everything possible to save the patient—everything except the most important thing of all, which is to stop the killer from refusing to leave the ER and continuing to stab the patient, again and again and again.

Bright green solutions merely keep stabbing the living planet again and again and again. We need to stop them.

Wild animals have responded as we would think—as we would, in our deepest hearts, hope—to this decrease in industrial activities, by coming out, at least a little bit, from their hiding places, from their refugia from this culture's war on nature.

And of course, they have, because the most important and profound rule of life on this planet is that *life wants to live*. And if we just allow it to, it will return, so long as we have not pushed it too far. It's already too late for passenger pigeons, Labrador ducks, sea mink, silphium, Mesopotamian elephants. Is it too late for salmon? Not quite yet. But give this culture another 10 years and it may very well be. Is it too late for piscine life in the oceans? Not quite yet. But give this culture another 15 years and it may very well be.

There's another image that I can't shake. I was a messy child. My mother would sometimes ask me to clean my room, and I wouldn't get around to it. She'd ask again, and then again. I would dilly-dally. Finally, she'd lose patience and say, "If you don't clean your room, I'm going to do it, and if I do it you won't like it, because I'm going to throw everything away." I cleaned my room.

Life on this planet is giving us this same choice. This way of living will not and cannot last. What we do now determines how much of the planet remains later. We can voluntarily reduce the harm caused by this culture now, and work to create spaces where nature can regenerate, or we can continue to allow—indeed, to subsidize—further destruction of the planet's ecological infrastructure. And while that may allow the economy to limp along a few more years, I guarantee that none of us—salmon, right whales, piscine life in the oceans, humans—are going to like where that takes us.

Here's one final image, though, to carry us forward through these difficult times. As I write this, I see, across a small open space in this dense redwood forest, a mother bear lying on her back, head resting comfortably against the base of a tree. The tree—maybe 120 feet tall—is one of many resprouted after an old-growth redwood was cut here about 100 years ago. On the bear's belly sprawl two cubs, suckling eagerly, stopping now and then, as children are wont to do, to squabble until she calms them with a soft sound. These bears, these trees, the flying squirrels who sometimes descend from the trees to check for scraps of food—and the magnificent dance between all of these beings and the thimbleberries, huckleberries, grasses, arthropods, fungi, and unseen bacteria—are here for now. And it is for them that I work, it is to them and not to the system destroying them that I give my loyalty, it is to them and for them that I dedicate my life.

That is the least I or any of us can do for the planet that—who—gave us our own lives, that—who—feeds us, clothes us, sings us awake in the mornings and to sleep at night—the planet who welcomes us at our beginnings and to whom we all return at our ends. And as Aldo Leopold, the father of wildlife ecology, made clear so many years ago, this is the right—and beautiful—thing to do.

RESOURCES GUIDE

BOOKS

Against the Grain: How Agriculture Has Hijacked Civilization by Richard Manning

Columbus and Other Cannibals by Jack D. Forbes

Deep Green Resistance: Strategy to Save the Planet by Derrick Jensen, Aric McBay, and Lierre Keith

Dirt to Soil: One Family's Journey into Regenerative Agriculture by Gabe Brown

Green Illusions: The Dirty Secrets of Clean Energy, and the Future of Environmentalism by Ozzie Zehner

Imperial San Francisco: Urban Power, Earthly Ruin by Gray Brechin

In the Absence of the Sacred: The Failure of Technology and the Survival of the Indian Nations by Jerry Mander

Monocultures of the Mind: Perspectives on Biodiversity and Biotechnology by Vandana Shiva

The Myth of the Machine: Technics and Human Development by Lewis Mumford

Rebels Against the Future: The Luddites and Their War on the Industrial Revolution, Lessons for the Computer Age by Kirkpatrick Sale

Rewilding the West: Restoration in a Prairie Landscape by Richard Manning

Sacred Cow: The Case for (Better) Meat by Diana Rogers and Robb Wolf

Techno-Fix: Why Technology Won't Save Us or the Environment by Michael and Joyce Huesemann

Tending the Wild by M. Kat Anderson

To Save Everything, Click Here: The Folly of Technological Solutionism by Evgeny Morozov

Wilding: The Return of Nature to a British Farm by Isabella Tree

FILMS

Bright Green Lies by Julia Barnes

END:CIV Resist or Die by Franklin Lopez

Planet of the Humans by Jeff Gibbs

Running Out of Time by Trevor Langham

Sacred Cow: The Nutritional, Environmental, and Ethical Case for Better Meat by Diana Rodgers

What a Way to Go: Life at the End of Empire by Timothy S. Bennett

ORGANIZATIONS

Basin and Range Watch
Buffalo Field Campaign
Carbon Cycle Institute
Deep Green Resistance
Elder Creek Oak Sanctuary
Fertile Ground Institute
Great Plains Restoration Council
Gurukula Botanical Sanctuary
Marin Carbon Project
Prairie Protection Colorado
Politics, Art, Roots, Culture (PARC)
RESTORE: The North Woods
Savory Institute
Wildlands Network

ABOUT THE AUTHORS

DERRICK JENSEN has authored more than 25 books, including *Deep Green Resistance, A Language Older Than Words, The Culture of Make Believe,* and *Endgame.* He is also a teacher, activist, and small farmer, and was named the "poet-philosopher of the ecological movement" by *Democracy Now!* In 2008, he was chosen as one of *Utne Reader*'s 50 Visionaries Who Are Changing Your World and won the Eric Hoffer Award. He is a cofounder of the organization Deep Green Resistance.

Jensen has written for the *New York Times Magazine, Audubon,* and *The Sun,* and was a columnist at *Orion.* He holds an MFA in creative writing from Eastern Washington University and a BS degree in mineral engineering physics from the Colorado School of Mines, and has taught creative writing at Eastern Washington University and Pelican Bay State Prison. He lives in Northern California on a property frequented by bears.

DERRICKJENSEN.ORG

LIERRE KEITH is a writer, small farmer, and radical feminist activist. She is the author of six books, including *The Vegetarian Myth: Food, Justice, and Sustainability,* and is the co-author, with Derrick Jensen and Aric McBay, of *Deep Green Resistance: Strategy to Save the Planet.* She is also a cofounder of the organization Deep Green Resistance.

Keith has been arrested six times for acts of political resistance. She lives in Northern California, where she shares 20 acres (including a restored one-acre meadow) with giant trees and giant dogs.

LIERREKEITH.COM

MAX WILBERT is a writer, organizer, and wilderness guide who has fought the Canadian tar sands megaproject and tar sands mining in Utah, resisted industrial-scale water extraction and deforestation in Nevada, advocated for the last wild buffalo in Yellowstone National Park, worked with indigenous communities in British Columbia, and participated in campaigns against police brutality and sexual violence.

He is cofounder of the Pinyon-Juniper Alliance and a member of the board of directors of Fertile Ground Institute for Social and Ecological Justice and Deep Green Resistance, for which he edits the Deep Green Resistance News Service and produces the podcast *The Green Flame.*

Wilbert has written for *Earth Island Journal, CounterPunch, Dissident Voice,* and DGR News Service; and he authored the introduction to the French translation of *Earth First! Direct Action Manual* and the German essay collection *We Choose to Speak.* He lives near Eugene, Oregon, in a communal living project.

MAXWILBERT.ORG

CPSIA information can be obtained
at www.ICGtesting.com
Printed in the USA
JSHW041001060521
14387JS00004B/4